The New Service Economy

SERVICES, ECONOMY AND INNOVATION

Series editor: John R. Bryson, *Professor of Enterprise and Economic Geography, School of Geography, Earth and Environmental Sciences, The University of Birmingham, UK and Distinguished Research Fellow, Foundation for Research in Economics and Business Administration (SNF), Bergen, Norway*

An ever-increasing proportion of the world's business involves some type of service function and employment. Manufacturing is being transformed into hybrid production systems that combine production and service functions both within manufacturing processes as well as in final products. Manufacturing employment continues to decline while employment in a range of services activities continues to grow. The shift towards service dominated economies presents a series of challenges for academics as well as policy makers. The focus of much academic work has been on manufacturing and until recently services have been relatively neglected. This is the first book series to bring together a range of different perspectives that explore different aspects of services, economy and innovation. The series will include titles that explore:

- The economics of services
- Service-led economies or enterprises
- Service work and employment
- Innovation and services
- Services and the wider process of production
- Services and globalization.

This series is essential reading for academics and researchers in economics, economic geography and business.

Titles in the series include:

The New Service Economy
Challenges and Policy Implications for Europe
Luis Rubalcaba

The New Service Economy

Challenges and Policy Implications for Europe

Luis Rubalcaba

Associate Professor of Economic Policy, University of Alcalá, Madrid, Spain
President of the European Association for Services Research (RESER)

SERVICES, ECONOMY AND INNOVATION

Edward Elgar
Cheltenham, UK • Northampton, MA, USA

Published by
Edward Elgar Publishing Limited
Glensanda House
Montpellier Parade
Cheltenham
Glos GL50 1UA
UK

Edward Elgar Publishing, Inc.
William Pratt House
9 Dewey Court
Northampton
Massachusetts 01060
USA

A catalogue record for this book
is available from the British Library

Library of Congress Cataloguing in Publication Data

Rubalcaba-Bermejo, Luis
  The new service economy : challenges and policy implications for Europe / Luis Rubalcaba.
    p. cm. - (Services, economy and innovation series)
    Includes bibliographical references and index.
    1. Service industries—Europe. 2. Service industries—United States. 3. European Union countries—Economic policy. 4. Globalization—Economic aspects. 5 Competition. I. Title.
    HD9986.A2R385 2007
    338.4094—dc22

                                                                2007025573

ISBN 978 1 84542 585 2

Printed and bound in Great Britain by MPG Books Ltd, Bodmin, Cornwall

To my wife, Fuencisla, and my four children:
Gloria Casilda, Leticia María, Luis and Isabel

'Freedom, Sancho, is one of the most precious gifts
that heaven has bestowed upon men'
Don Quixote – Miguel de Cervantes Saavedra

Contents

Acknowledgements

I would like to thank all those without whom this book would not have been possible. Firstly, I am grateful to the Foundation Rafael del Pino, and especially to its Director, Amadeo Petitbò, and its Vice-President, María del Pino, for their initiative and support for this project. In moments of intense workload, I always remembered the time when a former colleague in Alcalá, Professor Petitbò, a reputed expert on regulations and competition policy called me to suggest that I carry out this ambitious but attractive work. At that time, I was still working in the European Commission in Brussels, collaborating in the development of some of the services policies that I set out here. For this reason, my gratitude extends to my work colleagues in Brussels, particularly Ole Guldberg, Ronald Mackay, Peter-Boegh Nielsen and Samuli Rikama, with whom I had the opportunity to share and learn intensively during the almost two years I spent there.

I am indebted to Professor Mr. Juan Ramón Cuadrado Roura for my professional orientation towards the services economy. I began my university studies with him in 1990 and we have collaborated on numerous interesting projects since then. My gratitude also extends towards other departmental colleagues and Servilab, especially Professors Del Río, Mancha, Peinado, Mañas, Garrido, Iglesias and García Tabuenca.

In recent years, I have had the opportunity of establishing very enriching international scientific relationships. This has arisen particularly through the European Association for Service Research (RESER), of which I have the honour of being President, and in which we are working to promote research on services by several initiatives. I thank the work of the Council, but specifically to my closest collaborators, Professors Bryson, Stare and Monnoyer. Regarding my knowledge on services policies, I am indebted to many researchers, but I would like to especially mention Henk Kox, Ian Miles, Paul Windrum and Pim den Hertog with whom I am jointly working on some very interesting projects.

Finally, I wish to mention those persons who have helped me directly in the execution of this book. Firstly I thank the young collaborators who have participated in some chapters or have helped me to compile the statistics used: the PhD students Andrés Maroto, Stefano Visintin, Gisela Di Meglio and Jorge Gallego, and the PhD Nuria Fernández. Secondly, a special acknowledgement must be given to thank Jean Bergevin and Francisco Caballero (DG Internal Market and Services), Ronald Mackay (DG Enterprise and Industry), Mikel Landabasso (DG Regional Policy) and

Augustijn van Haasteren (DG Competition) from the European Commission, for the fruitful discussions we have had in some European Commission meetings and for the appraisal and comments in the chapters on internal market, complementary policies, regional policy and competition policy, respectively. Thirdly, I am grateful to all the anonymous advisers, for their useful suggestions, as well as to Matthew Pitman, from Edward Elgar, for his interest in this book. Finally, I thank Marta Mozo for her work as translator and proof-reader and also to Lia D. Shimada and Timothy Martin for their revisions of the final text. The author assumes full responsibility for any errors that persist.

Research Assistants and Coauthors

Andrés Maroto, in Chapter 4. PhD in Applied Economy, University of Alcalá and Servilab.
Gisela Di Meglio, in Chapter 3 – Section 3 – and Chapter 8. PhD student, University of Alcalá and Servilab.
Jorge Gallego, in Chapter 5 – Sections 4, 5 and 6. PhD student, University of Alcalá and Servilab.
Nuria Fernández, in Chapter 7. PhD in Applied Economy, University of Alcalá and Quasar.
Stefano Visintin, in Chapter 6 – Section 4 – and Chapter 9. PhD student, University of Alcalá and Servilab.

The research behind this book has been developed with the support of the Rafael del Pino Foundation

PART I

Analytical Framework for Services

1. Introduction – exploring the new service economy

This chapter introduces the book by presenting the rationale for a better understanding of the new service economy and setting out the objectives, scope and criteria underlying the research in the rest of the chapters. The chapter singles out what is new and deserving of special attention in the service economies and points up the main research-related questions. The structure and rationale of the book is presented through a linkage between economic facts, challenges and policy implications, with particular attention to the case of Europe.

1. RATIONALE FOR A BETTER UNDERSTANDING OF THE NEW SERVICE ECONOMY

Services represent a dimension which is present in our economic and social life. When visitors arrive in a modern city, they are to a large extent experiencing immersion in the service society and economy by visiting the historical monuments that encourage tourism through a complex web of services (travel agencies and tour operators, television programmes, magazines, etc.) and by enjoying local gastronomy, hotels and restaurants. They also visit shops (distributive trades) selling all kinds of goods and services. Alongside private traffic there is the public transport system, which enables movement and is the backbone of city life. Services are performed inside office buildings or in schools, universities, training centres and, of course, in leisure and cultural centres – a perfect way for visitors to end their day in the city. All of the above are service activities that are numerous and omnipresent in day-to-day city life. The elements of past agricultural or industrial societies are gradually waning. Nevertheless, without goods – food, buildings, machinery – the development of the services society would not be possible.

Nowadays, services represent around 70 per cent of developed economies, in terms of both employment and added value (see Chapter 3). All industrial companies require services to define, design, produce and distribute their products. Services are increasingly essential for a company's competitiveness, whether they are produced within the company itself or outsourced. It is not by chance that innovation; information- and knowledge-intensive services are more developed in countries with higher levels of competition and economic prosperity. In the area of consumption, the most powerful western countries are service-oriented countries, even though they are still paradoxically called 'industrialized countries'.

Despite the recent advances, services are still inadequately studied by researchers, underestimated by politicians and insufficiently exploited by many entrepreneurs. The perception of services as unproductive by some thinkers from the 18th century (e.g., Adam Smith, 1776) still persists in the common mind of the present society. Even today, in the centre of a society characterized by knowledge, information and intangibles, many still consider services as secondary activities to economic growth. Others currently give services the lowest role in economy: less productive, less innovative, less advanced regarding technology, a shelter for industrial unemployment or a specialization for those who cannot compete in what really matters, the goods economy. This idea is inherited from a materialist concept which, literally speaking, ostentatiously conflicts with the current reality.

Studying services means studying not an isolated economic sector but horizontal activities that affect all sectors of the economy. An emblematic case of integration between goods and services is the construction sector, which is sometimes classified separately either as an industry or even as a service. The aim of construction is to provide tangible goods offering a service to the users of houses, roads, office buildings, etc., so that the way in which services are linked to the use, supply and maintenance of these goods has taken on increased importance. There are also production-linked services (e.g. those of engineers, architects, draughtsmen, topographers, transport and logistics experts, etc.) that have a decisive effect on the quality and competitiveness of the final product. To these we can add services related to quality control, security and risk management, sales and obviously real estate and rentals. Unfortunately, understanding of these services directly associated with the production of goods is limited. Likewise, those goods required for services are equally important in many cases, including computer software, which needs hardware in order to be stored and to function. Integration between goods and services is a reality that calls for the role of intangibles and tangibles – and of the knowledge society in the production of goods – to be reconsidered. This applies not only to business services but also to many final consumer services, which are increasingly knowledge-intensive and have a growing importance in advanced societies, where culture and education are considered almost as basic goods.

Many aspects of services are still inadequately understood, and this is precisely what we are attempting to highlight in this book. Included among these aspects is the apparent low productivity or low innovative capacity of this sector. Common methods used in traditional industry in order to calculate productivity or innovation fail when applied in the same way to the service sector. The difficulties in defining product in the world of services or the forms in which innovation is developed mean that new and alternative approaches are required in order to attain a full understanding of the sector's dynamism and its contribution to economic growth. This is also influenced by the profuse interaction between services and globalization, although this too has been partly ignored due to the limited importance of services in international trade.

In this context, it is hardly surprising that economists have been the last to start studying and acknowledging the productive nature of services, although researchers from other areas such as economic geography, sociology, marketing or management have done so more openly. Economists have found it more difficult to abandon the traditional issues inherited from the most famous experts, who either considered services to be unproductive – as in the case of Adam Smith (1776), who stated that services did not generate value ('...seldom leave any trace or value behind them for which an equal quantity of service could afterwards be procured') – or of the theories that were developed as part of the goods economy and were therefore not specifically relevant to the services economy, as with the Neoclassical models. Moreover, the studies carried out by economists have been, and still are, hampered by such factors as the objective difficulty of applying the supposed reality-simplifiers (including product or price homogeneity) required to create models, as well as by the lack of comparable time-series statistics. That is one reason for the emergence of economists researching specific sectors strongly subject to a liberalization process (transport, finances, and communications). These economists apply certain regulation theories that can be empirically contrasted in sectors with a high level of economic and statistical information. The huge amount of economic-services regulation, particularly in network industries, has attracted the interest of researchers in the context of an economic policy that favours the liberalization and opening up of markets in many countries. However, important gaps still exist in research on many business and consumer services, despite the fact that these sectors are often highly regulated too. Closer attention has been paid to public services, although they could usefully benefit from even more.

In fact, from an economic policy perspective, there are abundant services regulations, although many of them are no longer justified. There are still a number of politicians and policymakers who, on the basis of outdated ideas, defend protectionist positions in services and manufacturing industry. However, the advance of liberalization and pro-competition processes in recent years has generally been of remarkable benefit to society, even though these processes have not always been implemented in the best possible way, i.e. with sufficient re-regulation or taking into consideration the interests of the main affected parties. The competitive opening-up of the service sector is still in full swing and debate on many aspects continues.

In Europe, the reduction of protectionism is being carried forward under the recently approved EU Directive for the internal services market – at both European level and, under the GATS negotiations, at global level. Many difficulties are encountered by these processes along the way.

Efforts are also being made to extend innovation policies and standards-rules to the field of services, so that – in line with the interests of the sectors affected – services are not excluded from the advantages that such policies have yielded in the goods market.

Within Europe, political interest in services centres on the Lisbon Strategy (2000), which is aimed at making the European Union the most competitive economy by 2010. The objectives were simplified and clarified in 2005 as a result of the modest progress made towards the objectives set out in the Lisbon Strategy – Kok report. However, the European Commission has insisted on relaunching the Lisbon Agenda, and together with the Member States has proposed national programmes to implement structural measures aimed at improving employment and growth. For the first time, services are included, as of 2004, in many of the measures and initiatives as a key objective of the Commission's political strategies, particularly as regards the internal services market but also in other important areas. Significant proof of the importance of sectoral aspects, particularly services, in the application of European policies is contained in the recent Commission report (Gelauff and Lejour, 2006), which assesses the five key Lisbon targets. One of these targets is the internal services market, and a sectoral analysis that includes services is carried out in the other four.

Taking as a basis the 'new' characteristics of the service economy ('new' in an incremental sense of novelty more than in a radical one), and without going into too much depth, the reasons for studying services – which to some extent justify this book – can be summarized as follows:

1. Services represent the major share of developed economies and are increasingly integrated in the overall production system: interrelations between industry and services are growing. Despite the traditional isolation of services in much economic analysis, when we consider the economy we are to a large extent referring to the service economy. Nevertheless, the growth of services does not negatively affect the growth of goods.

2. Services to support trade began in some few countries such as the UK and the US as these countries industrialized. However, unlike in previous decades, services nowadays play a much more active role in market integration and globalization. So much so that the phenomenon of services-offshoring has been posing competitive challenges to developed countries since the year 2000.

3. The creation of employment, added value and income is increasingly related to the good performance of services. This mainly applies to productive, innovative services and those with a competitive and

employment capacity. These three variables are not traditionally associated with services, although a correct approach opens up new possibilities and challenges consistent with the potential that has sometimes been hidden from traditional indicators and analyses.

4. Nowadays, many service markets and advanced economies, having been protected by public monopolies and protectionist regulations, are opening up to competition after being isolated from it. This change of scenario prompts us to reconsider the role of public intervention in these markets and the need for more determined efforts towards competition, opening and integration between neighbouring countries.

The basic new characteristics of the service economy can be complemented with some specific new EU developments. Services are required in order to achieve the European objectives for growth and employment, as specified by the Lisbon Strategy. However, a series of deficits and challenges concerning the services economy have been pointed out, and it is therefore necessary to identify, document and justify those policies most consistent with the real problems of the sector. A full understanding of services can be used to properly assess current policies and to make recommendations for future developments. In this direction, the European Commission is launching new initiatives as regards service policies, as can be seen in the 2004 renaming of DG Internal Market to DG Internal Market and Services. The best recent examples of how services have been moved to the top of EU agendas are the approved Framework Directive for an Internal Market for Services, the complementary policies for business-related services currently under discussion, and the work on services of general interest. The more prominent position of services at EU level opens up new policy scenarios allowing services to be monitored and understood in a more comprehensive way. Furthermore, the eastward expansion of the European Union and the prospect of greater liberalization of trade in services by the GATS constitute an arena for European services that extends beyond the borders of the old Member States. The inclusion of the new eastern Members to the European area and foreseeable advances in multilateral or bilateral international trade pose new challenges for sectors traditionally omitted from the international scene.

2. FROM CHALLENGES TO POLICY IMPLICATIONS

As indicated above, this book endeavours to combine economic realities, challenges and policies in a single volume. The main objective is to contribute to the understanding of the new service economy by means of its key dimensions and available empirical evidence. This in turn will allow us to deduce the existing need for improvements in economic capacity as regards employment, productivity, innovation and competitiveness. On the basis of the challenges identified, we will attempt to show the current policies implemented in Europe and their ability to respond to the requirements of the sector.

The book therefore sets out to meet several objectives. Firstly, it aims to provide a comprehensive picture and review of the importance and role of services in an advanced economy. All services are covered, although the focus will be on business and knowledge-intensive services. The recent new statistics on services will be used as key empirical support for different sections. For analytical frameworks, recent studies on services in the related literature are reviewed, covering the different perspectives of economics, economic geography and policy-related material. A survey on the economic policy for services is particularly needed. For international comparisons, the book compares different situations and patterns among various countries, but mainly between the EU and the US, at both economic and regulation/policy levels, with the focus on the competitive position of the EU economies.

Secondly, the book endeavours to provide new critical elements for reconsidering and going beyond traditional statements about services, e.g. their low capacity for productivity and innovation growth, EU services lagging behind those in the US, the limited capacity of services to operate in global markets, or the need for greater regulation and protectionism in services in order to guarantee quality and consumer satisfaction.

Thirdly, the book attempts to provide a comprehensive approach to all policies affecting services, from competition to internal market policies, from regulation to liberalization policies, and from regional to innovation policies. To do this, recent EU policies on services are explored and discussed.

Some possible answers to a series of questions are set out below as general hypotheses of this research. They will be directed towards the relevant subjects in each of the chapters.

1. Is it possible to single out a common feature among the heterogeneous service sectors and activities, thereby enabling us to extract useful implications that help us to understand their needs and challenges? Despite the very varied nature of the services comprising the service sector, can common aspects be deduced to define a particular 'ontology' of the service economy (characterized by interactive dimensions which are freely operated and co-produced by the parties: see Chapter 2). This dictates the need to approach the sector according to its specific nature.

2. Service sectors or service activities? The specific features of services cannot be directly associated with all service sectors. There are, for example, certain services for which the presence of the goods economy is relatively important and which display significant behavioural similarities with goods. Moreover, goods industries can assimilate service behaviours because their characteristics form a horizontal dimension in the overall

production system. In that sense we should seek out the specificity not of service sectors but of those service activities that can be developed within any industry or that are present in any economic activity.

3. Where is the structural change heading? Services are expected to assume a greater presence in all economic dimensions. The outsourcing process does not seem to have a limit, at least as far as the microeconomic integration between goods and services is concerned. However, a slowdown in their relative growth compared to that of goods industries could be foreseen in some countries.

4. Is the world moving towards a single services model? While a great variety of service behaviours by country and by sector is predicted, this could well be accompanied by a higher common dynamism of knowledge-intensive services and thus by convergence towards a less heterogeneous services model in Europe. A certain convergence between the US and EU service economies could be expected too.

5. Can industrial assessment criteria be transferred to the services world? Productivity, innovation and a competitive economy in services mean that traditional concepts applied to goods must be reviewed and less linear and more multidimensional categories, indicators and approaches established.

6. What is the situation of European services? The lack of a European service-oriented culture confident of its potential has had negative effects in Europe. As a result, we can identify a series of deficits and weaknesses, many of which are related either to insufficiently decisive political action or to action that is over-characterized by protectionist and conservative practices. In any case, globalization poses a key challenge for services.

7. Which service policies have been formulated and how can we assess them? Do they meet the needs of the sector and their ontological features? What is the European Union doing? European policies on services are extremely varied and diverse, at both national and EU levels. Sometimes they are a response to protectionist efforts, and sometimes they bring stiffer competition and market opening. In any case, more decisive proposals are required at both regulatory and non-regulatory (or complementary policy) levels. Liberalizing measures must be supplemented with other non-regulatory ones, and this requires greater concordance and coherence between them and between national and EU policies.

In order to deal with the aforementioned objectives and these working hypotheses, we try to corroborate or refute, on a methodological basis, the ideas arising from previous works or from new ongoing approaches. The method used is strongly linked to empirical evidence in the early chapters and to European Commission documents of policy practice in the others. The overall aim is to combine analytical, empirical and economic policy approaches in an organized manner.

The book is divided into three clearly differentiated parts. The first includes this introductory chapter (Chapter 1) and establishes the conceptual framework defining services and suggests an 'ontology' that develops their features (Chapter 2).

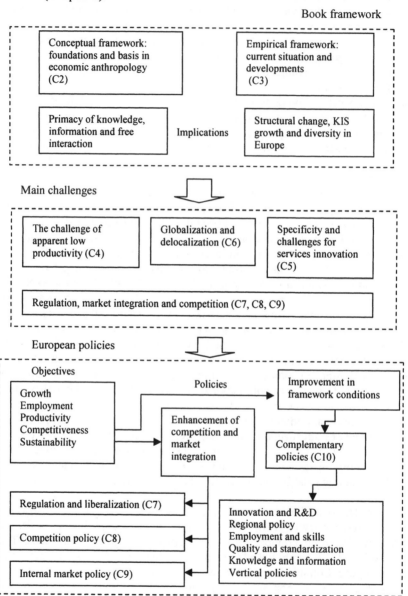

Figure 1.1 Rationale of the research

The second part begins with a chapter (Chapter 3) dealing with the empirical framework. Here the discussion centres on the hypotheses of structural change and growth of the service sector in advanced economies, as well as the existence or non-existence of convergence between these. Following the theoretical, conceptual and basic empirical framework, three chapters set out to refute the traditional assumptions regarding the low productivity of services (Chapter 4), their low innovative capacity (Chapter 5) and their low competitive capacity (Chapter 6), highlighting in each case those positive aspects of the traditional analysis that cannot be refuted. From the four empirical chapters, we deduce a series of challenges that characterize the new service economy in advanced economies, but mainly within the European context after a benchmarking exercise on the US economy. The third part consists of an initial chapter (Chapter 7) on service regulations and their impact within the OECD framework. After this we analyse the two basic EU policies aimed at favouring competition and market integration in Europe: competition policy (Chapter 8) and the policy on an internal market for services (Chapter 9). These three chapters set out the specific challenges of these policies, which are characterized by the EU's economic objectives and the corresponding legal system. The policy section of the book is then brought to a close with a brief overview of the various EU complementary policies on services (Chapter 10). Finally, the concluding section summarizes the main contributions of the book and the main implications for economic policy.

Figure 1.1 shows the logic underlying the order and structure of the book. Chapters 2 and 3, corresponding to different sections – theoretical-conceptual and empirical, respectively – combine to form the working framework on which is based the analysis of the main service dimensions in advanced economies and their challenges. This – from Chapter 3 to Chapter 10 – represents the core of the book. Chapter 7 onwards sets out the regulatory and non-regulatory services-related policies justified by the growth and employment objectives of the European Union, with the corresponding consequences on productivity and competitiveness.

3. RESEARCH PRIORITIES AND FOCUS ON PRODUCER SERVICES

As the reader will appreciate, the objectives, working hypotheses and methodological approach of this book are particularly ambitious. It is therefore only prudent to consider the limits of the work carried out and to modestly highlight its scope.

Firstly, although this is a sizeable book, it is not large enough to allow systematic discussion of all the difficulties and issues surrounding the service economy. Each of the chapters represents a complete line of research. Consequently, the book offers only a more or less limited contribution from these – on the basis of priorities subjectively chosen by the author – and a necessary overview of the current situation. Although every effort has been made to give the chapters a degree of uniformity, some issues are dealt with in more depth than others and some chapters include more novel elements than others.

Secondly, the book deals with services in as cross-cutting a fashion as possible, although it does refer to the situation of specific sectors. Sectoral chapters have not been included, since the priority was to study common elements and differences within services. While this results in greater formal coherence, the book will not meet the needs of readers interested in specific details or advances in a specific service sector (since there is no specific chapter on transport, communications, etc.). Only the chapter on competition policy has a sector-by-sector structure, as a way of illustrating particular cases that highlight the types of EU action promoting competition in those sectors. In many cases the book is able to document some common elements for service activities, but most of its chapters provide evidence, at detailed sub-sectoral level, of the highly heterogeneous nature of service activities, mainly among producer services and consumer services. Within the book's predominantly horizontal approach, producer services – in particular knowledge-intensive services and business services – are analysed in greater depth, as they represent the most dynamic areas in recent decades, and many of the most interesting competitive challenges can be found there. When talking about the new service economy, we talk mainly about the new dimensions of services carried out by producer services, even if consumer services and public services also contain many new elements and form an essential part of the current service economy, as shown in the recent book by Jansson (2006). However, the focus on producer services is deemed to be more appropriate to make the point of services as integrated activities within any economic activity; an essential characteristic of the new services economy. This implicitly means more focus on service production and intermediate consumption and less on service final consumption. A focus on service consumption as an element of the new service economy would take us into a different research project, or at least into a quite different approach.

Thirdly, the book is based on a fundamentally European approach, although its early chapters are international in scope and include comparisons with other countries, mainly from the OECD and particularly with the United States. A benchmarking is made between the EU and the US.

Fourthly, the analyses of economic service policies are limited to the sphere of those promoted by the European Commission. An overview and assessment of the service policies implemented in each of the European countries would have been extremely ambitious, and would call for a different approach in any future research. Nor have we made a detailed study of all the EU policies. The most horizontal policies have been chosen, and those of a vertical nature – e.g. transport, tourism or the information sector and communications – have been deliberately excluded, while at the same time remaining consistent with the approach followed in the empirical chapters.

Finally, the reader will certainly and inevitably find points and issues to which this book cannot give a response, thus leaving the way open for abundant future research.

2. Historical and anthropological origin of the service economy

INTRODUCTION

This second chapter aims to introduce the reader to the service economy by debating 'services' and explaining their operational role in society. In a certain sense, this chapter adopts an anthropological viewpoint; that is to say, it explains services through the dimension of human action in society. Services, therefore, are much more than just a simple economic sector. They are presented here as a dimension of all economic activities, which relates to the most typical values of economic creation: freedom, interaction, co-production and co-responsibility. The historical and anthropological origin of services is used to highlight the parameters behind their economy, and must be respected by political actions. Free interaction is the most distinctive element related to the creative and dynamic nature of services.

1. ORIGIN OF SERVICES IN HISTORY AND IN ECONOMIC THOUGHT

Services have frequently been considered as secondary activities. The origins of the perception lie not only with the thought and praxis of those responsible for economics or politics, but also in the broader history of economic thought. However, as will be discussed later in depth, this claim does not diminish the importance that services have had in society. Moreover, economic activity has always been related to the supply of a service: in a sense, economic activity is a service that has been revealed and discovered over time. The consolidation of services as an economic sector confirms the anthropological dimension within the service economy.

Services as a Dimension of all Economic Activities

Although the harvesting and hunting activities of the first hominids can be included within the primary sector, people living then would have understood these activities as a type of service performed by some members to benefit the community to which they belonged. All economic production is conceived and turned into a service to the extent that it is not the result of a mechanical, pre-established or instinctive process. Humans differ markedly from the animal world, which also tries to satisfy needs with limited resources. More specifically, humans adopt a progressive awareness of the resources available and, by discovering original solutions, find the necessary means to make the most of these. In their search for satisfaction, humans retain a conscious relationship with their desires and needs (some of which remain unfulfilled), and with opportunities for satisfying these through work. Human awareness of reality encourages a responsibility toward working in society. Main human activity consists of a jointly responsible working activity in the interests of the common weal. War, robbery or pilferage would be ways to accumulate wealth, but all are contrary to the sustainable development of a community. As humans consider their dominant position, they perceive the possibility of constructing a stable and peaceful society through work. Although this is not always the case, humans knows that violent conflict in the fight for survival is unnecessary to obtain scarce resources. Intelligence and self-awareness allow humans the corresponding understanding of their activities. Human action, especially regarding work, generates a service to the whole society. The service is a social dimension of joint responsibility in the workplace: one works 'towards' rendering a service with an end product, cause or need, and one works 'towards' the service to a person, family or town. Even the most individual activity transmits a kind of 'self-service', leading to a level of individual achievement.

Joint responsibility that is connected to services stems etymologically from the term 'service', which in turn stems from the Latin '*servitium*' and is related to '*servus*'. Historically, dependent relationships (i.e., servant–master, slave–lord) established hierarchical social relationships that would later extend to military, royal and governmental services. Services progressively changed from being understood only within a private sphere, to their inclusion within a social concept. The extension of this trend suggests that in democracies, political authorities work (at least theoretically) for the service of society. Therefore, services become the means and ends of political action. Similar parallels can be found with economic activity: enterprises also work at the service of the existing or created needs of consumers.

The development of advanced societies has run parallel to the development of the bilateral or multilateral nature of services. Not only will citizens serve their superiors and consumers their entrepreneurial interests, but the inverse will become increasingly important. Services require the active participation of all enterprises so that both economy and society can function. The features of co-responsibility, always present in the human workplace, acquire new dimensions in more competitive and demanding modern times. Consumers not only determine the success of some products, but they also participate more actively in the economic production itself. Unlike the systems of past centuries, citizens today also have the possibility of participating more actively in the politics of democracies. Economy and politics become more streamlined as services depend on and require an interaction between the two for their success.

A service, more than an economic sector, is a dimension of social activities that drives towards a joint achievement, to an interaction between people, and to an awareness of joint change. Goods produce a service, just as the economy is fuelled by services rendered by production, exchange and distribution between different agents. Economic growth is based on exchange and trust, which provide the foundations of specialization, money and the peaceful accumulation of income. The exchange relies on trust in a mutual service's existence within economic activity. In other words, the buyer uses the seller, and the seller uses the buyer. The importance of mutual service in economic relationships leads to the service economy, and also to the production of goods. Intensity and co-responsibility of the mutual service make distinct the production of a service, as its economic value does not necessarily require a tangible asset to express and generate welfare. The intangibles are the maximum expression of 'mutual services', which are also behind the tangibles.

Services as an Active Sector in the History of Economic Thought

The previous paragraph pointed out the value of services as a dimension of human activity from the origins of economy. However, services can also be valued as an economic sector. In ancient societies, upper-class Greeks and Romans held in high regard services relating to leisure, political power or education for the privileged. Work, especially manual work, was considered a non-leisure 'no-ocio' activity (this is the root from which the Spanish language derives 'negocio', its word for business) that was only to be performed by slaves. This was a period in which the production of goods depended on the production of services, such as political organization, defence, domestic services, religious services, leisure events or sport and circus shows, and even mercantile trade. Goods were at the service of an organization that was, to a large extent, already producing services.

The pre-eminence of services found in the social and economic organization of ancient times persists to the present day, although in highly changed form. Throughout the centuries, however, other non-service-related activities have been considered as more productive. Since ancient times and for many centuries, agriculture held a superior role, which manufacturing later claimed. Services registered a low economic consideration until well into the 20th century. Authors from the 17th and 18th centuries only seemed to hold commerce, transport and financial services in any sort of 'productive' regard.

Society's recognition occurred not suddenly, but through the long and difficult evolution of economic and social thought. Even today, 'industrialized countries' are those considered to be the world's most developed, with economies that include around 60–70 per cent services. This difference between thought and reality is due to four different factors:

1. The consolidation of the services sector in economy did not become evident until the 1960s–1970s, when industrial growth started to decline in favour of services. Economists logically focused on agriculture in an agricultural world, and on manufacturing in a goods-based world. It is therefore easy to see that progressive growth of services hid for centuries behind the expansion and development of goods-based activities.
2. The second factor, which links to the previous one, is the absence of statistics regarding services. The low level of concern for this sector was due to the pre-eminence of other, more attractive, sectors. Hence, politicians and statisticians did not take this sector into consideration. The lack of data concerning services and their marginal consideration in all statistics are two serious obstacles to capturing the interest of economists and, in particular, researchers.
3. A central part of classical economic thought has an enlightened cultural component. For the Illuminists, technical and economic progress, together with enlightened reasoning, would set humans free from their material and spiritual slaveries. In this context, services were seen only as 'immaterial' activities unable to contribute to the 'material' economic progress. Economy was defined in terms of goods. Due to production and distribution to fit with determinist laws, a determinist 'natural' order, similar to that applied in physics and mechanics,[1] was upheld in economy.
4. When services became so evident that they could no longer be put aside, the 'Rostowian'[2] development theories saw in services the ideal element to complete the developmentalist schemes in stages and the characterization of post-industrial society. Services went from being ignored or disregarded to being deified. The sudden inclusion of the services sector in the scene caused reactions that thwarted the realist consideration of the sector outside of Manichaean sectoral comparisons.

These four factors explain the long-term disregard shown by economists towards the services sector. The contrary factors are as follows: primarily, the unaided consolidation of the sector (the sector has obtained a position in society of its own accord); other factors such as improvements in the statistical situation (although still deficient); the overcoming of determinist schemes (due to the current consideration of economy as a social science based on human action and not on mechanical production); and the abdication of developmentalist dialectics among the sectors.

Before the 19th century, services were not considered in their own right. In general, they were perceived negatively, as they employed people in non-productive jobs. Mercantilists would become the exception to this perception.

As Sir William Petty (1690) observed from his statistical studies, 'there is more to be gained using manufactured goods than agriculture; and still more through commerce than through manufactured goods'.[3] With physiocracy, services are relegated to a non-productive category, against the productivity of agriculture.

Although this book will not engage in a thorough explanation, it is worth noting that classical economists also considered professions in the services sector as non-productive. Adam Smith (1776) recognized a distinction between two types of labour: that which produces a value connected to the goods to be exchanged, and that which does not produce a value. Hence, as services are immaterial, these do not produce any augmentation of wealth. Malthus, Say, Sismondi, Mill, Saint-Simon and Marx all had different opinions; some regarded services positively, although in general they upheld the negative view that had defined services throughout the classical era. Neoclassical and marginalist authors conceived their models of a general balance for a goods economy, acknowledging the difficulties involved in applying the Walrasian theory to services (D'Alcantara, 1987).

It was not until the 20th century that services were included completely in the group of productive activities. Fisher (1935, 1939), Clark (1940) and Fourastié (1949) were the first to introduce the services sector as the 'tertiary' sector of economic activity. They considered services to be productive; they verified Engel's Law and analysed the relatively low productivity of this sector with respect to the other economic activities. These works used substantial empirical applications.

The era of development during the 1950s and 1960s brought about the boom of post-industrial theses. Within the evolution of development 'by stages', services started to become the new standard of contemporary civilization, ended up replacing industry, and thus established a new order. Bell (1973) was the most famous author of this era. Apart from the channelled trend in sociology, the service economy focuses on explanations regarding growth in the sector starting from the differences of inter-sectorial productivities. Fourastié's pioneering studies were magnified and reinforced by Fuchs (1968) and Baumol (1967) (see Chapter 4 for details).

In the 1970s, economic thought ran parallel to the industrial crisis and the assimilation of industrial unemployment by the employment of services. This is why the 'tertiarization' phenomenon was analysed as a result of the 'de-industrialization' process from a viewpoint contrary to that prevailing in the 1960s. For example, Gershuny (1978) was considered the 'anti-Bell' (Delaunay and Gadrey, 1987) due to his analysis regarding consumer services and his concept of the self-service society, based on the pre-eminence of goods over services.[4] Aside from Gershuny, other authors studied the growth of the service sector as a consequence of technological innovations (Pavit, 1980), the displacement of the industrial sector by the public sector (Bacon and Eltis, 1976), the information economy (Porat, 1976) and a series of different factors such as the complementarity between goods and services, the increase of services compared with production or the industrialization of services (Stanback, 1979; Noyelle, 1983).

The 1980s were characterized by criticism of all the previous interpretations that ignored the complementarity between industry and services. In this decade, authors commented on the tertiarization of industry and the industrialization of the tertiary sector; *input-output* studies spread, and the business services sector came to be considered the most emblematic subsector of sectorial integration. Some of the current experts on business services contribute to a recent book edited by Rubalcaba and Kox (2007).

As old myths and dialectics receded, services started to be analysed systematically using specialized approaches. In the 1980s, and predominantly from 1987 throughout the 1990s, substantial efforts resulted in numerous and varied publications. A summary of these different working lines would require a whole chapter: aside from a few examples, this book makes no attempt to cover this vast research process (the author apologises for those experts not mentioned in this brief text).

The first main line of research (which was instigated by the authors (mostly economists) who studied *the factors and environment of growth of service)* describes, analyses and reinforces in its entirety the services sector and its relationships with economy. This block can be divided into three research fields. The first field could be named *income and structural change,* and is the most relevant for understanding services and related economic processes. Stigler's (1956) primary research in the late 1970s was the turning point towards understanding services from a realist point of view, and towards analysing and reinforcing the hypothesis of structural change (Singelmann, 1978, Gershuny, 1978). The second field of research is one towards which economists have veered: the *productivity and prices* of services. The growth of the sector has been justified traditionally by the differences of productivity between services and other sectors. In this sense, works by Fuchs (1968), and particularly by Baumol (1967) are worth mentioning, in light of Fourastié's (1949) pioneering studies. As Chapter 4 will discuss, the debate regarding productivity and prices was active throughout the 1980s and up to present times. Recent contributions are provided by Oulton, Pilat, Kox, Wolf, Fixler, van Ark, Gadrey and Griliches among others. Finally, the third research field focuses on the growth of services from the perspective of changes in productive systems, innovation, the inclusion of new technologies and industry–services relationships. This trend of *technologies, innovation and productive change* is heterogeneous, as it includes multiple disciplines and methods for tackling different questions. The 'Manchester school' (Miles, Howells, Boden, Tether, Windrum, Miozzo, Cunningham) has been particularly active in service innovation, together with other researchers in France (Gallouj), Germany (Hipp), Denmark (Sundbo) or the Netherlands (Den Hertog).

The second block of research corresponds to implications originated by the new service economy in *spatial relationships*. In this case, there are three clearly different lines of research. The first devotes itself to the study of international trade of services. During the 1980s, this study was linked to methodological and statistical problems, the Uruguay Round and positions for or against protectionism with regards to services. The second research line corresponds to the analysis of internationalization processes connected to services, resulting in a conceptual change regarding these processes and their implications. The third line of research has been linked to the spatial topics at international, regional and urban levels. Many authors, some of them experts in economic geography or regional economy, have studied the *international, regional and urban location of services*. Decisive works include those by authors such as Daniels, Illeris, Beyers, Wood, Bryson, Sjøholt, Marshall, Coffey, Polèse, Cuadrado, Senn, Stare, Aharoni, Nachum or Markusen, among others. A particular reference must be made with the heterogeneous and rich 'French school' of Gadrey, Bonamy, Barcet, Monnoyer, Philippe, Gallouj, Moulaert, De Bandt or May. Beyond the geographical dimension of services, some of these authors have also made in-depth research in other service research areas and have also focused their attention upon the macroeconomics of services, the study of relationships between services and their markets, as well as management and marketing aspects.

The 1980s and 1990s were also fruitful in other research lines related to services. These include the *characterization of services markets* based on their peculiarities, supply-demand relationships, analyses of *regulations* (especially in regulated sectors such as transport or communications) and national or regional *policies* for services. The field of *service management, business and marketing,* which concentrates the highest number of service researchers in the world, including the most important service-related international journals, also underwent important improvements which are not possible to report here given the limited space of this book and the high number of reputed researchers in this area. An interesting state of the service research, mainly from the management angle, has been compiled by Ganz and Meiren (2002).

2. CONCEPT, DEFINITION AND HETEROGENEITY OF SERVICES

Traditionally, the service sector has been defined within residual categories. Services do not represent either agriculture or manufacturing; they are part of the tertiary (as opposed to the primary or secondary) sector. The study's object (data) and its subject (thinkers) have frequently employed residual categories in an attempt to apply the same interpretative categories to services as to goods. The consequences of this phenomenon have been far-reaching. Along with some of the classical economists, some analysts today still hold the extreme view of services as unproductive activities.

An important classification of services from a positive point of view consists of enumerating their distinguishing characteristics: immaterial, transitory, unpredictable, etc. However, most of these characteristics retain the negativity that defines services not by what they are but by what they are not (not material, not durable, not storable, not transportable, not accumulative, etc.). However, negative definitions have faced abundant criticism (see, for example, O'Farrell and Hitchens, 1989). Hill's well-known article 'On goods and services' (1977) is a pioneering step towards a positive approach. He put forward the first positive difference between goods and services: goods are physical objects that are appropriated and are therefore transferable between economic units. However, a service provided by an economic unit represents a change to the condition of a person or goods that belong to another economic unit. Hence, the service is defined as a result.

In principle, services can be identified according to classic categories on types of goods:

1. Search goods, based on the selection of products, quality and diversification through attributes such as colour, style, consistency, smell, etc., whose quality can be evaluated prior to consumption;
2. Experience goods, based on information on opportunity, taste, durability, etc., and whose quality cannot be evaluated until after consumption;
3. Credence goods, whose quality cannot be evaluated even after consumption. Services in general belong to the latter two categories (Sapir, 1993a), and most business services (market research and consulting, for example) can be considered as belonging to the group of credence goods (O'Farrell and Hitchens, 1990). The role of credence in business services emphasizes the relational aspect of their services. In a positive way, the former concept of simultaneity of production and consumption leads to the current concept of interaction as the main characteristic of service co-production.

The 1990s saw the development of several positive interpretations of services, which connect to interactive aspects and demand, rather than merely to elements of supply. In particular, these interpretations have been applied to business services (Martini 1990, 1992; Sharpe and Wernerheim, 1996; Rubalcaba 1999; Gadrey and Gallouj, 1998). Although this chapter will not discuss them in detail, the accepted approaches stress elements such as changes or utilities produced and interactive aspects of the service and related agents.

Despite the attempts to define them, services possess a remarkable degree of heterogeneity. However, the diversity of service sectors does not obscure the definition of common features. The case of business services is a significant example of how uniqueness can be maintained alongside heterogeneity. These services have traditionally been defined as a subgroup.

The definition criterion is the type of clientele to which services are directed. These are not services for collective or individual consumers, but for productive organization, namely companies. This 'a priori' definition represents the role that the group of services carries out in the contracting company and the place that it occupies in the company's normal production line.

Business services can be defined as follows: they are real (not financial) activities that first influence the competitiveness of companies (they are not incompatible with the service provision to consumers) through their use as *intermediary inputs* in the value chain, and via *quality and innovation gains* resulting from the interaction between supplier, client and service, by complementing or substituting the in-house service functions. This definition aims: to serve as a positive definition, in counterpoint to the traditional negative definition; to introduce the function of the service in its own definition, in order to link its tertiary nature to a competitive aim (i.e., business services are interesting because of the effects they produce); to insert the sector's activity in the intermediary inputs of clients and the final outputs that incorporate gains (not necessarily positive, and even if they are only basic) in quality and innovation; and, finally, to highlight the service's interactive aspect, which is always co-produced between two or more parties.

Table 2.1 Negative vs. positive definitions of a service

Negative features	Positive features
Non-tangible	Usefulness or benefit of goods
Non-material	Usefulness or benefit of an action
Non-transportable	Simultaneous consumption and production
Non-cumulative	Change in a person or good
Non-quantifiable	Dialogue relationship
Non-durable / perishable	Interaction between supplier and user
Non-predictable	Transitive relationship

The heterogeneity of business services is based on different criteria. When taking about business services, these refer to large traditional services (such as accounting, law or engineering) and also to very recent services (such as those related to the Internet, temporary employment or telecommunications). Moreover, some business services are highly advanced (for instance, computing, electronic communication or R&D services), while others are highly operative (security, industrial cleaning or courier services). Another group comprises services of a high social and commercial involvement (advertising, fairs and exhibitions), together with services related to the field of business organization and production (advanced management and quality control services, respectively). Finally, there are intensive services in physical capital (specialized renting and leasing services), technological capital (Internet services), highly-qualified human capital (advanced consultancy services), and intensive services in low-qualified work (industrial building cleaning). Due to the array of situations, the common features of activities cannot be categorized by their age, for their advanced or operative nature, or for their intensive resources for certain production factors. This sector bases its uniqueness on three pillars: the ways in which companies use business services; the functions they develop in the industrial system, and the nature of the performance of business services. According to the method of use, business services are defined by their use as intermediate inputs in the value chain of companies. Whilst they are produced within the industrial or services society, or by specialized firms, these services are necessary for company production. In accordance with the role they perform, business services exercise a direct influence on competitiveness through the reduction of production costs and reverse benefit. This is due to higher product quality, improvements in business organization, broader technological exploitation, and informative infrastructure for commercialization. All in all, business services are justified by the benefits they bring to companies that want and know how to use them, regardless of the sector to which they belong.

The nature of the relevant business service is characterized by the result of a transitive co-production between the offerer, the petitioners and the results to be produced. Business services are distinguished by their genuinely interactive, and therefore personalized, nature. Even more standardized business services require a joint definition of the service and a minimal level of personalization, leading many to embrace integrated services (for example, some companies offer services for cleaning, security, restoration, etc. all in one customized 'package'). The most advanced business services, such as those rendered by management consultancy firms, cannot be explained outside the interaction of two parties acting in the service. In fact, the supplier can offer a service that complies with all expectations created only to the extent to which the petitioner is qualified for co-production. Consequently, business services are activities that contribute as intermediate inputs to the improvement of business competitiveness from interactive co-productions. This definition is a convergence between three levels: integrative (intermediate inputs); functional (impact on competitiveness); and ontological (interactive co-production). This conceptualization has led to the rejection of traditional trends that define services not by what they are but by what they are not (not storable, not tangible, not repeatable, etc.), and that classify them negatively (not agriculture, not industry, etc.). Despite the heterogeneity of services, some aspects of positive definition can be found.

3. THE CLASSIFICATION OF SERVICES AND STATISTICS

The heterogeneity of services becomes evident in their traditional classifications. They have often been defined as a mixture of what is not included in industry or agriculture (e.g. Fisher, 1935). The attempts to classify services from a positive viewpoint are many and diverse. In 1940, Clark popularized the phrase 'tertiary sector'. In his famous classification, he extended the scope of services to construction or energy, and replaced the phrase 'tertiary sector' with 'services'. Subsequent authors departed from Clark, such as Fuchs (1968), who excluded capital-intensive services from the services sector in order to define and classify services in terms of their employment intensity. In the same era, Greenfield (1966) identified the difference between services to end consumers and services to production, subject to intermediate demand. Noteworthy modern classifications include that of Browning and Singelmann in 1978 (distribution services, producer services, social services and personal services), Nusbaumer's functional classification in 1984 (marketable services, services performed in situ, durable services and non-durable services), and Ochel and Wegner's in 1987 (permanent and temporary services, reversible and irreversible services, private and collective provision of services, non-marketable and marketable services). In fact, most researchers writing on this subject have proposed their own classification, or have adhered, with reservations, to the existing main classifications.

Table 2.2 Main services needed for the running of companies (functional approach)

Business activities by function	Main business-related services
Administration	Management consulting
	Legal services
	Auditing and accounting services
Human resources	Temporary work
	Selection and supply of personnel
	Professional training
Financial intermediation	Banking
	Insurances
	Leasing and renting
Information management	Computer services
	Telecommunications
Commercialization and sales	Advertising
	Distributive trades
	Public relations
	Fairs and exhibitions
	After-sales services
Transport and logistics	Logistics
	Transport services
	Express mail services

Source: Contribution of the author in the European Commission (2003a, COM747) regarding business-related services.

The classifications made by international organizations have been used as a reference for services. Although until recently statistical breakdowns preferentially considered the manufacturing industry and the primary sector, the situation has improved considerably over the last fifteen years. Previously, it was unfathomable for the sector representing around 65–70 per cent of advanced societies to have an official statistical representation of under 20–30 per cent. Services did not have sufficient sectoral breakdown and were excluded from many major international statistics, for instance, some indicators of national accounting, foreign commerce, price indexes, innovation and technology. Gaps still exist today in the field of statistics, but the situation is improving gradually. One reason for this improvement was the adoption, at the beginning of the 1990s, of the Nace Rev.1 in Europe, which provided a more positive classification of services (for the first time, some services such as computer activities or telecommunications took more important positions). The ongoing Rev. 2 of Nace (expected for 2010) should result in greater attention paid to services, since the current version, especially in the area of business services, still contains too many additions and simplifications. Some strategically important activities such as management consultancy or fairs and exhibitions are dissolved into extremely aggregated categories. Moreover, difficulties arising out of the Nace rev. 1 extend to classifications used by all national and regional institutes of statistics. Statistically, these problems are similar to those services considered very poor. The sparse coverage of countries and regions hinders a reasonable understanding of the activity, and the information available is highly limited. The empirical chapters of this book will discuss these problems in greater depth.

It is worth noting that this distinction between economic activities becomes less clear if these elements are considered: the dissolution of boundaries; the intersection of clients in companies and final consumers; and the existence of multiple secondary activities, etc. In a strict sense, jobs classified within the service industries can be considered as manufacturing jobs, and many jobs in manufacturing industries can be considered as service jobs. The definitions and classifications tend to focus the attention on the main type of activity and product, more than on the type of employment or activity implied. As O'Farrell and Hitchens (1990) observe: 'part of the confusion arises from the practice of defining services by listing industries rather than trying to articulate the essence of service activity that all such industries share'.

Within the field of business services, some approaches have spread wider, looking for a greater functionality as an alternative to the official rigid ones. There are classifications according to motivation of the service use, establishing services the use of which is obligatory (through functional necessity), compulsory (through legal necessity), or knowledge-intensive (linked to new technologies or strategic areas). Classification according to the place of supply is also important. A distinction can be made between internally linked services, which are produced within the company, and externally linked services, which are produced outside. Finally, classifications by type of product or supplied expertise accompany classifications according to the market. These classifications by approach are useful for new studies on business services. However, they are extremely difficult to implement in traditional statistical systems.

Table 2.3 Classification of services activities by functions in the economic system

Production services	Social and economic function	Final consumer services
Wholesale trade, restaurants and hotels	Food, goods acquisition and distribution	Retail trade
Communication services Courier services Satellite TV services	Communication	Landline and mobile telephones, mail services
Marketing services Advertising agencies Professional fairs Internet services	Marketing, information and sales	Press and television Internet Consumer fairs
Consultancy, professional, engineering, quality control, computer, R&D and KIS services in general.	Information, knowledge, advice and innovation	Legal services, tax consultancy Internet services
Consultancy, engineering, quality control and business services in general	Production and innovation	
Selection of personnel, temporary work, training	Education Training Employment	Education system, schools, universities, nurseries
Banking and insurance Goods and car renting Office renting	Financing	Banking and retail insurance House renting
Transport services	Transportation	Passenger transport
Business travel Corporate and incentive travel Hotel agencies	Tourism	Hotels and restaurants Travel agencies
Audiovisual services	Leisure and culture	Sport and cultural events Leisure and culture services
Security services, cleaning services Facility management	Home and building care (real estate)	Security, house cleaning
Public business services Environment, waste exploitation, corporate social responsibility	Organization, health, welfare and social and environmental cohesion	Public services to citizens Health, personal services NGOs

The functional approach to services related to businesses also attempts to classify services based on their importance to business function, as does the European Commission Communication 747 (2003a) on business-related services. The concept used in this document is itself defined by the functions that services provide to productions that are included to improve business competitiveness. The commission's work implies a strategy for the development of services statistics, which are at the height of development and could lead to an advance in understanding the sector's interrelation with the entire economic system. Useful classifications and statistics are suggested initially to analyse not only services supply, but also demand and its relevant interrelations. Beyond classification of business-related services, Table 2.3 proposes a classification that integrates consumer services as well. To this end, social functions and economic functions are considered together.

4. SERVICE SOCIETY: POST-INDUSTRIAL SOCIETY OR SERVINDUSTRIAL SOCIETY?

The consolidation of the service economy is not a consequence of a breakdown in industrial economy. Recent research shows that the type of economy developing currently incorporates services and industry. The consolidation of services occurs with the inclusion – not exclusion – of industry. Services are imperative to a strong industrial economy, and they develop as a consequence.

That services are considered as a dimension of all economic activities could be better understood by observing the goods economy and the overlapping of goods and services. Just as goods need services and vice versa at a macroeconomic level (from which 'the tertiarization of manufacturing' and 'the industrialization of the tertiary' are derived), all products are good–service compounds at a microeconomic level. As Wood (1991, page 165) states: 'all goods and service production involves increasingly complex combinations of material and service inputs. Many modern goods are highly "customised", or service intensive, while some services depend heavily on material goods'. In this context, the differentiation of a product is reached by means of material–immaterial combinations within the good–service continuum.

The paradigmatic case of this integration between goods and services is represented by business services, which justify their existence as intermediate products joining industrial processes and end goods and services. Creation, design, production, and sales are phases in which services make themselves increasingly necessary with the shortening of product life-cycles.[5] Manufacturing companies tend to integrate more services linked to production and distribution in order to adapt better to their clientele.[6]

One result of the integration process of goods and services is the difficulty in establishing a division between the two.[7] Integration is not simply juxtaposition: it represents a complete transformation. The extent to which services and goods mix together and interchange with greater frequency and ease than in earlier times is not of vital importance. The true 'revolution' which the integration of goods and services represents is caused by the original transformation of goods into services and services into goods. In a new way, the goods become a service, while the service converts into goods.

It is possible to identify five ways in which goods are transformed into services. These correspond to the following five types of services incorporated in goods:

1. *Production services*. These are the services used to obtain, produce and distribute goods. They are added to the value chain of the goods, and affect its value added. 'Pure' physical goods can have a high selling price thanks to the services incorporated into the production process. In many cases, services for the production of goods may surpass the value added obtained in the 'material' chain starting from raw materials.
2. *Operational services*. These are services produced by goods independent of their use and enjoyment. The goods' function is carried out through the service, which the former provides.
3. *Functional services*. These give functional use to the goods. All goods have a functional use; this is intrinsically a service.
4. *Accompanying services*. These accompany the attainment, enjoyment and maintenance of goods and, on occasions, also their elimination.
5. *Differentiating services*. The peculiar 'good + service' composition provides an additional service that allows the user to differentiate him/herself from other consumers. This uniqueness may be real or imagined, and the fragmentation of mass consumption acts as its greatest protector.

These five types of services associated with goods act as a group and determine the depth of transformation. The example of television sets explains this point. The business services used for their design, production management, advertising and sale, among others, are production services incorporated in the end price and formulated in the supply function of the producer. In television sets, the service that offers various images and sounds is an operational service, comparable to the freezing service provided by a refrigerator or the alimentation service of an agricultural product. In functional services, the consumer's use and enjoyment now has an influence. From one standpoint, the television set becomes an instrumental good–service between operational services (uses provided by the good) and functional services (uses received by the consumer). The services that accompany a television are wide-ranging and cover anything from delivery to maintenance services. The differentiating service is the user's perception of uniqueness bestowed through owning a television with certain characteristics, which are combinations of goods and services. Interactive television, tele-shopping, cable television or the encoding of channels are the result of technologies and strategies applied to the integration of services in the television, thus producing its successive and uninterrupted transformation into a service.

Similarly, although less prominent in today's society, an equivalent relationship could be established regarding the change of services into goods (by means of productive goods, operational goods, etc.). The price of products serves as an example of this relationship. The price of a good is the result of an assessment of the services employed for its production and its consumption. For example, the selling price of automobiles (at the price which companies are willing to produce the quantity where marginal cost equals marginal revenue) takes into account the cost of the services, which are introduced into the value chain. In the same way, the purchase price (the price consumers are willing to pay for a determined quantity, maintaining the equality of marginal benefits) incorporates the user's appraisal of related services. In other words, business services (management, advertising, etc.) affect the price of automobiles as much as do repair or finance services. On the other hand, the price of a service becomes increasingly determined by the integration of goods in its production and consumption. In this way, a service such as security incorporates the price of the computers and instruments necessary to render the service, as well as the prices that certain goods pass on to consumers (emblems, uniforms, monitoring equipment, etc.). Such prices may be valued highly in terms of the opportunity cost. However, the intangible value of many services is growing faster than the tangible value.

The points raised above suggest a services society that does not exclude tangible growth or the goods economy; indeed, it reinforces them. Therefore, the services society cannot be considered as a post-industrial society, but rather a 'servindustrial' society to the extent that the whole industry (either goods or services industry) needs a services economy to develop fully. Table 2.4 shows the main differences between a manufacturing society, predominantly based on a goods economy, and a servindustrial society, where services control all areas of productive life – not only the organization, but also the markets. On the one hand, services economy goes together with greater flexibility of productive systems, the incorporation of ICT, the primary role of human resources and higher qualification requirements, and the predominance of the immaterial as a distinguishing element. On the other hand, services contribute to globalization by changing the market game rules into more competitive structures, and in more varied locations.

To close this section, it is worth noting that the strong integration between industry and services, of which business services are distinctive activities, contradicts the classifications and denominations that confront the major economic sectors. For example, the traditional classification of economic sectors (agriculture, industry, services) is giving way to a new industry concept that includes manufacturing, energy and construction as well as services. In fact, the Anglo-Saxon world is appropriately denominating industry to all productive activity (excluding agriculture); in contrast to industries formed by manufacturing industries and services, service industries. Following this change of orientation in the industry concept, this book adopts the Anglo-Saxon denomination, while understanding that services are part of the industry and never their natural alternative.

Table 2.4 Differences between a manufacturing society and a servindustrial society

	Element	Manufacturing society	Changing factors	Servindustrial society
PRODUC-TION	**Organization**	- Rigid production - Long assembly lines - Hierarchical organization - Few intermediary services - Vertical integration	Flexibility Specialization Incorporation of ICT	- Flexible production - Short production lines - Flexible organization and networking - Many intermediary services - Subcontracting and externalization
	Productive factors	-Primacy of capital over work -Monotonous, standard work -Information process on paper -Few qualifications	Higher qualification requirements Main role of human resources Global access to productive factors	-Primacy of work, creativity and knowledge -Automatic, standard work -Information processes with new technologies -High qualifications for blue and white collar workers
	Products	-Mass consumption -Standardization and massive sales	Predominance of the immaterial	- Goods–services integration - Product differentiation - Personalization and closeness to client
MARKETS	**Competition**	- Prices as a basic element - Pure competition	More competitive environment Market globalization and integration	Differentiation and quality as competition factors, apart from prices. Evaluations of quality, services and adapting to needs added to prices
	Structure	-Stable markets -Homogenous markets -National markets -Dominance of large companies	Business concentration: mergers and acquisitions Diversity in segmentation methods and monopolist power	-Turbulent and unstable markets -Fragmented markets -International markets -Dominance of large groups but also wide niches for SMEs
	Location	-Concentration in large areas -Closeness to production factors	Globalization	-Concentration in large cities -Closeness to clients and qualified work -Multilocation and offshoring

5. ECONOMIC ANTHROPOLOGY OF SERVICES[8]

The Dual Nature of Services

What emerges from the debate on definitions of services is the need to understand the nature of services. An understanding of their internal dynamics, and the ways in which they are distinguished from goods, facilitates the ontology that defines their rationale and explicit behaviour. To this end, this subsection hypothesizes that an 'existential' duality defines the nature of a service, based on examples mainly provided from the business service world. More specifically, this hypothesis maintains that services oscillate between becoming a 'pure' service and becoming goods. The formulation of this hypothesis is not strange, given the growing integration of goods and services. All goods imply a service and entail a service, while all services imply goods, materialization or some form of physical concretization. Many goods behave more like services than goods, and many services behave more like goods than services. Knowledge of the point at which a type of product, or compound of goods–service, proceeds as goods or service is highly important. This knowledge may establish a study of growth, markets and interrelations with other activities. The same effects of services in competition with companies will depend on implicit or explicit knowledge of their intrinsic nature. This hypothesis – of the duality between goods, service in any product – manifests itself in the following four types of tensions described below:

Tension between repetition and personalization
Companies that offer services try to supply the most standardized products possible in order to repeat the service. Repetition of the same service for different clients translates into savings in terms of labour costs, thus making the most of scale economies and leading to more opportunities for specialization and the reinforcement of brand image. On the other hand, client companies seek personalized services that adjust to the real needs of the company, make utility more effective, and place the company in a position of relative competitive advantage. In some cases, demand imposes as a condition that the supplier itself will not offer services to competitors. In the advertising sector, for example, large agencies aim to develop a client in each sector, as they cannot have several competing clients in the same sector. Consulting services may also follow this pattern in some cases. In short, all services fluctuate between interest in repetition in supply and interest in personalized demand.

Obviously, this does not mean that supply does not obtain benefits from personalization, nor demand from repetition. When supply is personalized, it manages to hold certain niche markets by creating a high level of client loyalty. Many small and medium-sized companies mobilize the resource of personalization in their competition against large, highly standardized service companies with strong brand images. Demand also benefits when it receives repeated services. On the one hand, it benefits from the type of service experienced previously. On the other hand, a repeated service is often associated with large companies whose strong brand name acts to guarantee service reliability. In some cases, clients buy a brand image – a name and not a service. On occasions, a service may be provided with poorer quality, as the name can be used to justify actions of doubtful cost effectiveness in the medium and long term.

As a result, trends towards closed products (similar to goods, standardized, with a predetermined result) crosses with trends towards open products (actions of personalized services that are subject to permanent changes). This range of possible service to choose reflects the dynamic of the service that characterizes a compound of goods and interactive services.

Tension between the bipolar and the multipolar

There is a linear relationship between two poles within the production of goods: the seller and the buyer. This relationship is fairly interactive at the point of production and consumer response regarding satisfaction produced by the goods. However, it is a unilateral relationship at the point of buying goods. In contrast, services have a permanently dynamic and interactive action throughout production. This is the 'servuction' indicated by Barcet (1987), and quoted in De Bandt and Gadrey (1994). The difference between goods and services lies not in the material nature of the product, but in the different way it relates to the material. In goods, form is manifested as a finite whole; in services, a movement implying a risk is generated. In other words, not all the effects are known. In a service, correction generates a new service. A service is an act, not an object.

This characterization of the nature of a service entails the shift from one bipolar, linear model to a multipolar, radial model. The most basic scheme of the service, within a linear relationship, is constituted by the consideration that the service introduces itself in the value chain of a company in the same way as any other intermediary input. The production of services such as consulting, advertising or legal advice tends to increase the value of the final product with the appropriate consequences for price, quality and the final margin of the company (Porter, 1990). In this simple relationship, the client will have to look for a function that other goods can supply in the provision of the service. The client tries to use intermediary services at the lowest possible cost in order to obtain a predetermined performance.

As Gadrey (1994) shows, the first industrialization of the service was produced in the 1960s–1970s by seeking scale economies rather than a passive and little fragmented clientele. Scope economies took their place in the 1980s, multiplying the number of services offered and introducing themselves less mechanically and less passively into client companies. Commercial functions and marketing are highly developed within the growing fragmentation. The 1990s were directed towards obtaining services prioritized with a high value added, automating the simple parts of the service and dealing with the problems of uncertainty with much more complex and individual solutions.

This development in services coincides with the strengthening of the multipolar organization of the service between agents, products and environments. The co-productions of knowledge-intensive services normally involve several agents – on both the demand and supply sides – that carry out several products and sub-products in changing environments, for which flexibility and co-production adaptation are necessary at all times. This trend toward multipolar organization does not eliminate the trend to produce the service within a bipolar linear relationship between supply and demand, and in which objectives, tools, stages and results are easily planned, controlled and evaluated, as they are in a goods economy. In this way, the linear models of service interaction between supplier and client tend to be complex and to multiply the number of phases or stages in the production process.

Tension between simplicity and complexity
Although some services are highly transitory and simple, such as the buying and selling of advertising space, most usually involve a degree of complexity and durability. In these services, and above all in the knowledge-intensive ones, co-production implies the establishment of a series of relationships and interrelations between goods, services and, especially, work. Even in standardized services multiple relationships (such as industrial cleaning) are created. In the example of industrial cleaning, this co-definition involves the following: setting up a suitable contracting system, making the cleaning materials available, selecting what is to be cleaned, co-ordinating the work with that of other services such as security, dealing with residuals, administration and management, etc. Much greater complexity can be found in knowledge-intensive services like consulting, information, etc.

The growing complexity of the service's relationships introduces the idea of covalence, as Barcet indicates (1991, page 64): 'this notion is used in chemistry to point out the connections which are made between atoms (or between ions) in order to obtain a combination or a chain whose value is determined by the different elements, knowing that, independent of their nature, each one has an essential place'. From this idea, Barcet first deduces that a service is obtained through a combination of different acts; and secondly (and more crucially), that 'the flow of money which circulates is not necessarily and strictly determined by the instantaneous activity flow' (page 65). Although at one moment the flow of money coincides with the flow of activity, the activity later falls into a dynamic to which the flow of money does not adjust, at least not instantly. This leads to conclusions on risk, stability and competition in the service systems.

Another fundamental aspect of the idea of covalence is that the service changes in nature when faced with a change in one of its areas. The interaction between agents defines a system of relationships that changes in nature with the incorporation of new elements into the system. This is a natural consequence of the concept of covalence: supply and demand constitute a double-linked service within an environment or system from which co-production emerges, and whose nature changes when faced with the introduction of any new element.

These systems are configured as internal objective factors in the relationship (contract), internal subjective factors in the relationship (conditions and development of service provision and development of expectations), as well as by factors outside the relationship (economic conditions, development of alternative experiences in the provision of similar services, etc.). A change in any of the system's elements can lead to a partial or absolute variation in the relationship, as a change to one element induces change in the other elements to the extent that one could talk about a variation in nature.

Within a framework system of relationships (contract, economic environment, fluidity of the relationship between those who co-produce the service, etc.) a company which has contracted a specific design service with a supplier sees the nature of this service altered. For example, innovation by a competitor can shoot down the design provided by the supplier, and therefore the new situation requires a radical change to the design's conception. Contracts, relationships and the vision of the environment all change. In this situation, types of service and relationships, which were offered by alternative companies to the original supplier, are particularly relevant: the latter could be replaced if a substantial change does not occur in the way it carries out its co-productive relationship.

Tension between security and risk
Risk perception – fruit of the co-productive and covalent character of services – differs from the case of goods. When goods are purchased the risk inherent in the quality of the product is reduced by the existence of guarantees, endorsements, standards, repair services and insurance. In some businesses, a simple statement from the client on defects perceived in the goods purchased is enough to change the goods or return the money. The process is not the same in services. First, the risk connected to purchasing the service does not have as many mechanisms for risk reduction. A service cannot be returned, as it was consumed during production, and is not an object open to sell and return. On the other hand, services have a process of endorsements, standards and accreditation that goes much further than the current process for goods.

In fact, services entail a risk implicit in their nature: the uncertainty associated with a co-productive action whose objectives and tools can vary when faced with external change. Goods are repaired, resulting in a return to the previous situation. In most cases, a service cannot be repaired, as that would imply a new service. Repair is based on a different philosophy: its nature changes. Market research is not repairable in the strict sense of the word. If it has been wrong and the results are incorrect, a new study can be undertaken to investigate other factors previously excluded. In this way, it can meet the previous demands more precisely. The new study will vary in nature: workers, interlocutors, interviewees, methodology, etc. Time is already a factor of change in many services. Of course, the consequence of the risky nature of many services can be serious for both customers and providers.

The growing complexity of service relationships implies the vulnerability of the systems of co-production. The cluster of multipolar relationships that emerges causes the interdependence of some elements with others to increase, and augments the risk of a fault in the whole system. The vulnerability of the complex systems described by Giarini (1987; Giarini and Stahel, 1993) reflects how certain risks stand out in the service economy. This explains the internal tendencies of services towards simplification and bipolarization, such as the mechanism to reduce risks and make complex service relationships more similar to the mechanical relationships of goods. There is, therefore, a trend to produce secure service products controlling the risky nature of services, even if this control will never be fully possible.

The Logic of Participation and the Asymmetry in Duality

The consumption of goods is basically unilateral in nature if the consumer is considered just the final destination of the product, and this is compared and selected according to rational capacity. The potential development of these goods is already determined a priori: the value of use depends on the duration of time and the evaluation of the results of the goods (such as in the purchase of a car that can work out well or badly), demonstrating that the potential development of the goods was already contained at the time of purchase (the car was good or bad).

The consumption of a service obligatorily has an interlocutor, which prevents the application of the same reasoning to the consumption of goods. In this case, it is important to create a fruitful relationship that cannot be pre-established. The potential development of this relationship unfolds over time; it is not fixed at the time of purchase or contracting, but is verified according to the intelligence the two parties apply in co-production. In this sense, services are more ephemeral in nature, as they change when faced with a new phenomenon (as was deduced above regarding covalence), whereas goods, by nature, do not change unless a radical transformation or dilapidation of goods is carried out consciously after purchase.

The human reason applied to the service alters its nature: the service is the fruit of a combination of rational faculties. The reason applied to the goods can, at most, maximize the utility produced, but it cannot alter its nature. Services are configured with a meaning that depends on the intentions, agreements and potential of the participating agents. On the other hand, goods are configured with a meaning that is only altered when the service is applied. For example, the consumption of petrol is an act that contains the meaning of the goods in question: the nature of petrol cannot be altered, although it may be used for purposes other than for its original intent (e.g. incendiary use). In contrast, the discovery that petrol can be used in manufacturing and cars was possible thanks to human rationality applied to the task of observing and researching (in other words, a service).

Services not only change in nature over time, but also serve to change the nature of goods. However, the opposite is not true: goods alone cannot alter the nature of a service without the existence of another service. Advertising, design or consulting are altered by the incorporation of new information and communication technologies, but this alteration is only possible through redefinition of the system of co-production that the agents determine. Goods provoke, but do not determine, an alteration in the nature of services.

In short, services unfold a hidden potential at the point of the first co-productive act, whereas in goods a predetermined potential unfolds. In a certain sense, it is a service that makes goods unfold their potential, but always connected to the material object of the action. In a service, a connection is needed not with a physical object, but with an initial act, from which follow new acts laden with elements that cannot be predetermined and are hard to control. One possesses goods; but one can never totally possess a free service. In a slave society, domestic service only has a predetermined performance in accordance with the wishes and orders of the master. In a free service, the will of both parties and mutual understanding are fundamental to attaining the satisfaction of both parties. Even so, satisfaction will never be entire, as what remains hidden in the potential of the service always supersedes what is revealed while it becomes an act.

In this way, expectations for the possibility of a service's continued growth are much greater than in the possession of goods. Goods are possessed, and possession leads from the human condition to the economic law of decreasing marginal utility. The more one has, the less additional satisfaction one gains. In contrast, the service provision leads to another service provision, with a new set of expectations and relative levels of satisfaction. For this reason, goods and their advertising increasingly try to offer a different service; they attempt to change their apparent nature, although the real nature stays the same. They attempt to stimulate novel attraction, even if their objective is to sell the same, unchanged product: to stimulate, via the recourse to new goods, the provision of a service. In this way, many industrial manufacturers are like traditional large services that attempt to stimulate this attraction: banking, transport, retail, and tourism.

In contrast, knowledge-intensive services wage much more local battles, from barricade to barricade, from need to need, from service to service. It is a battle in which the decisive arms are not directed against the decreasing marginal utility and the possible innovations (clearly identified) of other services. Instead, they are employed against markets fragmented by different economic activities, different levels of expectation, the degree of uncertainty in the markets, reputation, loyalty, tradition and, in general, all the problems related with the lack of information. In knowledge services, the markets reflect the behaviour of a service much more than in traditional standardized services, which contain more similarities to the large manufacturing industries (proof of this is the growing concentration of traditional services). In knowledge services, the consequences of continuous potential (not predetermined) and participation (as a feature superior to possession) come to condition all aspects of the dynamics and markets.

Asymmetrical nature

Bearing in mind that the following chapters will study the characteristics of services, this section summarizes the subject of the present point and the hypothesis on the duality of services (becoming goods and becoming 'pure' services). The first tension indicated how a service tends to be personalized due to the fundamental interests of demand and to be repeated in the basic interests of supply. The second tension showed the shift from linear, bipolar relationships to multipolar and radial relationships. The third tension was produced in simple systems of co-production similar to those of goods and complex co-production systems characteristic of covalent systems. The fourth comes from the tension between the security that characterizes goods, and risk and vulnerability implicit in many services. One final tension occurred between the continuous unfolding of a service's potential and the prior revelation that characterizes goods, associated with the difference between possession and participation – two different modes of applying economic reasoning and logic.

However, this duality manifests itself in a series of tensions can give a biased result. The trend towards personalization prevails over standardization; multipolarity supersedes bipolarity; complexity grows at the cost of simplicity; increased risk reduces secure and predetermined production; the hidden element in services is greater than what is revealed; participation is greater than possession. In the case of business services, at least there is an asymmetrical duality: in all its ontological dimensions, the process of becoming a service predominates the process of becoming goods. Table 2.5 summarizes the typical features.

These results lead to some interesting implications. If services, specifically business services, are characterized by strong interactive processes rather than by associated products, then policies should address agents who interact, rather than products which are delivered. An enterprise that seeks to enhance knowledge services provision should know those who participate in the final production of services, what qualifications and aptitudes they have, how their co-productive capacity can be improved, how they are related to the parts implied by the service, etc. It would not be useful to focus all its performance objectives in the small measurable part of labour/output that is hard to value. Added to this, any generic valuation attempt would not be very helpful unless it is part of a case by case study, service by service and person/team by person/team.

Table 2.5 Shaping the ontology of services

Tensions	Features of the service ontology
Repetition vs. personalization	Dynamic balances between supply and demand. Personalization control in KIS
Bipolarity vs. multipolarity	Service as an act, not an object. Servuction, dynamic and interactive action.
Simplicity vs. complexity	Covalent systems. Changes in conditions. Changes in nature. Complexity in KIS
Security vs. risk	Return difficulties. Uncertainty and insecurity. Vulnerability.
Possession vs. participation	Not pre-established potentialities. Changing expectations.

6. THE VALUE OF FREEDOM AND THE FREE INTERACTION IN SERVICES

Orio Giarini and Walter Stahel (1993) state that the limits of growth coincide with the limits to certainty. Sticking to old certainties is hardly the best way to face a future full of uncertainties. Three conditions are necessary: recognizing the services economy as the battlefield where the real opportunities for a future growth can be found; regaining faith in producer-offerers and their high-risk activities; and identifying risk as a positive factor in which uncertainty is the condition for reconstruction.

It is true that the growth of services connects to ways of dealing with uncertainties: activities emerge to increase confidence in times of risk or change (services such as insurance, lawyers, consultants, or those related to personnel, training and education). Just as trust makes an increase in profit, exchanges and speculations, today this trust (thanks to services) moves the economy towards new development stages.

However, many obstacles inhabit this path. Contrary to the assumed norm, there is distrust firstly *towards* services economy and, secondly, distrust *of* the capabilities of services that are the foundations of the boundaries for growth. The distrust *towards* services is the reason why services have been largely ignored in economic thought for centuries, and to some extent still are today. The distrust of the capabilities of services has generated defects in markets, services and in their regulation. The lack of confidence in services markets justifies regulations and also brings forward their limits and distortions. It was thought that the services markets, which were not very productive, needed more regulations and protection than did other sectors. This was the very action that limited development possibilities. As will be seen in Chapter 7, the excess of protection, resulting from distrust or a 'conservative' method of facing risk and uncertainty, has hindered its development.

Services develop fully in an environment of freedom and limited protection. At times, however, the regulation or protection of certain activities under certain circumstances is necessary. Freedom is a key dimension of the services economy. This chapter shows how services have been defined by a series of terms corresponding to their particular ontology: co-production, interaction, personalization, co-responsibility and participation. All these highlight the role of two or more parties in building the economy. To ensure the correct provision of service, at least one offerer and one petitioner must agree to their transaction plans with an active and free attitude.

Freedom is essential to reach an optimal service provision. Freedom can be understood as the attitude towards satisfaction of a desire under conditions suggested or imposed, as the case may be, by reality (an environment, a market, an offer). The service economy's development is hindered by regulated circumstances or situations with a centralized decision system or a system that does not stimulate production. The quality of the service depends on the freedom allowed (motivation for freedom) for the practise of a co-responsible economic action (in co-production with others). Given their incentives, it is no wonder that the employees of many companies providing knowledge-intensive services are highly qualified. At times, they enjoy a high level of autonomy in decision-making (i.e., partners in consultancy or auditing). Even the success of numerous services SMEs can be appreciated in light of their freedom to act. For example, under certain circumstances, a small service company may offer more possibilities than does a large company.[9]

Freedom can also be understood as market freedom. It is hardly surprising that advanced and free countries, where an incentive system based on the respect for freedom exists, lead in advanced services. Obviously, there are poor or developing countries with highly centralized systems that specialize in tourism or public administration services, although not in many advanced services. The services introduced by advanced countries, from centralized and non-democratic countries, used to be those of medium or low added value, where the reduction of costs is the first element in the decision for relocation or the growth of a specific sector.[10]

Market freedom also plays a role in a developed and democratic world. The services economy slows down when interventionist or protectionist approaches that do not favour competition are maintained. Those companies operating in open markets are obliged to exercise their freedom to reach certain goals. Within a protectionist framework, in the absence of conditions that offer incentive to find new challenges, everything tends towards standardization and petrification. In general, market freedom motivates individual freedom. Admittedly, sometimes the openness of competition can devalue the quality of the service, but this depends on the way in which markets open up to competition and the role of existing regulations on the markets. As discussed in Chapter 7, liberalizing without regulating does not guarantee the establishment of an incentive system that, by favouring the exercise of individual and company freedom, improves the quality of services.

The State holds the responsibility to guarantee conditions that favour service interaction. This implies the guarantee of competitive conditions in those markets allowing freedom in all offers and products, in the plurality of provision methods, in the diversity of association systems (heterogeneity of legal status in services societies), and in the public–private complementarity needed (i.e., to avoid exclusion from public offer and to guarantee the subsidiarity principle). These freedoms require the State's decisive commitment to increasing capacity of services within increasingly competitive and uncertain environments.

7. CONCLUSIONS AND IMPLICATIONS

This chapter has discussed the fundamental features of services from two points of view: contextual ('servindustrial' economy) and conceptual (definitions and classifications). The transformation of the old service economy into the new service economy has been discussed in the context of the growing integration between goods and services. The chapter has presented services as a dimension of any economic activity that has evolved gradually towards a more dominant and complete place in modern society.

Services are many and heterogeneous, but they share common features that define them positively, without the need for residual and marginal categories. The effects they produce in societies and the interactive nature of co-productions constitute basic elements for definitions and classifications. The co-productive character of many services is used to present a service ontology, mainly applicable to interactive business and consumer services. Within the inevitable ambivalence of becoming standardized goods or becoming personalized services, the new services economy reaches its full height. Services are developed actively within an ontological asymmetry that shapes the most dynamic changes in current economies. Personalized services, multi-polar and 'covalent' relationships, risk aversion and uncertainty, or the participation logic in the destination of the service, are some of the categories that make the economy and the internal order of services explicit. Many services cannot be considered as goods-oriented activities in the same way as are other manufacturing or goods sectors.

There are several managerial implications from the discussed relationship between services and freedom. Firstly, freedom can be regarded as a basis for launching and performing a service, from the motivation phase till the impact assessment. Secondly, the freedom to choose different options may allow firms to plan different scenarios for services provision and different frameworks depending on different service types and levels of interactions. Besides, it is important to consider the role of motivation to support the freedom to choose the best option in each case and the role of human capital in performing high-level interactions. The interactive nature of services drives the issue of freedom as an essential feature to reach an optimal services provision.

From the policy point of view, the promotion of freedom is considered an important constituent to develop service-friendly policies. Economic policy implications can be obtained from the prevalence of services. Multilateral or bilateral interactive processes must be taken into account in the formulation of any service policy. If there are problems regarding the possibilities and developments of co-productive relations, the preservation of free competition becomes a crucial matter. This is especially true when those characteristics typical of services force them to operate in segmented or low-competitive markets. If innovation generated by services radically depends on the staff that produces them, then policies concerning education, professional training, and R&D are decisive, particularly for the development of effective innovations and intangible comparative advantages. If quality depends more on the supplier than on the product itself, policies should favour qualifications, training and the best conditions so that qualified service professionals operate. If risks and uncertainties are high, some systems for reducing vulnerability and guaranteeing results (e.g. standards, performance of contracts) should be promoted. The provision of public services should take into account the agents, needs and possibilities of public and private interaction. The State should guarantee the conditions in which free interactions promote more and better services for economies and societies. All these points will be considered in further chapters, Chapters 10 and 11 in particular.

NOTES

1. It is not by chance that the origin of the modern economic thought coincides with the Industrial Revolution and the enlightened cultural process. This convergence led to interpretation of the new situation based on 'certainty,' in the sense used by Giarini (1987, 1988) to explain the stress of those times to the related conception of static balanced situations in the absence of risk.
2. And also the inclusion of the services sector as the tertiary sector.
3. Quotation taken from Petty (1690).
4. The contribution of Gershuny implies a serious reverse for the developmentalist concepts, although he ended up proposing a dialectic scheme between the service society and the self-service society.
5. See, for example, Coffey and Bailly (1990) or De Jong (1992).

6. See, for example, Ochel and Wegner (1987).
7. See, for example, Marshall (1988).
8. This section is based on a previous work (Rubalcaba, 1999; Chapter 1).
9. This viewpoint has been verified by many high-qualified workers in large services companies who end up founding their own companies.
10. Multinational companies are a prime example, as in the case of tourism and hotel chains, which may be established in poor or developing countries too.

PART II

Facts and Challenges in the New Service Economy

3. Growth and employment in services

INTRODUCTION

European economies are advanced economies, and this is why they are also services economies. In developed countries, the service sector has evolved continually over the past thirty years, modifying the structure of employment and the composition of value added. Agriculture and the manufacturing industry have gradually been losing their relative importance; nowadays, services companies generate about 70 per cent of value added and employment in the most developed countries. As stated in the previous chapter, the service economy has not necessarily grown at the expense of the industrial economy, but within a type of 'servindustrial' society where interrelations between goods and services are of primary importance.

This chapter analyses the reasons underlying the growth of services and related employment, particularly in Europe. Moreover, this information is contrasted with the situation in the United States, and the issue of the convergence or divergence towards a single model of structural change is set forth. These analyses will be carried out through an approach that is basically empirical, and that tries to provide new evidence regarding various issues. The main working hypotheses are linked to the following three points:

1. The growth of employment in services can be accounted for by using an extensive number of causes as explanatory factors, which cannot be reduced to the income–productivity dichotomy. No single factor alone can provide the bulk of the explanation.
2. There are some significant differences between the situations in Europe and in the United States, although a rapprochement generated by a higher economic integration and globalization is currently occurring.
3. The situation in Europe is heterogeneous, and convergence in the structural change can be referred to only in a limited way.

The statistics available are essentially those of National Accounts, collected by the OECD (Stan Data Base) and compiled by the Groningen Growth and Development Centre (60-Industry Data Base). These statistics will be used to corroborate the hypotheses listed above, although given the diversity of sources used and the non-convertibility of data using purchasing power parity (PPP),[1] these data present some problems regarding international comparability. Nonetheless, these statistics constitute the best information sources existing currently. When possible, the results obtained have been compared cautiously to other similar international works and to OECD works based directly on the STAN database, with no significant distortions. Eurostat data have been used complementarily when necessary.[2]

1. IMPORTANCE AND GROWTH OF SERVICES

According to Eurostat, services in the EU15 represented 71.9 per cent of gross value added generated in 2004, and explained 72 per cent of employment. These values are considerably higher than those registered in the mid 1990s. By 1995, the weight of the tertiary sector in community value added was 67.6 per cent, while employment reached 67.7 per cent. Taking the data of the EU25 into consideration, it can be observed that the participation of services in 2004 is slightly lower than that of the 15 countries: 71.4 per cent in the case of value added and 70 per cent on employment.

For a better international comparison, the OECD data (Table 3.1) can be used. In virtually all countries considered, the expansion of the tertiary sector can be noted, more specifically regarding employment. Services stand out in the economies of the Member States in contrast with those of Korea, Turkey or New Zealand. In these regions, the sector under analysis registers less than 70 per cent in value added and employment. The EU15 values, particularly regarding employment, are lower than those of the United States, although they are not very different to those registered in Japan, Australia or Canada. Within Europe, however, the situation among countries is not homogeneous. Luxembourg, the United Kingdom, Holland, Belgium, France and Denmark lead in services, which have been growing continuously since the 1970s and currently exceed 70 per cent of value added and employment. On the other hand, the development of the service sector in Portugal, Greece and Spain has moved forward at a slower rate and, as a consequence, is more limited. This situation is heightened in the case of Member States incorporated into the Union in 2004, such as Hungary, Slovakia, the Czech Republic and Poland. Although there are some differences among them, it is possible to note that services represent, on average, just over 60 per cent of value added and less than this value in the case of employment.

The rapid growth of the services sector in the 1980s and 1990s is a result mainly of the important performance shown by some specific services markets rather than of the total decline of industry or agriculture. In countries such as the United States, world leader in services, industry has not registered a clear loss of jobs until 2000, but new jobs have concentrated mainly in the services sector (but important losses have started after 2001). The situation in Europe is different, as the continent has undergone a larger industrial crisis and an undeniable process of deindustrialization. In any case, services have been used not only as a shelter sector for employment, but also as a guarantee of fluidity in specialization changes. The whole economy requires these changes in order to be competitive, although as discussed later, in Chapter 6, the function of 'employment reserve' is progressively less guaranteed.

Table 3.1 Percentages of services in OECD economies

Country	Value added 2003	Employment 2004	VA growth 1993–2003*	Empl. growth 1994–2004*
Luxembourg	78.8	77.5	0.8	1.1
USA	76.5	78.4	0.6	0.7
France	75.9	72.6	0.4	0.6
Belgium	73.0	73.1	0.6	0.3
UK	72.0	76.4	0.7	0.8
Holland	71.8	76.6	0.6	0.5
Denmark	71.8	73.1	0.1	0.7
Australia	71.0	74.9	0.4	0.5
Mexico	70.4	59.1	0.5	1.3
Germany	70.1	66.6	0.7	1.2
Sweden	70.1	75.2	0.3	0.5
Switzerland	69.6	72.6	0.5	0.7
Italy	69.6	64.5	0.6	1.0
Greece	69.5	64.9	0.7	1.5
Portugal	69.1	56.5	0.7	0.2
Japan	68.0	67.1	1.0	1.1
Austria	67.6	67.2	0.1	1.3
Spain	67.2	64.0	0.4	0.6
Poland	66.5	53.2	2.3	1.8
Finland	65.5	69.3	0.3	0.6
New Zealand	65.5	69.8	0.2	0.8
Canada	65.4	75.0	-0.4	0.1
Hungary	65.4	61.5	0.6	0.7
Slovakia	63.5	55.9	1.0	1.1
Norway	60.8	75.6	-0.4	0.6
Turkey	58.5	43.0	1.4	2.5
Czech Rep.	58.5	56.3	0.8	1.1
Korea	57.2	64.4	1.1	1.8
Ireland	56.2	65.9	-0.1	1.0
Average EU15	**69.9**	**69.6**		
Average NM**	**63.5**	**56.7**		
Average rest	**66.3**	**68.0**		

Notes: * Exponential growth rates of participation. ** New members of the EU with available information: Hungary, the Czech Republic, Poland and Slovakia.

Source: Based on *OECD in Figures*, 2005 edition.

Table 3.2 shows the main statistics of the EU15 Member States regarding services. On the basis of this table, three broad categories explain the bulk of the relative participation of the sector in value added and employment of the European economy. Distributive trades, public services and business services represent more than 40 per cent of the total value added generated by the EU15, and almost 50 per cent of employment. Among these, business services have experienced the highest growth in the last two decades. Distributive trades and public services slightly increased their contributions to value added and employment between 1979 and 2003. Business services, in turn, doubled their participation in the total value added. During this period, the boost has been more noticeable in employment, where the contribution of business services was 4.6 per cent in 1979 and 11.4 per cent in 2003.

Table 3.2 Main data regarding services in the EU15, 2003

Sector	Value added			Employment		
	Thousand million Euro (*)	Relative %	Rates (**) 1979/2003	Thousand	Relative %	Rates (**) 1979/2003
Total sectors	9.540	100	2.2	171.167	100	0.6
Agriculture	154	1.6	1.0	6.679	3.9	-3.1
Manufacturing	2.516	26.4	2.2	42.055	24.6	-1.0
Distributive trades	937	9.8	2.3	25.943	15.2	0.9
Hotels and restaurants	229	2.4	1.1	8.347	4.9	2.3
Transport	455	4.8	2.4	7.191	4.2	0.5
Communications	247	2.6	5.7	2.613	1.5	0.1
Banking and insurance	576	6.0	2.5	5.392	3.2	1.3
Real estate	1.057	11.1	2.7	1.758	1.0	3.3
Business services	1.067	11.2	4.2	19.460	11.4	4.4
- Renting of machinery and equipment	90	0.9	5.0	563	0.3	3.4
- Computer and related activities	183	1.9	6.6	2.450	1.4	6.1
- R&D services	37	0.4	2.4	632	0.4	1.8
- Professional services	472	4.9	3.8	7.037	4.1	3.8
- Other business services	286	3.0	3.9	8.778	5.1	4.8
Public services	1.914	20.1	1.7	39.731	23.2	1.5
Social and personal services	342	3.6	2.5	8.136	4.8	2.5

Notes: * Current prices. ** Exponential annual growth rates, value added at constant prices, 1995.

Sources: Based on National Accounts Statistics, collected by the OECD (STAN) and the GGDC.

Interactions between services and the other economic sectors are strong. In fact, without dynamic and well-established financial, communication, distribution and transport mechanisms, the general economic system could not operate efficiently. For this reason, the great dynamism shown by services holds relevance for sectors (including manufacturing) that use them as intermediate inputs. In dynamic terms, it is observed that the real value added of all services sectors (with the exception of hotels and restaurants and public services) grew to a greater extent than did that of agriculture and manufacturing during the period 1979 to 2003. Communications and business services registered the highest annual growth rates, with 5.7 per cent and 4.2 per cent respectively. Within the latter category, it is worth highlighting the strong increase of computer and related activities, whose value added augmented 6.6 per cent. Moreover, the renting of machinery and equipment has increased by 5 per cent per year during this period, and professional services and other business services have also shown significant annual growths of almost 4 per cent.

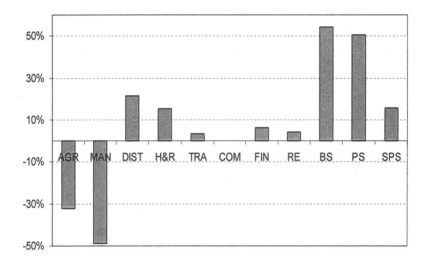

Notes: AGR: agriculture, MAN: manufacturing, DIST: distributive trades, H&R: hotels and restaurants, TRA: transport, COM: communications, FIN: banking and insurance, RE: real estate, BS: business services, PS: public services, SPS: social and personal services.

Source: Based on National Accounts Statistics, collected by the OECD (STAN) and the GGDC, see Table 3.2.

Figure 3.1 Relative contribution of business services to the aggregate growth of EU15 employment, 1979–2003

Regarding employment, services showed themselves to be the driving force from 1979 to 2003, as unlinked activities registered negative annual growth rates. Within the tertiary sector, business services reveal the highest employment growth rates (4.4 per cent per year). As in the case of value added, computer activities (6.1 per cent), followed by other business services (4.8 per cent) and professional services (3.8 per cent), have been the primary promoters of these services. In contrast, communications registered the lowest employment growth rate within the services sector (0.1 per cent). According to the data, business services appear to be one of the most dynamic sectors, which can be explained by several factors that will be analysed in greater depth later in this book. Figure 3.1 illustrates that the total annual employment growth between 1979 and 2003 (0.6 per cent) is almost divided in thirds: one third for business services, another third for public services, and the last third for distributive trades, hotels and restaurants. Within business services, operational services account for nearly 26 per cent of total employment created. In comparison, professional services account for 18 per cent, and computer services, 8 per cent.

Heterogeneity within Europe

Although services are quantitatively predominant in the whole Community economy, their profiles are not the same for all Member States. In the United Kingdom, the Netherlands, Luxembourg, Belgium, France, Denmark and Sweden, the relative weighting of services in employment exceeds that of the European Union, according to the respective specialization indices shown in Table 3.3.[3] Excluding Denmark, all these countries, plus Italy and Germany, also exceed the European average for employment in knowledge-intensive services (KIS), which include computer and related activities, research and development, and professional services. Moreover, together with Finland, these countries lead in computer-related services.

Luxembourg takes the first place in KIS. It has experienced an increase of 9.75 per cent in employment in this activity compared to the whole European Union since 1993, when France led in this area. The case of Ireland also deserves remark, since it registers the second highest employment rate in KIS between 1993 and 2003 (7.8 per cent), followed by Austria (6.6 per cent). In fact, the Irish and Austrian specialization index in KIS increased constantly over a decade. Portugal and Poland, in contrast, lag behind in this sector. Ireland, along with Luxembourg, also stands out regarding IT services, with annual employment growth rates of almost 16.5 per cent and 12 per cent respectively during the period under analysis. Greece and Portugal remain less specialized in this area, although they have experienced important increases in recent years.

Without taking Denmark and Sweden into account, countries leading the services world also stand out in producer services. Again, Luxembourg easily surpasses the European average, and Poland together with Portugal turns out to be relegated. With regard to public services, Sweden and Denmark register much higher rates than the European average, while Luxembourg, Poland and the Czech Republic lag behind.

Table 3.3 Indices of employment specialization*, 2003

	Total services (1)	Producer services				Consumer services		Public services (6)
		Total (2)	KIS (4)	Computer services	Network services (5)	Total (3)	Hotels and restaurants	
United Kingdom (UK)	1.10	1.18	1.08	1.21	1.00	1.19	1.35	1.02
Netherlands (NL)	1.09	1.15	1.11	1.00	0.95	1.02	0.75	1.07
Luxembourg (LX)	1.08	1.75	1.28	1.17	1.41	0.91	0.95	0.69
Belgium (BE)	1.07	1.22	1.16	1.12	1.23	0.83	0.68	1.23
France (FR)	1.05	1.15	1.09	1.27	1.02	0.85	0.73	1.22
Denmark (DK)	1.05	0.95	0.90	1.07	1.12	0.94	0.64	1.32
Sweden (SW)	1.05	0.92	1.15	1.50	1.16	0.89	0.55	1.40
EU15	1.00	1.00	1.00	1.00	1.00	1.00	1.00	1.00
Germany (DE)	0.99	0.99	1.12	0.89	0.98	1.00	0.89	0.99
Finland (FI)	0.96	0.86	0.91	1.31	1.24	0.83	0.65	1.23
Italy (IT)	0.93	0.88	1.03	1.14	0.80	1.01	1.04	0.78
Ireland (IR)	0.92	0.90	0.78	0.81	1.10	1.03	1.31	0.90
Spain (SP)	0.91	0.76	0.59	0.52	1.02	0.93	1.26	0.84
Austria (AT)	0.90	0.91	0.96	0.88	1.14	0.97	1.12	0.87
Slovakia (SK)	0.86	0.72	0.55	0.50	1.47	0.97	0.55	0.93
Hungary (HUN)	0.86	0.76	0.58	0.56	1.50	0.89	0.73	0.98
Greece (GR)	0.85	0.77	0.62	0.16	1.24	1.04	1.37	0.78
Portugal (PT)	0.84	0.58	0.44	0.27	0.59	1.12	1.04	0.87
Czech Rep. (CZ)	0.80	0.86	0.89	0.72	1.35	0.88	0.70	0.74
Poland (PL)	0.76	0.68	0.48	0.31	1.20	0.86	0.36	0.75

Notes: * Relative per cent of employment in the country/Relative per cent of employment in the EU15. (1) Total employment in services (ISIC rev. 3, 50 to 99); (2) Includes transport, communications, business services and financial services (ISIC 60 to 67, 71 to 749); (3) Includes distributive trades, hotels, social and personal services (ISIC 50 to 52, 55 and 90–93); (4) Includes computer and related activities, professional and R&D services (ISIC 72, 73, 74.1–74.4); (5) Includes transport, communications and energy (ISIC 60 to 64, 40–41); (6) Includes public administration, defence and social security, education, health and social work (ISIC 75, 80, 85).

Source: Based on OECD and GGDC data.

Poland, the Czech Republic, Slovakia, Hungary, as well as Greece and Portugal are less specialized in terms of tertiary employment. Nevertheless, an ascending trend has been observed in most of them in the 1990s. Regarding services value added, the new Member States are those most behind compared to the EU15, although the growth rates of the specialization indices are positive for all of them between 1993 and 2003. Except for the Czech Republic, these countries possess the lowest figures in KIS employment, but the specialization indices show important improvements compared to 1993. In contrast, their speciality focuses mainly on network services such as transport, communications and energy (the only sector where employment percentages exceed those of the EU15).

Countries such as Greece, the United Kingdom, Ireland, Italy, Portugal, Austria and Spain are more specialized in tourism than the European Union average. Except for Austria and Spain, these countries lead consumer services employment.

Although Poland still lags the farthest behind in these fields, all the new Member States registered positive growth rates between 1993 and 2003 in consumer services employment.

It is important to note that, in 2003, the United Kingdom was the only country with indices above one in all sectors under analysis. Hence, together with the Netherlands, it became one of the European leaders in services. In fact, as discussed later, its productive structure – as well as that of other Member States – has characteristics similar to those of the United States.

2. EXPLANATORY REASONS FOR THE GROWTH OF SERVICES

Due to the numerous factors affecting dimensions of the services sector, this section aims to prove that one sole argument is insufficient to explain the boost experienced by the sector in the last thirty years.

Here, the two classical reasons for services growth will be explained: its difference of productivity compared to other sectors, and the effects of the income increase of developed countries. Both arguments date back to the 1940s (Fisher, Clark, Fourastié, Rostow) and have been used up to present times.

Apart from verifying the validity margin to understand their effect almost seventy years later, this chapter will tackle the most recent explanations developed since the 1980s.

This chapter will also consider the role of the progressive flexibility of production systems, the incorporation of new technologies, human capital, interrelations with industries and business services, outsourcing, globalization and governmental regulations in this process. Finally, these different explanatory factors will be summarized and classified.

Productivity

Researchers have mainly cited the relative productivity of services to explain the sector's growth, and this reason is still used in many areas. Although its development dates back to the 1940s from works carried out by Fourastié, it was not until the 1960s that the thesis reached its peak with Baumol (1967). The issue's importance and the implications derived from services productivity justify the dedication of an entire chapter to this topic. Briefly, this section will discuss empirical evidence supporting or refuting the thesis of growth in Europe due to the relatively low productivity.

The so-called 'Baumol's disease' explains the uneven growth of sectors due to relocation of resources towards more or less productive sectors. This resource relocation affects the total aggregate growth, which at the same time is depleted by the uneven growth.

Services, which have difficulty with incorporating technological capital, consider labour as a good in itself, and have high price and income inelasticities. They tend, however, to adopt the salaries of more productive sectors, playing the role of a stagnant sector.

One way to check this theory, as did Wölfl (2005), is to compare the growths of productivity in manufacturing and services, thus demonstrating lower growth in services productivity (this growth being only half that of manufacturing) and higher growth in employment. According to the latest data available, labour productivity in the agricultural and manufacturing sector increased 3.1 per cent and 3 per cent correspondingly in the EU15 during the period 1993 to 2003, while such a growth in services increased by 1.1 per cent.

During the same period, employment registered negative growth rates in the primary and secondary sectors (2.4 per cent and 0.4 per cent respectively), while services showed an employment growth of 1.8 per cent over the increase of total employment (1 per cent).

Another method for verifying Baumol's thesis is to compare directly the employment and productivity growth rates of intra- and inter-sectors. The relationship between relative employment and relative productivity growths in the EU15 is shown in Figure 3.2, where the evolution of different sectors between 1979 and 2003 can be observed. The productivity rate seems to explain 53 per cent of employment rate in a highly significant correlation of - 0.7.

Computer and related activities, communications and renting have grown to a larger extent regarding employment than would correspond to a higher productivity rate. In the case of hotels and restaurants, the opposite occurs. These results draw attention to the validity and limits of the traditional productivity theories concerning the sectors and indicators analysed.

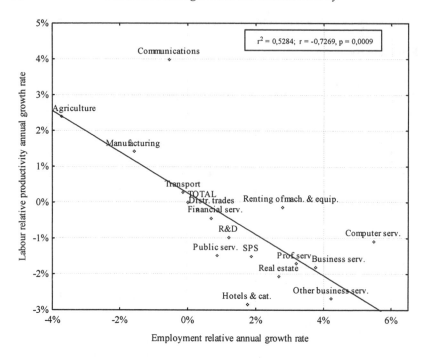

Source: Based on OECD and GGCD National Accounts Statistics.

Figure 3.2 Relationship between relative productivity growth and relative employment growth, EU15, 1979–2003. Cross-sector comparison

When dynamic cross-country comparison is performed, the negative relationship between relative productivity growth and relative employment share is maintained. In the case of services, the higher growth of employment corresponds to the lower growth of productivity in the time period 1979–2003, when taking the EU15 into consideration (R: -0.5, P: 0.04). This result becomes more solid with the exclusion of Ireland from the estimate (r: -0.64, p: 0.009, as shown in Figure 3.3), and even more so when three new members of the EU are considered in the period 1993–2003 (r: -0.67, p: 0.002). The cross-sector relationship previously described in Figure 3.2 is reproduced at a cross-country level in Figure 3.3. These two figures suggest that the Baumol thesis may still hold validity for the service sector as such. Nevertheless, similar analyses of specific service sectors provide different results. A solid negative relationship between employment share and relative productivity growth does not appear in disaggregated service categories, except in the case of knowledge-intensive services in the period 1979–2003 and in producer services in the period 1993–2003. Relative productivity and relative employment growth in manufacturing may be positively correlated between

1979 and 2003, and between 1993 and 2003, but these estimates are not statistically significant. In most sectors, non-significant correlations dominate.

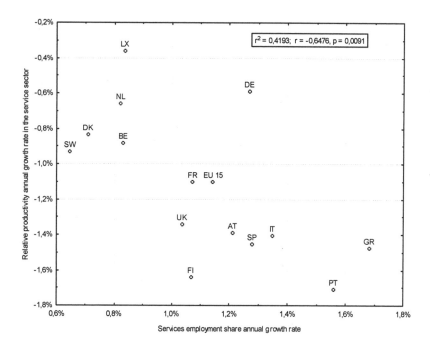

Notes: For country abbreviations, see Table 3.3. Ireland has been excluded as it is a statistical outlier.

Source: Based on OECD and GGDC data.

Figure 3.3 Relationship between relative productivity growth and employment share growth, EU15, 1979–2003. Cross-country comparison

A static cross-country analysis shows a direct and significant relationship between the weighting of services in employment and their productivity in 2003: levels of labour productivity are higher in those countries where services represent an important ratio of total employment (Figure 3.4). The same occurs in the case of KIS: the service-orientated countries reach higher productivity levels.

However, this is not verified in the case of manufacturing, where an inverse and significant relationship is observed between employment and productivity in the year 2003. This result does not agree with traditional theses that state that those countries where services play a very important role should register lower relative productivity.

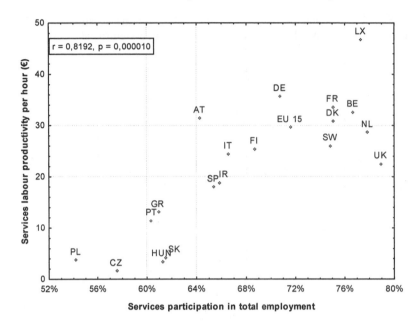

Notes: For country abbreviations, see Table 3.3.

Source: Based on OECD and GGDC data.

Figure 3.4 Productivity of the services sector, 2003

Income

Another explanation for services expansion, which is a result of the well-known Engel's law, is the increased income level in developed economics. In those countries with higher income per capita, the participation of the services sector in employment is also higher. This fact has been proven on many occasions, such as in the works carried out by Maddison (1980) or more recently by those of the OECD (2005a). The reason for this is that the final demand of some services registers high income elasticity, particularly those services contributing to the improvement of the quality of life such as leisure, education, health, travel, etc. At the same time, demographic changes in the richest economies, more specifically related to their aging populations, have increased the demand for certain services such as health and personal services. Finally, the welfare state in some developed countries has affected the demand for public services, particularly education and health services. The various factors explaining services consumption correspond to aspects as different as price and elasticity, education and preferences, trends of self-consumption, and self-service or life cycle effects.

Figure 3.5 illustrates the strong positive relationship between GDP per capita measured by PPS and participation of services in total employment. The case of value added upholds this correlation. This figure indicates that countries with high income levels – such as Luxembourg, the Netherlands, the United Kingdom, Belgium or Denmark – uphold high services contributions both to employment and to the total value added of their economies. In contrast, income and participation in employment and value added in Poland, the Czech Republic, Slovakia and Hungary are low. The case of Ireland is remarkable, as it has a relatively high level of GDP per capita, and the services sector participation is much more important in employment than in value added.

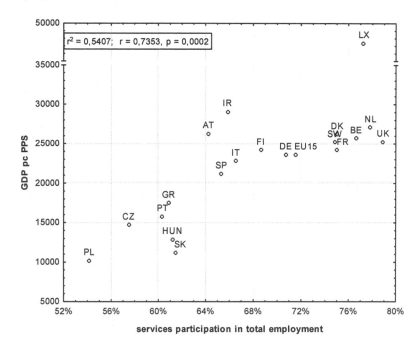

Source: Based on OECD, GGDC and Eurostat data.

Figure 3.5 Employment in services and GDP per capita, 2003

It is worth noting that this general relationship becomes less evident with the inclusion of more countries in the sample. In particular, the evidence decreases when taking into consideration the value added of emerging highly productive countries and weighting of the manufacturing industrial sector. These factors explain the low correlations that Wölfl (2005) obtained by including Ireland or Korea (R^2 of 0.35 against 0.54 of the previous figure). A lower correlation even exists when tertiary data are included within groups of countries. Some small, rich countries (i.e., some Arab countries) have a low-developed services sector while many poor countries have a high level of services participation due to the strong presence of tourism and public services in their economies. These observations induce more in-depth analyses by activity sectors.

A more disaggregated analysis reveals a solid relationship between income levels and the weighting of knowledge-intensive services in employment. Again, the outstanding countries are Luxembourg, the Netherlands, the United Kingdom, Belgium and Sweden, in contrast to less-advanced Slovakia, Poland, Hungary and Portugal. It is interesting to note that, when considering the value added in KIS, the correlation with income remains positive, as in the case of employment, but is not statistically significant.

The dynamic analysis reveals a lack of correlation between income growth and relative employment growth in the different service categories during 1993–2003, except for the case of computer services. Nevertheless, robust correlations arise when absolute employment growth is considered, especially in total services, consumer services, public services, KIS and computer and related services. Moreover, a direct correlation with producer and network services can also be observed, although with slightly reduced significance in these cases. The relationship is not statistically important with regard to the hotel sector. As expected, the most notable relationship is explained through consumer services (income explains almost 70 per cent of the variance), and the lowest relationship through producer services. Except for the relationship with hotels and restaurants, these results – when total employment growth is considered instead of growth of shares – confirm the thesis of income importance as an explanatory factor of some services.

Basically, limits to income and productivity as explanations of services growth suggest more structural explanations. These alternative explanations include services in the whole productive system, which has been facilitated by the increase of flexibility, the incorporation of new technologies and the emergence of new qualifications and the need for labour specialization. These issues are clearly interrelated, and this book will explain them separately in a later section.

Services as an Intermediate Demand: Productive Flexibility, Specialization and Outsourcing

According to the previous data, business services appear to be one of the most – if not *the* most – dynamic sectors of the European economy in recent decades. The dimension of business services in the value added of economy has gradually increased throughout the last two decades. It doubled between 1979 and 2003, exceeding that of distributive trades. This sector's progress is due mainly to professional services and, to a lesser extent, to computer activities and business services.

Business services have become essential to the general performance of a business. Several factors explain this role: outsourcing carried out by companies engaged in various activities; the development of small production units that use external services to complement their own resources; the need for greater business flexibility; the pressure of knowledge-based economies requiring specialized services; and many other factors (Rubalcaba, 1999; Kox, 2002; OECD, 2005a) related to the whole of services, as discussed earlier. Amongst these, one specific reason explains the emergence of services as an intermediate demand: the changes in the productive systems, which explain their use and, where relevant, their outsourcing. Changes in productive systems refer to a higher flexibility of the production processes, which can be associated with new specializations that lead to more professional services and, therefore, to processes of services use and outsourcing.

Due to their dynamic nature, production systems evolve continually. Flexibilization represents the key element of what many would call a new productive 'paradigm'. In a sense, the introduction of new information and communication technologies, the integration of goods and services, and other processes of change are based on flexibilization. Although flexible systems have existed since the industrial revolution (Gertler, 1988), it must be acknowledged that the foundations for a completely new working environment are being laid out (Giarini and Stahel, 1993). The initial theories put forward by Taylor (1911) and Fayol (1916), based on the efficient organization of work from its hierarchical and formal aspects, remain obsolete in those productive systems where the issue of information and metainformation play a predominant role. In this context, new concepts of programming, communication, excellence, Z theory, re-engineering, etc. derive from the limited rationality principle introduced by Simon's organization theory (1945).

The concepts of flexible specialization (Piore and Sabel, 1984) and flexible integration (Cooke, 1988; Valery, 1987) have turned the word 'flexibility' into the new name of the industrial production game. The emergence of this flexible productive environment makes possible the development of the services economy by means of the incomes resulting from the specialization and organizational changes. Flexibility constitutes an explanatory factor for the growth of certain services, largely due to its facilitation of flexible and integrated specialization. As production is organized in more horizontal and decentralized units, in which departments, companies and offices increasingly share production, production services have gained the necessary space for their development.

In part, the incomes in specialization derived from the flexible production system have been channelled towards outsourcing, as in the case of services. The most important issue regarding services outsourcing is that it has served as a key argument to explain the growth of business services, to the extent that their expansion was the mere result of an employment transfer from the industrial sector to the services sector.

Table 3.4 Outsourcing: advantages and disadvantages

Reasons	Advantages	Disadvantages

Transactional costs	* Decrease in transaction costs
	  - production costs
	  - information and search costs
	  - policy and performance costs
	  - labour and other costs
	* Use of scale economies
	* Use of scope economies
	* Use of network economies
		* Problems of moral hazard and adverse
		  selection
		* High cost of specialized services
		* Opposing transaction costs
		* Waste of classical advantages of
		  internalization: technical and
		  management economies

Potential costs	* Adaptation to the uneven demand
	* Elimination of possible labour
	  conflicts
	* More adjusted cost estimates
		* Problems regarding follow-up, control
		  and assessment of services
		* Cost control difficulties
		* Technological dependence

Quality and expertise	* Improvements in the quality of
	  service
	* Acquisition of specialized
	  knowledge by transfer
		* Possible lack of sufficient experience
		  and specialization
		* Generalist and theoretical knowledge
		* Difficult introduction of solutions
		* Insufficient transfer

Production organization	* Flexibility
	  - substitution of fixed costs by
	    variables
	* Concentration on key tasks
	* Independence
	* Assistance in complex businesses
		* Lack of independence and
		  confidentiality
		* Possible increase of internal conflicts

Market penetration	* Passive, active and instrumental
	  modes
	* Access to new geographical,
	  segmented and socio-economic
	  markets
		* Possible lower market control

Governmental intervention	* Specialized assistance for tax,
	  accountant, legal, etc. regulations
	* Cost reduction of labour
	  protectionism
		* Conflicts with internal personnel

Source: Rubalcaba (1999).

In fact, many manufacturing companies have delegated some tertiary activities – such as financial, research and development, and logistic activities – to service-specialized suppliers delivering these at lower costs or with higher quality standards. According to the OECD (2002a), the outsourcing of information technologies registers the fastest growth in the European Union, particularly in the United Kingdom, France and Italy. De Groot (1998) made a first move to standardize outsourcing processes of services activities by manufacturing companies, and to analyse their effects on economic growth. In a previous work (Rubalcaba, 1999), the advantages and disadvantages of outsourcing are defined, explaining the coexistence of outsourcing processes occurring simultaneously with re-internalization processes, although the latter are less significant than the former (see Table 3.4). In the aforementioned work, related literature is also analysed, which essentially explains the growth of business services as a complex phenomenon. As concluded in other recent works (Rubalcaba and Kox, 2007), outsourcing only partly explains this growth.

Kox (2002) analyses the effects of labour division using services outsourcing processes. A broad technological change, such as that involving ICTs, enables the distribution of work, more outsourcing possibilities and a higher use of specialized services. The new social division of work creates an ascending movement of the economy's production function. Within this framework, an increase of inputs facilitates a higher level of economic growth. Empirical evidence supports this situation. By using the same sample for different countries, François and Reinert (1995) discovered that those countries where services producers played a more important role over the total of intermediate inputs within the manufacturing sector also registered a higher GDP per capita.

Beyond the debate and the explanation of outsourcing, the growth of business services deepens the understanding that rather than growing apart from industry, services have become deeply interrelated within it. Without manufacturing companies as clients of services companies, the boost of the sector would be hardly comprehended. The reverse is also true: without the delivery of essential services for business competitiveness, European and American manufacturing industries would have virtually disappeared, moving to countries with lower labour costs. Business services offer new comparative advantages to industrial and services sectors, and their sources and conveyors of innovation allow for improvement of business productivity and competitiveness. Some specific business services have facilitated the assimilation of technological innovations or the production of non-technological innovations, which are necessary to enhance productivity.

The following table shows the total use of intermediate services in the European economy among other manufacturing areas. The highest average of intermediate inputs from a total of 40 areas (25 are manufacturing services) corresponds to general business services (Nace 74), followed by financial services, distributive trades, chemical products and transport. In other words, services dominate goods with regard to intermediate inputs in the total economic categories. The results are even more favourable for producer services if manufacturing industries are divided into a smaller number of areas. The relatively low positions of ICT services can be explained by the relatively low expenditure in these services by the majority of industrial areas. However, recent data for some specific countries confirms an increase of their weighting as intermediate inputs, also in the case of manufacturing.

According to Pilat and Wölfl (2005), deep interrelations between services and manufacturing cause an increasingly diffuse distinction between the two. On the basis of the analysis of input–product, it is understood that the weighting of services value added in manufacturing has increased over time, and around the mid–1990s accounted for a quarter or more of the total output of this sector in some countries. A progressive participation of workers of the manufacturing sector in activities related to services is also indicated. In fact, this percentage in Holland reached 50 per cent in 2002. Despite this higher complementation and interrelation, both sectors differ with regard to their profiles within economy. While goods companies interact to a large extent with the other industries, both as input suppliers and users, tertiary activities are more independent. The majority of intermediate inputs needed for their production come from the services sector itself.

Table 3.5 Total use (*) of intermediate inputs in the EU15 economic categories, 1995 (**)

Position	Top 10: most used intermediate inputs	%	Position	Other intermediate services inputs	%
1	Business services	**14.5**	12	Real estate services	**5.5**
2	Banking, insurance	**10.2**	18	Social and personal services	**5**
3	Wholesale and retail distribution, repairs	**9.3**	19	Construction	**4.9**
4	Chemicals, excluding pharmaceuticals	**8.6**	20	Postal and telecommunications services	**4.8**
5	Transport and storage	**8.1**	25	Computer services	**4.3**
6	Iron and steel	**7.5**	28	Machinery and equipment rental	**4.2**
7	Manufactured metallic products	7	32	Research and development	**3.5**
8	Pulp, paper, printing and publishing	**6.9**		Social and health work	**3.4**
9	Mining and extraction	**6.9**	35	Hotels and restaurants	**3.2**
10	Electricity, gas and water supply	**6.3**	38	Public administration and defence	**2.9**
			39	Education	**2.9**

Notes: * Direct + indirect through the use of the IOT inverse matrix and technical coefficients. ** Average intermediate use of each sector in 40 economic activities (15 of services and 25 of goods).

Source: Based on Eurostat, IOT tables.

Other works with input–output tables have emphasized the integration between services and manufacturing by using direct use coefficients. The European Commission (2004) concludes that 29 per cent of all intermediate inputs of business-related services are aimed at the manufacturing industry, 2 per cent at the primary sector, 11 per cent at the public sector, 12 per cent at other consumer services and 46 per cent at the utilization by the group of producer services sectors. The manufacturing industry, in turn, only devotes 12 per cent of its intermediate inputs to business-related services. Therefore, the integration between goods and producer services is asymmetrical, since services are more integrated in manufacturing than the other way round. However, as Wölfl (2005) showed, the interrelation is symmetrical when considering the group of services and the group of manufactures within the framework of the OECD. In this case, the total destination of services is taken into consideration: 56.4 per cent to final use, 6.2 per cent to exports, 24.4 per cent to self-consumption, and 8.5 per cent to the intermediate industry use. In contrast, the manufacturing sector assigns the same proportion to final consumption (although much more to external than to internal consumption) and to self-consumption, and 10.6 per cent to the intermediate use of services. Again, there are differences when considering the group of services compared to the group of producer services. In the case of the latter, recent econometrical studies of the input–output tables for various countries proved the positive impact of using KIS within the economic system (in productivity, innovation and production) (Camacho and Rodríguez, 2007). This positive impact is also ratified for the group of business services, despite differences by sector and by country (Baker, 2007).

Finally, it is worth noting the significance of producer services in the explanation of the sector's apparently low productivity, as well as the positive indirect effects caused by the productivity returns of client sectors, particularly the manufacturing industry. This issue is analysed in more depth in the next chapter.

New Technologies and Innovation

Technology and innovation are key elements for boosting the economy. Even from different perspectives, no school of economic thinking (Classical, Neo-classical, Keynesian or Structuralist) has denied this evidence (Freeman and Soete, 1987). New information and communication technologies, in particular, have implied a revolution in the tertiary sector. It is important to note the time coincidence of the huge technological progress of the last twenty years, the consolidation of services economy and the emergence of advanced services. This coincidence suggests that substitutive processes have not reduced the growth of services, and could even have contributed to their expansion. Services are usually considered as isolation activities of the industrial substitution processes. However, verification and criticism of this thesis requires a sector-by-sector analysis. Thus, there are examples and counter-examples that contrast or juxtapose depending on the economic activity and location. Banks, for instance, have automated many services, thus saving personnel costs. At the same time, however, increasing complexity of financial markets and greater competition has led the financial sector to develop closer contact with clients, and to invest more in personnel.

Services industries have reached the operational leverage achieved by manufacturers some years before, to a large extent due to technology (OECD, 2000a). Other sectors (apart from financial services) that have benefited from scale economics derived from the increasing use of new technologies include health and distribution services, distributive trades and telecommunications. One of the services sectors most closely linked to this process is business services. The most advanced of these services are often defined as technological information services. Their relation to technology – or rather, to the information transmitted through technology – can be clearly observed through analyses of those services behind e-economy. Some of the most characteristic aspects of current global transformations are, undoubtedly, changes undergone in the Internet world and in trade and electronic businesses. These changes are so important that experts and businesspeople suggest that the period of expansion experienced by the North American economies in the 1990s is due to *increases in productivity* and to lower unitary labour costs that can be explained by the technological revolution. They have also suggested that the growth differential in Europe and the United States during the second half of that decade can be explained in the same way. It is worth mentioning that those differentials enabled the possible transfer of this kind of American revolution to Europe. Taking these expectations into consideration, it is not a coincidence that Internet companies experienced dramatic increases in the value of their shares. Many of these companies were operating on losses and with excessive capitalization. The strong rectification of the e-economy occurred in the second half of 2000 and 2001–2002, when the North American economy and business services suffered a significant drop in performance. The problems affecting many Internet companies have led to various issues regarding the overestimate of company-generated financial benefits, rather than a more general criticism regarding new technological developments. The value gradually became linked to a new or reviewed idea of value, created around the concept of services value (Giarini, 2002).

In the context of the 'new technological revolution', some services have been and are essential to these change processes. Telecommunications, computer-related enterprises and leisure companies lead technological markets in international stock exchanges, and they promote and act towards the development of e-economy. These services companies have played a direct and significant role in the globalization process. However, there are other, more discrete services that are ignored by the media but that are nonetheless also behind these changes. For example, advanced services linked to engineering, computer and related activities, and electronic commerce are three business services most strongly associated with the 'technological revolution.' They facilitated the production, expansion and use of new technologies that have become the infrastructure for e-economy technologies. Many new services, such as ICT services, have been and still are the main forerunners of new Internet-related businesses. At the same time, their growth is based on the incorporation and improvement of this technology. Technologies have also paved the way for new services. These services, which are more marketable and grow even at distance, such as those resulting from the offshoring process, will be analysed in Chapter 6.

In summary, technological changes promote the emergence of new tertiary activities by means of innovation processes, although innovation has more dimensions than just the technological. Chapter 5 will address services innovation and define the methods by which services contribute to innovation and vice versa, heightening the role of an innovative environment in the growth of services. These different innovation needs explain the growth of various types of services.

Human Capital and Qualifications

To a large extent, the growth and development of services are based on human capital. It is a known fact that production in the tertiary sector has a higher amount of qualified labour than in manufacturing (Messina, 2004 and OECD, 2005a). In the late-1990s, the proportion of university and non-university workers contracted by the services industry was three times that of the secondary sector (OECD, 2000b).

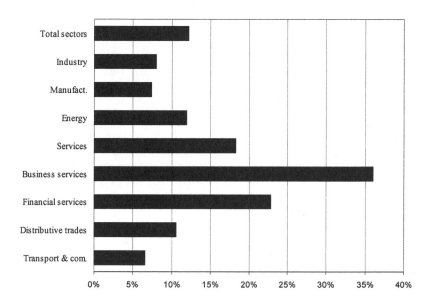

Note: Average data for EU15. Industry excludes manufacturing, and services exclude public administration. Business services include: real estate, rentals and other business services. Distributive trades includes: wholesale and retail distribution and repairs of motor vehicles.

Source: Based on Eurostat data.

Figure 3.6 Percentage of higher-education employees by economic activities, EU15, 2000

However, heterogeneous situations exist within the manufacturing and tertiary sectors. In the area of goods production, the highest ratio of university workers is registered in gas, electricity and water supply. On the other hand, producer and social services require higher qualifications. More specifically, all business services are intensive in human capital and, to a lesser extent, financial services, as shown in Figure 3.6. Nevertheless, while some business services require highly skilled staff, such as management consultants, others use low-skill employees, as in the case of industrial cleaning.

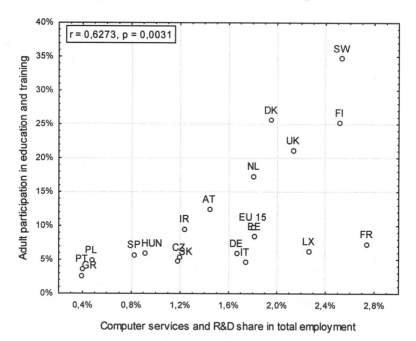

Source: Based on OECD and Eurostat, LFS.

Figure 3.7 Human capital and knowledge-intensive services

In all cases, services are produced by a labour factor that is inevitably involved in an interactive process with the client. Not surprisingly, the growth of business services has been associated with the accumulation of expertise and specialization processes (for example, Stanback, 1979; Stanback *et al.*, 1981; Wood, 1991). The increase of flexible, skilled and, to a certain extent, multipurpose workers explains the emergence of certain advanced services based on the accumulation of expertise. Therefore, a relationship between the training and specialization level and the allocation of advanced services could be expected. Figure 3.7 illustrates the positive and firm relationship between the employment dimension in computer and related activities and R&D

services, and the level of participation of adult population in continuous training activities. Sweden, Finland, Denmark and the United Kingdom lead in this respect, while Greece, Portugal and Poland lag behind. In any case, training is a relevant issue for all types and skill levels of services, even for low-skill ones.

Since human capital is at the core of services organizations, it is essential to give preference to contributions to improved recruitment, contracting, motivation and management. Personnel care has resulted in services that organize training, learning and recycling courses. In addition, the contracting and recruitment of personnel is increasing in importance. As the management of human capital has increased in its complexity, it has created alternatives for different contracting possibilities. Additionally, human resources are immersed in a continuous specialization process, which explains the growth of many related business services. In recent decades, the specialization of human resources can explain part of the boost of business services, the engines for growth in the tertiary sector.

Nowadays, several companies and countries show a lack of highly skilled workers. Hence, governments are studying new ways of improving the qualification of their labour forces through the use of different instruments. These instruments range from educational reforms to incentives for companies and individuals to invest in continuous training. Therefore, as Chapter 10 will explain, the key to developing human capital is a broad educational policy to promote multidisciplinary long-term education.

Globalization and Trade in Services

Competitive pressures associated with market globalization have changed the relationships among companies, increasing the need for modernization and promoting interaction. In this sense, internationalization contributes in part to the increase in demand for services (Illeris, 1989; Coffey and Bailly, 1990; Howells, 1988; Cuadrado, Rubalcaba and Bryson, 2002; OECD, 2005a). Its results, however, are limited, and the final part of services destined to trade is only 6 per cent within the OCDE (Wölfl, 2005). The internationalization process increases the size of businesses, facilitates the distribution of labour and the obtainment of scale economies and specialization, and establishes the need for incorporating services for production (François, 1990). Chapter 6 deals with this issue in depth, verifying the role of globalization in the growth of services, and vice versa. In this section, only the relationship between the services trade and tertiary economies will be discussed. Trade in services should be more developed in service-orientated countries for obvious reasons. Those countries generating more value added and employment in services should be those in the best position to export and import services. At the same time, those countries registering a higher level of trade would consider this a decisive factor to explain their own specialization towards the sector.

OECD[4] data indicate that countries with the most tertiary-orientated economies are the United States, Australia, the United Kingdom, Holland, Belgium, France, Denmark and Sweden, with rates of over 70 per cent in value added and employment. The presence of services in global trade is lower than expected due to its presence in economy; on average, 22–24 per cent against more than a 68 per cent of participation in added value and employment. This imbalance could be explained by different reasons, such as the existence of natural and artificial barriers to the trade of services, or the statistical deficiencies hindering a global coverage of this phenomenon. However, the influence of these factors potentially differs depending on country, as some have a more service-orientated trade than others. Regarding services exports, the maximum level is produced in countries such as Spain, Denmark and particularly Greece (due to a large extent to the tourism industry). Imports, in turn, are heavily biased in favour of services in countries such as Ireland, Denmark or Austria. By analysing the levels of growth in recent years, it can be observed that the highest growth, besides the economic powers such as the United States or Japan, occurs in small countries such as Ireland, Greece or Denmark.

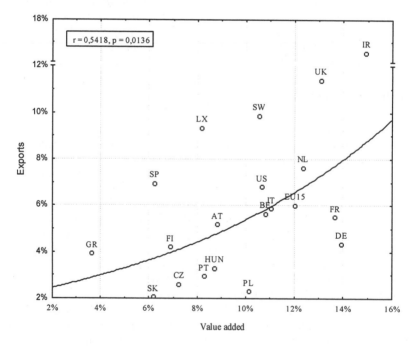

Source: Based on OECD and Eurostat.

Figure 3.8 Contribution of business services to value added and international trade (exports), 2002

A simple association between levels of services shares in the economy and levels of growth of international trade in services cannot be established. Employment and value added in services are variables that do not correlate with any others in commerce, according to the respective correlation coefficients. However, there are some positive links when the analysis concentrates not on services as a group, but on specific sectors such as business services. In the case of the business sector, there is a positive relationship between the level of economy and the level of trade regarding both imports and exports, with an emphasis on the former (see Figure 3.8). What seems to be evident is that variability in services trade is much higher than variability of the service economy (which is currently quite low, especially regarding value added) among developed countries. The lack of association implies that abundance in a sector is not a guarantee in itself for a certain competitive capacity, leading to the need for a customized analysis of competitiveness indicators and factors to be conducted. Neither does the competitive capacity seem to be much related to a specific development of the sectors in terms of relative weighting.

To a large extent, a higher presence of services in the world market can be explained on the basis of the foreign direct investment, which exceeds that of manufacturing in recent years. Due to these flows, services providers have consolidated their commercial presence in foreign markets. However, it seems more appropriate to consider services as facilitating and promoting instruments of globalization, rather than as direct beneficiaries of this process. The exceptions are those directly linked to market integration, as in the case of some business services. Chapter 6 will analyse in detail the process of globalization, offshoring and market integration, and its interrelation with services.

State, Regulations and Institutional Changes

The last block of explanatory factors covers the role of the State, institutions and social changes. The State is influential in various ways. Its existence alone comprises an important activity sector of approximately 23 per cent of European economies regarding employment, and 20 per cent of value added. This sector has also registered a high growth since the 1960s, although a certain deceleration occurred in the 1990s. Between 1979 and 2003, the public sector grew 1.7 per cent in terms of value added and 1.5 per cent in terms of employment, whilst between 1993 and 2003, those growth rates were 1.5 per cent and 1.2 per cent, respectively. Obviously, participation levels vary by country: in Sweden, Denmark, Finland, Belgium and France, the presence of the public sector is higher, representing approximately 30 per cent of total employment, while in Luxembourg, the Czech Republic and Poland, governmental participation in employment is around 16 per cent.

Reform processes of the public sector look for reductions in costs and dimensions, as well as modernization of public services. In view of this, over the past fifteen years governments have proceeded to liberalize services sectors which previously operated under monopolistic conditions or, in many cases, in low-competitive and restricted markets. The opening of certain markets (such as telecommunications) explains the growth in some parts of the sector, particularly in productivity and efficiency gains. A similar case could be stated regarding air transport, although not with regard for other sectors not yet operating in low-integrated and low-liberalized markets (Chapters 7 and 8 will focus on this issue). Within regional areas, local administrations have also promoted the growth of services related to local services or services promoted as a part of the regional development system.

Apart from the existence of public services and the management of services in liberalization processes, the public regulation is in itself a growth factor for some services, particularly business services. Services that have grown concern law, accountancy, tax counselling, audit, or product or environment quality. On many occasions, governmental regulations promoted their growth to guarantee high functioning of law practitioners, accounting, the tax system or the preservation of the environment and consumers' guarantees. Obviously, had it not been for coercive, obligatory rules, some business services from the 1980s would not have developed. The emergence of the so-called 'third sector', or non-profit sector, is another method by which the State and social institutions can influence services. In the last thirty years, non-governmental and development aid organizations, along with foundations and other social, educational or health institutions, have strongly increased in number throughout the world. This area has an increasingly higher weighting in the services sector, and implies the practice of subsidiarity by governmental institutions in favour of social institutions. Both the state and social institutions have a public service nature, and those services traditionally supplied by government in the 20th century (education, health and development aid) are now increasingly supplied by profit and non-profit making private entities, under similar – and, many times, higher – efficiency conditions (Vittadini and Barea, 1999).

Finally, private institutions, families and villages have also undergone social changes that have boosted the growth of specific services. The urbanization of advanced societies has evolved in conjunction with the following: higher population concentrations in residential areas; changes in concepts of family, resulting from the massive incorporation of women into the labour market; and to the strong migratory flows from the 1950s and 1960s within the old EU15 (although, Eastern Europe aside, in recent decades almost all countries have acted as net receivers of immigrants). All these changes have caused city life to become more expensive.

Less free time is available, and new services are now required for this new situation (for example, the boost of kindergarten, nursery and domestic services in the 1980s and 1990s). This coincides with the aging of the European population, which is only partially compensated by immigration.

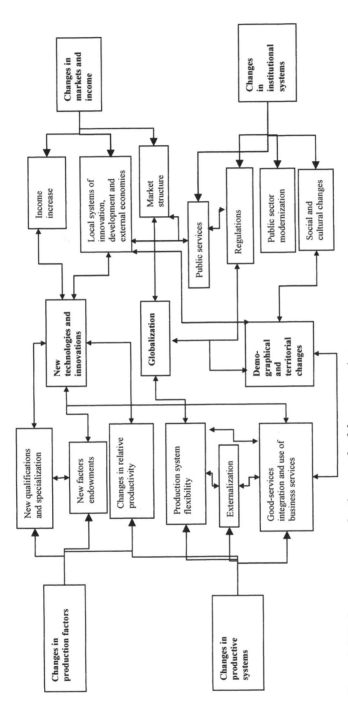

Figure 3.9 Explanatory reasons for the growth of the new service economy

Changes in the demographic structure lead to the promotion of social and health services, pensions expenditure, and private pension insurances. These, in turn, affect the expansion of parts of the health sector, the financial sector (i.e., pension funds) and social services for immigration assistance, among others.

Summary of Explanatory Factors

In order to summarize and put into order the group of factors under analysis, four types of essential changes (previously described) can be distinguished: changes in production factors (mainly labour and human capital); changes in productive systems (flexibility and integration goods-services); changes in markets and income (due to economic growth and external economies); and, finally, changes in institutional system (public services, regulations, cultural and social changes). For each of these factors, three decisive elements of current societies interact: the incorporation of new technologies and innovations, globalization, and demographic and territorial changes. These three elements of socio-economic change simultaneously cause and affect the afore-mentioned four driving forces of structural change.

In addition, some aspects interact with each other but cannot be assigned a specific explanatory dimension. These include not only the three factors of socio-economic change (ICT, globalization and social and territorial change), but also many other, individual elements under consideration.

3. DIFFERENCES AND SIMILARITIES BETWEEN SERVICES IN THE UNITED STATES AND EUROPE[5]

This section compares services between Europe and the United States. In the latter, the services sector is more developed than in Europe, which drives us to analyse to what extent and in which activity subsectors. The size of the EU's agricultural and manufacturing sectors is larger than those in the United States. In 2003, they represented 1.6 per cent and 26.4 per cent of the total EU value added respectively, while these values in the United States were around 1.2 per cent and 22.5 per cent.

Regarding the services sector, the situation is quite the opposite. Temporal evolution shows that throughout the last two decades, the participation of the American tertiary sector in employment – already above 80 per cent – and in value added exceeds that of Europe.

An interesting difference in the behavioural patterns of services between both regions is worth mentioning; in the United States, the participation of the tertiary sector in employment has exceeded that of value added since 1979, although an approach is observed in the late 1990s. The opposite occurs in the EU15, namely, the weighting of services in value added is more important, but their participation in employment has increased continuously since the late 1980s, as shown in Figure 3.10. This explains why the gap between the size of employment in the services sector in the United States and Europe has reduced over time, from 15 per cent in 1979 to 9 per cent in 2003. Meanwhile, this difference has remained at around 4 per cent in the case of value added in services.

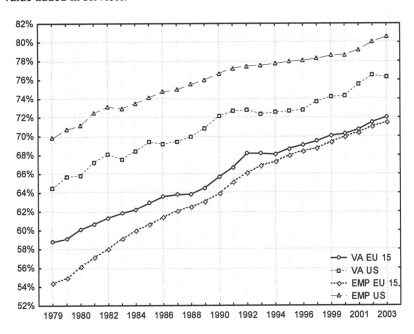

Source: Based on OECD and GGDC data.

Figure 3.10 Participation of services in value added and employment. Evolution between 1979 and 2003, US vs. EU15

Taking into consideration the different categories of services, it can be concluded that the North American economy exceeds that of Europe in virtually all cases, regarding value added and employment (Table 3.6). Only in the case of transport can a clear advance of the EU15 in both variables be noted. Moreover, the value added in real estate and business services is slightly higher in the latter, as well as employment in public administration and, slightly, in computer and professional services.

In terms of long-term growth, the predominance of the United States is also evident. Dynamic analyses suggest that the United States grew to a larger extent than did Europe between 1979 and 2003. The promoters of this growth have been primarily business services, which register high growth rates in almost all areas. Moreover, distributive trades and financial services – principally in the case of value added – have contributed to this growth. In the case of Europe, the enhancement of the role of business services (particularly IT and communication services) is also remarkable. In the United States, the growth of business services held special significance in the 1980s, while in Europe their growth occurred in the 1990s, when the gap between both areas reduced. Between 1979 and 1993, employment in North American business services increased 6 per cent per year, while during the period between 1993 and 2003; such the increase was just at 3 per cent. Regarding the EU15, this growth was lower in the first period, but around 5 per cent in the latter.

Table 3.6 Comparison of data regarding services in the United States and Europe, 2003

	Value added				Employment			
	relative %		Rates (*) 1979/03		relative %		Rates (*) 1979/03	
	EU 15	US	EU 15	US	EU 15	US	EU 15	US
Total sectors	100	100	2.2	2.9	100	100	0.6	1.4
Agriculture	1.6	1.2	1.0	3.9	3.9	1.7	-3.1	0.1
Manufacturing	26.4	22.5	2.2	3.0	24.6	17.8	-1.0	-0.4
Distributive trades	9.8	12.3	2.3	4.6	15.2	16.7	0.9	1.3
Hotels and restaurants	2.4	2.5	1.1	1.4	4.9	7.3	2.3	2.3
Transport	4.8	2.8	2.4	3.2	4.2	2.9	0.5	1.7
Communications	2.6	3.0	5.7	4.0	1.5	1.8	0.1	0.3
Banking and insurance	6.0	8.9	2.5	4.5	3.2	4.3	1.3	1.6
Real estate services	11.1	10.5	2.7	2.8	1.0	1.3	3.3	1.6
Business services	11.2	11.0	4.2	4.6	11.4	11.8	4.4	4.3
- Renting of machinery and equipment	0.9	0.4	5.0	5.6	0.3	0.5	3.4	3.1
- Computer and related services	1.9	2.0	6.6	10.0	1.4	1.3	6.1	8.2
- R&D services	0.4	0.5	2.4	3.3	0.37	0.42	1.8	2.6
- Professional services	4.95	4.94	3.8	2.9	4.1	3.9	3.8	3.2
- Other business services	3.0	3.1	3.9	5.1	5.1	5.7	4.8	4.9
Public administration	7.0	7.9	5.8	5.5	6.9	5.3	0.5	0.6
Social and personal services	3.6	3.7	2.5	2.4	4.8	5.9	2.5	2.4

Note: * Exponential annual growth rates, value added at constant prices, 1995.

Source: Based on OECD and GGDC data.

4. CONVERGENCE OR DIVERGENCE IN EUROPE

Are European countries following a common trajectory regarding services and their different subsectors? To analyse the existence of convergence, this book will study on the one hand, the time profile of dispersions of relative participations of services in total employment (sigma convergence), and, on the other hand, the equation estimates (beta convergence).

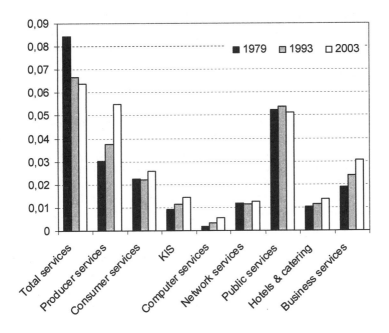

Source: Based on OECD data.

Note: * Standard deviations calculated for the EU15.

Figure 3.11 Standard deviations in the participation of the different services sectors in total employment*

In the long term, a lower dispersion can be observed between the fifteen countries of the EU compared to the total contribution of the tertiary sector in employment. Standard deviation has fallen from 8.5 per cent in 1979 to 6.4 per cent in 2003, as shown in Figure 3.11. In the case of public services, a decrease of national dispersions in 2003 can also be perceived, although to a lesser extent. However, in all the other services categories, the situation is the opposite and regional differences widen. Employment in computer and related services, for example, has evolved unevenly among the countries. In

1979, these services represented between 0.7 per cent and 0.05 per cent of total employment, while in 2003 the range was extended to 2.1 per cent and 0.2 per cent. In both years, Greece had the lowest participation, while France (in 1979) and Sweden (in 2003) registered the highest rates. Over the last two decades, hotel services, producer services, knowledge-intensive services and business services also accentuated their differences, with particular significance in the latter three cases. Dispersions fluctuated with regard to customer service, although an increase can be observed in 2003 compared to previous years.

From an analysis that takes into consideration a more limited period of time and includes the four new Member States, it can be concluded that (with the exception of consumer services) national differences have increased in the same services subsectors. However, in the tertiary sector as a whole, public and network services have reduced their differences.

Table 3.7 measures the level of convergence in the employment levels of the tertiary sector among the European economies using convergence equations. It analyses the relationship between annual employment growth in different services sectors and initial participation level in total employment for different periods of time. A negative relationship could be due to convergence between countries, for instance a downward trend of the initially highest participations and an upward trend of the lowest. In the longer term, for the period 1979 to 2003, the fifteen countries of the EU converged at knowledge-intensive services, computer and related services, business services and public services. These are the only cases for which values are statistically robust.

Nevertheless, and as mentioned previously, dispersions did not reduce in that same period for KIS, computer and business services. This trend could mean that, despite rapid growth, some countries that lag behind in these activities still cannot match the more advanced, continually growing economies. In the other categories, the relationship between variables is positive in some cases and negative in others, but is not significant. In the short term (1993–2003) and within the same group of countries, a solid converging relationship in computer and related services can be observed. Regarding public services, a certain level of convergence can be noted if 10 per cent is accepted as the significance level.

When the analysis includes the four new Member States, two negative, statistically significant relationships emerge, although to different degrees. The most robust relationship emerges for business services, while a less significant relationship is present in computer services. It is worth mentioning that in the group of fifteen countries between 1979 and 2003, convergence in this sector becomes less intense with a limited time range and with an extension of the group of countries considered. On the other hand, within the category of producer services, a divergent relationship emerges for the twenty countries considered from 1993 to 2003.

Empirical evidence regarding national convergences seems to prove that many services models exist within the tertiary scheme in force in the EU15.

In fact, several patterns can be observed in the employment levels of different subsectors among groups of countries. Some economies, such as Luxembourg, the Netherlands, Finland, Sweden and the United Kingdom, behave differently with respect to most European countries in computer and related services. Luxembourg and the Netherlands, together with Ireland, also show a divergence in KIS. This group of countries is characterized by a higher productive specialization than the EU15 average and the significant growth of employment in these categories throughout the last decade. To a certain extent, their employment structures are similar to those of the United States, and are characterized by high participation of technological and knowledge-intensive industries. Some authors refer to these countries as 'excellence centres' and talk about a new European model characterized by investments in new technologies of rapid diffusion, rather than by the wide social coverage typical of the welfare State (Aiginger and Landesmann, 2002). At the other extreme are Portugal, the Czech Republic and Slovakia, which despite their growth in the last decade, differ from the rest of European economies in their poor performance in computer and related services.[6]

Table 3.7 Convergence equations in employment for EU15 and extended EU

Sectors	EU15+US 1979–2003		EU15+US 1993–2003		EU19+US 1993–2003	
	r	R2	r	R2	r	R2
Total services	-0.279	0.078	-0.144	0.020	0.103	0.010
Producer services	0.258	0.066	0.409	0.167	0.447**	0.200
Consumer services	-0.026	0.000	0.165	0.027	0.044	0.001
KIS	-0.754*	0.569	-0.391	0.153	-0.363	0.131
Computer services	-0.730*	0.532	-0.541**	0.292	-0.411***	0.169
Network services	0.038	0.001	0.179	0.032	-0.239	0.057
Hotel services	0.149	0.022	0.289	0.083	0.280	0.078
Public services	-0.717*	0.514	-0.456***	0.208	-0.217	0.047
Business services	-0.639*	0.408	-0.393	0.154	-0.476**	0.227

Notes: *significant at 1 per cent; ** significant at 5 per cent; *** significant at 10 per cent.

Source: Based on OECD and GGDC data.

The lack of beta convergence coincides with the lack of sigma convergence. However, in the case of KIS, there is a kind of convergence of the first type, but not of the second. Some countries have converged greatly since 1979, starting from very low levels (Ireland, Italy, Finland and Austria), although other countries (such as Spain, Portugal and Greece) reached levels of employment participation of around 3 per cent in 2003 – values that the most advanced countries had already registered by 1979. This is why there is a higher statistical deviation, which is due to the greater distance between the extremes. In 2003, countries including Belgium, Luxembourg, France, Germany, the United Kingdom and Holland registered percentages of around 7 per cent. The great dynamism of KIS and their current importance in economic growth are behind this convergence process concerning structural change.

5. CONCLUSIONS

The processes of structural change in recent decades have turned developed economies into services economies. Many European countries have already exceeded an achievement level of 70 per cent services in employment and value added, and the United States leads the trend towards reaching 80 per cent. Empirical work carried out in this chapter confirms the multiplicity of explanatory factors of services growth, although no decisive theory exists for its explanatory capacity. Even the integration of goods-services, which may be the most important factor at present, must be considered together with the others.

The specialization differences within services demonstrate the coexistence of some explanatory elements that act differently by country. Traditional ideas associate services growth with both their lower apparent relative productivity and higher levels of income. Although there is some validity to these theories, current evidence and recent data impose serious limits on this generalization, particularly in the case of productivity. Despite some inter-sectorial cases, in the majority of areas, employment growth does not significantly correspond to lower productivity growth. The correlations between income per capita and services employment are obvious and significant, especially in consumer services.

In all cases, productivity and income reveal other underlying elements that act as driving forces on services: changes in production factors, changes in productive systems, changes in markets and changes in the institutional system. These changes are related to factors such as information and communication society, globalization and demographical and territorial changes. Among these factors, some stand out: integration between goods and services, which has increased the intermediate demand for business services; the interrelation between new technologies, innovation and services; the importance of human capital and qualifications (particularly in advanced services) and specialization; the role of international trade and investment; and finally, through its regulations and institutional changes, the role of the State in the economy. Moreover, the influence of statistical factors is, to a certain extent, present in the advances experienced by services as a sector.

Large enterprises traditionally considered manufacturers became tertiary companies when their production of services exceeded a certain threshold.

The services structure in Europe (EU15) and in the United States is relatively similar, although the latter stands out due to its higher intensity in services growth and, particularly, its higher contribution of business services, financial services, and distributive trades. With regard to KIS, the allocation in both areas is quite similar, although slightly higher in the United States. In services employment, Europe is catching up with the United States, although not in value added. As discussed in the next chapter, this discrepancy indicates the existence of productivity differences.

Europe holds great diversity. Although the general trend (between 1979 and 2003) has been towards a lower disparity in services as a whole, the divergence has increased in the sector's main areas. From sigma and beta convergences a single model of structural change can not be deducted, although a certain convergence process among countries seems to exist in some cases of computer and related services. These two types of convergence offer different results when considering KIS, thus indicating the sector's great dynamism in the context of increasing relative differences among those countries with higher and lower allocations of these activities. In summary, convergence is more significant in long-term (1979–2003) than in medium-short term (1993–2003), within EU15 and the US than a larger set of countries (including new EU member states) and in business and public services than in consumer and network services.

NOTES

1. There are two main types of problems: (1) different methodologies used in different countries, and (2) lack of official price indices, deflators and PPP by activity sectors. These problems result in work conducted without the necessary tools for international comparability, and the use of estimates built for this purpose, as is the case for several value added deflators.
2. The statistical work for drafting this chapter has been substantial. The author appreciates Gisela Di Meglio's help with statistical compilation and analysis.
3. In all countries except for Sweden, the participation of services in value added also exceeds that of the EU15.
4. *OECD in Figures*, 2004 edition, Paris: OECD Publishing.
5. This section is a first approach based on data set out in the introduction. Due to methodological difficulties, no full comparability by services categories is possible (for example, in the sector of distributive trades). However, the data lead to a first approach to the sectorial structure of both areas. In the case of Europe, EU15 will be considered. As main co-author, Gisela Di Meglio has participated heavily in the drafting of this section
6. For further reading on services in Eastern European countries see Stare (2005 and 2007).

4. Productivity in services[1]

INTRODUCTION

The previous chapter introduced productivity to explain the growth of services. One of the most conventional statements in economics, with regard to the services sector states that, as a whole, this sector has a lower productivity level than the other productive sectors, and that its growth is always quite slow. Such a statement is based initially on the personal nature of many services, which makes it difficult to substitute the work-for-capital factor and the incorporation of technical progress. From this approach we can derive the relative lower productivity as an explanation of the growth of the tertiary sector, although the previous chapter established this statement's limits. Here, we will look in greater depth at issues related to services productivity, from methodological aspects regarding the value and meaning of the work productivity indicator, to measurements of services production and productivity. The latter gives rise to serious difficulties when analysing the relationships between productivity and services. Analysis of the existing statistics reveals an alternative approach to this controversial issue, thus contributing unexpected results when taking into consideration the traditional theory. In order to identify better the challenges of the European economy, we will also conduct a comparison with the United States.

1. RELATIONSHIP BETWEEN PRODUCTIVITY AND SERVICES[2]

With regard to the relationship between the progressive growth of services in the economy and their low productivity, the most important advances are due to three works carried out by W. Baumol (1967, 1985, and 1989). Baumol showed the difference between the sectoral productivities as a result of the role played by the work factor in each of the activities. In 'progressive' sectors (which Baumol identified in principle with manufacturing), work is a means, while in 'stagnant' sectors (identified as a part of services) work is used as an end. At times, quality is highly important, which leaves only a small gap for the introduction of technological innovations and extreme productivity gains. Therefore, in an economy where wages are established according to the growth of productivity (mainly in the manufacturing sector), costs in these less dynamic sectors are relatively higher over time. If the demand in these sectors is not affected by their relatively higher prices (low elasticity demand price), a continuous flow of labour force will move towards these activities. However, in the stagnant sectors, where demand is affected by price increases, the possibilities of new jobs will tend to disappear. In this way, Baumol explains the gradual disappearance (except for subsidies) of sectors such as theatre, handicraft, haute cuisine, and so on. He also explains the pressing problem of public services (sectors that are clearly stagnant) with respect to predicted growing deficits 'which no one should be responsible for, as they are part of a trend that nobody can stop'. The well-known Baumol's 'disease' brings about a decrease of economic growth due to its influence on productivity, while at the same time prices in services increase.

The persistence of this dynamism and the increasing weight of the services sector within the economic activity lead to the idea of a decrease in the general growth rate. This decrease is mostly due to the slow growth of productivity in the services sector and its influence on the total productivity of factors. This relies on the hypothesis of the low growth of productivity in the services sector or, at least, on the fact that traditional measures of productivity are suitable for the services sector.

Many recent empirical works (see Oulton, 2001; Wölfl, 2003, 2005, 2007; or Maroto and Cuadrado, 2006a, among others) have tried to provide a contrast to this series of relationships in the services sector. The aggregate evidence for the majority of developed countries suggests a negative relationship between the growth of aggregate productivity and the weight of the tertiary sector, not only in terms of production but also in terms of employment. Some economies (such as Korea or Ireland, which have registered the highest growths of productivity in recent years) are also those where services activities represent a lower percentage over the total. In contrast, countries with high percentages of services over total production and employment, such as the United States or France, show lower growth rates of productivity. This same trend can also be observed in a wide group of the most developed economies. Obviously, the different ways in which services may be incorporated into production processes may bias these results. In any case, the argument is usually based on the traditional idea that services are characterized by a low productivity growth in comparison with other productive sectors. However, as we will consider below, this hypothesis has been recently refuted by numerous authors, and mainly by the empirical evidence itself.

In recent years, as other authors have criticized or have even contemplated that Baumol's disease has been 'cured', Baumol has corrected and redefined his positions[3] by distinguishing between types of services. In general, criticism and reviews are based on the following points:

1. The need to take the indirect effects, measures and indicators of services productivity into consideration (Rubalcaba, 1999; Wolff, 1999; and

Rubalcaba and Kox, 2007), as a result of the conceptual and statistical debate arising over the last ten years, from the works by Gadrey (1996) and other French authors, and up until the most recent works developed by the OECD and other international organizations.

2. The need to take into consideration the role of other elements – not just the labour force – to explain the growth of services and conditioning their productivity. These theories, which currently include the explanation for the growth of services, are very broad and cover many factors. This is true for factors connected to the nature of services, the organization and segmentation of their markets, or the peculiar substitution relationships between work and capital (De Bandt, 1989; Kox, 2002).

3. The need to limit the application of Baumol's theories solely to end-use services and not to those assigned to intermediate use: although the same services industries have stagnant productivities, the movement of resources towards them must be interpreted not as the result of a fall, but as an increase of productivity (Oulton, 2001). On the other hand, a lower services productivity can be a reflection of the higher productivity generated in the companies using them (Raa and Wolff, 1996; Fixler and Siegel, 1999; Kox and Rubalcaba, 2007a).[4]

4. And finally, recent empirical approaches highlight the role of the strong productivity in some services branches, especially those related to ICT in Europe (O'Mahony and van Ark, 2003; van Ark and Piatkowski, 2004) and in the United States (Stiroh, 2001; Triplett and Bosworth, 2002). In the latter case, strong productivity is due to an unprecedented expansion of the total productivity of factors. One possible explanation is the presence of growing returns of scale in these kinds of tertiary activities, which would contradict Baumol's theses (Wölfl, 2003).

2.   THE CONCEPT AND MEASUREMENT OF SERVICE PRODUCTIVITY

Despite its limitations, the indicator traditionally used to measure productivity in the services sector is the relationship between production and labour force, also known as 'apparent labour productivity' or 'relative labour productivity' (OECD, 2001a). However, when analysing the services sector, the value and significance of this indicator could be also questioned; the value added of a certain number of services sectors, especially in the case of non-sale services, is practically equivalent to the use and costs of the labour factor. For this reason, there is a direct relationship between how the production and evolution of productivity per employed person are estimated (De Bandt, 1989; Gadrey et al., 1992).

The problems associated with productivity measurement related to the tertiary sector are as important as those related to the meaning and concept of productivity and the links with service quality and service performance (Gadrey, 1996). The increase in the percentage registered by the services sector in advanced economies, in terms of production and employment, together with the relatively slow growth of the real production in such a sector, has led to the importance of services productivity registering an increase over the last years. However, there are still only a limited number of studies regarding comparisons at a global level. International comparisons in services productivity began with Paige and Bombach's (1959) work comparing the United Kingdom and the United States. No subsequent works were carried out, including all the services branches, until those performed by the Groningen University within the framework of the ICOP project. Schreyer and Pilat (2001) offer a general study of the issue regarding current productivity measurement in each of the services branches.

Measurement problems regarding output, prices and quality in services activities do not differ to a great extent from those in the case of goods (Kendrick, 1985). However, these problems are more significant regarding services, particularly due to the lack of primary activities such as census or price surveys. Therefore, when we tried to measure production and productivity in the services sector, we previously faced a conceptual problem of how to define quantity, quality and prices (Griliches, 1992). These problems refer to the definition of the product and to the identification of changes in the services quality and in prices, as well as the lack of data regarding the services sector, which has resulted in the historic underestimation of production and productivity growth in tertiary activities (Baily and Gordon, 1988; Slifman and Corrado, 1996; Gullickson and Harper, 1999; Sharpe et al., 2002; Vijselaar, 2003).

According to these theories, it seems that an important source of the growth differential of productivity between goods and services could be found in the above-mentioned measurement problems. Wölfl (2003) considers that these problems or biases regarding the measurement of services productivity are to be found in three different areas: in the selection of inputs; in the selection of outputs at current and constant prices; and finally, in the method of aggregation between sectors. Intuitively, the arguments in favour of this type of errors are not very complex. The first block of possible errors to be considered when trying to measure productivity in services is found in the selection of inputs. In the case of apparent labour productivity, this firstly means the measurement of the labour factor in terms of the total number of employees or the total number of hours worked. This problem could be significant, particularly when dealing with the hours worked by the self-employed or part-time employees (OECD, 2001b). In general, the conclusive differences between productivity growth in manufacturing and services are greater if they are measured in terms of employees rather than if worked hours are taken into consideration (McLean, 1997; Wölfl, 2003).

The second question regarding the selection of inputs is the relationship between the labour factor and the intermediate factors. This possible bias is particularly important in the case of the outsourcing or externalization of services production. Within the OECD countries, there is clear evidence that a growing part of services production (defined as all the services production, independent of the sector where it is produced) occurs in the services sectors (Heston and Summers, 1992). This information complicates the comparisons between goods and services productivity, due to the fact that externalization is generally a problem related to changes in the vertical integration between services and goods-producing units.

Nevertheless, the most controversial element in economic literature regarding the measurement bias within the framework of services productivity is the selection of outputs at current and constant prices. The first problem is the definition of output in some services, such as financial services, which is not necessarily the same in all countries (Griliches, 1999; Sichel, 1997). The second problem related to this issue is the calculation of the value added at constant prices. For example, in many services activities it is difficult to isolate price variations that are due to quality changes from those due to pure price changes, and therefore, to adjust the price indices in terms of quality. As a result, different measures have been used to calculate the value added in constant terms (OECD, 1996). The impact of the use of different price indices in the measurement of services production and productivity has been analysed in depth within economic literature (Baumol, Blackman and Wolff, 1985; Berndt et al., 1998; Eldridge, 1999; Lebow and Rudd, 2001; Wölfl, 2003). In recent years, a predominant example of measurement errors in services induced by prices is the impact of the selection of the price index in ICT-related sectors (Schreyer, 1998 and 2001; Pilat et al., 2002).

Finally, the third component in the possible bias regarding the measurement of productivity growth in the tertiary sector relates to the estimation of the aggregate productivity growth. In this case, there are two channels through which this services bias can be transmitted to the aggregate indicator. The first channel is the proportion, within production and employment totals in the economy, of services activities that underestimate the growth of their productivity. The second channel relates to the role of some services activities, such as financial, business, transport and telecommunication services, which are in demand by other sectors.

Other problems linked to the measurement of productivity in the services sector are: the lower quality of data regarding this sector, mainly due to the lower coverage of census and surveys in this type of activities; and the importance of some services activities such as personal and business services in the black economy. These two problems hinder the estimation of productivity in these activities and can lead to biases in the data studied.

Although the intuitive understanding of these types of measurement biases or errors is not very complex, the undertaking of accurate analyses regarding the dimension and direction of these measurement errors is much more complicated. The impact of the use of inappropriate deflators or incorrect production measures, for example, depends to a large extent on the models and data used at a sub-sectoral level. For this reason, the majority of studies carried out until now concentrated on specific activities within services, and thus their conclusions cannot necessarily be generalized for the rest of the services. Hence, national statistics offices and the OECD have tried to face the problem of production and productivity measurement in the services sector since the 1990s, carrying out tasks related to all the possible errors previously described (OECD, 2001c, 2002b, 2002c).

3. SERVICES PRODUCTIVITY GROWTH

The services sector currently accounts for more than 70 per cent of productivity and employment in advanced economies. Despite this increasingly important role, however, services growth in productivity has been slow in the majority of these economies, resulting in a need to achieve higher dynamics and more power in the sector. If the objective is to increase the use of this sector's labour force and produce a higher growth in productivity, services will need to contribute to a larger extent than in recent years. Such has been the case of the United States, Australia, Canada and Luxembourg, but in other countries such as Italy, France, Holland or Spain, the contribution of the services sector to the growth of productivity has been low (Wölfl, 2005).

Table 4.1 illustrates the growth rates of productivity per employee in the European Union, the US, Japan and some other countries of the OECD, for the period 1980 to 2002, and for the reduced period 1996 to 2002. The results show that the growth in productivity accelerated in the second half of the 1990s in countries such as the US, Greece and Ireland. In contrast, productivity growth slowed over the same period in the other European countries, Japan and Korea. If we analyse the productivity growth in the services sector, we can observe that, again, the US and Ireland register an increase in their growth rates at the end of the 1990s. In this case however, other European countries such as the United Kingdom, Italy and Spain, also registered a rise in their growth rates per employee in the services sector. As indicated in the previous section, although empirical studies at a global level have pointed out the existence of an unbalanced growth between manufacturing and services as a sectoral aggregate, this statement is not as univocal when different services sectors are analysed. The aforementioned positive performance of the services sector in some countries, refuting to some extent the sector's traditional image, is not homogeneous in all services activities. The productivity growth rates of branches related to communications, transport, financial services and some business services[5] are similar to those registered by the most productive industries (such as machinery- and equipment-related ones). The rapid growth in employment in the services sector in many developed countries during the 1990s was due primarily to the dynamics of some market services such as telecommunications, transport, distributive trades, financial services, insurance and business services.[6] One of the main characteristics of these services is the rising use of technologies boosting productivity, such as ICT, which has resulted in a growth of labour productivity in countries such as Australia, Japan or the United States (OECD, 2005b).

The remaining employment increase in advanced countries has been promoted by social and personal services – including health and education. Some of these services – mainly health and personal services, as well as hotels and restaurants – have undergone small growths of productivity observed, and therefore do not achieve the positive dynamics of the others. They act in the way suggested by the traditional theories regarding services.

The fact that productivity in some services branches has registered high growth rates in recent years does not necessarily mean that these activities have also contributed significantly to the growth of aggregate productivity. The direct contribution of services sectors to the productivity growth in the European Union is illustrated in Figure 4.1. Productivity growth is defined as the increase in the value added per unit of employment used. Given that the direct contribution of some services activities to the growth of the value added was considerably lower than their contribution to the employment growth, we can deduce that the direct contribution of some services sectors such as social and personal services, hotels and restaurants and business-related services, to the growth of the aggregate productivity should have been relatively poor. Superficially, this could have a reducing impact on the growth of the aggregate productivity, which has led some researchers to conclude that the growth of these tertiary activities contributes to the stagnation of growth in the long term (Baumol's disease), whose limits have already been mentioned.[7] Nevertheless, despite these decreasing trends, it is worth highlighting that the high level of relative productivity still persists in some services branches such as communications, financial services and public administration services.

Over time, the contribution of services will have to increase in many developed countries, while that of manufacturing companies will fall and these will turn progressively into services companies (Pilat, 2005). Moreover, a more productive and competitive services sector is also important to complement the operation of the manufacturing sector, due to the increasingly important outsourcing and globalization processes, as mentioned in the first section of this chapter. This rising role of services highlights the implementation of policies that take into consideration this growing contribution of services to the aggregate economic operation. Therefore, the regulatory reforms and the openness towards commerce and foreign direct investment in services are important in this respect, as this sector has traditionally been less exposed to the competitive pressure exerted by manufacturing industries (as we shall see in the following chapters).

Table 4.1 Productivity growth per employee by country

Sectors	NACE Code	UE-15		US		Japan		Spain		Germany		France		Italy		UK		Ireland		Korea	
		80-02	96-02	80-02	96-02	80-02	96-02	80-02	96-02	80-02	96-02	80-02	96-02	80-02	96-02	80-02	96-02	80-02	96-02	80-02	96-02
Agriculture	1,2,5	4.4	3.2	3.7	4.3	1.9	1.6	4.2	3.9	5.7	4.2	4.5	2.9	4.4	2.4	3.5	4.3	2.7	0.7	5.2	3.5
Manufacturing	10-37	3.7	6.1	5.5	12.3	3.1	2.6	3.1	0.8	3.4	6.1	1.7	3.6	1.4	0.2	5.4	7.2	8.0	9.5	13.5	29.4
Energy	40-41	3.6	5.7	1.6	1.3	2.6	3.7	3.7	6.3	2.8	5.7	3.5	2.8	2.5	4.2	7.3	9.7	7.9	7.0	13.1	15.0
Construction	45	1.0	0.6	1.6	1.3	-0.4	-1.2	1.6	-0.4	0.2	0.7	0.6	-0.4	0.4	0.6	2.2	1.7	0.9	4.0	2.6	0.9
Services	**50-95**	**0.8**	**0.8**	**1.0**	**2.4**	**1.6**	**0.8**	**0.3**	**0.3**	**1.0**	**1.0**	**0.5**	**0.3**	**-0.1**	**0.0**	**1.0**	**1.7**	**1.5**	**2.1**	**1.9**	**1.7**
Dist. trades	50-52	1.3	1.0	3.8	7.0	2.8	-0.4	0.5	0.5	0.7	0.1	1.6	0.0	0.3	0.2	2.5	3.4	1.0	2.7	3.9	4.0
Hotels and restaurants	55	-1.3	-0.8	-0.8	0.6	-1.0	-0.2	-0.2	-1.2	-3.1	-4.3	-2.4	0.1	-1.7	-0.9	-0.2	0.4	0.0	1.8	0.1	1.7
Transport	60-63	2.2	1.3	1.4	1.2	0.5	-2.0	2.3	1.4	2.6	3.2	1.9	1.5	1.8	-0.5	2.4	-0.0	4.9	6.8	2.8	2.7
Communications	64	6.3	8.6	3.8	6.1	7.4	8.7	3.9	4.6	8.1	14.9	5.5	6.3	7.5	9.1	5.5	7.8	2.9	1.0	11.4	13.6
Financial services	65-67	1.5	2.0	2.1	5.3	5.2	4.1	1.4	2.1	2.0	3.6	2.4	-0.2	0.6	1.5	1.3	3.0	2.2	-0.9	4.6	6.6
Real estate	70	-0.9	-0.9	1.2	1.2	0.9	2.5	-1.1	-6.3	-0.6	-1.3	0.5	1.9	-2.6	-1.8	-3.8	-1.3	-0.1	5.4	-4.0	-2.2
Business services	71-74	0.1	-0.2	-0.2	1.0	4.4	2.8	-0.5	-0.4	0.1	-0.9	-0.4	-1.4	-2.6	-0.9	0.8	2.8	-0.7	0.7	-0.2	-5.2
Public Services	75	0.7	0.7	0.3	0.3	1.3	1.1	0.2	1.2	1.1	1.1	0.7	1.5	0.8	0.8	0.8	-0.4	0.9	-1.6	-0.3	0.0
Social and personal services	80-95	0.0	0.2	-0.4	-0.5	-0.1	0.4	0.1	0.3	-0.3	-0.2	-0.3	0.2	-1.3	0.3	0.5	0.5	2.6	2.2	0.5	-2.2
TOTAL ECONOMY	**1-99**	**1.6**	**1.2**	**1.4**	**2.3**	**2.6**	**1.8**	**1.7**	**0.7**	**1.6**	**1.4**	**1.5**	**0.8**	**1.4**	**0.7**	**2.0**	**1.8**	**4.2**	**5.8**	**5.3**	**4.1**

Source: Based on GGDC data.

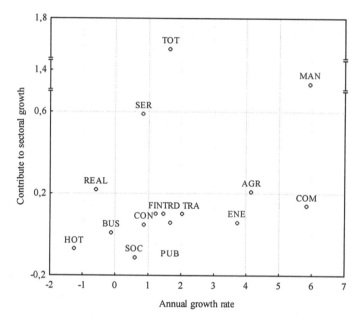

Source: Based on GGDC data.

Figure 4.1 Contribution of services to productivity growth, 1979–2003

The comparison between the evolution of productivity in manufacturing and in services as an aggregate sector supports the most traditional theories that emphasize low growth of productivity in the latter sector. However, when analysing the evolution of services by activity sectors, a clear dualism emerges. Some activity areas register the same, or even higher, productivity growth rates than the average rates registered in the manufacturing sector and in its most dynamic sub-sectors. Moreover, and beyond the statistical and measurement limits described in the previous section, the empirical evidence regarding services productivity highlights the need to improve its associated policies.

Some characteristic factors (such as the intensive utilization of labour force, innovation obstacles, low intensity of competition, smaller size of service companies, or inherent differences of the labour market) demonstrate the need for a strong services policy that takes a long term vision into consideration. However, these measures must not be implemented separately from the rest of the sectors, due to the interdependence of many services (business services, financial activities, transport and communications) with manufacturing industries, and the benefits arising from this connection in terms of aggregate growth.

4. SERVICES PRODUCTIVITY CONVERGENCE AND DIVERGENCE: EUROPE AND THE US

In the last section of this chapter, we compare the labour productivity in both Europe and in the United States. In recent years, many authors have shown the limits and differences in productivity growth of Europe compared with that of the United States, not only at an aggregate level (HLIG, 2003; Kok et al., 2004; European Commission, 2003b; Maroto and Cuadrado, 2006b), but also in specific economic sectors or sub-sectors (O'Mahony and van Ark, 2003; OECD, 2004a; van Ark et al., 2003a, b). Thus, the objective of this section is to analyse the situation of the services sector in order to find out whether the EU15 is also behind the US in terms of productivity in this sector.

Table 4.2 Productivity levels per employee, EU15/US (1 = same level)

	1979	**1985**	**1990**	**1995**	**2000**	**2003**
Agriculture	0.38	0.29	0.35	0.50	0.39	0.41
Manufacturing	0.84	0.85	0.87	0.89	0.66	0.45
Energy	0.55	0.58	0.60	0.64	0.78	0.79
Construction	0.89	1.03	1.14	1.13	1.16	1.22
Services	**1.07**	**1.05**	**1.10**	**1.15**	**1.04**	**0.98**
Distributive trades	1.23	1.03	1.10	1.07	0.87	0.79
Hotels and restaurants	1.62	1.77	1.71	1.66	1.55	1.49
Transport	0.77	0.84	0.91	0.98	0.96	0.83
Communications	0.71	0.79	0.91	1.00	1.14	1.14
Financial and insurance services	1.19	0.95	1.11	1.08	0.76	0.64
Real Estate activities	1.80	1.63	1.51	1.37	1.18	1.18
Business services	1.21	1.37	1.32	1.39	1.24	1.11
Equipment rental	2.68	3.55	3.88	2.87	2.56	2.17
IT services	1.10	1.33	1.03	0.89	1.05	0.82
R&D	1.33	1.58	1.40	1.42	1.30	1.30
Legal, technical and advertising	0.89	0.98	0.97	1.05	1.06	0.95
Other n.e.c.	1.75	1.86	1.68	1.81	1.35	1.31
Public Administration services	0.57	0.58	0.59	0.63	0.66	0.64
Social and personal services	1.25	1.23	1.23	1.31	1.36	1.38
TOTAL ECONOMY	**0.93**	**0.95**	**1.01**	**1.06**	**1.00**	**0.97**

Source: Based on GGDC data.

Productivity and the use of the labour force are the two key elements when explaining the differences of per capita income at an international level. The interest taken by many developed countries regarding these aspects in recent years is, at least partially, due to the strong growth of the US economy from the mid-1990s and the stagnation of the convergence process of the other developed economies. Most research shows that productivity is the main element determining the gap of GDP per capita between the US and other advanced economies, which include the majority of the European economies (European Commission, 2003b).

In terms of productivity levels per employee[8] (Table 4.2), the services sector situation in Europe is slightly below that of the United States, in the same way as is observed at an aggregate level in 2003. However, the situation in the manufacturing sector is much worse, due to the fact that American productivity in this type of activity is significantly higher than that of Europe (more precisely, 55 per cent). Within the framework of the services sector, although considerable statistical differences must be taken into consideration between both economic areas, almost all areas (except for distributive trades, transport, financial and Public Administration services) register higher productivity levels in Europe than in the US. Nevertheless, we can also observe how the surplus in favour of the EU has been reduced since the mid-1990s, only excluding communication-related activities.

Taking into consideration evolution, we can clearly observe the change experienced from the second half of the 1990s. From this point onward, European levels in the services sector (higher than those of the US until this point) fell until becoming slightly lower than American services in 2003. On the other hand, in the manufacturing sector, the differential in 1995 in favour of the American economy has increased significantly since then. When analysing growth rates, European productivity showed superiority over the whole economy during the period 1979–1995. Between 1985 and 1995, almost all the important sectors showed a better performance in Europe than in the United States. However, in some services such as IT or R&D services, productivity growth rates in the US were higher than in Europe. From the year 1995, we can observe a shift in this situation, as American productivity began its 'boom' (European Commission, 2001; O'Mahony, 2002; Collechia and Schreyer, 2001). The differential with respect to Europe increased significantly in many sectors, mainly in those related to ICTs – ICT users rather than producers, where the EU has demonstrated a positive performance.

In Figure 4.2, which summarizes the above, we can observe the performance in terms of productivity per employee regarding the different economic sectors and sub-sectors in Europe, compared to the US. A minor convergence process has been registered concerning the whole economic aggregate, in view of the fact that there was a level of productivity inferior to that of the US in the year 1979 but that the annual average growth rate from then onwards has been superior to that of the American economy. However, the productivity per employee in the US was still slightly higher in 2003 than that of the EU15, so differences between both economic areas persist in aggregate terms.

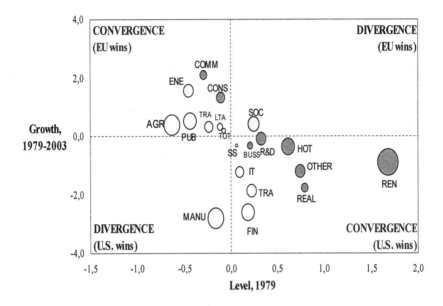

Notes: In the horizontal axis, we can see the relative differences in the productivity level per employee in 1979 between both areas [(EU level – US level)/US level]. The vertical axis shows the differences in the growth rate for the period 1979–2003 between both areas [EU rate – US rate]. The size of the circles shows the relative differences in the level of productivity per employee in 2003 [(EU level – US level)/US level]; when the difference is positive – in favour of the EU – these are shaded, whereas those without shade refer to the negative difference – in favour of the US. Abbreviations correspond to the sectors included in Table 4.2.

Source: Based on GGDC data.

Figure 4.2 Descriptive convergence in productivity per employee EU–US (US data = 0)

The services sector, in turn, has also experienced a slight convergence process during this period, but in favour of the American tertiary sector in this case. From an initial higher productivity level in Europe, lower growth rates have been reached despite the fact that the current productivity level is still slightly higher than that of the US. In the manufacturing sector, a divergent process in favour of the American economy has taken place. This is caused by the fact that, considering the higher level in 1979, the growth rates have also been higher during the period under analysis, so the differences are significantly broader. The opposite phenomenon has been experienced by energy and construction industries – sectors where a convergent process has occurred. The case of construction is a different situation, as its productivity levels in 1979 were lower in Europe, and in 2003 exceeded those of the US. In the primary sector, although a certain convergence has occurred compared to the US, productivity levels are still relatively lower in Europe.

If we analyse the different services areas, social and community services have experienced a process of divergence in favour of the US. In the remaining services activities, a process of convergence has taken place between both economies. Some services stand out, such as those related to communication, transport, public administrations and some business services, such as legal, technical and advertising services.

All these areas have shortened the gap regarding American productivity levels due to higher growth rates (in the case of communication services, these are currently above those of the US). On the contrary, we find hotels and restaurants, distributive trades, financial services, real estate activities and some business services, such as those related to IT, R&D, equipment rental and others. Although these business activities start with higher productivity levels than those of the US, they have experienced lower growth rates than the latter, so the differences have been shortened or the situation has changed radically, as is the case of distributive trades, financial or IT services, where levels in the US are above those in Europe, the same as in the aggregate services sector.

5. CONCLUSIONS AND IMPLICATIONS

Various relevant conclusions can be drawn from the analyses carried out in this chapter. Firstly, it seems clear that the analysis regarding productivity in the services sector is the core of an increasing debate, principally regarding its definition and measurement. The lack of data for its subsequent analysis can be added to the conceptual problems encompassed in the study of services productivity. The importance of these issues regarding measurement is due to the implications of services productivity over the multifactor productivity and the aggregate economic growth of any current developed economy.

With regard to the empirical relationship between services and productivity important differences emerge at sectoral level. Data concerning productivity growth per employee in the majority of countries shows important differences between a more progressive and dynamic manufacturing sector on the one hand, and an almost 'stagnant' services sector' on the other, according to the traditional ideas related to productivity and services. However, the services sector itself cannot be considered unproductive, according to the empirical evidence. If we disaggregate the analysis of the services sector, the performance pattern of some tertiary activities does not agree with the traditional assumptions about services productivity.

The heterogeneity and dualism within the tertiary sector in developed economies are significant. Many services register productivity growths that are typical of highly productive manufacturing industries. This is the case of transport, communication and financial services, and also, to a lesser extent, of distributive trades. Likewise, ICT-related services and some business services seem to have indirect positive effects on the productivity growth of other sectors and activities, and thus on growth of the aggregate productivity in the European economies. However, some services still register a nil or even a negative growth in their productivity despite the increasing use of technologies and the rise of competition. Regarding the United States, we can verify a convergence process in many sectors, with European productivity registering high relative growths in sectors such as telecommunication, professional or transport services. In contrast, the United States surpasses Europe in sectors like distributive trades or financial services with higher relative growths.

In summary, the challenges regarding productivity in Europe are: the relative backwardness of some services areas; the development of growth potential in those areas with higher growths outside of Europe; and the development of business services, whose use rebounds indirect effects onto the productivity of the sectors that use them.

There are significant overall views to explain, both in the positive and negative sense, the performance of services productivity, either as a whole or by activity sectors. Among them, we can find: physical capital (and capitalization processes and improvement of capital–labour relations); innovation (showing clear differences with the manufacturing sector, as we will see in Chapter 5 regarding service innovation); the qualification and training of employees in the sector; the existence of regulations and factors preventing free competition (analysed in greater detail in Chapter 7 regarding services regulations); the inferior dimensions of business services (in relation to manufacturing); and some specific characteristics of the labour market. These factors are not displayed equally in all services areas or in all countries, but the existing differences are those which arise from the heterogeneous performance of productivity in the different services activities and economies.

This is, however, just a starting point. The effect of errors in the definition and measurement of productivity in services on the aggregate economic growth, as well as the heterogeneity in terms of productivity within the sector itself, need a far deeper analysis. Not only political-economic authorities, but also service market protagonists themselves (companies and public organizations) have a wide area in which to act and achieve improvements in their respective productivity growth rates. For this very reason, many countries are now developing policies and studies aimed at the improvement of these aspects, and international organizations are working together with national offices in order to improve the information and its analysis in numerous areas, such as financial and insurances services, or business services. This is the way to better measure the productivity of services and to extend the knowledge regarding growth factors and international differences that underlie the operation and growth of productivity.

NOTES

1. Andrés Maroto has participated in this chapter as main co-author.
2. This section is based on a paper that will be published in the *Service Industries Journal* (volume 28, number 3) under the title, 'Services Productivity Revisited', by Maroto and Rubalcaba. The authors thank the Journal for permission to use this section in this book. The forthcoming journal article will complement this chapter by providing different insights into the contribution of services to overall productivity and by analysing the role of cycles and trends in the productivity debate.
3. Baumol himself (1989) configures a new classification of services, according to productivity, where sectors with a low productivity growth co-exist with services registering productive growths that are equal to or higher than those of manufactured products. Along the same lines, more recent studies show that only one third of the services sector can be identified as low productivity growth activities, while the rest includes sectors registering similar growth rates (transport and storage) or even higher (telecommunications) than the manufacturing sector. More recently, Baumol draws conclusions that highlight the importance of services and their innovation to economic growth (Baumol, 2000).
4. These results force us to reconsider previous literature on this subject. While the manufactured goods sector has increased – primarily due to improvements in technical and technological efficiency (productivity gains that will be translated into higher wage increments, and consequently, into increases of costs related to less progressive sectors of the economy) – the rapid growth registered in the services sector can be explained by the increase of capital and labour factors.
5. Over the 1990s, the annual average productivity growth was around 10 per cent in communications, 4.5 per cent in financial services, and about 2.5 per cent in distributive trades and transport services in the majority of developed countries (Wölfl, 2005).
6. During the 1990s, these services accounted for approximately 60 per cent of total employment in the field of OECD countries (OECD, 2005a).
7. Regarding some specific services branches, such as business services, Baumol's limits of original interpretation are even more important than in other services sectors, as shown in the works carried out by Oulton (2001), Wölfl (2003) and Kox (2002, 2004). Baumol's model focuses on consumer services, while business services are intermediate consumptions for other industries. Also, the possibility exists that the business services industry indirectly increases the productivity of other industries. This may be a consequence of the knowledge generated, and the possibility that underestimation problems are overlooked.
8. In constant dollars of 1995, based on GGDC data. It is worth mentioning that the comparison of levels has many more problems than the comparison of growth rates, given that the methodological differences between countries are more

predominant. This is especially significant in some services such as distributive trades, where productivity measurements are different. Even so, this must be considered as a provisional approach. In the case of trade, McGuckin et al. (2005) proved that the differences in favour of the United States are real and not just due to statistical effects.

5. Service innovation

INTRODUCTION

This chapter introduces the reader to the concept of innovation as a key factor in the service economy. The productivity problems defined in the previous chapter could be partly related to the deficits in the service innovation system. Technological shifts and innovation have always lagged behind economic growth, and the same pattern occurs when dealing with the tertiary sector. Common sentiment, however, persistently upheld services as generally less innovative and less productive than other industrial organizations. This chapter will show (as did the previous chapter) that these principles are far less prevalent than before, and that heterogeneity exists within the different types of services. Firstly, the basic issues relating to service innovation (definitions, concepts and measurement difficulties) will be presented, followed by the main European and OECD data concerning service innovation and R&D. Thus, this chapter aims to identify the European challenges in this field.

1. INNOVATION, GROWTH AND SERVICES

Since the beginning of economic science, economists have linked innovation with economic growth, and Joseph A. Schumpeter was the author who placed it at the forefront. As a growth factor using processes of creative destruction, innovation has taken shape as one of the most significant explanatory elements for long-term growth. According to Schumpeter (1942), innovation is the essential boost of an evolving capitalism, provided that it maintains its underlying entrepreneurial nature.[1] After Schumpeter, the developing growth theories used Solow as their basis, placing technological progress – and therefore innovation processes – at the core of economic analysis. With new theories of endogenous growth (Romer, 1986, 1990; Lucas, 1988), technological progress is fully integrated as an endogenous variable, which is explained by learning- and knowledge-related elements, among others. The value of intangibles, and therefore the related services, would form part of these elements.

In recent years, an alternative approach to the neoclassical theories has come to light. Evolutionist growth models create another concept of innovation within growth by looking at the integration of economic and non-economic factors (culture, institutions, and sciences). Evolutionist theories have been the preferred field of the specialists in service innovation. Services have developed within innovative systems as another dimension that linked to the whole economic system, especially by means of knowledge-intensive services. In this respect, important contributions have arisen, such as those by Antonelli (1999), Miles (1999), Boden and Miles (2000), Metcalfe and Miles (2000), Muller (2001) and Zenker (2001).

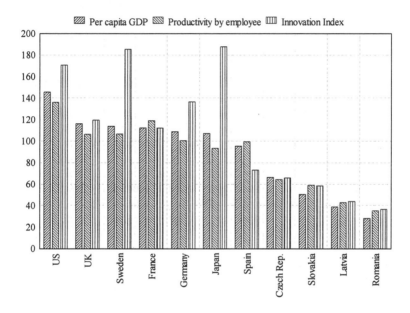

Source: Based on Innovation Scoreboard 2004 and EUROSTAT data.

Figure 5.1 Per capita GDP, productivity and innovation rate, 2004 (EU25 = 100)

In all cases, the different approaches acknowledge the importance of innovation to economic growth. Service innovation also has a particular relationship with productivity and organizational efficiency, which are essential channels for the transmission of their effects to growth. Figure 5.1 shows the existing relationship between these economic variables at an aggregate level.[2] Those countries reporting higher innovation indices in their economies also present major levels of per capita GDP and productivity. Therefore, when the value of the innovation rate is lower, such as in the case of the Czech Republic, Slovakia, Latvia and Romania, the figures regarding national production and productivity are also reduced. The different correlation values calculated for the three variables under analysis show their relevant dependence, when considering the observed correlation level.[3]

Service innovation affects growth by means of three key mechanisms:

1. As services constitute 70 per cent of advanced economies, their innovation process will be essential for the group of innovative systems and their impact on growth.
2. Certain services were and are essential in the development of some technological innovations.
3. Business services, especially KIS (Knowledge Intensive Services), are used as intermediate inputs in production, due to their positive effects on the innovation of those companies that make use of these services. This includes impacts on manufacturing that provide products for the service sector.

The other sections in this chapter refer to the first of the aforementioned mechanisms. The second mechanism summarizes the arguments put forth in Chapter 3. The third mechanism was discussed and summarized in previous work (Rubalcaba, 1999). The strategic role of business services in industry is associated with their innovative nature. This function can be better understood by analysing the five types of innovation that promote business services: technological, organizational, strategic, commercial and operational (see Table 5.1). Some of these terms are the modern expressions of the innovative aspects as defined by Joseph A. Schumpeter. According to Schumpeter, innovation includes new products, new processes, new forms of organization, new markets, and new sources of inputs to production (Schumpeter, 1939).

We will take technological innovation as an example. The incorporation of technologies and their improved usage are the first consequences of innovation produced by business services. IT services are those most related to technological innovation, although electronic communication, engineering, computer-assisted design and certain telecommunication services could also have the same or higher importance. All these services contribute to a real and effective technological innovation: *real* because a high percentage of technology usually remains out of those companies which do not understand its potential use, due to the lack of accompanying services; and *effective* because if there were no services linked to new technologies, they would be under-used.

Business knowledge-intensive services have achieved an important role in modern economies and national innovation systems (Kox and Rubalcaba, 2007b; Windrum and Tomlinson, 1999) that favour the modernization of a country's knowledge base. This achievement becomes evident in two ways: on the one hand, due to technological innovations (in subsectors with important levels of intensity in R&D such as engineering, software and research), including those of an organizational type and those related to business strategy, marketing and management of human resources (Boden and Miles 2000); and on the other hand, due to the diffusion of knowledge for developing best practices for solving the most common business problems encountered by different customer organizations, and for orientating them towards a relevant efficiency. Knowledge-intensive services provide the intangible elements (know-how, software, organizational skills, R&D capabilities, and so on) which have become the key motivating elements for the creation of value, since according to Grubel (1995), a substantial part of growth in the total factors productivity can be understood from the increase of specialization in the production of inputs.

Table 5.1 Business services innovative functions

Innovative functions	*Main innovation components*	*Business services (some representative activities)*
Technological Innovation	▪ Major technology incorporation ▪ Major utilization of existent technology ▪ Technological adaptation to the business necessities ▪ Efficiency in the information and communication advanced processes ▪ Routine processes automatization ▪ Productive structures flexibilization ▪ Improve in quality	▪ Computing services ▪ Engineering services ▪ Design services ▪ Communication services ▪ Electronic on-line communication services ▪ Quality control services
Organizational Innovation	▪ Efficiency in the internal organization ▪ Integration of the control and coordination processes ▪ Improve in selection, training and utilization of human factor ▪ Improve in different functional specializations	▪ Management consultancy ▪ Legal audit and services ▪ Personal services (selection, training and part-time jobs)
Strategic Innovation	▪ Flexibility for dynamic environments ▪ Positioning in complex markets ▪ Strategic information on alliances ▪ Information on product adequacy ▪ Information on allocation and markets ▪ Defence in a conflictive legal environment	▪ Management services ▪ On-line services ▪ Audit services ▪ Legal services ▪ Fair and exhibition services ▪ Market studies
Commercial Innovation	▪ Competitive product design ▪ Innovative commercialization ▪ Major utilization of opportunities ▪ Seek and form links with clients ▪ Innovative marketing ▪ Image consideration	▪ Design services ▪ Exhibitions ▪ Advertising ▪ Direct marketing ▪ Public relations ▪ After-sale services
Operative Innovation	▪ Functional work division ▪ Key tasks concentration ▪ Operative consideration ▪ Image consideration	▪ Language services ▪ Courier services ▪ Security services ▪ Operative services

Source: Rubalcaba (1999).

From a service economy perspective, it is understood that innovative processes do not form, transmit or produce the same effects as those generated in a manufacturing environment, which are much more linear and are directed straight at products or at productive processes. Intangible aspects, which are results of the interactive nature of services, help to explain the peculiar way in which services innovate, are innovative, or enable other sectors to take advantage of innovation capabilities. All in all, the wide possibilities of technological change opened by an appropriate system of innovation are reinforced by the service economy (Miles, 2000), although some differences persist, depending on the type of services involved (Howells, 2001). Advanced services do not generate innovation in the same way or with the same intensity as do more traditional or operational services.

2. CONCEPT AND FEATURES OF SERVICE INNOVATION

There are various basic definitions of innovation in services. For example, the definition adopted by the Publin group[4] tends to simplify the concept as innovation related to all relevant change processes. Alternatively, van Ark et al. (2003c) establish a lengthy definition of innovation in services, including its main kinds: 'A new or considerably changed service concept, client interaction channel, service delivery system or technological concept that individually, but most likely in combination leads to one or more (re)new(ed) services functions that are new to the firm and do change the service/good offered on the market and do require structurally new technological, human or organizational capabilities of the service organization'.

Table 5.2 Modes of service innovation by main types and supply or demand approach

	Innovation in services (supply approach)	**Service innovation (demand approach)**
Services companies	Innovative services companies (Mode I)	Use of innovative services companies (e.g. external KIS) (Mode II)
Services activities (any sector)	Innovative services activities (Mode III)	Use of innovative services activities (e.g. internal or external KIS) (Mode IV)

Note: KIS = Knowledge-intensive services.

First, there is a need to distinguish between innovation in services and service innovation. The first concerns the innovative change within the service activity or sector itself. The latter refers to the innovative change in those organizations or companies that use innovative services or those engendering innovation. It is worth highlighting that the majority of the approaches conducted to date refer to modes I and III, and that there are sparse approaches concerning modes II and IV. However, quantitative approaches are based on mode I, and some of them on mode II; the lack of data regarding services activities hinders quantitative approaches to modes III and IV.

In recent years, the literature regarding innovation has explored different taxonomies. The categorization to product, process and organizational innovation first emerged from J.A. Schumpeter's work (1934). Specifically for services, Miles and Howells distinguish between product innovation (goods or services), process innovation, organizational innovation, and innovation in client interaction as a specific type. F. Gallouj (1994) distinguishes between vaporization, anticipation and objectivization innovation processes, on the basis of the function carried out by each type of innovation.

Van Ark et al.'s works (2003c) develop the difference between several types of technological profiles, and also distinguish among three types of non-technological innovation: new services conceptions, new interfaces with clients, and new systems of service delivery. These latter authors also drew a distinction between innovation guided by the supplier, the client, the company itself, the use of services or by paradigmatic changes. In this respect, the customer–supplier duality is found in the delivery of services, where customers are suppliers of significant inputs to the innovative process (Fitzsimmons et al., 2004). Another approach, based on that of Soete and Miozzo (1989), is developed further by Hipp and Grupp (2005). This approach shows the differences between four key categories on the basis of their intrinsic characteristics and their innovation processes: knowledge-intensive, network-intensive, scale-intensive and external innovation-intensive.

These taxonomies (some more analytical, some more sectoral-level classification) are intended for the service economy. However, many could be extrapolated to the goods economy, as they include services activities in their productive process, and also share an outstanding multidimensional scope. Different authors have emphasized the particular features of service innovation in comparison to innovation in manufacturing. The text below summarizes some notable aspects on this subject.

In this respect, there is a strong interaction between producer and consumer in service activities. This interaction partially diffuses the distinction between product and process innovation, which is more evident in manufacturing (Miles, 1995). The relationship with clients constitutes one of the basic and typical elements of service innovation; its co-productive nature is preserved in the processes generated by many service innovations (Miles, 1999). As a result of its co-productive nature, this feature is upheld in processes generated from many services innovations. Some business services channel their innovations from externalization and outsourcing.

Table 5.3 Specific and non-specific features of innovation in services

	Common features of goods and services or specific of goods and valid for services	Specific features, although non-exclusive of innovation in services	Exclusive features of innovation in services
Modes of innovation	• Innovations of processes and products • Technological innovation	• Organizational innovation, innovation of relationships with clients, and distribution and marketing innovation	• Innovation by the use of innovative advanced services
Place and mode of generation	• Specialized units	• Interaction between provider and client	• Sometimes, co-production between provider and client
Features of the inputs	• Highly-skilled labour force	• Low use of physical capital compared to human capital	
R&D	• Important source of innovation	• External and accurate R&D	• Low relevance of R&D in services
Features of the innovative output	• Externalities (spillovers): social return higher than private • Indivisibility: easy transmission without damaging supply		• Intangible results
Risk and appropriation	• High-risk investments: uncertainty • Disincentives to investment by easy imitation and free-riding. • Difficulty to determine demand • Sparse efficiency of patents • Costs and risks that result in market failures	• Difficulty to patent and apply regimes of intellectual property • Low visibility for potential clients • Rights by means of copyright vs. patents	• Risk associated to intangibility • Investment used to be considered an expense • Imitation as an easy and complex phenomenon at the same time, depending on the type of innovation
Import	• High import costs: (complex and expensive election, assimilation problems, requires experimental R&D, loss of leadership)	• Import by means of mobility and recruitment of innovative personnel and methods of information treatment	• Payment of royalties and rights is just one of the numerous modes of import of innovation in services
Impact of innovation	• Productivity and competitiveness factor	• Higher impact in quality than in apparent productivity	

Some consumer services, in turn, direct a part of their innovations towards self-service, in line with what Gershuny (1978) stated many years before. The interaction required in service co-production may imply that innovation has its own features, conducts and needs, such as the greater importance of human and organizational factors as competitive elements, in comparison to manufacturing sector (Evangelista et al., 1998; Tether, 2005). Services require greater consideration of the organizational aspects, beyond the traditional product and process innovation methods (Gallouj, 1994, 2002; Gallouj and Gallouj, 1996; Gadrey et al., 1995; Sundbo, 1998). This is due to the high content of intangible and informative elements associated with these services products and processes, through the transmission of knowledge and skills rather than through the purchase of machinery or technology (F. Gallouj, 2002).

Service innovation is interrelated to goods innovation through a process of 'encapsulation' as described by Howells (2004), whereby non-technological factors and the information intermediaries are of higher importance. As a consequence, service innovation can be considered to be multidimensional in developing new concepts, new interfaces with clients, new systems of provision and new technological options (den Hertog and Bilderbeek, 1999). Accordingly and from a multidimensional approach, services are more innovative than generally believed.

Innovation in services has a series of non-specific features in common with innovation in manufacturing (Table 5.3). Specific features can be divided into those exclusive of services and those shared with goods; that is to say, those stemming from the service economy but present in the goods economy. These characteristics lead to the identification of the challenges that must be overcome for a service-specific innovation policy.

3. STATISTICAL SOURCES AND THEIR LIMITATIONS

Among the different sources for studying innovation in services, the following represent the main ones:

- R&D data and related indicators in the ANBERD database of the OECD and New Cronos from Eurostat. Science and technology statistics also provide interesting information.
- The survey on service innovation CISIII carried out in 2001–2002, whose data has only recently become available, and only for certain countries. Some problems regarding data comparability, liability and confidentiality persist. In addition, some countries provide limited information (e.g., the United Kingdom and Ireland). Possibilities for drawing comparisons with the CISII are restricted, due to methodological changes and different time referents.

- Surveys: Innobarometer, regarding entrepreneurs' opinions, is the only large-scale source to create compound innovation indicators, although it does not allow temporal series given the methodological changes from one year to another.
- innovation Scoreboard: collection of European innovation indicators, on the basis of several databases, including the previous ones.

In the statistics regarding innovation, the conventional definitions of the Oslo Manual[5] are used. These definitions are problematic when considering services, as the wide range of their characteristic innovation sources are not taken into consideration. This can be seen in taxonomies in which there are serious difficulties in the measurement of organizational innovation. In addition, an added difficulty in the case of services exists when differentiating between the three types of basic innovation, as the frontiers are not always delimited. The Frascati Manual (OECD, 1993) defines R& D as creative work undertaken on a systematic basis in order to increase the stock of knowledge (including knowledge of humans, culture and society) and the use of this stock of knowledge to devise new applications.[6]

It is not easy for services companies to identify and to define the 'systematic base' in the absence of R&D processes formalization. In services, a part of R&D is not statistically registered (for example, because it is not conducted in a R&D department or because such a department does not exist), and many programmes of innovation investment are not included in R&D. At present, there are debates on whether the definition of R&D is appropriate or whether it should be modified or re-created specifically for services. It seems there is at least a margin for its revision, so that the registration level of the innovative activity in services can be improved. However, more research appears to be necessary (Miles, 2005).

In general, the statistical difficulties in studying innovation in services can be summarized as follows: problems in the definitions and their coverage; difficulties with identifying innovation in services in the same way as the majority of academic studies regarding innovation in services and related typologies; over-orientation of the CISIII toward manufacturing, which excludes the analytical and statistical needs required to meet the key aspects of innovation in services (Rubalcaba, 2004)[7]; lack of statistical sources complementary to the CISIII; lack of statistical continuity in the use of KIS as an innovative source; bias of the current approach toward supply rather than demand; statistical ignorance with regard to internal service innovation within manufacturing and services companies; lack of distinction between product-innovative services and goods; non-existence of a vertical approach specific to certain services sectors; sparse knowledge and limited number of statistics regarding organizational and non-technological innovations; absence of statistical continuity about modes, conductors, obstacles and impacts of different types of service innovation; insufficient disaggregation of R&D statistics (concepts, programmes, companies, etc.); limited knowledge of the service area (services activities and services companies) participating in

national and EU R&D programmes; and problems of statistical coverage
(countries providing just a limited amount of data and comparison problems).

4. INTERNATIONAL PROFILES OF SERVICE R&D[8]

R&D expenditure is a classical indicator of the innovative potential of a
country. Although this is only one of the inputs necessary to achieve
innovation, and although its approximation is relatively limited in the service
domain, R&D continues to be the most comparable and widely used
statistical indicator in the field of innovation.

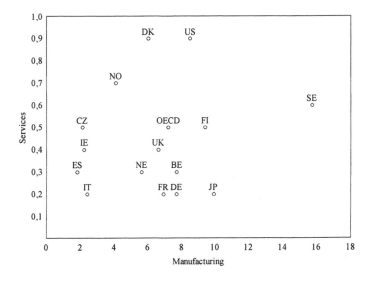

Source: Based on the OECD databases ANBERD and STAN.

Figure 5.2 Intensity in R&D on the basis of value added, 2001 (%)

In 1998, services accounted for about 17 per cent of total business sector
R&D in the OECD area – an increase of 2 per cent from 1992. Presently,
approximately 80 per cent of total R&D is carried out in the manufacturing
sector (OECD, 2001d). In this sense, service R&D intensity in European
countries averages around 10 per cent in the manufacturing sector (Figure
5.2). The United States provide the highest degree of significance to service
R&D (of which an important part is allocated to defence); while in contrast,
some of the main European economies, such as Germany and France, register
lower levels than expected. Nordic countries such as Norway, Denmark,
Sweden and Finland play an outstanding role, and maintain important levels
of R&D intensity in services. In 2000, 48 per cent of total business R&D

developed in Norway was carried out in the services sector, and 37 per cent in the case of Denmark (OECD, 2001d). In some other European countries, the level of service R&D is also highly relevant, given the reduced level registered in manufacturing. This is true for the Czech Republic, Ireland, and Spain, where the amount of service R&D is more than 15 per cent over the manufacturing R&D level.

Table 5.4 Annual growth rates of the R&D internal business expenditure 1995–2003 (%) (*)

	Total economy	MAN	SER	BS	COMP	DIST	TRAN
Belgium	3.1	:	:	:	:	:	:
Canada	3.8	3.5	5.1	8.2	7.5	-0.1	-1.8
Czech R.	4.6	2.4	10.2	7.8	:	:	:
Denmark	9.0	7.3	12.1	:	14.9	-4.2	24.2
Finland	10.3	9.9	12.7	14.1	20.8	18.7	6.7
France	2.0	:	:	:	:	:	:
Germany	3.8	3.2	14.7	16.0	30.4	11.2	10.9
Greece	7.0	8.9	6.3	9.0	12.9	-10.1	23.1
Hungary	4.9	5.0	23.6	25.6	28.3	52.3	-9.3
Iceland	17.7	10.7	25.2	28.6	14.1	:	12.0
Ireland	6.3	1.7	23.6	30.5	31.8	28.5	-9.7
Italy	1.9	0.0	12.5	10.2	14.7	33.6	7.8
Japan	3.7	2.6	21.7	:	:	:	6.6
Holland	2.7	2.1	7.3	11.7	22.9	5.5	-17.2
Norway	4.3	3.8	4.6	5.5	13.8	3.4	-0.7
Poland	-2.3	-3.2	-1.2	-8.9	19.6	-44.8	4.7
Portugal	12.2	7.6	19.8	24.0	29.0	27.1	-6.2
Slovakia	-1.7	-5.0	0.7	0.5	:	:	:
Spain	8.6	3.8	23.6	25.2	17.3	45.0	8.9
Sweden	4.7	4.1	7.0	8.1	19.1	11.5	-36.6
UK	2.4	2.2	:	:	5.7	:	:
US	3.9	:	:	:	:	:	:
Average	**5.1**	**3.7**	**12.8**	**13.5**	**18.9**	**12.7**	**1.5**

Notes: * Exponential growth rates in R&D spending at constant prices. MAN: manufacturing; SER: services; BS: business services; COMP: computer services; DIST: distributive trades; TRAN: transport services.

Source: Based on the ANBERD database, OECD.

Thus, as a whole, the intensity of service R&D remains below the levels registered in manufacturing. However, as shown in Table 5.4, between 1995 and 2003 R&D business expenditure grew to a greater extent in services sector than in manufacturing. This trend is characterized by the role of some business services, particularly computing services, which have experienced a notable growth during this period, as well as distributive trades. This affirmation holds true for all analysed countries, except in the case of Greece (partially as result of the reduction in the levels of R&D investment in the distribution sector in this country). Available data also suggests that the behaviour of R&D growth in services varies considerably from one country to another, although in those regions where this development rate is outstanding, as in the case of Iceland, Hungary, Ireland, Spain and Portugal, this major increase is due, to a large extent, to significant increases in business services.

Finally, the growing participation of services R&D reflects at least four key factors:

- *More research*: Firstly, service sectors are increasing the use of new technologies and developing more and more complex services functions and processes within the company.
- *Companies outsourcing*: Manufacturing companies sometimes purchase (or externalize) R&D when locating their laboratories in a remote corporate entity or when they purchase R&D services from another private company.
- *Government outsourcing:* Frequently, governments purchase R&D instead of conducting it themselves.
- *Measurement*: R&D statistics in the service sector have notably improved in some countries. The increasing participation of services in R&D is partly the result of changes undertaken in statistical practices, and partly the result of better sampling (Young, 1996). In addition, an important statistical bias is related to those primarily manufacturing companies that recently surpassed the 50 per cent mark of their turnover in services. Their activities, including R&D, are classified currently as integrated in the service sector.

5. INNOVATION IN SERVICES: EUROPEAN INNOVATIVE PROFILES

General Performance of Innovation in Services

This section completes, mainly on the basis of data included in the third European survey on innovation (Community Innovation Survey – CISIII[9]), a situation analysis of the innovating profile comprising the European entrepreneurial and institutional system, comparing innovation activity in both industry[10] and service sectors, considering existent differences among countries – mainly between southern and northern European regions –, analysing the most significant outcomes in order to understand those challenges service innovation has to face and tackle, and briefly discussing some policy implications to promote European competitiveness and economic growth.

Table 5.5 Indicators regarding innovation by activity sectors in 2005

Indicator / Sector	Total economy	IND	SER	DIST	TRAN	FIN	BS	IT	ICT
Ranking (*)	:	13	16	21	24	19	6	3	2
Share of higher-education employees	13.1	8.3	20.6	11.2	8	30.1	51.4	50.9	29.4
R&D expenses as percentage of the added value	1.7	:	0.52	:	0.59	0.27	2.13	6.12	7.93
Share of companies with internal innovation	35.4	38.1	31.5	27	19.6	42.7	50.8	58.4	56.7
Percentage of SMEs collaborating with others	5.8	5.6	6.2	3.8	2.7	7.1	15.2	14.6	15.0
Innovation expenses as % of the turnover	2.06	3.13	0.95	0.44	1.19	0.6	5.42	4.18	5.80
Share of sales of new products in the market	6.4	7.8	5	3.3	5.8	5.6	10.6	12.7	17.7
Proportion of companies carrying out training	17.7	16.7	19.0	13.5	12.8	26.0	35.0	38.1	35.5

Notes: * The Ranking indicator produces a certain value that summarizes the general performance of each activity sector before the different variables that measure their innovative nature, and they are put in descending order according to their tendency towards innovation. IND: Industry; SER: Services; DIST: Distributive trades; TRAN: Transport; FIN: Financial services; BS: Business services; IT: Information and technology services; ICT: Information and communication services.

Source: Based on the European Sector Innovation Scoreboard, 2005.

Before going into a more detailed analysis of the CISIII database, some key indicators collected from the European Sector Innovation Scoreboard 2005 are shown in Table 5.5. Business services in Europe, and more specifically ICT (Information and Communication Technologies) and computing services, reveal a strong innovative position within the group of economic activities, thus presenting levels of innovation even highly above those registered in the industrial sector. On the other hand, the service sector as a whole is, in general, less innovative than the industrial sector, although differences are less significant than could be expected a priori. Some variables such as the percentage of companies that innovate, the innovation expenditure level and proportion of new products' sales in the market, register higher values in industry than in services. However, indicators such as the percentage of higher-education workers, the level of cooperation between SMEs and also the proportion of companies that carries out training, acquire a higher relevance in the case of services. Consequently, most recent statistical information contradicts the traditional assumption presuming a minimum innovative profile to services within the economy.

Innovative Companies[11] and Innovation Activity

The previous section shows how services, business services in particular, carry out larger R&D investments than expected. These results are confirmed by present CISIII analysis, which points out that the percentages of innovative companies in this sector are extremely positive.

Business services register the highest percentage of innovative companies in the economy, with a 62.7 per cent over the total of organizations in the sector, followed by financial services with 52.8 per cent. A substantial part of these business services is considered to be innovative, and no other significant economic activity has achieved such dynamism. Obviously, a certain statistical bias could influence these results depending on the composition of business services companies included in the sample. For example, an over-representation of ICT services can provide different results than those obtained with a higher presence of traditional professional or operational services. Nevertheless, the high rates obtained constitute a clear example that business services are highly innovative activities. The proportion of innovative organizations continues to be higher in the industrial sector (47.9 per cent) compared to the service sector as a whole (40.7 per cent).[12] Services, in turn, stand out from the industrial companies as far as the introduction of new products in the market is concerned, while the industrial sector shows a stronger trend than does services towards the attainment of process renewals.

Germany displays the major share of innovative firms in the EU, both in services (57 per cent) and in industry (66 per cent), whereas the percentage of innovative enterprises in southern countries such as Spain, Italy and Greece remains below 40 per cent. Some northern countries, such as Denmark and Norway, register the highest percentage of companies that regenerate or extend their range of products in the market. On the other hand, innovation in companies from countries of southern Europe, such as Portugal and Spain, focus more on the introduction of new or enhanced processes, as a consequence of the relative backwardness shown in their levels of productivity compared to other, more economically developed European regions. These advances regarding new processes, which bring with them cutbacks in production costs, indicate a way of increasing international competitiveness levels.

Table 5.6 Percentage of innovative companies, 2000 (%)

	Total economy	IND	SER	DIST	TRAN	FIN	BS
Belgium	50	59	42	46	25	38	71
Denmark	44	52	37	36	25	47	54
Germany	61	66	57	52	40	75	77
Greece	28	27	33	30	22	22	60
Spain	33	37	25	21	19	48	48
France	41	46	34	23	41	59	49
Italy	36	40	25	20	16	42	49
Luxembourg	48	49	48	43	36	53	69
Netherlands	45	55	38	40	22	49	57
Austria	49	53	45	35	23	74	94
Portugal	46	45	50	47	44	72	72
Finland	45	49	40	43	26	:	55
Sweden	47	47	46	54	23	48	60
Iceland	55	54	56	39	53	68	75
Norway	36	39	34	35	14	44	51
Average	**44.3**	**47.9**	**40.7**	**37.6**	**28.6**	**52.8**	**62.7**

Notes: IND: Industry; SER: Services; DIST: Distributive trades; TRAN: Transport; FIN: Financial services; BS: Business services.

Source: Based on the Eurostat database, CISIII data.

The main innovation activities, both in services companies and in industrial organizations, include the acquisition of equipment, personnel training and functions of internal R&D. The latter are particularly remarkable regarding business services, where, on average, 71.7 per cent of the European organizations in this sector acknowledge the deployment of tasks related to internal R&D as part of their innovation effort, while this percentage is reduced to 55.1 per cent for industrial companies, and to 43.8 per cent for total services. Financial services, in turn, are re-confirmed as the economic sector which develops external R&D activities to the largest extent (29.2 per cent of companies), whereas this percentage only reaches 24.9 per cent in the industrial sector.

Finland and Denmark are those countries where the highest percentage of companies develops R&D activities, with values above 64 per cent regarding internal R&D and 32 per cent in external R&D. In 2001, almost 71 per cent of R&D expenditure in Finland was financed by the business sector and over 60 per cent in Denmark. The annual growth rates of R&D investment in both countries were around 2.15 per cent between 1998 and 2002, which proves to a certain extent the strong innovative effort, above the average European levels, made by the companies in these two Scandinavian countries.

Again, as an example of the relevant innovative capacity of business services, it is worth mentioning that while there are about 4.5 per cent of employees involved in internal R&D tasks in industrial companies, this percentage reaches 11.6 per cent in the case of services organizations (information technologies, software, consultancy services, and so on). Despite this fact, the industrial sector keeps an average of employees who work in R&D activities above the levels registered in services, which indicate in some way the more explicit link between R&D (input) and innovation (output) in this former sector.

The proportion of companies developing activities for the introduction of innovations in the market and staff training is higher in services than in the industrial sector, as a consequence of the strong relationship between services and knowledge and informal interaction. However, as previously stated, the percentage of companies developing internal R&D activities is higher in the industrial sector than in services, despite the positive performance of some business services. In this key variable lies the proportional difference between both sectors, which greatly depends on the individual way in which services organize their innovation processes. These processes are not generally focused on specific R&D departments, as in the case of the industrial sector, but by means of the work in different functional business areas.

Data also reflect that while the procedure of implementing changes in the corporate image of a company is more characteristic of the industrial sector than of the service sector (37.5 per cent vs. 34.9 per cent), the latter makes stronger efforts towards the fulfilment of advanced management techniques, the improvement of its organizational structures, and the achievement of changes in concepts and in marketing strategies. Financial services and business services are the economic activities where the majority of companies, to a greater or lesser extent, achieve improvements in their company's strategic structure. About 40 per cent of companies in these two sectors acknowledge the implementation of advanced management techniques and changes in concepts and marketing strategies, and over 55 per cent register changes in their organizational structures. All this demonstrates that more than half of the services companies in these two sectors declare to have carried out changes in their corporate strategies; this percentage is around 42 per cent in the case of industrial organizations.

On the one hand, these strategic and organizational business changes are more extensive in companies from Luxembourg, Germany and Austria. On the other hand, the ratio of companies undertaking changes in their business appearance or image is higher in South European countries such as Greece, Spain and Italy.

Inputs and Outputs

In the European economy as a whole, companies find the greatest innovative source within themselves and their relationship with clients and suppliers. In the three aforementioned cases, the industrial sector approaches such sources to a greater extent than do services. In contrast, services companies, to a higher degree than do industrial companies, exploit as innovation sources their own competitors and other companies of the same sector (34.4 per cent), conferences and professional meetings (37.4 per cent) and organizations within the business group to which they belong (28.7 per cent). This latter variable demonstrates one of the main differences between the industrial sector and the service sector, with almost 29 per cent of services companies resorting to companies of the group as agents facilitating innovation, while in the case of industry, this percentage falls to 19.7 per cent. Business services are the activities that register the highest use of innovative sources, including clients, universities and national research centres. Financial services, in contrast, more frequently use competitors and other organizations of the sector as their innovation source, with a percentage of more than 39 per cent of companies (that is, six points above the levels registered in the industrial sector). Some differences can also be found in the innovation sources used by companies, depending on their country of origin. In countries such as Sweden, Norway and Finland, firms tend to pay more attention to their relationships with clients (79.8 per cent of companies in Sweden), universities (20.8 per cent in Finland), and other national research centres (16.6 per cent in Norway). Moreover, the proportion of companies that resort to other companies of the group or to the organization itself as agents facilitating innovation is more significant in these Nordic countries. On the other hand, southern countries that register low levels of intensity in R&D (such as Spain, Greece or Portugal) use, to a higher extent, innovation sources such as equipment and material suppliers, and fairs and exhibitions. A high percentage of industrial companies (over 45 per cent) consider that the interaction that occurs at these fairs and exhibitions is a significant element towards achieving innovation. In contrast, only 35.2 per cent of service organizations favour these interactions.

Patents

The intangible nature of many services innovations creates challenges for Intellectual Property Right (IPR) systems (Miles et al., 2000). The industrial sector continues to be the activity sector that requires a higher degree of intellectual property protection measures (around 17 per cent of companies), although the percentage of services companies that resort to this type of procedures has grown in recent years reaching 11 per cent. Evidence can be seen in the fact that in economic activity as a whole, business services register the highest use of copyrights (20 per cent) and trade secret rights (37.4 per cent), whereas distributive trade services favour procedures such as trademarks (28.7 per cent) and registrations of design patterns (15 per cent). In this respect, it is worth mentioning that, as a consequence of the aggregate between transport companies and communication companies illustrated in the CISIII database, this activity area registers very low levels regarding patent application in the survey, even though the percentage of telecommunication firms demanding protection for their inventions is among the highest in the economy.

By country, companies from Sweden, France and Finland apply to a larger extent for intellectual property protection through patents, while the opposite occurs in Portugal and Greece, where intensity levels in R&D are low. Sweden has the highest amount of companies that apply for copyrights (40.9 per cent), while the proportion of companies seeking for protection through trade secret rights is higher in Finland (48.7 per cent) and in the United Kingdom (55.6 per cent).

The two aforementioned Nordic countries, Sweden and Finland, lead the development of patents in Europe. They are also the world leaders, and not by chance, in R&D expenditure as a percentage of their GDP, exceeding already in 2003 the 3 per cent objective included in the Lisbon Strategy. Thus, although it has been previously stated that the innovation capacity of services depends, to a greater extent than the industrial sector, on inputs such as knowledge, human capital, and new organizational changes, R&D continues to be an essential factor in the explanation of some output variables, as in the case of patents. This fact poses the latent challenge present in Europe of generating increases in R&D investments in order to achieve a more innovative and dynamic service activity that, supporting around 70 per cent of the total European economy, can be used to set out the foundations for future economic growth.

Effects

Three main effects can be highlighted, with regard to innovation and innovative systems introduction: (1) an increase in the range of products (affecting about 56 per cent of industrial companies and about 58.5 per cent of services companies); (2) an increase in the market share (52.7 per cent and 54.6 per cent); and (3) an improvement in the quality of products offered (64.3 per cent and 64.4 per cent). These effects have a greater impact in the service sector, particularly with concern to business services and financial services. However, the majority of the outcomes measured by the CISIII as a consequence of innovative activity carried out by the companies are largely highlighted in the industrial sector. These outcomes include increased flexibility and production capacity, and reductions in labour costs, and so on.

By taking into consideration two critical effects – quality and costs – of corporate innovation, the uneven introduction of innovation in the organizations of the different activity sectors can be better appreciated. Therefore, while 68.5 per cent of business services and 66.2 per cent of financial services acknowledge improvement in the quality of their products, this percentage is around 64.3 per cent in the case of industrial organizations. However, while 40.4 per cent of industry companies report to have achieved significant reductions in their labour costs per unit produced, the value for the service sector is around 27 per cent. This data once more reflects the high technological dependency of industry in the creation of scale economies in order to readjust its labour costs.

Southern European organizations, mainly from countries such as Spain, Greece and Portugal, register a higher impact index as a consequence of the introduction of innovative elements. It is worth clarifying that this fact does not mean that the real impacts are higher in these countries, but that the impression given by the companies surveyed denotes such assumption. This could even be a sign of a lower development of service innovation in these countries. Therefore, when a low number of innovative companies in a certain region coincides with lower levels of market competition, the impacts are deemed to be more positive than when the activity is developed in a more dynamic environment, in which innovation must be more radical in order to register a significant effect.

For a high proportion of the surveyed companies, innovation had important positive repercussions on the quality of products and services offered (85.3 per cent in Greece), on flexibility and production capacity (57.2 per cent in Spain), on labour costs (45.6 per cent in Portugal) and on approaches towards production norms and standards (60.1 per cent in Greece), among others. Ultimately, southern European states could reach competitiveness and technological development levels characteristic of more advanced European regions. On the other hand, and by means of innovative methods, companies from France and the Benelux area achieve significant impacts regarding the number of products offered and notable increases in their market shares.

Obstacles

As can be appreciated in Figure 5.3, in the industrial sector and service sectors, the main obstacles for the introduction of innovative activities in European companies are: high cost of innovation; the economic risks entailed; the lack of qualified personnel; and the difficulty in finding financial support. According to the data arising from the CISIII, organizations most affected by these four factors are those related to business services. Therefore, it is worth noting the significant difference between the level of business services that stress the lack of financial sources as an obstacle for the launching of innovative activities (43.8 per cent) against those levels registered in the industrial sector (31.2 per cent) and the service sector as a whole (29.1 per cent).

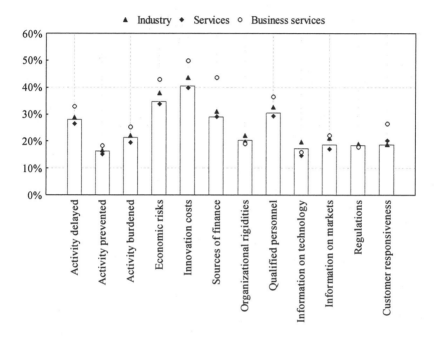

Source: Based on the Eurostat database, CISIII.

Figure 5.3 Percentage of all innovative companies affected by obstacles to innovation

An analysis by country suggests that companies hindering the development of innovation procedures as a consequence of the various obstacles tend to be from Austria and Germany, and from southern countries such as Spain, Greece and Portugal. With regard to Austria and Germany, the main difficulties that business innovation must tackle are economic risks, which affect more than 60 per cent of organizations in the case of Austria, organizational inflexibility (36.3 per cent in Germany), high costs of innovation (67.6 per cent in Austria), lack of qualified personnel (54.6 per cent in Germany), and high levels of standards and regulations (36.4 per cent in Germany). In the case of the mentioned southern European countries mentioned above, the factors that hinder the progress of innovative activity include lack of financing, limited information regarding markets, consumer indifference toward innovation, and lack of technological information.

Excessive regulations hinder innovation in 23.3 per cent of transport services organizations, compared with lower percentages registered in industry (19.2 per cent) and the service sector as a whole (18.5 per cent). This information suggests that, despite the progressive opening of the transport market in Europe in the last decade, the regulatory weighting carried by this sector has important negative consequences in the development of its innovative activity.

Public Programmes

With regard to the proportion of companies receiving public support from different administrations, financing levels are much higher in the industrial sector (30.1 per cent) than in services (16.8 per cent). As far as the latter sector is concerned, business services register the highest amount of public assistance (27.4 per cent), while financial services register the lowest one (4.5 per cent).

Table 5.7 Percentage of the total innovative companies receiving public funding

	Total public funding		Funding from local and regional authorities		Funding from central government		Funding from the EU		Funding from EU's 4th or 5th RTD	
	SER	IND	SER	IND	SER	IND	SER	IND	SER	IND
Austria	25.7	50.6	14.6	25.3	15.1	39.2	6.9	15.2	6.2	8.3
Belgium	15.1	29.2	10.2	24.2	5.2	4.3	3.2	4.7	2.0	1.6
Germany	13.9	26.4	10.1	15.7	5.4	14.3	2.1	5.7	2.0	3.1
Denmark	6.5	7.7	:	:	:	:	6.5	7.7	3.5	4.8
Spain	18.1	30.8	13.8	22.8	6.3	11.7	3.4	4.8	3.2	1.8
Finland	27.0	50.8	3.0	8.9	23.2	45.4	6.0	8.1	1.8	5.6
France	17.6	28.9	7.1	10.4	12.4	23.9	6.7	6.2	3.8	2.9
Greece	23.5	33.9	2.6	3.7	15.5	17.0	17.0	16.0	14.5	8.9
Iceland	4.8	11.9	0.5	:	3.8	10.1	2.1	3.1	2.1	2.6
Italy	26.0	43.8	15.7	24.9	7.8	20.2	7.3	6.9	3.0	2.6
Luxembourg	11.1	27.4	0.4	1.3	9.2	26.7	2.7	2.0	1.4	2.2
Netherlands	18.9	45.1	3.3	4.7	15.8	40.5	3.5	5.4	1.9	2.1
Norway	17.6	26.1	2.8	3.4	14.4	23.2	1.5	2.4	2.4	2.8
Portugal	15.4	36.2	0.1	2.2	7.7	15.3	11.1	26.0	6.7	18.2
Sweden	18.6	20.3	8.5	7.7	3.7	3.5	7.3	9.6	8.4	9.2
UK	8.1	12.5	:	:	:	:	:	:	:	:

Notes: SER: Services; IND: Industry.

Source: Based on the Eurostat database, CIS III.

Table 5.7 shows that in Finland, Italy and Austria, public investment reaches a higher percentage of companies compared to the rest of the Member States (41.7 per cent, 40.7 per cent and 39.4 per cent respectively). On the contrary, Denmark remarkably registers the lowest financing degree, with only about 7 per cent of the organizations.

In northern European countries such as Finland and Holland, measures launched by the central government are fundamental for the development of business innovation, while in Mediterranean countries such as Spain and Italy, a significant number of companies are financed by regional or local organizations, probably as result of a higher national administrative decentralization. Greek companies, in turn, are notable for the important support obtained through the European Union budget.

Business services companies obtain more benefit from financing policies governed by the European Union and the fourth and fifth Framework Programme (10.9 per cent and 9.1 per cent of companies respectively), mainly as a consequence of the strong support given to consultancy companies over recent years. On the other hand, financing provided by different central governments and regional and local authorities is aimed, to a large extent, at the industrial sector, and affects around 21 per cent and 12 per cent of organizations, respectively.

Hence, one of the main challenges that the service sector must face in Europe is the weak support of public financing towards innovation. The industrial sector, and thus technological innovation, is still considered the priority of innovation policies in various countries, despite the fact that some positional changes can be observed in recent years.

Comments on the CISIII Analysis

The particular nature of service innovation activity is an important explanatory basis for some of the main results obtained from the realized CISIII based analysis, and explains to a certain extent the differences arising in comparison with industrial sector. On the one hand, evident intangibility, dependence on the human factor and knowledge, and difficulties of standardizing a product are some of the specific features of services affecting the origin, development, application and impacts of their innovative activity within economy. On the other hand, innovation in services is characterized by apparent blurred concepts of process, product and organizational innovation, pronounced multidimensional and inter-departmental nature within the companies, important inclusion of informational elements, and relative complexity when observing its effects in the market.

Section 5 has presented an analysis of innovation's current situation regarding European companies, particularly those within the service sector, thus becoming a complementary study to previous approaches such as that carried out by OECD (2005c). The analysis set out is to complete the CISIII based study, placing a specific emphasis on differences between countries – mainly between southern and northern European regions – and to point out those more significant challenges that service innovation in Europe has to tackle.

6. PROFILES IN EUROPE AND THE UNITED STATES

The CISIII does not enable a comparison between European countries and the United States, although in view of previous works regarding service innovation, it is possible to deduce some important conclusions regarding the innovative performance of both areas. Howells and Tether's study (2004) deals with the different behaviour patterns regarding innovation followed by services organizations in Germany, France, Spain, Italy, the United Kingdom and the United States. These behavioural differences could be explained, as specified in the study, by means of two principal views. On the one hand, the existent possibility that the results are partly due to methodological issues (effects of survey adequacy and interpretation, language differences and differences in selection and response systems). On the other hand, the views that emerge from the analysis could have been originated from the real differences in the innovation strategies of companies.

The study highlights the tendency of French services companies, in contrast with their German counterparts, to incorporate, to a greater extent, innovation of an organizational type and to carry out changes in their relationships with clients. In contrast, Italian services companies tend to accumulate innovation in processes, organizational structure and relationships with clients. Spanish services companies tend to have higher levels of innovation in distribution processes and larger technological and ability changes. Finally, services companies in the United Kingdom profusely use distribution innovation and carry out significant changes in client relations.

These differences could be partly explained by different socioeconomic environments. As mentioned by the authors, they are also due partly to a 'catch-up process' whereby European countries with lower levels of innovation in services companies within the whole economy (France, Spain, Italy, the United Kingdom) converge toward the levels already reached in Germany. That is to say, the organizations from countries in innovative positions that are less important in their national corporate structure are introducing and making more efforts to achieve organizational, procedural, distributive and technological innovations, among others. In doing so, they are able to reach, for example, some German levels.

Similarly, the study also highlights a trend in which services companies in Germany are now striving for innovation to a larger degree than are their American counterparts; they are approaching to a certain degree the innovation levels present in the US economy. Therefore, US services organizations have shown (compared to the German organizations) a lower trend toward incorporating innovation in their production and distribution processes, as well as changes in their relationships with other entities.

The main view derived from the previous assertion is that European companies are currently introducing changes already used in the US as a tool for approaching the innovation levels achieved in the American economy. On the basis of the data included in the European Innovation Scoreboard 2005, it is possible to observe the significant distance between Europe and the US regarding innovation levels, in favour of the US. This distance, however, tends to stabilize. The major deficiencies in terms of innovation between US and European companies are observed in indicators such as the volume of patents granted by the United States Patent and Trademark Office (USPTO), the percentage of higher-education population, and the level of R&D private expenditure. A recent report (EIS Expert Report, 2005) also remarks on the European deficit compared to the US in relation with R&D expenditure, scientific production, the integration of universities in the innovation process of the country and the participation of European companies in the investigation and patent generation process at an international level. The superiority of US multinationals in innovation has also been considered by the OECD (2005c).

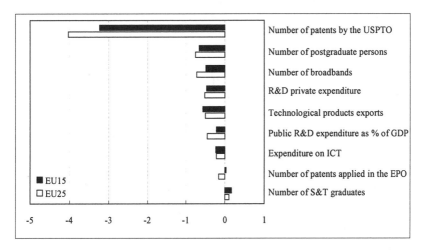

Source: Based on the European Innovation Scoreboard, 2005.

Figure 5.4 Difference in innovation indices of EU15 and EU25 compared with the US

Despite the information that emerges from Figure 5.4, the catch-up process (mentioned previously) regarding innovation between the US and Europe could be occurring gradually. The report by Howells and Tether (2004) states that while 54 per cent of the European services companies admitted to having made significant production and distribution changes in products and services, the percentage in the US only amounted to 29 per cent. Moreover, the percentage of European companies that introduced significant new production or distribution technologies was around 53 per cent, versus 40 per cent in the US. 34 per cent of the European organizations acknowledged significant development of personnel skills, compared to 18 per cent registered by the American companies. Over 60 per cent of the US services companies admitted to not having introduced any change in their organizational structure, as opposed to just 25 per cent in Europe.

In any case, it is worth highlighting that this is a relative phenomenon, as European services companies could possibly register their levels of innovation from a much more positive perspective than that of their US counterparts. An explanation for this fact, provided by the authors of the aforementioned analysis, is the potential difference between strategies carried out by the European companies and by those in the United States. US services organizations tend to develop individual advances and continuous innovations, which may not be recognized, thus focusing on the fulfilment of an established group of activities and the improvement of their results. On the other hand, European companies are more determined to adapt to their environment, maintaining higher levels of capability to change into a different set of activities. These changes tend to be more discontinuous, thus achieving higher acknowledgement than those developed in cumulative models, as in the case of the US (Howells and Tether, 2004).

7. SERVICE INNOVATION, ICT AND E-ECONOMY

One of the basic reasons why services are not considered very innovative or productive is their apparent difficulty with incorporating technological innovations. However, as Chapter 3 highlighted, there is a close interrelation between services and technology, to the extent that both have developed in parallel in many activities. The STEP Report (Haukens, 1996) concluded that services sectors were major users, originators and agents of transfer for technological and non-technological innovations, thus playing a major role in creating, gathering and diffusing organizational, institutional and social knowledge.

Moreover, the work developed by the international network, established from the KISSIN project of the IV Framework Programme (Wood, 2001), was used for the international acknowledgement of KIS as engines of technological and non-technological innovation. Other research works also stress the complementary relationship between service innovation and technology (Licht and Moch, 1999; Gago and Rubalcaba, 2007). The CISIII does not enable the integration of technologies in the analysis in an adequate manner, although the role of services in the innovation process has been confirmed in works about the CISIII, both contemporary (OECD, 2005c) and previous (Green et al., 2001).

Table 5.8 Services and the e-economy, 2003 (%)

		Online sale (1)	Online purchase (2)	Online sale impact: sales volume (very positive) (3)	Online use impact: obtained costs (very positive) (4)	General e-business importance for a company (significant part) (5)
ALL SECTORS	Total	15.9	46.1	14.9	12.5	12.0
Textile	Total	5.2	22.7	1.0	13.8	7.0
Chemistry	Total	8.6	50.7	4.1	3.8	7.3
Electronic	Total	13.6	58.8	33.7	13.4	13.9
Transport	Total	17.0	65.3	1.2	21.3	5.5
Retail	Total	17.4	38.4	13.9	7.0	7.1
Tourism	Total	36.9	46.7	14.1	14.0	18.1
ICT Services	Total	23.7	74.3	8.8	15.9	30.6
Business services	Total	11.1	50.0	31.2	11.4	16.7
Health-related services	Total	12.4	47.6	0.5	15.4	8.6
Handcraft and trade	Total	3.2	23.7	9.9	11.1	6.3
ALL SECTORS	Total	9.5	31.1	17.2	15.6	12.4
Micro	0-9	8.9	29.9	17.6	15.9	12.4
Small	10-49	16.8	45.8	15.5	13.4	11.8
Medium	50-249	15.9	51.3	8.5	11.3	14.5
Large	250+	19.2	56.2	16.1	10.1	14.0
TIC services	Total	15.3	74.7	21.7	18.7	26.4
Micro	0-9	15.0	74.4	22.3	18.7	25.9
Small	10-49	19.8	79.5	18.0	18.9	34.3
Medium	50-249	19.5	70.8	9.2	13.7	25.6
Large	250+	29.9	72.6	4.4	13.7	33.6

Notes: (1) Share of enterprises that sells through the Internet or another channel of online distribution. (2) Share of enterprises that acquire goods and services online. (3) Share of enterprises that admit to obtaining positive effects on sales volume (with online sale; excl. DK/NA). (4) Share of enterprises that admit to obtaining positive effects on costs (acting online; excl. DK/NA). (5) Share of enterprises admitting that e-business constitutes a significant part of the work methodology.

Source: Based on E-watch 2003, European Commission.

As Chapter 3 considered, global processes of technological changes adopted by companies and businesses in communication and information societies have led to increased competitiveness at a worldwide level. Organizations of the e-economy that are a result of this technological revolution have increased their productivity and reduced their labour costs – a phenomenon that is more significant in the United States than in Europe. The more prominent introduction of information and communication technologies in the services organizations in the US compared to Europe might partially explain the existing economic growth differences between both regions in the 1990s, as O'Mahony and van Ark (2003) remarked. Table 5.8 shows the use of e-economy by European services.

ICT services and tourism stand out from the entire group of economic activities, due to the high percentage of companies using the Internet as a sale and distribution channel for their products. Moreover, there is a high proportion of companies from these sectors including e-business as an important part of their working methodology. The exercise of e-economy itself is also remarkable in other services sectors such as business services, where 31.2 per cent of the organizations admit to having had positive impacts on their sale levels, and in the transport sector, where 21.3 per cent of companies acknowledge effective impacts on the reduction of their costs. On the other hand, small companies are those benefiting the most in their sales volumes and production costs thanks to on-line trade management.

8. IDENTIFICATION OF CHALLENGES AND CONCLUDING REMARKS

Despite the fact that innovation plays a key role within the service sector, only recently have extensive theoretical and empirical approaches to this subject been conducted. In fact, the majority of studies regarding innovation have used the industrial sector as a reference, putting the tertiary sector to one side. This is based on the traditional idea of a limited area in the service sector for the incorporation and use of technology, and hence a limited margin for technical change and innovation, with the inevitable consequences for the development of this sector in the economy. From an empirical perspective, the lack of relevant contributions is associated with the difficulties that arise in the study of technological change and innovation in the service sector, and the non-existence of standard criteria to define these concepts.

Nonetheless, recent developments clearly undermine these arguments. Services companies are an increasing subject of deliberate attempts to innovate, as a means to increase cost efficiency levels, quality levels or the development of new services types. In this respect, there is a group of advanced services within the heterogeneous tertiary sector that, far from adopting a passive role in improving economies' competitiveness and modernization, become innovation-generating, innovation-driving and innovation-transmitting elements. This is the main point on which numerous contributions regarding services and innovation are based, stressing the related innovative importance of other, not strictly technological aspects.

As previously stated, even though innovation in the service sector is founded mainly on organizational and information factors, R&D continues to be a significant indicator of its innovative activity in this sector. Although the intensity levels in service R&D are reduced regarding the investment levels in the manufacturing sector, the annual growth rates of internal business expenditure of services in R&D have been higher than those registered in industry over the last decade. This phenomenon can be understood as a result of four possible actions: improvements in statistics and statistical bias; increased investment in technological and more complex processes within the service sector; increase of outsourcing in R&D activities by the manufacturing sector; and similar increase by central governments.

In Europe, services sectors such as business services and the financial sector register a higher innovation density level than manufacturing. Business services frequently present superior levels than those of the industrial sector in variables such as, among others, the introduction of new products to the market, the protection of intellectual property through copyrights and trade secret rights, the implementation of new corporate strategies, the improvement in the quality of products, or the percentage of people involved in R&D tasks. In this sense, it is also worth mentioning the relevant differences in innovation behaviours of the different sectors within the services field. Hence, more traditional or operational activities such as transport and communications generally register lower percentages of innovative activity.

In any case, the manufacturing sector still registers the highest proportion of innovative companies in the market, despite the high levels of innovative activity in services sectors such as business services. The difficult task of measuring service innovation, in a sector with many diverse activities and different innovation processes, is an obstacle to the service organizations' acknowledgement of their own innovative operations. Moreover, statistical sources that facilitate the analysis of service innovation activity in economy are sparse; they generally adopt a methodological approach that is more applicable to goods than to services. As a consequence, one of the main challenges that any innovation policy, including services, must tackle within its scope of action is to improve the deficient statistical information system.

The significant difference between financing percentages in the different sectors by the institutions could also have a determining effect on the results. The evident higher support provided to manufacturing, at least at both European and national levels, to the detriment of some service sectors – politically considered as less productive and innovative – may influence the innovative potential of services. Similarly, recent works (Rubalcaba and Gallego, 2006) suggest that pro-industrial and technological orientation of R&D programmes can explain the gap.

The cross-country analysis shows significant differences regarding entrepreneurial innovation levels between northern and southern European countries. In this respect, northern European regions, in comparison with those in the south, develop more internal R&D; apply more for intellectual property protection; maintain an important innovative relation with external agents (clients, universities, R&D centres, etc.); and realize a superior number of innovations in market. Companies from the south of Europe, in turn, register greater relative impacts as a result of the introduction of innovative elements in their productive systems. This latter fact might point out the relative productivity backwardness of regions from the south with regard to other more economically developed European countries.

This phenomenon repeats itself at a Europe–United States level: recent efforts on innovation may increase more rapidly in Europe than in the North American economy, thus maintaining an effective comparative advantage. In fact, this advantage, which became apparent in the 1990s, seems to be the result of better innovation performance, major introduction of information and communication technologies (ICT), and higher productivity levels in the US economy, which to a certain extent might explain the higher economic growth ratios shown by the US since mid-1990s. Although some possible catch-up process may occur, more research is needed on this subject.

Throughout this chapter, the innovative capacity of services, their fruitful relationship with technology, and the significant place taken by KIS have been outlined. The implications of economic and innovation policy regarding these issues are analysed in Chapter 10.

NOTES

1. This author was not very optimistic about entrepreneurship, given the monopolistic concentration processes.
2. A similar relationship at the services level has been dismissed due to methodological problems in the elaboration of indices in some countries, particularly where sample biases presumably arise.
3. The coefficient of correlation between productivity and per capita GDP is 0.953; between per capita GDP and innovation rate, 0.595; and between productivity and innovation rate, 0.6. All are significant at 1 per cent.
4. Research group within the fifth European Framework Programme, directed to the research of innovation in the public sector.
5. Product innovation: any change in the product leading to the improvement of features offered to the client (with or without a technological dimension). Process innovation: the provision of an important change to the manufacturing processes of a product. Examples include new equipment, new management and organizational methods, or both types together. Organizational innovation occurs when significant changes are made in the organization, coordination and behaviour of the human resources implied in the production and commercialization of a product. Such changes could be applied to the hierarchy, culture, strategy and policy of companies.
6. Three activities are observed: 1. Basic Research: theoretical or experimental work mainly carried out to acquire new general knowledge on the principles underlying the phenomena and events observed, without any particular application or

immediate use on sight; 2. Applied Research: original research carried out to acquire new knowledge with a specific practical objective. 3. Experimental Development: this is a systematic work, based on the existing knowledge gained by the research and practical experience, directed towards the production of new materials, products and mechanisms; to install new processes, systems or services; or to improve substantially those already produced or installed.

7. The CISIII is, in particular, subject to the attention of many services researchers, despite the fact that a more appropriate approach is needed regarding the services sector. However, one can state that the CISIII is a great advance when compared to previous surveys which initially focused only on manufacturing companies. In addition, some organizational issues were introduced, although many questions concerning the innovation of advanced services are not yet covered, and the indicators are still heavily biased toward traditional innovation sources.

8. Jorge Gallego has collaborated in the drafting of sections 4, 5 and 6 as co-author. Sections 4 and 5 are mainly based on a paper to be published in the *International Journal of Services Technology and Management*. The authors thank the journal for permission to reproduce part of it in this book.

9. Data from the CISIII database provided in this section corresponds to the values of innovative companies. The percentages referring to the different activity sectors reflect the average value of each indicator in the year 2000 for the following sixteen countries: Austria, Belgium, Germany, Denmark, Spain, Finland, France, Greece, Iceland, Italy, Luxembourg, Holland, Norway, Portugal, Sweden and the United Kingdom. The information available for each of the previous countries has received the same level of significance or relative weighting in the process of calculating the aggregate values or indicators presented in this chapter, in contrast with the procedure followed in other previous works, as in the case of the OECD report (2005c).

10. The term 'Industry' is understood in this section as manufacturing plus energy and other non-service sector and non-primary sector in the economy: the non-services industries all together.

11. Innovative company: that introducing new or significantly improved products and processes onto the market.

12. It is worth mentioning that this data is partly biased due to the fact that about 60–80 per cent of services organizations included in the CISIII belong to the least innovative sectors (distributive trades and transport and communication companies), so there is an underassessment of the total participation of the business services and financial sectors (OECD, 2005c).

6. The globalization of services and offshoring

1. INTRODUCTION: SERVICES IN THE GLOBAL ECONOMY

A few decades ago, globalization started to become a problem, although also an opportunity, for countries that witnessed how their agricultural or manufactured goods industries had to face increasingly stronger competition. From the oil crisis in the 1970s to the materialization of the so-called emerging economies in Southeast Asia, the relocation of factories to developing countries caused alarm in developed countries, which became concerned about the increasing de-industrialization of the rich world. The still-industrialized countries gradually started to change into service economy countries. This was generally considered a hindrance to growth, given the intangible nature of services, associated with lower rates of capital and technology, extreme dependence on labour and labour's role within the slowdown of total productivity. The scarce capacity to participate in international trade was also included among the negative points related to the services sector, except for tourism and transport. A service-based economy seemed to head towards lower competitive potential at a global level. A few decades later, the economic reality and economic thought countered many of the above-mentioned suppositions, either totally or partially, as stated in the third chapter. In the last few years, within this context, where services search for their place in the economic reality, a new issue has arisen. The present trend towards externalization and international contracting of services has again set off the delocalization alarms, but this time with respect to services, as occurred in the 1970s and still occurs today in the manufacturing business. International offshoring caused a huge loss of potential jobs, amounting to hundreds of thousands of jobs in Europe and the United States.[1] Economists try to pacify politicians with the old Ricardian and Neoclassical theories regarding the benefits of international trade and the advantages of specialization, even when sometimes this change in specialization seems very hard: in the 1970s, industrial unemployment was palliated by services.

Which sector will now absorb services unemployment? Will a fourth sector appear? The service offshoring phenomenon is serving to intensify the interest in countries such as India or China, or makes Europe contemplate, more intensely, the United States, the world leader in the export of services, with a much higher trade balance than Europe, although their huge trade deficit in goods is not compensated by this. Is Europe competitive in services? Who can replicate or compensate the competitive advantages of countries such as India? In order to answer these questions, we have to consider a prior issue: the identification of service sectors with their comparative advantages and disadvantages, and the analysis and explanation of the evolution of international trade.

This chapter aims to clarify the European case, as well as to state the basic framework regarding the relationships between services and globalization, where we must stress the role of business services and advanced services as the axis of the new competitive positions. Service offshoring does not refer to tourism, but mainly to knowledge-intensive service related to information technology and operational and back-office services. This chapter provides empirical evidence regarding European trade and investment in services, once a framework of analytical understanding is exposed justifying the interest of 'tertiary' sector competitiveness in a global economy. This study comprises several sections, including this introduction as the first. The second section outlines the analytical framework suitable for understanding trade and investment relations between globalization and services, followed by a section concerning the types of services globalization. In the empirical part of this chapter, the most important data regarding trade and services foreign direct investment (FDI) in Europe are provided. Then, we present the main results and compare them with those of the United States, Japan and emerging countries, in order to study the competitiveness of services in Europe. The chapter ends with the presentation of service offshoring or global sourcing, as well as their challenges and opportunities.

It is worth highlighting that the empirical sections of this chapter have met substantial statistical difficulties. Statistics regarding the international trade and foreign direct investment of services are complicated, as these only include, from the estimates of the balance of payments, a restrictive part of the real transactions, among other limitations. It is also difficult to obtain the indices that could inform about the competitive capacity of each type of service, particularly when long and homogeneous series are required from different countries. Therefore, the empirical results presented in this chapter are obviously subject to the limitations of the statistics they are based on.

2. RELATIONSHIPS BETWEEN SERVICES, COMPETITIVENESS AND GLOBALIZATION

Words such as globalization, trade, competitiveness or services have been regularly used in economic literature in order to highlight the challenges of the environments within which economies had to develop at the beginning of the 21st century (e.g., Aharoni and Nachum, 2000; Beyers, 2007; Camacho et al., 2007, among others). It is clear that we are immersed in a global economy, where the manner of thinking and acting has changed radically in recent years.

Within this framework, companies can find suppliers, clients and structure and organization methods in a wider range of places in the world. Moreover, technology and new communications can result in a considerable saving of time and money for many economic agents. This global economy is accompanied by global trade, deduced from the new open opportunities resulting from the increase in the exchange of products, knowledge, international arrangements, foreign investment, etc. And following trade is competitiveness, understood in a merely commercial sense. Thus, the most competitive countries in a specific sector are those with the highest market share within the global economy.[2]

In this context of factors promoting competitiveness, services are not immune. For example, business services increasingly become essential factors for competitiveness within the global environment (European Commission, 2003a; den Hertog et al., 2007). In general, services contribute to economic globalization, although they are also affected by such a globalization, being obliged to participate in dynamics which break the traditional and frequent market segmentation. Therefore, in order to tackle the relationship between services and globalization, it is important to recognize two directions: services have an influence on globalization (and within the business area, on competitiveness; due to this a company, a sector or a country can be more or less competitive) and globalization influences services (the global economy where all compete with or against all, which impels services to respond to internationalization challenges). Obviously, both directions are interrelated and have some common explanatory elements.

The Contribution of Services to Globalization

The services sector is essential in the current globalization processes (e.g., Bryson et al, 2004; Bryson and Daniels, 2007). The contribution of this sector to the attainment of a world dimension of economy can be summarized by classifying the activities into three groups:

1. Services that make globalization possible by establishing transport and communication networks, thus facilitating travelling, international trade, purchase and sale of goods and services in other places. Some of these are traditional services, for example commercial transport by road or by sea, and some others are modern services such as telecommunications that apply new technologies. All of them establish links between geographically distant places and constitute the basic infrastructure that makes globalization possible. The improvement of these services in the last decades and the decrease in prices is what leads to what some call

'death of distance', which refers to the recent exponential reduction of costs and time required for dealing with physical distances. This has been an advantage not only for producers, but also for consumers.

2. Secondly, there are business services that support the internationalization of the activity. A modern company will hardly succeed in a global economy if it does not use business-related services properly. Sometimes, the company will require services for the direct advice regarding its international strategy or the legal and tax aspects of its transactions abroad. Others will provide assistance in foreign trade or in efficient recruitment and contracting of personnel.

3. And thirdly, there is a group of consumer services offered within global economy. The most globalized ones are audiovisual and cultural services such as cinema. However, also the international dimension of leisure and sport services is growing, as well as tourism-related services, which are consumer services par excellence. Obviously, distributive trades or e-commerce services are also included, facilitating the distribution of goods and other services to the global market.

Figure 6.1 shows the group of services promoting economic and social globalization. Evidently, business and consumer globalization are interrelated. Among all the relationships, those held by business services stand out predominantly. The weight of services in the most advanced countries shows to a certain extent their relationship with the competitive capacity of economies. This is how services contribute to business competitiveness:

1. Influence on productive factors. Services affect productive factors by facilitating a global access to capital and the production of globally competitive technical innovations, to the labour force and the use of new global skills in local markets, as well as to the obtaining and control of global knowledge. A wide range of services contributes to this, from the recruitment and contracting of personnel to ICT or engineering services. In turn, financial services provide an easier access to global financial capital (credit, saving and investment).

2. Influence on markets. Business services steer the export and trade of goods (consultancy, marketing, fairs and exhibitions) towards new markets or towards the adaptation of goods to local needs, in which distributive trades and internet services also play a role. Services also facilitate the achievement of a global reputation by means of trademarks, franchises or CSR services.

3. Influence on locations. Transport, communications and information services have allowed the possibility of studying new business locations, which could lead to services relocation and offshoring of processes, both high- and low-skilled.

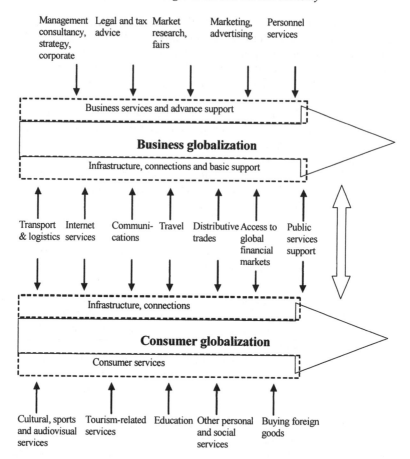

Figure 6.1 Services and globalization

Globalization can be defined as an individual case of market integration. The historical processes defined show the way to a higher integration and globalization of markets, although these concepts are different. Two markets can be completely integrated in a specific region without global companies or a maximum level of globalization. On the other hand, globalization always implies a higher integration of markets, but it does not seem to necessarily lead to a formal and real integration among a series of markets. Integration takes place between two or more countries, with the establishment of formal links in order to reinforce their commercial bonds. Globalization occurs among all countries: it refers to a way of thinking and acting not restricted to a specific country or set of countries.

The contribution of services to globalization can also be detected by means of five stages of different levels of world integration. These stages are superimposed, so that the new integration factors are added to the previous ones.

- First stage: *International exchange.* From the beginning of civilization, societies and their economies have been interrelated, generating several social, economic and cultural exchanges. The fairs that took place between the 10th and 12th centuries are an example of the contribution that services made to the first stages of globalization (Rubalcaba, 1994).
- Second stage: *Internationalization.* This is the link between countries, which is produced primarily through the use of international trade and the mobility of production factors. Companies become more international, as do their workers and capital. The goods industry is leader in this stage, although general production and other professional services go hand in hand with this expansion.
- Third stage: *Transnationalization.* When the wars in the first half of the 20th century were over, a process of European reconstruction began and with this came the boom of transnational companies (later to be called multinationals). Expansion by means of foreign direct investment added to the mere commercial expansion. So much so that, with the crisis of the 1970s, this led to a significant beginning for industrial relocation and the surfacing of new competitive countries (predominantly in Southeast Asia). In this context, the concept of outsourcing is established and services continue to grow, generally within the large companies, offering alternatives to reduce costs or increase quality to confront the competitive challenges of the crisis. Furthermore, many services companies accompany their clients in this international adventure. Then, the second modern wave of globalization, in which we are immersed, begins.
- With *Globalization,* services in the 1980s stopped playing a complementary role in the processes of change and market integration. Countries leading globalization are those where the majority of their value added and employment are in the services sector. Moreover, the business services sector emerges intensely, encouraged by an increasing externalization of tertiary activities previously provided within the big trade companies. Globalization implies a new way to understand business and companies within an environment which tends to coincide with the one of the whole world. Therefore, the first global companies arise, even today limited in number and restricted to some activities of very homogeneous goods, such as oil. At the dawn of the 21st century, services companies started to extend their international strategies on a global scale, as well as services externalization to developing countries.

These four phases have grown in continuity and complementary way. There is no replacement dynamism in there. Globalization implies firms transnationalization – setting-up abroad –, which means that international companies need to buy – provision of foreign factors – and sell abroad – international exchanges –. Business services play a role in each of these dimensions for which globalization is the final one where value chain is generated in different places, making international fragmentation of production possible, as well as the own firm management. A particular case of economic reality suitable to promote globalization, to a certain extent, is given by *Areas of economic integration*. These areas create formal and legal bonds with the aim of obtaining a single market based on common borders and customs, common regulation and administrative guarantees for free trade among a set of countries.

Services contribute decisively to the market integration and business competitiveness. In some cases (communications, transport, tourism) they bring together geographically distant realities; in other cases (legal services, strategic consultancy, language services, fairs and exhibitions, etc.) they approach realities that are distant from the economic and socio-cultural points of view. Unlike goods, where globalization creates a conflict or an alternative between what is local and what is global, services benefit from a complementarity that tends to surpass this conflict in certain cases. The existence of some services is due to economic, social, geographical or cultural diversity. As tourism requires the existence of different destinations, language services need the variety of languages, and fairs need the variety of companies, products and innovations. Many services contribute to integrating markets through diversity, and this is highlighted in the case of the European Union. Services facilitate the completion of a single market, and promote the real integration of markets and economies. Services are large promoters of what is known as 'glocalization': the aim of globalization is a better 'location', understood as an improved adaptation to regulatory, economic, social and cultural parameters of the region where companies operate. It is the way of doing things on a large and small scale. Glocalization solves the conflict between supporters and detractors of globalization by offering a process tailored, at least potentially, to local requirements.

The Influence of Services Globalization

Services contribute to and are affected by economic globalization, which forces them to participate in a dynamism that breaks the traditional segmentation of markets existing over the centuries. There are many factors that have promoted the internationalization of services activities. Among these, we can list those factors related to the traditional macroeconomic theories explaining international trade, the specialization factors linked to the provision of factors and related prices, microeconomic elements characteristic of business competitive strategies, the technological change that facilitates the provision of distance services, other more qualitative dimensions associated to the change of productive systems, the so-called 'service relationships' and the complementarity and substitution between different forms of services internationalization, especially between trade and foreign direct investment. The openness of markets due to the national political action – new regulations, more liberal and favourable for competition – or the international political action – Strategy for the Internal Market of Services, at a European level, and GATS, at a global level – has also been an incentive to modify the borders of markets that have been divided for years.

Within the process of services globalization, some activities adapt better to the international situation, while others, whose local dimensions are limited, do not have a cross-border expansion. Business services are protagonists, some of which allow the presentation of a relatively high level of trade due to the influences of ICT or to the standardization of production. On the other hand, it is more complex for final consumer services in general to go beyond local markets where they usually operate as niches. In the following section, we will summarize the key dimensions of services globalization, followed by the existing empirical evidence.

3. KEY DIMENSIONS OF SERVICES GLOBALIZATION

Challenges and opportunities of service globalization have given rise to a wide variety of forms of internationalization, international trade being just one of these forms. Trade has a dual function: from one viewpoint, it is a way of services internationalization since it allows an international approach; from the other, we can state that international trade interacts with the rest of the dimensions of services globalization so that its complementary nature tends to dominate the substitution effects and any services internationalization generates a kind of international trade. These relationships are described below.

Services globalization takes many forms, implying in all cases a global concept of the market that involves the internationalization of productive inputs and intra-firm activities. For consumers, globalization implies a wider capacity of use and enjoyment of goods and services, originating from anywhere in the world.

The methods of services internationalization are characterized by the ontological features explained in Chapter 2, such as the tension between the need for standardization and the global reputation of services and the need for differentiation (a product is never identical in all markets) and customization (due to the interactive nature of services). Both aspects imply that a service has to be altered to fit the requirements of a foreign market. This means that service 'internationalization' implies 'nationalization', that is to say, the adaptation to normative, economic, social and cultural and parameters of foreign countries or markets where they operate. This difference means that the global movements of services are not so much associated with cross-border movements as with the transmission of processes, knowledge and techniques or with the exchange of residents and non-residents and the transfer of workers and technology.

Classical forms of internationalization include cross-border international trade and capital movement, to which foreign direct investment, as well as international merger and acquisition processes contribute.[3] However, there are other dimensions to take into consideration including the following which form part of the definition of international trade: the movement of the labour factor – temporary movement of workers is extremely important in many types of services – and the displacement of consumers out of their borders – mainly in consumer services–. Services combine sectors where the displacement of suppliers and consumers is commonplace and there have been many typologies of services classified according to these movements (e.g., Sapir, 1993a, b). Although there is another group of components regarding services globalization outside of the official definitions which are comprised of those groups transferring knowledge, information, standards, and innovations (of products, processes or organizations) that are superimpose on the different forms of trade and investment (Rubalcaba and Cuadrado, 2002a, b). Trademarks and franchises are some examples of these other components, which are so influential within the uncertain framework of services markets, where reputation is associated with quality and the ways of generating confidence in consumers or buyers, thus becoming an essential tool for globalization. And finally, another form of services globalization is collaboration networks among companies of different countries, even though these do not have formal agreements of purchase, acquisition or direct trade between the parties.

All these dimensions are interrelated. For example, a consultant travelling from one country to another to share knowledge contributes to service globalization through client transactions and the diffusion of a brand and a reputation associated with a firm. During this type of 'service trade', networking and knowledge transfer will occur and the co-production of an international service will result in adaptation to local conditions. This process of adaptation will lead to further opportunities to develop service trade, as the acquired experience may result in the provision of services to other foreign companies (Wood, 2001; Rubalcaba and Gago, 2001). These interrelations explain some of the complementarities between, for example, international trade and FDI, or the role of international provision of services with and within foreign affiliates.

In general terms, business services internationalization creates cross-border trade, intra-firm trade included, which can follow or precede FDI, although some times a similar path is established (Roberts, 1999) while, in general, the relationship between trade and FDI, especially in services, is very heterogeneous, i.e. it varies by category of services (Pain and van Welsum, 2004; van Welsum, 2003a, b, 2004).

International Trade

Not all the exposed dimensions related to service globalization develop in a linear manner. The existence of certain limits to service globalization promotes a divergence between certain ways of internationalizing and others. In particular, empirical evidence underlines the limits to cross-border internationalization of services. Figure 6.2 shows the evolution of services trade within the total trade in goods and services. In Europe, the percentage has remained steadily between 18 per cent and 22 per cent. The situation in other geographical areas has been similar. The paradox emerging from the comparison between these data and the ones on value added is here evident once more.

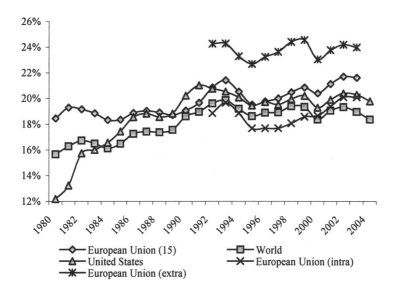

Source: Based on WTO (2005).

Figure 6.2 Percentages of services trade (exports + imports) in total trade, 1980–2004

The low threshold in the growing importance of services trade cannot be explained as a lack of dynamics in the sector but is due to the even larger growth of world trade in goods. International trade in services has been very dynamic during recent years but not dynamic enough to keep up with international trade in goods. Trends in the 1990s do not seem to allow a different scenario in the coming years, even if services have behaved more regularly in recent years and other commercial services (business services mainly) have shown constant growth. It is noticeable that a decrease in world trade took place between 2000 and 2001, but a recovery has been registered between 2001 and 2004.

These empirical results are used to introduce the question of differences between the goods and services trade. The importance of the human capital factor in the services trade questions the validity of traditional models of international trade (Petit, 1986), and stresses the consideration of elements related to cultural and social advantages (Riddle, 1986; Daniels, 1993): the relative abundance of production factors or raw materials acquires a less weighted explanation. This is due to the weight of expectations, reputation and prestige in the international services markets (Aharoni, 1999). Switching costs are high and confidence is crucial, as stated in Chapter 2.

Table 6.1 Key data on international trade in business services. EU15 to extra-EU15 trade, 2005

POST	Shares % (X+M) in total services	Balance Net (X-M) millions of euros	Cover rate X/M	Annual growth rate % 95/05 (X+M)	Growth X/M 05 – X/M 95 difference
100 Goods (*)	280.57	16808000	1.02	6.75	-0.04
200 Services	100.00	11876372	1.03	8.28	0.06
205 Transport	24.44	3030647	1.03	7.28	0.13
236 Travel	21.99	-28413656	0.70	6.62	-0.24
981 Other services	52.55	36874542	1.21	9.58	0.19
245 Communication services	1.96	-1141499	0.85	8.47	0.07
249 Construction services	2.33	3496057	1.51	0.27	0.08
253 Insurance services	2.62	3244826	1.40	8.03	-1.60
260 Financial services	5.80	16082693	2.19	13.81	0.72
262 Computer and information services	3.43	8316878	1.97	14.37	1.14
266 Royalties and license fees	6.94	-10620661	0.66	11.56	0.15
268 Other business services	25.96	15308296	1.17	10.80	0.23
287 Personal, cultural and recreational services	1.38	-293431	0.94	2.96	0.26
288 Audio, visual and related services	1.11	-452322	0.90	4.37	0.39
289 Other personal, cultural and recreational services	0.26	159229	1.18	-0.53	-0.14
291 Government services	2.13	2481382	1.37	1.57	-0.12
982 Services not allocated	1.02	384839	1.11	8.36	-1.42
Business services (#)	29.39	23625174	1.24	11.14	0.31

Notes: * 2004 data. # Computer and information services plus other business services (services between affiliated enterprises are excluded).

Source: Eurostat, New Cronos, 2007.

Table 6.1 confirms the predominance of goods on service trade and the fact that the latter is not presenting any catch-up patterns. The most traded service categories are the transport and travel services, but if business services are accounted all together they are converted into the service activity with more international transactions. It has to be noticed how EU 15 was, in 2005, a net exporter in most of the principal economic sectors, a negative balance is met only in few activities: travel; communication services; royalties and license fees; personal, cultural and recreational services; audio, visual and related services; all activities where the USA are the world leader. Business services are once again at the top of the list when considering the growth rates; in fact the sector with the highest growth rate between 1995 and 2005 is the computer and information services followed by the royalties and licenses fees.

Direct Investment

In foreign direct investment, goods only account for the 27 per cent of the amount of the value of FDI in services (28 per cent of total inwards, 25 per cent of total outwards, see Table 6.2). The preference of services for FDI versus trading has a clear effect on these statistics where services FDI (72 per cent of total) have a weight in coherence with its total weight in the economy (70 per cent).

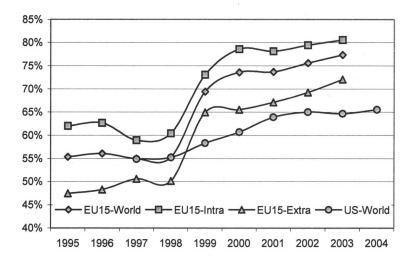

Source: Based on Eurostat, balance of payment statistics (2006).

Figure 6.3 Percentages of services in total foreign direct investment (FDI) stocks

Within this role of services in FDI, with respect to the 'minor' quantitative importance as an economic sector, financial services provide 61 per cent of total service FDI, business services represent 22 per cent and telecommunications represent relative share at 4 per cent. However, this picture was not the same a few years ago. In 1996, FDI was more important in goods than in services and the composition of service FDI was less dominated by financial services (40 per cent), business services represented 28 per cent and telecommunications only 1 per cent. In just five years, the composition of FDI in Europe has shifted towards services and in particular towards financial and telecommunications services compared to distributive trades. These trends are also influenced for the changes between 2001 and 2002.

Table 6.2 Key data on foreign direct investment in business services. EU15 to Extra-EU15. Stock position outward and inward, 2003 and growth 1996–2003

	% services (in + out) 2003	Outward/ Inward 2003	Outward % Annual GR	Inward % Annual GR
9999 Total	139	1.4	19	18
Total Goods	27	1.4	8	9
5095 Total services	100	1.3	26	23
5295 Distributive trades and repairs	7	1.3	16	7
5500 Hotels and restaurants	1	1.2	22	12
Transport (*)	7	3.2	41	27
6420 Telecommunications	4	4.6	53	29
6895 Financial intermediation	61	1.3	32	29
7395 Real estate and business activities	24	0.9	19	22
7000 Real estate	2	1.0	13	19
Business services	22	0.9	20	22
7200 Computer activities	1	2.2	49	18
7300 Research and development	0	3.0	18	6
7400 Other business activities	20	0.8	18	22
9995 Other services	2	1.9	7	8
9996 Not allocated	3	1.8	63	92

Notes: * 2002. GR: growth rate.

Source: based on Eurostat, New Cronos, 2006.

Interesting results concern in fact the relationship between outward and inward investment. The coefficient outward/inward has been built to evaluate the net investment positions in Europe. This is not a fully equivalent indicator to the one on international trade, the market quota export/imports. To obtain an advantageous export/import rate is a clear economic and political objective. The ratio outward/inward investment can be interpreted in two different ways. High outward investment can be considered as a loss for the countries that could have benefited from that investment being made domestically. On the contrary, high inward investment represents the positive capacity to attract capital, indicating certain international competitiveness. On the other hand, only the most powerful countries have the capacity to invest strongly abroad. To a certain degree, in this age of globalization, a country needs to be strong both in inward FDI (more resources to itself) and outward FDI (more scale economies and competitive conditions when new or part of the local production is transferred elsewhere).

In Europe, outward FDI towards third countries is higher than inward foreign investment towards Europe for every sector. This relationship is slightly stronger in goods (coefficient 1.4) than in services (1.3). In services, the outward/inward investment is higher in telecommunications (4.6), transportation (3.2) and research and development (3.0). Other business services (0.8) and business services (0.9) are in a more balanced position. Except for Other services and Other Business Activities, all the ratios have grown between 1996 and 2003. In 1996, distributive trades, hotels, telecommunications and computer services showed more inward investments than outwards stocks (the ratios were less than one).

Taking a look to the evolution in the last years it can be noticed that average annual growth rates between 1996 and 2003 have been extraordinarily high. The boom of the 'new economy' running up to April 2001 brought huge investments in telecommunications and computer services: from Europe more outwards than inwards. Investment in all services grew strongly. As has been seen in Table 6.2 it was not only the 'new economy' leading the figures, other high technology services gathered importance in the same period. Transport, financial and computer activities became a field open to foreign expansion for European companies and investors, which increased their presence abroad by 41 per cent for the former sector, 32 per cent for the financial services and 49 per cent for the latter.

The process of globalization sees Europe as an actor more inclined to the expansion toward new markets than a receiver of investment from abroad; all the most important activities registered indeed greater outward than inwards FDI growth rates. The active role of Europe in the globalization is not surprising, it had to be expected that this phenomenon would be led by the developed economies. What is surprising is the fact that analysing some data registered by the USA the figures are reduced and the patterns take the opposite direction: the growth of the inward FDI had been more consistent than the outward one in most of the sectors from manufacturing until computer services. This has to be read as an index of the attractiveness the

North American service sector is exercising on foreign investors. However, some of these trends seem to have changed after 2002 for many services, although official statistics do not yet offer detailed data on FDI flows or stocks for the recent 2003–2006 period. The overestimation and the consequent collapse of the 'new economy' influenced a decrease of FDI in ICT activities so relative figures and shares were already somewhat adjusted in 2003 data.

Table 6.3 Basic data on merger and acquisitions, 2003

	Number of operations between 1993 and 2003				Average value of operation Extra-EU
	Purchases	**Sales**	**Difference Purchase/ sales**	**Intra-EU 1993– 2003**	
Total of sectors	16590	1739	9.5	16618	135 368
Primary sector	147	9	16.3	71	374 379
Manufacturing	7745	723	10.7	7379	136 877
Network industries	1951	194	10.1	1885	218 093
Distribution	1301	157	8.3	1940	143 079
Financial and real estate	2278	194	11.7	1840	160 014
Business services	2615	361	7.2	2925	55 599

Source: DG Economic and Financial Affairs data base, 2003.

An increasing part of FDI is due to the growth of mergers and acquisitions (M&A) in the second half of the 1990s. According to this indicator and the DG ECFIN data base recording major M&A operations, M&A in services account for 50 per cent of total operations, although the average value of operations in goods was not significantly higher than in services (due to the impact of operations in networking industries). Within the services financial and real estate services, that presented a total of 2472 operations of merging and acquisition, and in the period which goes from the year 1993 to the year 2003, and business services, 2976 operations, show the highest share of processes while the group of the other services and the distribution seem to be affected by the phenomenon in a less extended way.

Once the situations in the field of international trade and foreign direct investment in services have been analysed, it can be concluded that the establishment of a subsidiary with productive and exporting capacity is often found at the end of a long process where non-international companies start with local exports and gradually open to the rest of the world (Roberts, 1999) strongly maintaining diverse local markets. However, these companies never or almost never reach a process of complete globalization, such as that produced in some manufacturing companies or those specializing in oil-derived energy products. The global strategy facilitates the homogeneity of products, while services are essentially very different and their success depends on a good adaptation of the service to local needs. This is the reason why there are only very limited global companies in the services world, and they are basically concentrated in the financial, communication and software sectors.

In the report regarding the top-100 non-financial companies in the world, no more than 20–25 per cent are services companies: their markets are very local and it would be complicated for them to divide on a global scale. The advantages of being a multinational company are important not only in goods, but also services (Enderwick, 1989), although lesser in the latter (Dunning, 1993), which are moved to act by reactive rather than proactive behaviours (Gusinger, 1992). Also, the artificial obstacles which exist in the services trade contribute significantly to their timid international behaviour.

Due to their specific characteristics, services cross boundaries more as a direct investment than as a product, therefore, for example, a services multinational is presented in a different way to a goods producer, which tends to concentrate production with localizations that associate wide scale economies at low costs and with a strongly developed distribution network. Services multinationals are companies that offer their products to a global market, but by means of a network of subsidiaries and branches whose highest extension and level of market penetration will show their international relevance. For that purpose, multinationals of the sector develop their expansion strategies by introducing locations where services are offered principally and directly in the objective markets. A review on these concepts from an empirical viewpoint will be presented later on in this chapter.

The prestige of an international supplier enables firms to forge relationships of trust that are often better than those reproduced by local firms. This factor explains the success of most multinational service companies, but also the limitations for a global provision, as services need local staff to manage and lead the service provision. A suitable combination between a global reputation and local reputation is a balance requested by multinational firms. That explains why service companies use mergers and acquisitions to expand quickly in international markets. Alternatively, a new investment needs time to obtain a local reputation upon which the service is built.

As stated before the increasing role of outsourcing processes at a global scale is still limited to selected activities, especially in activities within the businesses services such as operative standards services (e.g., call centres) or qualified standardized international trade business services (accountancy, billing, information, computer services) where the need for local reputation is of minor concern. The links between reputation, innovation and knowledge intensive business services are particularly strong (Wood, 2001), providing a value added package that increases the performance of users.

4. TRADE COMPETITIVENESS OF EUROPEAN SERVICES[4]

Services competitiveness can be understood from a wide concept of competitiveness, including the sustainable development of the sector and its capacity to create employment and social welfare. However, this wider definition is implicitly included in all the chapters of this book and in the identification of the challenges that the European economy must face. This section is focused on competitiveness in its commercial sense, through the classical indicators of market shares or percentages in the world market.

The European Services in the World

A. Overall world performance (WTO data). A comprehensive presentation of the state of the world commerce in services, in order to identify the main actors at world level, can be carried out through the observation of the WTO data on international trade in commercial services (all services excluding governmental ones). If we consider the EU15 as a unique actor (later on in Chapter 9 we will discuss the limitations to this supposition) the Union is shown to be the economy with the largest market shares of trade in services, with a quota constantly between 18 per cent and 20 per cent of total world exchanges. It is followed by the US, which maintains a quota between 14 and 16 per cent since the half of the 1980s. In the first years of the new century the US share is sharply declining and this is also the case of Japanese trade (the third largest service economy), which started to decline its market share since the mid-1990s. These decreases are accompanied by the raising role played by recently developed economies such as the Indian or the Chinese. Their growing importance in the world market becomes even more relevant if we take into consideration that in the examined periods the total exchange of services grew at global level at the average rate of almost 7 per cent per year.

From an analysis conducted at national level it can be observed how the United Kingdom, Germany, Japan, France and Ireland are world's leading countries in other commercial services according to WTO[5], producing export values among the highest in the world, although their world shares in exports and imports have decreased (still above 4 per cent from around 7 per cent in exports in 1995), indicating the increasing role of other competitors. Among the large countries, only the United Kingdom, following the US pattern, increased its market shares between 1995 and 2004: from 8.3 per cent to 11.8 per cent of total world exports, but this rise occurred between 1995 and 2000, and since then the share remains unchanged. To a lesser extent, Spain has also increased its shares: from 1.7 per cent to 2.5 per cent in exports and from 2.4 per cent to 3.2 per cent in imports. An important increase in export market shares has taken place in India, following the off-shoring trends that occurred between 1995 and 2004: from 0.5 per cent to 3.1 per cent. This phenomenon brought India into the top ten economies in service exports, with a commercial value of more than 30 billions USD.

Apart from other trade services, the WTO data allow the analysis of tourism and transport categories. In both cases, and for the year 2004, the United States is again the country with the highest market share, 15.3 per cent and 11.7 per cent respectively. The highest differences are registered in the next group of countries. Therefore, while this group in transport services is comprised of Germany (with 6.6 per cent of the share), Japan (6.4 per cent), United Kingdom (5.2 per cent) and France (5.1), Spain stands out in tourism services, with a world share of 7.4 per cent, above France (6.5 per cent), Italy (5.7 per cent) and Germany (4.4 per cent). The Spanish international scope in this type of services is especially remarkable due to its high dynamism in the last years; in fact, it held the fourth position in 1995, with a share of 6.3 per cent, below France and Italy.

B. EU vs. US vs. JP benchmarking (Eurostat data). The Eurostat data allow a more detailed analysis by activities. In order to assess the situation of the international services trade of the EU15, in comparison with the United States and Japan, we have taken into consideration four indicators: the volumes of trade and investment of EU15 and the US; and three other additional indicators: the coverage rate, referring to the relationship between imports and exports in the year 2002, the variation of these rates during the period 1996–2002, and the growing of exports in that same period.

Figure 6.4 shows the volume of trade and investment of the EU15 and the US. In international trade, for most service sectors, the EU15 volumes are larger than the US ones. The largest difference is in computer services. For the US, the largest dominance is produced in royalties and licence fees. In business services, differences in volumes between the EU15 and the US are much larger in imports than in exports for business services, information services in particular.

In FDI, the situation is more differentiated. The EU15 inward FDI for total business services is very high compared to the US, while the situation in outward FDI is exactly the opposite. In real estate, and to a lesser extent in R&D, the US volumes are larger in inwards, the same as in many other services sectors such as telecommunications, transport, distributive trades or hotels and restaurants. In telecommunications and transport the outwards FDI in EU15 are impressive compared to the US. In conclusion, many services in the EU can be very competitive according to this first indicator, since they surpass the US volumes in exports, imports and inward FDI. In growth terms, except in hotels, restaurants and distributive trades, in all other sectors in the figure with available data, EU inward and outward investments have grown more than the US inward FDI (and also more than US outward FDI in many sectors). This is an indication of the competitive position of many European business services compared to the US ones, which is not the case in many manufacturing and other services activities.

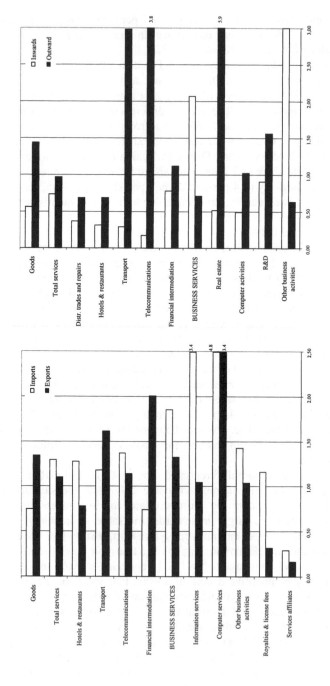

Source: Based on Balance of Payment Statistics, New Cronos, Eurostat, 2004.

Figure 6.4 Volumes of trade in investment in EU15 and the US (rates EU15/US; 1=volumes are the same)

When services are compared to goods from the perspective of the most selected competitiveness indicators (Table 6.4), the first aspect to be highlighted is that the European Union has been the economic area with the lowest level of discrepancy in coverage rates, both in growth levels and rates. In other words, the coverage rates in goods and services, as well as their evolution in the last years, have been very similar. On the contrary, the United States and Japan present very different situations. In the first, the coverage rate of services is higher than goods, which shows the increased American trade deficit (compensated by the services surplus to a large extent). In Japan, deficit is registered by services (coverage rate of 0.72), against the goods surplus (1.32). As regards the growth rates of services and goods exports, the most important ones have been experienced in Europe (8.1 per cent and 7.6 per cent). In the USA, although coverage rates of exports have been lower, services have registered a higher growth (4.8 per cent against 3.7 per cent of goods). In Japan, services exports grew more than manufactures (4.8 per cent against 4.0 per cent).

The differences are even more obvious when analysing the behaviour of the various services branches, which allow us to draw a preliminary map of strengths and weaknesses. This comparison is basically restricted to the EU15 and the United States, since the statistical coverage for Japan is only available for some services branches.

Therefore, the greatest strengths in the European Union (backed by high coverage rates, growth and exports) lie mainly in computer and financial services, which were especially dynamic between 1996 and 2002. The situation of public administrations, legal services and R&D is also considerable.

The best records in the United States occur in advanced services implying a high investment in Information and Communication Technologies, which illustrates the advantages of an earlier investment in these types of technology in the US. These advantages foster other changes within the organization (for example, in management strategies or in the introduction of re-engineering processes) and, in the end, will result in a higher productivity and competitiveness (Van Ark and McGuckin, 2002). As examples, we can mention R&D, technical, information or telecommunications services. As well as these, the US is outstanding in other services including: royalties, construction, leasing and tourism.

The superiority of the United States in the competitiveness of many services can be related, to a large extent, to the weight of their multinationals. The number of companies leading business services, transport, trade or TIC is similar on both sides of the Atlantic Ocean, although the average market value in America is usually double that of European companies. In contrast, the European weight in financial services and telecommunications is very considerable. In Europe, there are also around a hundred non-financial service firms among the Top 500 and 22 business service companies are listed: seven software and computer service companies and 15 other business services. In the US, the number of service companies in the top 500 ranking is slightly higher since they have few companies in telecommunications (only 12 versus 30 in Europe) and in transportation (only seven versus 19 in Europe) but many more in other services such as computer services (e.g., 27 US versus 7 EU in computer services).

Table 6.4 The situation of the EU vs. US and Japan in the global services market

Sectors	Coverage rate 2004			Differences in coverage rate 1996–2004			Growing of exports 1996–2004		
	EU15	**US**	**Japan**	**EU15**	**US**	**Japan**	**EU15**	**US**	**Japan**
Goods	1.02	0.55	1.32	-0.06	-0.21	0.06	6.98	3.74	3.97
Services (total)	1.10	1.15	0.72	0.03	-0.41	0.20	7.58	4.75	4.83
Transportation	1.11	0.72	0.75	0.12	-0.36	0.11	7.46	2.51	5.23
Tourism	0.77	1.35	0.29	-0.24	-0.30	0.18	3.71	1.99	12.94
Other services	1.29	1.28	0.99	0.13	-0.55	0.29	9.13	7.22	3.44
Communications	0.93	0.94	0.73	-0.01	0.54	-0.01	8.67	3.58	-13.62
- Post	0.83	0.46		-0.03			0.65		
-Telecommunications	0.96	1.00		0.60			3.78		
Construction	1.52	3.15	1.43	-0.18	-4.43	0.20	-0.21	-1.86	2.10
Insurance	1.51	0.20	0.31	-0.84	-0.10	0.06	8.04	16.64	10.08
Financial	2.41	4.41	1.66	0.63	1.58	0.71	11.34	12.49	5.77
IC services	2.30	3.29	0.48	1.15	-3.28	-0.02	21.29	11.09	-1.72
- Computer	2.11	2.32		-3.54			11.54		
- Information	4.51	9.24		1.31			10.43		
Royalties	0.70	2.20	1.15	0.14	-1.94	0.47	11.05	6.30	10.96
Other business services	1.25	1.42	0.89	0.07	-0.20	0.22	9.06	9.51	0.21
- Distributive trades	1.48			0.39			7.05		
- Leasing	1.04			0.17			10.31		
- Various business companies	1.21	1.42		-0.02	-0.20		9.64	9.51	
-- Legal, management. accountant	1.09			0.12			14.58	20.9*	
--Marketing and advertising	0.75			0.07			9.77	5.8*	
-- R&D	1.15			0.00			13.09	49.2*	
-- Technical	2.01			0.32			6.22	4.8*	
-- Other services	1.24	1.95		-0.54	-0.12		6.97	7.95	
Services between subsidiaries	1.02	1.28		0.07	-0.19		8.76	10.16	
Personal, cultural and leisure services	0.76	23.71		0.42	7.99		13.50	12.42	
- Audio-visual	1.38			0.64			3.53	5.9*	
- Other personal	1.56	0.57	1.78	0.11	-1.01	0.74	3.33	-1.25	8.93
Public administrations	1.63	0.55	1.32	0.55	-0.21	0.06	12.86	3.74	3.97

Notes: * 2002 data.

Source: Based on Eurostat data, Balance of Payments, 2007.

Table 6.5 Services in the market value of top World, European and American 500 companies

Market value by sector / Sector	Global 500 N° of firms	Data 2004 Market value $m	Data 2004 Global Ranking	Europe 500 N° of Firms	Data 2003 Market value $m	Data 2003 EU Ranking	US 500 N° of firms	Data 2003 Market value $m	Data 2003 US Ranking	EU / (EU+US+JP) N° of Firms (%)	EU / (EU+US+JP) Market value $m (%)	Data 2003 Ranking Share EU in Triade
Banks	65	2 591 665.5	1	76	876 485.3	1	39	809 401.8	2	44	48	7
Pharmaceuticals & biotechnology	23	1 504 255.3	2	16	465 610.4	4	23	917 070.2	1	25	31	16
Oil & gas	31	1 487 874.0	3	21	594 192.0	2	29	523 754.1	6	38	52	6
Telecommunication services	36	1 467 881.8	4	30	517 602.3	3	12	295 203.2	12	63	53	4
Information technology hardware	34	1 300 001.6	5	7	124 224.8	10	32	595 592.0	4	14	16	30
General retailers	24	765 522.5	6	14	91 217.6	15	25	533 135.0	5	22	14	31
Insurance	20	761 448.7	7	18	160 398.0	7	22	397 076.8	9	38	27	19
Software & computer services	15	746 348.1	8	7	53 309.2	25	27	597 614.3	3	13	8	33
Media & entertainment	22	630 035.6	9	25	133 224.7	9	24	415 843.2	8	40	22	28
-----------------	--	-------	--	--	-------	--	--	-------	--	--	--	--
Health	18	434 373.5	13	12	44 407.5	28	29	373 114.8	10	27	10	32
Life assurance	12	218 845.1	19	11	70 302.8	21	7	74 861.5	23	58	47	8
Support services	9	209 417.6	21	15	64 753.5	22	14	150 243.7	16	45	29	18

Source: Based on Financial Times, 2004.

Market shares of European business service companies in leading countries (EU+US+Japan) are particularly low (8 per cent in computer services, 29 per cent in other business services) while telecommunications and banking are among the highest (53 per cent and 48 per cent; see Table 6.5 for further information).

The results for market shares in the top segment of the markets show that the role of services in global businesses differs according to regions and countries. That means that there are limitations to service globalizations that depend, not on the nature of services, but on the framework conditions operating in different geographical areas: market size and market fragmentation among different countries, different business models, entrepreneurship, economic, social and cultural differences, etc.

Place held by the Emerging Countries

In order to assess more concretely and meticulously the role of emerging countries in the international trade of services, the analysis will firstly concentrate on the shares in the so-called other commercial services (excluding transport and tourism), as it is in this category that the present offshoring trends occur to a longer extent and where, consequently, the real possibilities of the emerging countries as services export centres arise. Therefore, Figure 6.5 shows the relationship between the export rate of other commercial services in percentages over the world total in 2004 (horizontal axis), and the growth of this rate registered between 2000 and 2004 (vertical axis).

The relationship between the export rate in these services and recent growth is quite uneven. From a detailed analysis of Figure 6.5, we can deduce the existence of a triple relationship level depending on the magnitude of the 2004 rate. Therefore, there are strong contrasts between those countries with lower rates, which happen to be emerging countries, alternating between countries with extremely high, positive variation share rates (for example, Russian Federation or Hungary) and those whose rates are on the decrease (Mexico, Turkey).

These varied results should be interpreted in the sense that the international trade of services offers opportunities to these countries, although there is not an inertial logic that these are the net winners; the end result will finally depend on their capacity to take advantage of such opportunities. A second level of relationship links these countries with average export rates. In this case, there seems to be a correlation (although quite weak) between a higher growth and a higher level of rates.

Finally, the countries with a higher market share (the United States and the United Kingdom) have not been the most dynamic ones in recent years. In fact, the United States has slightly decreased its share, while the United Kingdom has remained stable.

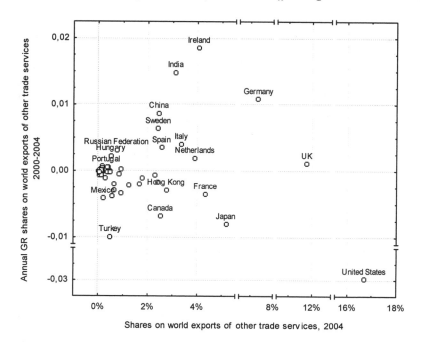

Source: Based on World Trade Organisation data, 2006.

Figure 6.5 Leaders in trade of other commercial services (exports in % over the world total) in 2004 and recent dynamics (growth rates 2000–2004)

Ireland stands out among all the countries represented in the figure. It is a country combining a considerable export rate in 2004 (4.0 per cent), with a much accentuated growth rate during the period 2000–2004. From this, we can conclude that the 'Irish miracle' is also expressed in the evolution of the market share of these services, or even more so, the force of this type of services in international markets is, at the same time, a cause and a consequence of this 'miracle'.

A combination of different factors, such as a qualified labour force, a clear commitment to R&D&I and the knowledge society, as well as a favourable legislation and tax treatment of investment, has increased the level of international reputation and the attraction of foreign investment in highly tradable and added-valued services, which has been a decisive lever for the attainment of this success. In its turn, Spain is located in a *warm area*, its market share in 2004 being 2.5 per cent and the variation rate of its shares approximately 1.5 per cent. Spain and France are much related, in a certain sense, to the growth of Morocco as an emerging exporting country of other commercial services.

5. THE MIGRATION OF SERVICES: THE EMERGING ROLE OF OFFSHORING

The role of emerging countries within the flow of international services is strongly linked to a series of events that have frequently attracted the attention of economists during recent years. Offshoring would be the term defining all of them, although there are different dimensions.

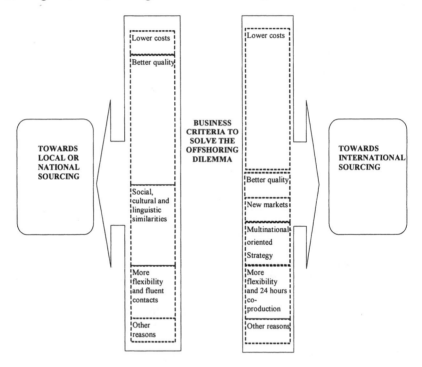

Figure 6.6 The offshoring dilemma

Sometimes there is a certain confusion using the terms delocalization, externalization, outsourcing and off-shoring. This can clarify the use of some of the terms:

- Delocalization means the transfer of certain activities once produced in a given place, to other places. However, currently this term is restricted mainly to regional flows (e.g., intra-EU flows).
- Outsourcing is the contracting out of productive activities, manufacturing or services, new or previously produced in-house.
- Externalization means any transfer from in-house activities to external companies. It is mainly an organizational change.

- Off-shoring is the outsourcing of services in other countries or areas. For Europe, off-shoring is the international sourcing to extra-EU countries.
- Off-shoring can also be related to international insourcing in multinational companies established abroad. Offshoring covers both international outsourcing and international insourcing (van Welsum and Vickery, 2004). Sometimes these two subcategories are grouped in the 'global resourcing' definition (McKinsey Global Institute 2003; global insourcing is named captive offshoring). The distinction between the two ways of offshoring is based on degrees of control between enterprises or subsidiaries.

Enterprises in different countries with different history, languages and commercial partners look for different strategies to solve the dilemma between local or national sourcing and international offshoring. Figure 6.6 shows this dilemma and the elements enterprises take into consideration when choosing between the two options. An OECD (2004b) report explained that to compete with the internal cost savings achieved through internal offshoring and offshore joint ventures, multinational outsourcers (i.e. providers of outsourced services to others) moved part of their activities offshore through FDI and subcontracting. With multinationals accessing the same cost base, indigenous offshore-based firms responded by opening front-office operations in developed country markets in order to compete in the country of origin of outsourcing with the multinational enterprises (MNE) providers of outsourced services. This, in turn, has compelled MNE providers of outsourced services to extend their offshoring activity. This is an example of the type of explanations behind the business criteria to solve the offshoring dilemma.

In August 2003, the *Financial Times* published a famous article[6] that summarized the services being provided in India, South Africa, Australia, Malaysia, Singapore and China. These productive destinations for services had resulted in the migration of thousands of people: in the financial sector alone Europe migrated 730 000 jobs, the United States 850 000 and Japan 400 000.[7] A forecast for 2015 was published at the end of 2003: 3.3 million white-collar jobs (500 000 in IT) would move offshore to countries such as India.[8] The Forrester study (Parker, 2004) reports that more than one million jobs will move offshore, the UK being the main active country in the process. Farrell (2005) and McKinsey Global Institute (2005) estimate that actual offshore employment will reach 4.1 million jobs worldwide in 2008 and reach an estimated 1.2 per cent of total demand for labour services from developed countries. Unfortunately, all these figures cannot be confirmed or negated by official statistics due to the lack of data in the European statistical system. Indirect measures, like the ones from OECD, based on occupations data, estimate a 20 per cent of total employment potentially affected by offshoring in developed countries (van Welsum and Vickery, 2005).

The offshoring of services to countries like India also has its limits. As reported in *The Economist* in March 2004, 'A lift to India', non English-speaking countries have more difficulties in keeping a service provision on a general scale.[9] The language is of course an important factor, but not the only one: the cultural and socio-economic environments play a role. The historical links of India with the English-speaking tradition has facilitated exchanges of people and knowledge so India has thus become a natural place for large-scale outsourcing. In continental Europe, similar trends are continued by some multinationals, but generally a lack of common behaviours still predominates. European enlargement will bring new opportunities for concentration of the offshoring process inside Europe. The new member states are already exporting services based on cheaper jobs – lower wages – to current member countries, within a relatively close cultural and social framework. They are already starting becoming a reference for international outsourcing in Europe. The new countries could assume a role similar to that played by India, Mexico, Brazil or Malaysia. The competitiveness of countries like Hungary or the Czech Republic in the offshoring of information technology services has already awakened the interest of stakeholders and researchers (see Stare and Rubalcaba, 2005).

The A.T. Kearney Report gives an attractiveness index for IT offshoring.[10] The leading countries according to the index are (from the best performance): India, Canada, Brazil, Mexico, Philippines, Hungary, Ireland, the Czech Republic, Russia, and China. The presence of Canada and Mexico, close to the US, among this list of countries suggests that something similar can be extrapolated to many or most of the new EU Member States. German firms send roughly 60 per cent of their 'offshore' work to Eastern Europe, and only 40 per cent to India, even if in Indian services are 20 per cent cheaper. Another recent classification from a McKinsey study also includes the new Member States among the country players in the offshoring world. Most European offshoring projects remain on the European continent (UNCTAD-Roland Berger, 2003), while India and Ireland become the dominant producer countries in BPO and IT offshored services with impressive world shares of 12.2 per cent and 8.6 per cent respectively (McKinsey Global Institute, 2005).

An OECD study estimated an annual growth after 2001 of 20 per cent in ICT services outsourcing. In the same study it is highlighted how the higher rates of growth of the phenomenon are expected in sectors such as finance and accounting, market research, administrative and corporate services. The role of differences in wages and labour costs as the main explanatory driver cannot be neglected. 'A body called Accountants in India recently estimated that a qualified bookkeeper or entry-level staff member in the US cost about \$30 an hour, including all the overheads (employee benefits, computers, office space, continuing education and so on). Experienced accountants got 50 per cent more. In contrast, a qualified, college graduate accountant, trained in standard business management applications could be hired for about \$8 an hour in India' (Robert, 2004). There are however other important reasons explaining offshoring, in particular in India, where the offshoring of R&D services cannot be explained by reduced costs alone.

Recent evidence is pointing out the difficulties and increasing limitations of some offshoring activities. The return of some services home started with Dell in January 2003 when the company brought back some tech support services (T. Krazit, *Network World,* 12 January 2003) after corporate customers complained about the quality of service they were receiving from workers in other countries. An article published by A. Bednarz, 'The downside of offshoring' (*Network World,* 7 May 2004) stressed that poor communication, cultural differences and lack of expertise can derail engagements: 'What's the big deal? Unrealistic expectations about cost savings, loss of control over intellectual property and management gaps are among the issues that can derail an offshore outsourcing project'. From the same article we acknowledge that even if the expectations of the economic actors are leaning towards an increase in their use of outsourcing, the other side of the coin shows a high number (21 per cent of the interviewed) of companies prematurely terminating an offshore arrangement. The most common causes behind this *back home* phenomenon relate to the difficult relationships with the provider.

The supposed cost-saving is not always a reality for firms as in some cases the effort required to transfer the knowledge, at technical and managerial level, leads to a loss in productivity in the first year up to 20 per cent. This evidence is not in contradiction with the fact that, according to the UNCTAD-Roland Berger sample of 500 European companies, 8 per cent with experience of offshoring are satisfied with the results, reporting cost savings in the range of 20 per cent to 40 per cent.

The increasing business evidence limiting offshoring to certain services, under certain conditions to certain countries is confirmed by recent Eurostat data on international trade. There is not a net import position of EU15 to Asia either in ICT services or in most other services. The India case for ICT, where most of the offshoring processes have taken place, is more an exception than a rule.

Taking into consideration data on international trade of services, the positive coverage rate of EU15 ICT services international trade can be noticed in all major commercial areas, even in the US (after 2002), except in India, where the difference between small exports and huge imports is impressive (limited but increasing cover rate of 0.32 in 2003). In new member states service exports to the EU15 are more important than imports but this is not the case for ICT and other business services where EU15 exports dominate and grow at very high rates (Table 6.6). The growth of Indian exports of ICT services has been very important during recent years (1996–2005) but its imports from the EU are increasing as well. In the shorter period 2001–2005 growth of EU15 exports has been more intense than imports, even in countries such as India or the new member states, mainly in ICT and other business services. In India a certain shift is registered from ICT exports to other business services exports.

In any case, the figures are still very limited comparing the total trade of ICT services intra and extra-Europe. Off-shoring and outsourcing to/from Asian and other countries are a very important and increasing phenomenon but it is necessary to go beyond the myth and consider the still limited magnitude.

Table 6.6 Data on international trade of total services, ICT and other business services from EU15 to other major partners. Growth rates (%) 1996–2005 and 2001–2005

	Partner								
	Intra-EU15	Ext-EU15	NMS*	US	Asia	Hong Kong	Japan	India	World
Total services GR 1996–05									
Exports	7.6	8.1		6.6	7.9		3.9	11.3	7.8
Imports	7.2	7.5		6.3	7.2		5.2	11.6	7.3
ICT services GR 1996–05									
Exports	22.7	18.6		16.2	23.8		19.2	34.8	20.9
Imports	14.8	12.2		11.1	16.8		13.2	34.2	13.8
Other business services GR 1996–05									
Exports	8.1	10.4		8.5	10.1		8.7	13.3	9.2
Imports	9.7	8.8		10.6	7.5		6.3	12.2	9.3
Total services GR 2001–05									
Exports	4.9	5.9	14.0	0.5	8.9	13.9	1.3	16.6	5.3
Imports	3.9	3.4	5.2	-1.5	5.2	4.4	0.6	11.2	3.6
ICT services GR 2001–05									
Exports	10.9	7.9	22.5	8.5	8.7	1.8	-0.5	29.7	9.7
Imports	7.2	2.4	-2.2	-0.7	2.3	-25.3	-1.0	5.1	5.4
Other business services GR 2001–05									
Exports	4.1	8.9	9.1	-0.9	15.9	30.4	11.9	30.4	6.4
Imports	4.7	2.3	6.0	-0.3	3.9	1.1	0.5	15.8	3.7

Notes: * Includes Czech Republic, Estonia, Latvia, Lithuania and Hungary. Data refer to the period 2001–2003.

Source: Based on international trade statistics, Eurostat, New Cronos, 2007.

6.   DISCUSSION ON GLOBALIZATION, OFFSHORING AND POLICY IMPLICATIONS

Because of its magnitude, the globalization phenomenon is not immune from political reactions. The delocalization of the production in particular had been, and still is, at the centre of the political debate with different contributions sustaining the multiple points of view. The most protectionist positions, adopted by some politicians in some countries, seem to suggest that the migration of manufacturing and services jobs to other countries represents an evil in itself that must be avoided by the strengthening of borders and reviving traditional industrial policy. This position contrasts with economic theory that has demonstrated in very diverse ways that trade and specialization are at the origin of the wealth of nations; it is senseless to prevent what is the natural course of events. The migration of services outside Europe or the United States results initially in an employment loss that, on the other hand, tends to be compensated by greater effectiveness and the lower prices of the service provision. The benefits should serve to generate other new services jobs, probably better paid and more specialized. The more advanced countries desire, as benefits from outsourcing processes, to contribute to replacing manual manufacturing or services activities (blue collar) with the more qualified activities (white collar) where labour conditions are better. The benefits derived from replacing a part of traditional industry by services – at the same time, the remaining industry has become more competitive – can also be replicated within the services sector. As has been indicated by most experts on industrial delocalization, this is not a problem in itself. The only major problem is the capacity to move resources towards specialization strategies, towards new activities, whether industrial or services.

Besides the advantages derived from each country's specialization, offshoring reports direct benefits for both the host and provider countries. In the first case, the advantages are clear (employment, income, wealth, tax collection) but in the second, it is important not to underestimate the effects of cost reduction by contracting companies, exports generated by the new needs coming from companies abroad and the transfer of incomes and profits by those national companies in foreign countries.

The debate on whether the offshoring of services to low-cost countries is good or bad for an advanced economy such as Europe's leads to the question of what are the advantages and economic and policy implications for service globalization. Globalization means, among other things, four major changes: more competition (international competition in particular), more available markets (the world becomes the target market both from the provision of resources and from the sales points of view), more movement of resources (more transfer of workers, technology, knowledge) and finally more interrelations with ICT in order to procure a global provision of services or a global organization of service enterprises.

As a result of globalization, enterprises develop new competitive advantages which contribute to reinforcing globalization trends. Companies can be more productive, by obtaining a better ratio between outcome and income. For example, companies develop more economies of scale or scope when they operate at a larger scale. In general, price reductions resulting from globalization are significant, and that is always a way to become more competitive, even if prices in services competition do not have the same strategic role as in goods competition. In services, to offer a wider range of services or to increase the quality of services can provide a greater competitive impact.

Other macroeconomic advantages spring from these points. Globalization of service activities brings new employment in those areas and sectors that are competitive, and promotes migration of services jobs from those countries or sectors that are not very competitive. The employment balance between new jobs and migration of jobs should be considered as an indicator of competitiveness, but in any event, a change in specialization should always be possible to counterbalance the negative effects of off-shoring. Otherwise, a related-market failure (e.g., skills shortages) or a related-state failure (e.g., rigid labour regulations) would require policy actions.

Globalization of services should also bring lower prices and therefore, less inflationary pressures, especially in more standardized services. This factor is becoming a driver of trade and investment throughout the major commercial areas of the world. All these effects are also combined with new regional dynamics. Globalization produces a twofold effect at geographical level: a further concentration in those countries, regions or cities which are already the leaders of the service economy – reputation breeds reputation, from the geographical point of view too – and trends towards decentralization, mainly towards low-cost countries, regions or cities, in standardized services (delocalization or offshoring). In doing so, new geographical areas can emerge as new competitors in some service sectors, although this fact does not yet threaten the dominant positions of leading areas since forces towards concentration are still too strong.

As a consequence of these impacts, globalization of services should lead to productivity and competitiveness gains all over the world, having an impact on economic growth and economic development.[11] The advantages are to a certain extent based on international trade theory and comparative advantage. The studies carried out using economic theory apply different models to producer services, based on the applicability of the theories on trade in services.[12] The traditional models for international trade, based on the relative comparative advantage theory and Heckscher-Ohlin-Samuelson type, explain that a country will specialize in products for which it has a relative abundance of positive factors. Exchanges will enhance the production and consumption possibilities of the countries through the access to goods or services produced in relatively favourable framework conditions. The cost and intensity of factors are the two parameters that explain trade and specialization. It can be supposed that business services follow this logic when they are intensive in capital (leasing), or highly qualified workforce (knowledge-intensive services), or in low-skilled workers (operational services). Production can be expected to be located in countries that provide the production factor with greatest endowment, in that they are more intensive, creating trade with other countries. In spite of the generic validity of this argument, the classical models have been criticized because of the unrealistic nature of a number of the suppositions and the co-existence of trends towards both specialization and despecialization (Landesmann and Petit, 1995).[13]

This is not the place to survey deeper into the abundant literature on the advantages and disadvantages of globalization.[14] What this chapter wanted to stress so far is a twofold summary of the aforementioned ideas that on the one hand the impacts of globalization and internationalization of service activities are positive in many respects. New opportunities are created for dynamic service companies, dynamic regions and dynamic countries bringing a further boost of productivity and employment growth rates. Even when projections indicate the migration of millions of jobs to low-wage countries, what these projections do not take into account is that, for example, globalization of software and IT services, in conjunction with diffusion of IT to new sectors and business, will yield even stronger job demand in developed economies for IT-proficient workers (Mann, 2003). There are no reasons to fear liberalization of services trading when goals and instruments are clear (see Cuadrado, Rubalcaba and Bryson, 2002). On the other hand it has to be borne in mind that sometimes it is not easy to take advantages of new challenges such as changing of specialization patterns when delocalization or off-shoring trends happen. Some market failures in the free provision of services are the results of state failures, normally translated into protectionist measures. For this reason, it is necessary to promote both the liberalization of service activities and the provision of complementary policy measures that can both limit the negative effects and achieve the most from the new competitive challenges.

The economic and business advantages of international trade in business services, acknowledged in most studies, should be evaluated considering that it is necessary to clarify several points:

1. The effects of internationalization cannot be generalized in all sectors and regions. The different activities and sectors are affected differently according to their specific conditions, maturity, degree of present concentration, growth dynamism, etc. Equally, the effects on countries, regions or cities are necessarily different. Trade in services raises many new issues because of their strong contribution to regional development in uneven scales and concentration patterns (e.g. Daniels, 1993; Daniels and Moulaert, 1991; Illeris, 1996; Beyers, 2005; Leo and Philippe, 2005; Bryson et al., 2004).

2. The framework conditions in a given region or country are very important in getting the most out of globalization. According to the study from the McKinsey Global Institute, 'every dollar of corporate spending shifted offshore by an American firm-mostly, now, to India-generates $1.13 in new wealth for America's economy. However, when a German firm moves a euro to a cheaper place to buy services, its home economy is on average 20 cents worse off' (*The Economist*, 15th July 2004). One of the key reasons for such substantial difference is found in labour markets: 'In America, McKinsey estimates that around 70 per cent of workers ousted in favour of offshore alternatives find new work within six months. In Germany, however, the re-employment rate is only around 40 per cent.

The reason? Above all, Germany's thicket of labour laws, which discourages firms from hiring workers who may prove a hard-to-shed liability. Admittedly, these same laws – which are increasingly under fire – also make it harder for German firms to shed workers to take advantage of efficiency-enhancing offshoring. The lesson: offshoring may be an easy target for politicians, but if they have flexible labour markets it may actually be a good thing, not just for big firms, but for everyone'. As stated in a recent report for Germany (Farrell, 2004), 'Germany's political leaders should view offshoring not as an economic threat but as an important opportunity for the nation's businesses, consumers, and shareholders'.

3. All the positive effects are attenuated by the following secondary effects: there are extremely narrow and weak markets that diminish the effects of internationalization; the pressures of competition can have a negative influence on specific places where there is no comparative advantage; etc.

4. The changes in specialization or in the provision of competitive advantages are not possible on some occasions due to the market forces, registering some policy complementary to those of market liberalization and international trade being required (Chapter 10).

5. Not all countries react in the same way when faced with the advantages of the liberalization of the international trade of services and some associate the GATS negotiations with goods negotiations.

GATS Negotiations

The General Agreement on Trade in Services (GATS) is at the same time the service economy globalization framework and a driver for its development. After almost fifty years since the first multilateral trade agreements on goods, WTO members decided to support the world service trade expansion through the settlement of an agreement based on transparency and a progressive liberalization of the sector. The GATS is an achievement of the Uruguay Round of trade negotiations (1986–1993) and went into effect in 1995. The reason why the agreement took so long to be signed, with respect to the General Agreement on Tariffs and Trade (GATT), has to be found, once more, in the particular features of service trade and in the high range of activities classified within this category. Up to the 1990s most of the services that nowadays are provided worldwide, were traditionally considered domestic activities (hotels and restaurants, personal services, and so on) or directly related to the fulfilment of the obligations governments have towards their citizens (health services, telecommunications, transport, and so on). Furthermore natural monopolies, due to the high fixed establishment costs and to the strategic relevance some service has within modern economies, existed in most of these activities. Therefore the weakness of the service international trade is not surprising at all. The rapid technological evolution affecting some services and their commercialization, the fact that some of them are not in a position of natural monopoly anymore, the delay of the public sector with respect to the necessities of dynamism of many sectors and of the population, sharply increased international transactions and evidenced the need of an international framework in this field.

In order to adapt its structure to the several forms undertaken by the internationalization within the sector, the agreement classifies service trade under four different forms. In addition to international trade, this four-pronged definition includes consumption abroad, commercial presence and natural person movement. As stated before, the GATS scope is to drive international trade expansion through the application of the transparency principle and a progressive liberalization. The principle affirms the idea that low levels of uncertainty are a favourable endowment for trade. It is for this reason that signatories committed to make public all the changes in regulations that could affect international commerce. It has to be noticed that GATS explicitly affirms the intention of not influencing governments' decisions about regulation or regulation changes planned to meet policy objectives or particular needs. In fact, due to the importance of the sector and the relevance of the regulations, any rule affecting the existing frameworks would mean the self-destruction of the agreement that, anyway, evidences the key role played by national regulations in the internationalization of the sector. The second pillar consists in signatories' obligation to take part in successive rounds of negotiations with the intention of promoting a progressive liberalization toward the service internationalization. This process will pass through a greater market inclination toward services produced in foreign countries and toward the establishment of foreign providers in national markets.

Despite the existence of sector specific or country specific exceptions, the GATS covers all the measures affecting services exchange. This means that all kinds of law, regulation or procedure operating at international, national or local level carry on with the obligations signed in the agreement. The mentioned measures regard all kinds of services, which had been classified in 12 core sectors further subdivided into 160 sub-categories, with the only exception of the provision of services in the exercise of governmental authority (public administration, security, etc.). Restrictions also affect services directly related to air transport.

In addition to the transparency principle and to the obligation of intervention when discriminations in service provision and market accession occur, one of the central tools of the agreement is the most-favoured-nation (MFN) principle. This concept had been developed within the international goods trade, in order to avoid power-based distortions between countries with different international weight. It often occurs that an economically strong country achieves favourable conditions in bilateral agreements because of disparities in contractual power, and that these conditions could not be reached by single 'minor' countries. Under the MFN principle, conditions conceded to one country are automatically extended to all the other commercial partners.

The GATS implies the WTO obligations to control national legislations on service trade, to create a working group with the aim of presenting recommendations on requirements and procedure for the homologation of professional qualifications and technical standards and the setting of international disputes.

The increasing volumes of international service trade and the way in which globalization has been affecting the tertiary sector in recent years have been endorsed by the GATS. Anyway the agreement has to be considered a first step toward the creation of a complete legal framework in international commercial law. According to plans, more negotiations started after the date the agreement took effect. Nonetheless progress over the last years in this kind of settlement has been slow and spasmodic. After the failure of the Seattle ministerial conference of 1999 the greatest improvement was reached by including in the Doha Agenda of 2001 an agreement to open new negotiations on services. As will also be seen later when discussing the European single market for services, the international accord on such an important issue in terms of employment and value added is always a long process that has to concern many connected interests and is therefore difficult.

7. CONCLUDING REMARKS

Five main challenges have been stated in this chapter:

1. Services are not just receivers of globalization outputs, but also their active agents. Business services and consumer services promote the current globalization wave and its effects, shortening distances, supporting activities regarding business internationalization, making the diffusion of international consumption and leisure products possible. In particular, advanced business services intervene in key domains, orienting the global strategy of companies. Europe requires competitive services in order to become a strong player on the international scene.
2. The globalization of services is understood from a multidimensional perspective, where cross-border trade has a lower position compared to direct investment and other ways of globalization. Due to the nature of services, and despite the emergence of ICT, which has led to more tradable services than one decade ago, there are still limits to the traditional goods internationalization. Artificial barriers to the services trade also play their part. In all respects, the present trends seem to indicate growing complementarity among service globalization methods with differences by sector type.
3. Comparing the situation of the European Union with the other two economic world powers, United States and Japan, the panorama presents lights and shades. In total volumes, the European position is clearly

positive in the majority of services. As regards to the growth of services exports during the period 1996–2003, the goods rate in Europe is outstanding, although a certain distance from the United States' rate comes into view. Taking into consideration that the coverage rate of the United States is higher than the European one, and that its goods deficit does not show clear moderate indications, it is very probable that the North American privileged situation will persist, or even grow, in the future. The main challenges seem to exist in those services related to ICT, knowledge society and royalties, while the European strengths are in financial and insurance services. In any case, the North American coverage rate in services shows a decreasing trend, thanks to the vigorous development of importation and to the new emerging countries. This means an opportunity for Europe in the sense that it could provide a larger future trajectory to its exports, although it could also be seen as a threat. The presence of services is lower than goods regarding multinationals, although the number of large firms in Europe and the United States is similar. However, the stock-exchange values of the ones in America are considerably higher than of those in Europe, and there are some sectors with significant European absence.

4. While treating the globalization phenomenon particular attention has to be devoted to global sourcing processes and service offshoring in particular. The increasing role of some Asian locations providing both qualified and low-skilled business services is a matter of concern to business men and politicians in Europe. Services could eventually follow the delocalization path initiated by manufacturing firms some decades ago. However, the advantages of offshoring processes are important both for importers and exporters of these services. The point is that countries such as the Member States of the European Union should be ready to specialize in those new sectors in which they can offer competitive advantages. Re-specialization processes will have to take place also within the service sectors and within business services. These offshoring trends are mainly explained by lower costs in low-wages countries, although other additional reasons do exist. For example, R&D services in India offer high quality in addition to cheap services. Even if current statistical evidence shows that offshoring processes are limited to certain sectors and certain areas, current trends call for action. Europe has to look for the framework conditions in which services can operate in a competitive way. European countries will have to provide high levels of quality and specialization although some of them can also be competitive by providing services at lower relative costs. The present situation is not static and the dynamism of the EU25 business services, supported by improved framework conditions, holds the key to a more competitive Europe. The outstanding cases of Ireland and some new EU members such as the Baltic States are important, although they are rather exceptional within the group of 25. Recent works (van Welsum and Reif, 2006) show that the potential employment affected by offshoring (20 per cent of the OECD countries) is not negatively correlated to the

importance of business services, but in a positive way to the exports of those services, which reinforces the positive aspects of the phenomenon.

5. There is no doubt about the advantages of the internationalization of services, even if some re-assignment processes have to be developed. The globalization of services produces both macroeconomic effects and business and microeconomic effects. Based on traditional and new theories on international trade, it is possible to identify gains in productivity, employment, prices, innovation and economic growth. Policy implications are derived since barriers between markets should be reduced to a minimum-represented by the efforts to create an internal market for services and the GATS negotiations. Complementary policy measures are necessary to cope with existing market failures, e.g., innovation, skills – and to guarantee equal opportunities for all enterprises, SMEs and less developed regions in particular. All these policies will be covered in the policy chapters presented in Chapters 8, 9 and 10.

NOTES

1. 3.3 million of white-collar for 2015 and half a million of information technology according to *The Economist*, 2003; more recently, 20 per cent of total employment is potentially affected by this event (van Welsum and Vickery, 2005).
2. Competitiveness has been defined and analysed in previous works in a broader and more specific economic sense (Rubalcaba, 2002), and also from a stricter commercial point of view, directly related to costs and prices, which could be called 'competitive position' and derives from other kinds of approaches (Rubalcaba and Gago, 2001).
3. International organizations use the classification of 4 modes of international trade defined by the WTO: Mode 1, cross-border supply; Mode 2, consumption abroad; Mode 3, commercial presence; Mode 4, presence of natural persons.
4. Stefano Visintin has participated in the drafting of this section as co-author.
5. All commercial services except for travel and transportation, where most of them are business services.
6. Give Roberts and Edward Shines (2003) 'Service industries go global: how high-wage professional jobs are migrating to low-cost countries'.
7. Another example is provided by the business sector process outsourcing (BPO) employing 200 000 people. It must be emphasized that this, without being a large figure, has grown rapidly in few years and has great prospects for future growth. The link between the migration of business services and the world of financial services is clear. Banking and insurance have been at the forefront of the complex outsourcing processes in human resources and information technologies. The financial world has been the preferred client of the BPO outsourcers. The reduction in costs has been the leitmotif for its contracting in countries like India.
8. 'Offshoring: Relocating the back office' *The Economist*, 11th December, 2003.
9. The case of India is rather special, with several active cities sharing the leading role. Bangalore is India's premier international trade location but has seen double-digit wage rate increases in recent years; as a result Hyderabad and Chennai (Madras) are emerging as service provider cities. Rated above Bangalore as the city

of choice for service offshoring, Delhi and its local government are focusing on developing quickly. Mumbai also has some important services, but costs and pollution are high.

10. Reported in *The Economist*, 'The Geography of the IT Industry', 11th July, 2003.

11. From the macroeconomic point of view, a wide set of interrelations between service trade and competitiveness can be found in a previous work (Rubalcaba and Gago, 2001).

12. This is based on a previous contribution (Rubalcaba, 1999). A true examination of these studies is beyond the scope of this work. Studies that have sought to apply economic models to trade in services are, for example, Landesmann and Petit (1995), Dearforff (1985), Bhagwati (1987), Sapir and Lutz (1981), UNCTAD (1989) and Markusen (2005).

13. Markusen (1989) indicated the application difficulties in a market with few competitive characteristics. His recent model (2005) on white-collar offshoring proposes some simulation models to clarify existing ambiguity in the area and approach the gains of trade for different countries. Nusbaumer (1987a, b) highlighted how the supposition of available technology runs counter to the objective of many services, based precisely on the non-availability of technology. Melvin (1989) and François (1993) pointed to the difficulties of the supposition of mobility of factors at an international level, stressed the need of reinterpreting the traditional models, and came to the conclusion that liberalization is beneficial for the gains in specialization derived from trade. This can be confirmed by the specialization of large multinationals that have benefited from the mobility of people and a degree of standardization of the service (Aharoni, 1993). In this way, the growth and specialization of hotel chains, American Express and airline companies can be explained, as can, to a certain extent, Accenture's specialization in integrating systems, McKinsey's in management or BCG in strategy. Trade, specialization and comparative advantages are all terms that are closely linked. For firms, these advantages can be translated into (Daniels, 1993): production of market-cost specialized knowledge, development of scale or scope economies, maintaining of highly specialized staff, reinforcement of corporate identity and reputation, and variations in the access to inputs and markets.

14. Among the many works on globalization those by Joseph Stiglitz (2002), *Globalization and Its Discontents* (New York: Norton) and J. Bhagwati (2004), *In Defence of Globalization* Oxford University Press are recommended. About the differences between international competitiveness in business and competitiveness in nations the works of Krugman (e.g., 1996) are important in a conceptual framework where changes in specialization are possible and advantage of changes in relative comparative advantages are recognized.

PART III

Policy Implications and Service-Related Policies in the European Union

7. The regulation of services and its reform[1]

INTRODUCTION

Public intervention in the economic field, within the context of market economies, has oscillated throughout history and, since the end of the 1970s, has entered a pro-market stage. Due to its geographical extension, many authors consider this stage to be a turning or even a breaking point.

From a theoretical point of view, the neoclassical hypothesis of market failures has been the greatest exponent of the presence of the public sector in the economic activity. This hypothesis justifies public intervention in the market system, which alone is unable to reach a Pareto-efficient equilibrium. Such inability is the consequence of certain phenomena, including the presence of public goods and services, externalities, asymmetric information, and natural monopolies. However, within the framework of the current global economy, new market failures that affect companies related to advanced technologies and network services, such as network economies, have arisen.

Empirical analyses, however, have demonstrated that market failure theory only provides a partial explanation for the generalization of the state, and regional or local intervention in certain historical periods (such as in the years following the end of the Second World War). This statement has led to the development of theories that can be considered complementary. The joint interpretation of these theories has justified to a greater extent the presence of regulation and public companies, which are recurrent models of public intervention in market economies.

Regarding regulation, its main objective is to guarantee a production level that is socially desirable when the market mechanism is unable to achieve it alone. For this purpose, regulatory authorities adopt control measures for different variables, mainly prices (with methods such as regulation according to rate of profit, CPI-X, etc.), quality (usually by the establishment of minimum standards and issuing of quality certificates), protection and promotion of competition, and, to a lesser extent, investment-related aspects.

In recent decades (since the end of the 1960s), the economic role of the public sector has been reinterpreted within the context of so-called regulatory reform, based on three essential concepts: de-regulation, re-regulation and privatization.

From the sectorial perspective and since late-1970s, industrial activities have been the first to be affected by regulatory reform in the leading countries (the United Kingdom and the United States). However, the services sector, which to a large extent was traditionally protected from internal and international competition, has also been subject to a process of regulatory reform. This is due to the fact that the evolution of the activities included within their framework directly determines economic competitiveness, given the high percentage over total activity, and indirectly, by means of their increasing association with the industrial sector.

Generally speaking, an improvement has been observed in terms of productivity and welfare in those countries that have tackled regulatory reform, although identifying the effects that result from those changes is not always easy. In this respect, European legislation aims to ensure that EU companies are competitive, and that their structural policies commit to a simplified regulation for the promotion of growth and employment creation. Ultimately, European legislation aims for sustainable development by supporting the objectives established by the Lisbon Strategy for 2010. Initially, the simplification processes have been applied to priority industrial activities, but the intention of the Commission is to extend these to the services sector.

This chapter is structured as follows. Firstly, the reasons justifying regulation are set out from a theoretical perspective. Special reference will be made to tertiary activities, as well as to the reasons behind the reform process, which has resulted in the reduction and re-interpretation of markets. Secondly, the predicted consequences of this process will be established. Thirdly, on the basis of data provided by the OECD, an analysis of the evolution and current situation of regulation in the services market will be carried out. Fourthly, this chapter will test the hypothesis that a higher level of regulation is normally accompanied by a lower level of efficiency and a lower increase over time. Finally, the EU policies toward better and more efficient regulations are presented.

1.   ANALYTICAL FRAMEWORK OF SERVICES REGULATION

In this first section, the basic concepts, typology and explanatory factors that justify services regulation will be described. To begin with, some brief basic definitions will be provided. The term 'regulation' can have several meanings that, despite their differences, all highlight its role as a regulatory activity (of an economic or administrative nature) carried out by a government or its regulatory agencies with the aim of establishing and enforcing an action framework for the economic agents in order to improve the efficiency of the allocation of resources or pursue criteria of social justice or equity. As established by the OECD (Conway et al., 2005), regulation is perhaps the most pervasive and dominant form of state intervention in economic activity.

De-regulation, in turn, includes the disappearance of inefficient regulations in the market, namely those regulations which constitute a burden, either because they are obsolete or because they are technically inappropriate, due to their generation of costs that are higher than the achieved social benefits. However, de-regulation does not refer to the total disappearance of public rules defining the context in which economic activity develops (structural regulations) or that define the behaviour of the economic agents that participate in the market (conduct regulations).

In fact, efficient regulations are not the only ones that remain; new regulations also appear in the context of re-regulation. In practice, the new economic situation requires a new regulation by which the public sector will try to achieve efficiency, and will intervene exclusively in those cases where it is strictly necessary. This regulatory activity tends to concentrate on aspects such as consumer protection, health, physical security, access to basic goods and services, the environment and, especially, competition policy. In fact, according to the OECD, the main aspect of the regulatory reform in recent years has been the introduction of competition in markets.

Finally, the term 'liberalization' refers to the rationalization of the effective regulation present in the market. This does not necessarily imply the total elimination of regulations, but their re-interpretation with the aim of keeping the efficiency of those remaining in the market, thus improving their previous situation. Consequently, the liberalization process includes both de-regulation and re-regulation.

Table 7.1 Types of regulation

Category	Types of regulation	Examples
	Ownership	
		▪ Public companies / private companies ▪ Ownership restrictions (participation, foreign investors, etc)
Structural regulations	Entry regulations and the right to carry out activities	▪ Competition policy ▪ Regulation of private monopolies ▪ Contracting-out monopoly to the private sector ▪ Corporatized public monopoly ▪ Public monopoly
Conduct regulations	Establishment of incentives in the market by regulatory agents	▪ Ownership rights ▪ Price fixing ▪ Establishment of services standards and rules ▪ Information improvement
	Command-and-control regulation	
	Process regulation	▪ Requirements to companies for risk taking

Market regulation has been characterized by its remarkable variety. Consistent classification attempts exist throughout the economic literature, including those provided by the OECD, the United Nations and various authors. Table 7.1 gathers some of these contributions (e.g., OECD, 2002d) and determines a regulation typology.

What justifies the growth of regulations in advanced economies? More specifically, what justifies services regulation? The starting point for answering these questions is the model of perfect competition, which holds that, given an income distribution, competition leads to the highest possible level of social welfare. However, this situation represents an exception rather than the norm in economic practice: the presence of a series of economic factors, which condition market efficiency (market failures), issues related to equity that justify public intervention, or political and institutional factors.

Firstly, economic factors will be considered. Situations in which the market does not operate appropriately, thus generating inefficiency, are especially evident in the case of tertiary activities when a series of failures arises:

1. *Existence of public goods and services.* Within this group of products, the so-called social goods and preferential goods can be distinguished.

- *Social goods and services* (more generally known as 'public goods') are joint-supply and non-price excludable goods. Justice and defence services, for example, traditionally have been considered to be included within the category of public services. The general feature of these services is that private provision is lower than that which is socially desirable (as a consequence of the presence of free riders), so the public sector has normally been in charge of their provision (although not necessarily of their direct production). Basic services provided by public administration represent the most evident example in this area. In a context where, of late, international relations have gained a great importance in the so-called globalization process (manifested by growing trade, foreign direct investment and capital movements), even the existence of global public goods – whose scope gives them a universal nature – has been considered.
- In contrast, *preferential goods or services* fulfil, at least partially, the characteristics of private goods, although citizens exhibit irrational behaviour with respect to their demand. This is the case of services such as education, where it is estimated that citizens are not sufficiently aware of the positive effects generated in the medium and long term. Therefore, demand tends to be lower than is socially desirable; as a consequence, the public sector establishes a minimum regulation.

2. *Externalities.* When there are external effects, the utility or *production* function depends not only on elements which can be directly *controlled* by the consumer or provider, but also on other factors out of this direct

control. In the case of airports, for example, the delivery of airport services generates negative externalities related to atmospheric or noise pollution, but can also generate positive externalities to the extent that the presence of an airport is a strong attraction for the establishment of surrounding business centres.

It seems logical to think of the role of the public sector, when there is an externality, in creating and guaranteeing a system of property rights, enabling the agents to internalize the externalities generated, and thus maximizing the profits obtained (Coase, 1960). However, the conditions required are sometimes highly restrictive and very difficult to achieve in practice, hence alternative strategies are set out. Cullis and Jones (1987) suggest some possible alternatives: fiscal action or establishment of a tax in the case of negative externalities; regulation; subsidies to those affected or to those generating the effect so that they reduce – or promote, in the case of positive externalities – production or use alternative methods to control the externality in question; and also the direct production of the goods or services generating the externality in the public sector.

In the case of business services, Kox and Rubalcaba (2007a) analysed the effects of social externalities. External effects arise when transactions between suppliers and buyers of business services have welfare effects for other producers or consumers that are not taken into account by the transaction partners. External effects are not reflected in the costs and prices of the business-services products. As a consequence, the market price for the delivered service is – from the social perspective – either too high or too low. The following section will first mention some branch-specific externalities, and then discuss more general externalities, whether positive or negative.

Intervention in markets for a number of knowledge-intensive business-services products has long been based on the social externalities that go along with these services. Specific examples of such services and the social externalities involved are:

- Accountancy: safeguards reliable financial information, which is essential for trust in capital markets and the financial system as a whole;
- Legal services (lawyers, notaries): upholds the legitimacy of the constitutional state and the legal system;
- Engineering: safeguards the liability of technical systems;
- Architects: upholds the amenity value of the urban environment, and the quality and aesthetic value of housing and other buildings.

3. *Natural monopoly.* A natural monopoly arises where production minimizes costs when concentrated in a single company. Therefore, it is more profitable that the whole market demand is satisfied by a single company than shared among several competitors. In other words, the

natural monopoly is defined as the industry in which the cost function is sub-additive.

However, as Baldwin and Cave (1999) indicate, the determination of an activity area as natural monopoly is an extremely complex process. Moreover, a situation of natural monopoly can be altered over time, when some changes occur in demand or technology, and are reflected in production and cost functions. By its nature, when a natural monopoly is controlled by a private company, it will produce a lower quantity than the social optimum and at a higher price than is competitive. The benefit to consumers will therefore be reduced (which will be superior to the total production cost, regardless of whether production is attractive to the private company), resulting in incentives for the intervention of the public sector, responsible for the provision of the goods under the most favourable conditions for consumers.

Network services have traditionally been the paradigmatic examples of natural monopolies. However, technological advances and variation of demand have caused a change in the market situation, which, alongside the verification of a lower efficiency in those situations where market power exists, has led to a re-definition of those markets.

4. *Asymmetric or imperfect information.* Those agents participating in the market do not have access to the same information, so the negotiating role in the exchange process is uneven. The most generalized problems in this field are known as adverse selection and moral hazard. In some professions, such as medicine and law, attempts have been made to find a solution to the difficulties generated by adverse selection through obligatory obtainment of certificates or licences, which enables customers to receive a minimum level of information about providers. The most recurrent example of moral hazard is found precisely in the services sector (where this market failure is more common), in the market of vehicle insurance. Coverage of car accident risk can result in a less preventive attitude of policyholders. Therefore, the average accident rate of the population insured is higher than the average of total population. The methods used in this field to increase and homogenize the existing information for all market participants are essentially concentrated in the requirement of certifications, licences, product standardization, etc.

5. From the perspective of equity, the provision of the so–called 'universal services' or 'services of general interest' is suggested. These are essential services to the extent that they provide security, equal opportunities, or respond to other 'social responsibilities', guaranteeing their access by low-income citizens. In such cases, the public sector is responsible for the provision of these services, whose characteristics (large highly–specific investments, scale, scope and density economies, mass consumption, high politicization and little supplying agents) prevent the market from becoming the most appropriate allocation method. According to the EU Green Book on Services of General Interest, this concept covers 'a broad range of different types of activities, from certain activities in the big

network industries (...) to health, education and social services'. These are the basic needs of population, to which an access must be guaranteed under favourable conditions.

Apart from these economic factors, other political factors can explain regulation – although the political and economic aspects are not entirely independent. The aforementioned basically prevents the application of the so-called public interest theory. This is clearly insufficient to explain the important regulatory generalization that occurred after the Second World War, despite the general perspective from which the concept can be defined, especially on the European continent. Other parallel theories related to private interest have been alleged (within the framework of Public Choice or the economic theory of regulation and rent seekers). Moreover, institutionalist theories provide other factors that determine regulation, based on the existence of social and institutional conditions that affect the behaviour of economic agents. Systemic failures also provide powerful arguments for service-related policies and related regulations due to lack of service-friendly innovative systems, financial shortages, or institutional asymmetries at regional level. In conclusion, the joint consideration of the previous arguments, which to a large extent are complementary, explains the recent regulatory trends.

2. STRUCTURAL AND REGULATORY REFORMS: FACILITATING FORCES

Towards the end of the 1970s, the public sector witnessed a dramatic change in the interpretation of the need for intervention in the economy that resulted in a more prominent market. The main objective of structural policies, as generalized from an international (irrespective of the governing political party in power) and sectoral perspective, has been the minimization of public intervention in order to reduce the negative effects generated by the excess of regulation. The trigger of this reform is a combination of a series of factors usually considered as determinant to the regulation policy (Baldwin and Cave, 1999). In this case, they introduce pressures towards changes in favour of a higher liberalism, as shown in Table 7.2.

Usually, consideration of only one of these six factors is not enough to explain the change of direction of regulations. Hence, it will be necessary to consider them jointly in order to achieve a satisfactory explanation. The relevance of each factor varies according to the countries' characteristics. For example, when considering Spain, the international factor or the changes in the economic context are particularly significant in a context of political-institutional change and integration of the Spanish economy in supranational organizations.

Table 7.2 The driving forces of the regulatory reform

Force	Description
1. 'Force of the ideas'	Predominance of neoliberal ideas (Friedman, Hayek, Peacock, etc.)
2. Pressure of particular interests	Disappearance/simplification of regulation is requested to the extent it benefits interest groups or particular individuals.
3. Public interest	Elimination of a regulation with higher costs than social profits implies an increase in social welfare, favouring public interest.
4. Market globalization	Pressures exerted by international trends and requirements of international organizations and agreements.
5. Changes in the economic context	The dynamic condition of market structure can make regulatory measures obsolete.
6. Regulation failures	Information problems, regulator capture (especially important in services, Gönenç et al., 2001), 'short-sighted' regulation, etc.

Source: Based on Baldwin and Cave, 1999.

These elements trigger a process of change in the interpretation of the role of the public sector (either national and territorial, or even supranational) in markets within the context of the regulatory reform. Petitbò (1999) describes this process as having three key features:

- Firstly, he states that the elimination of the inefficient regulation (due to the inappropriateness or obsolescence of its contents) becomes a prevailing need in the markets. However, de-regulation does not imply a total disappearance of public intervention. In fact, a parallel re-regulation process is required, which highlights regulations related to quality, consumer protection, the environment, market transparency, competition promotion and protection and, to a lesser extent, the universality of services and the maximum prices of goods, which are investment requirements for facing future demand and services. Despite its evident advantages, this de-regulation has been put into practice at a slow pace, as a consequence of the opposition shown by the groups that benefit from the legislation in force in the markets. These groups usually hold sufficient power to put up resistance, or at least delay the liberalization of the affected sectors.
- Secondly, and on the other hand, regulatory power is intended for reduction, as regulators introduce high levels of uncertainty in the market.

Therefore, it would be easy for participating agents to make decisions on the basis of pre-established and public parameters that provide information on regulations in force in a transparent market.

- Re-regulating activity is often associated with privatization processes, which represent another aspect of the liberalization process. The privatization trend has gained great importance at a global level in the context of regulatory reform as an option of micro-economic policy intended to improve the market's performance. Hence, this would promote economic growth and competitiveness to the extent of allowing a more efficient use of productive resources, provided that it facilitates the transfer of these from inefficient public activities to more efficient private activities.

Throughout the last decade, as reform process has undergone changes, the intensity of each role has been altered. Firstly, privatization adopts a priority role which has progressively been pushed into the background, as government participation in direct production has been notably reduced. Subsequently, it gains importance in the pro-competitive regulation process.

3. EFFECTS OF REGULATION AND LIBERALIZATION

Theoretical and empirical positions (among others Vickers and Yarrow, 1991; Ros, 1999; Li, 1999; Nicoletti and Scarpetta, 2003) show a direct relationship between the level of market regulation – particularly that which limits competition level – and the growth observed in the total productivity of factors. Estimates carried out by the OECD in the late 1990s foresaw that the rationalization of regulations in Spain would mean an approximate profit of at least 4–5 per cent of the GNP. Additionally, taking into consideration the dynamic effects on investment and technological innovation, these values increased notably. According to the conclusions reached by Scarpetta and Tressel (2002), regulation restricting market competition reduced innovation incentives and, consequently, potential growth in the medium and long term.

On the basis of the principle that 'the defence of economic rationality of public interests advises the de-regulation all that has been unnecessarily regulated' and the negative effects generated by an excessive and inefficient regulation, Petitbò (1997 and 1999) summarizes the positive effects of the regulatory reform process as follows: - Price reduction, which will result in a fall in inflation rates in the medium and long term, therefore contributing to the macroeconomic objective of inflation control. - Increase in production. In line with this, the study carried out by Esfahani and Arkadani[2] reveals the negative relationship between the GDP per capita, expressed in purchasing power parity (PPP), and the percentage represented by public companies over the total GDP in the early 1990s. According to this evidence, the elimination of public intervention leads to the forecast of an increase of the GDP per capita. This effect will also have positive consequences on economic growth and employment – in this latter case, under the condition that the labour market is sufficiently flexible. A work by Messina (2006) shows that market regulations hinder the development of dynamic sectors such as services industries and influence negative consequences on employment. The different studies analyses show that the existence of an excess in market regulation leads to a slow growth, a limited capacity of job creation and an upward trend in price evolution. In this sense, empirical evidence demonstrates that an initial reduction in employment and salaries could occur as a result of the deflationist effects of the introduction of short-term competition. In the long term, however, the emergence of new opportunities and the consequential variation of supply will allow an increase in employment and in the real income level. In fact, several studies, such as McKinsey Global Institute (1993), establish that Europe's high unemployment is due partly to the lack of competition in many goods and services markets, especially in the latter. - Widening of the range of goods and services supplied, and an improvement in quality. - Improvement of assignative efficiency. A reduction in the differential marginal cost-prices is observed, so extraordinary profits tend to approach zero. - Real salaries show an upward trend in view of the slight reduction or stability of nominal salaries and the price drop. - Reduction of producer surplus (in case of perfect competition, this will be zero). - Increase of consumer surplus. In absolute terms, this increase is higher than the fall of the producer surplus, so a net income of general welfare is produced. - Introduction of dynamic competition, as competition favours an innovative economic climate. In fact, empirical evidence defends a positive correlation between the competition level and the research and development effort (Bassanini et al., 2001).

In conclusion, the existence of an excess in market regulation leads to slow growth, a limited capacity for job creation, and an upward trend in price evolution. These problems are lessened by regulatory reform, which at the same time boosts the aforementioned positive effects.

4. SITUATION AND EVOLUTION OF REGULATION IN SERVICES MARKETS

Recent Evolution of Regulation in Services Markets

According to the information provided by the OECD PMR Data Base and the analyses carried out by this institution on the basis of this data (Nicoletti and Scarpetta, 2005a, b; Conway et al., 2005), the levels of regulation in all OECD countries in recent years (from 1975 until 2003) have been significantly reduced,[3] particularly in those countries where the starting regulation was more restrictive in the year of origin (such as Spain, Greece,

Italy or France). The main elements of this fall include the decrease of obstacles to competition, decrease of rule-control-sanction regulation, lower intervention in the choice of public and private companies, and reduction of barriers to trade and investment.

Figure 7.1 shows the evolution throughout that period in the European countries with available information regarding the aggregate level of regulation in the above-mentioned database. The level of regulation is restricted between 0 and 7, where the value 0 represents the lack of regulation and 7 is the maximum level of regulation in the country.

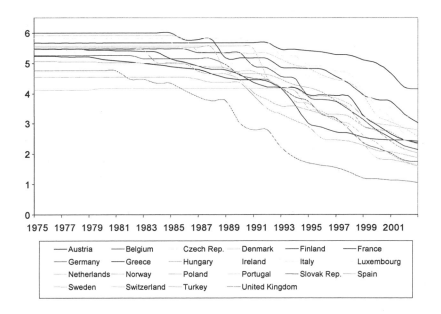

——Austria	——Belgium	Czech Rep.	Denmark	——Finland	——France
——Germany	——Greece	Hungary	Ireland	Italy	Luxembourg
Netherlands	Norway	Poland	Portugal	——Slovak Rep.	Spain
Sweden	Switzerland	Turkey	United Kingdom		

Source: Based on PMR Data Base.

Figure 7.1 Evolution of regulation in the European countries, 1975–2003

In contrast, no homogenization has occurred between regulations in the different countries under analysis. However, the intensity of reform in goods markets is less intense than in non-manufacturing industries, and more specifically in the tertiary sector. The decrease to a higher de-aggregation level suggests the evolution of regulation by services sectors.

The following figures (Figure 7.2) set out the framework of those activities related to airlines, telecommunications, electricity, gas, postal services, rail and road transport, and professional services. The general trend, as previously expounded, repeats in all cases: a significant drop in the levels of regulation registered. However, different patterns can be observed depending on the activity in question, with regard to two elements: (1) the time when the reform was put into practice, and (2) its intensity. Therefore, the reform has led to very significant changes in some sectors such as telecommunications which was started it in the early 1990s. In other sectors, such as postal services, the reform was implemented later and regulation has been much lower. In the particular case of the European Union, this evolution occurred within the framework of the completion process of the internal market for services, as established in Chapter 9.

As previously stated, the process of regulatory reform is based on three basic factors: de-regulation (on which this study essentially focuses), re-regulation (whose main element is pro-competitive regulation) and privatization. Despite the regulatory reform carried out in the 1980s and the 1990s, which has implied a reduction in the level of market regulation, a notably high regulation level can still be observed in the European markets.

The analysis of the indices provided by the OECD, reflecting the regulation level of goods markets, reveals that the lowest regulation levels are registered in the Anglo-Saxon countries, where the de-regulation, privatization and re-regulation processes were implemented earlier. Over-regulation indices are especially apparent in Mediterranean countries (Italy, Greece, France, Spain and Portugal). From a sectoral perspective, there are significant differences between services sectors (Conway and Nicoletti, 2006) and services such as professional or network services are still over-regulated; so there is still a broad liberalization margin for the following years.

This liberalization process is particularly relevant if the positive relationship between the excess of regulation and the level of market production and efficiency is taken into account, as stated in the economic literature. On the basis of this observation, the hypothesis that those countries with higher regulation levels register lower efficiency levels, and are therefore less competitive, can be proposed. Taking into consideration the important weighting of services in national productive structures, the specific connection between the regulation level of services activities and their efficiency level can be also asserted.

Network Services

The network services sector is a specific case, where the traditional presence of monopolies – usually public – has conditioned its evolution. Network industries are characterized by the existence of infrastructures, which constitute a necessary input for their production or distribution and give rise to high fixed costs, leading to a natural monopoly. According to the previous approach, network industries include, for example, fixed telephony, rail, air and road transport, electricity, water, gas and postal services.

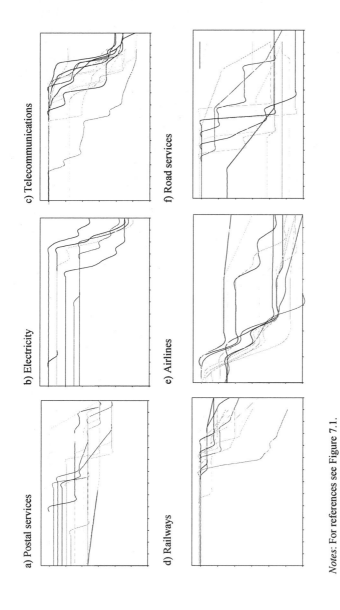

a) Postal services

b) Electricity

c) Telecommunications

d) Railways

e) Airlines

f) Road services

Notes: For references see Figure 7.1.

Source: Based on PMR Data Base.

Figure 7.2 Evolution of regulation in services activities, 1975–2003

Other situations also justify the regulation of these activities, such as the existence of externalities with the network connection or the consideration of strategic sectors or equality criteria, to the extent that these are considered fundamental to the population, beyond market failures. The changes that have occurred in recent decades regarding demand and technological conditions in which these activities are developed have allowed and boosted a restructuring of public intervention in such sectors. Moreover, governments (mainly in Europe) must face tax restrictions, which limit the availability of funds to finance the creation of the aforementioned infrastructures. This situation has led to a reform with which each sector and country has dealt differently. Nevertheless, there is a shared objective of improving the efficiency of activities, in which the intermediate objective of liberalizing the network activities is established. The action taken by the public sector has usually been as follows: to divide the industry into activities and to isolate all those which are non competitive, and then to introduce competition into the potentially competitive activities that use a component characteristic of market power as an input for transformation or distribution processes. At the same time, a significant number of traditional public monopolies have been privatized in the liberalization process. However, both were not always carried out in parallel time periods, meaning that the common result frequently has been the allocation of market power to a private company, with the subsequent loss of efficiency. The public sector, however, continues to control some companies operating in these industries, often those related directly to the component that introduces market power. In conclusion, the level of regulation is reduced in this sector, mainly regarding the entry obstacles to industry, regardless of whether the public sector still controls some of the companies or components of network services.

As shown in the Appendix, those sectors where a higher advance has occurred regarding the liberalization of activities include telecommunications and electricity. In this context, between 1998 and 2003, public control in the telecommunications sector was eliminated from companies or elements in four European Union countries – Spain, Italy, Ireland and Denmark – as well as in the United States and Korea. Despite this trend, 76.67 per cent of countries continue to maintain ownership or control of at least one of the companies operating in the market or its components. In electrical activities, the percentage of markets with public presence is even more significant (83.33 per cent), and in fact, the privatization of elements that in 1998 were under public control has only been carried out in the United States. The network services where public control is less representative are mainly those related to road transport, while water production is at the opposite end of the scale; in 1998, only the United Kingdom entrusted all the activity to private companies. Within this framework, the regulatory role has been re-interpreted, as independent regulatory organizations have gained growing importance. Experience reveals that the activity put into practice by these regulatory agencies, in sectors as significant as telecommunications or energy, has been clearly positive (OECD, 2002d).

Professional Services

The regulation of professional services has also maintained an upward trend, although this is not as generalized as in network services. In fact, some countries with a significant experience in European Union integration, such as the Netherlands, France, Ireland or Italy, have increased the regulation level of these activities.

Table 7.3 Causes of regulation increase in professional services

Country	Activity	Instruments
Finland	Legal services	Regulations on advertising
	Engineering services	Entry regulation: licences Educational requirements
France	Legal services	Entry regulation: licences
	Architectural services	Educational requirements Regulations on advertising
Ireland	Architectural services	Regulations on prices and fees
Italy	Accounting services	Licensing Educational requirements
Sweden	Legal services	Licensing Educational requirements
Portugal	Accounting services	Entry regulations Conduct regulation
	Legal services	Conduct regulation
Belgium	Architectural services	Licensing Educational requirements
	Engineering services	Regulations on advertising
Luxembourg	Architectural services	Educational requirements Regulations on the form of business and inter-professional co-operation Entry regulations
		Conduct regulation

Source: Based on OECD data.

Those activities included in this regulation behaviour vary in each country, but generally speaking, there have been two major methods used for the control of these activities: licences for market entry, and educational requirements to carry out the service. On many occasions, regulations have been self-regulated by professional bodies, sometimes for ensuring quality safety, and other times just for objectives related to intervention and protectionism.

Public Companies and Privatizations

One of the most representative policies of the regulatory reform, mainly throughout the 1990s, has been the privatization policy. This policy concentrates its efforts on services activities after gaining extensive experience in the industrial sectors. The British are pioneers in this respect. Towards the end of the century, however, public services companies still held a significant presence, especially in so-called network services (telecommunications, rail, water, electricity and air). Urban and interurban transport sectors were among those that maintained public companies within their structures in the late 1990s.

Justifications for the international wave of privatization concentrate principally in three key areas: cash reasons (Megginson (2004) states that the importance of this objective has represented a global-level reality); redistribution of income and wealth (empirical evidence demonstrates that the objective of redistribution is far from achieved through the sale of public companies to the private sector, even in those places that give, such as Great Britain, special relevance to these processes); and the improvement of efficiency (politics and specialized literature stress the efficiency objective).[4] Fernández (1995) identifies this as 'the objective most clearly achievable through privatization', although he clarifies that 'the sale of public companies is not enough (...), but the authorization of competition promotion measures is also necessary', which supports the perspective highlighted by the OECD. However, it is advisable not to forget that privatization is a political decision, thus implying political motivation.

Despite the arguments, the analysis of literature reveals that the open debate concerning the issue of whether ownership is relevant or not is far from settled. Therefore, some authors (for example Holland, 1972) support the importance of ownership, as public companies lead to the attainment of certain social and economic goals (namely, to search for social profitability, which is not always easy to measure, against the economic profitability pursued by the private sector). On the other hand, some authors associated with the theory of ownership rights also defend the importance of ownership, although they outline a negative feature of public companies: their inherent inefficiency (Veljanovski, 1987). Between these two extremes, many works uphold the argument, at least in theory, that ownership makes no difference (Clarke and Pitelis, 1994). Nevertheless, from an empirical point of view, the majority of studies carried out conclude that the private sector is more efficient and obtains higher profits in similar activities developed in competitive markets. The performance of mixed companies, however, is sometimes worse than that of private and public companies (FEDEA, 1987). This is not as clear when the focus is on non-competitive markets: in this case, neither theory nor experience provides determining arguments in favour of private ownership. Privatization could result in an improvement in efficiency, or the private monopoly could show a higher trend in the abuse of market power by increasing prices and even suffering a loss in quality. One example of this type of privatization, which includes loss of quality, can be found in rail transport in the United Kingdom. A consortium hires the lines, signals and stations to the 28 private companies that comprise the British railway service; this privatization provoked a clear decline in the service quality.

In conclusion, privatization *per se* from an essentially theoretical perspective does not guarantee important achievements in efficiency. These are more directly related to the level of competition, as will be explained below, where an increase tends to improve the output of public and private companies. However, this does not mean that ownership is irrelevant: as already discussed, public ownership implies a different behaviour to that of public productive units, which do not favour efficiency. A process of competitive opening and appropriate regulation are unavoidable factors that complement privatization (Vickers and Yarrow, 1991).

Airport services are an example of tertiary activities in which a change of the traditional model of public intervention is imposed. These strategic multiproduct activities are characterized by: failures (activities provided under a quasi-monopoly); the existence of essential facilities (a determining asset for the delivery of the service and one which is not easily replicated by competitors); externalities (both negative and positive); and the presence of scale economies and difficulties of asymmetric information. The latter resulted in the traditional airport management model remaining intact even though liberalization was already taking place in other sectors. However, in the late 1980s, the possibility (or the perceived need) of including the airport sector in the private sector led to the sharing of competence with the public sector, leading to new management models. The most generalized pattern of participation of the private sector in airport activity is the maintenance of infrastructures under public control, and also management by a private entity. However, there are also airports under private ownership and operation: some small and non-strategic airports traditionally were included in this category until 1987, when the privatization of the British Airport Authority (BAA) led to the complete privatization of seven airports. The orientation of airport regulations, when the state gives up the direct control on such services or co-participates in this task with the private sector, centres principally in the following areas: (a) rate regulation (examples include the application of price regulation under the RPI-X formulation in the airports of New Zealand or Australia, as well as those regulated by the British Civil Aviation Authority (CAA); (b) security levels; (c) planning of future investments mainly in new airports; (d) environment; and (e) quality levels.

5. RELATIONSHIPS BETWEEN REGULATIONS AND EFFICIENCY

Empirical evidence and the conclusions reached thus far all lead to this proposition: those countries with a higher level of regulation (particularly economic regulation) in the goods market maintain a higher effective regulation of services, resulting in a more reduced efficiency level in the overall economy. This general approach is based on three ideas:

- The efficiency of services activities is higher in those countries that register a lower level of regulation in these activities.
- A lower regulation level in services markets also coincides with higher efficiency levels in the overall economy of these countries.
- The regulatory reform carried out in recent years has contributed to an increase in efficiency levels in services sectors.

The data used to contrast these hypotheses comes mainly from two different sources: EUROSTAT and OECD. The information related to the levels of intervention in the goods markets by the public sectors has been extracted from the PMR Data Base (OECD), while data regarding value added at factor cost, investment and employment comes from EUROSTAT and OECD. Countries included in the analysis are those with data available for the year 2003 (with the exception of Belgium in all sectors, whose data corresponds to 2000, for the output and labour and employment inputs, and Germany in the case of the hotel and restaurant sector). The sectors chosen are those services sectors with available information in EUROSTAT: Hotels and Restaurants, Transport, Storage, Communication and Real Estate, and Renting and Business Activities.

The methodology chosen to carry out the study is the Data Envelopment Analysis (DEA), normally used in the study of efficiency levels of public and non-market activities. Selection in this case is based on the inclusion of the regulation level in the markets of the country in question among the non-traditional inputs, and on the advantages provided by the DEA. This methodology provides a series of significant advantages:

- Unlike the case of parametric approaches, this methodology does not require a specific functional form, which makes the analysis more flexible and avoids possible biases in the specification. In other words, the results offered by the DEA are less affected by possible errors than econometric models when specifying the functional form (Pascual, 2002). On the basis of this hypothesis, a specific boundary can be built for the decision units that, within the sample, show improved behaviour. In other words, those that from the allocation of certain productive factors show a maximum production or reach a specific production quantity and at the same time use the least possible volume of inputs (or the minimum allocation of factors used in order to reach a certain product unit). Any deviation outside this boundary means inefficiency. Therefore, inefficiency of each unit will be measured by establishing its distance from the boundary, so that each unit will be compared with other real efficient units or linear combinations of other efficient units. Consequently, the relative efficiency of the decision unit is measured and compared to those which present the best behaviour in the sample.

- Consistent with this approach, it is not necessary to make a supposition regarding the distribution of disruptions or error terms. In contrast, the possible influence of random factors is not taken into consideration.
- Stochastic analyses establish a boundary related to the most favourable behaviour on average, as non-parametric measures try to determine the best possible behaviour for each observation. In other words, it establishes 'the possibility of respecting the productive features of each centre in a complex context'.
- Additionally, the DEA enables the consideration of various inputs and outputs.
- From a more technical perspective, the interpretation of this methodology is simple and can be easily adapted to different technological suppositions.

However, the DEA methodology also has some weaknesses:

- The main disadvantage of this envelopment analysis is its lack of statistical tests to contrast the consistency of the results obtained.
- It does not take into consideration the component of random error, which can affect the company in question. In fact, it establishes that the extent to which the company does not reach the boundary of the group of productive possibilities is due only to its inefficiency.
- Moreover, the results are highly sensitive to the presence of 'extreme' observations, in positive terms. The presence of this type of decision units moves the boundary away from the remaining observations. Therefore, these will register very low relative efficiency indices.
- DEA methodology does not offer a criterion to select the variables to be included in the analysis. This selection has to be based on a purely economic reasoning.

The mathematical exercise involves solving a linear program for each observation in order to determine (when an orientation towards the factor is adopted) the minimum quantity of necessary factors to reach the quantity of production observed. On the basis of this referent, a radial index of efficiency is set up, which establishes that the inefficiency of a company enables us to know the proportional reduction that can occur at the same time in all the inputs without reducing production.

Minθ

s.a.:

$$\sum_{j=1}^{N} y_{sj}\lambda_j \geq y_{si}, \quad s=1,...,S$$

$$\sum_{j=1}^{N} x_{mj}\lambda_j \leq \theta x_{mi}, \quad m=1,...,M$$

$$\lambda \geq 0. \quad j=1,...,N$$

Table 7.4 Efficiency and regulation

	Productive efficiency in the services sector	Productive efficiency in economy	Regulation of goods markets	Regulation of the services sector	Regulation of professional services	Regulation of network services
Austria	0.877	0.776	1.4	2.2	2	2.4
Belgium	0.604	0.89	1.4	2.6	2.1	2.1
Czech Republic	0.21	0.236	1.7	3	2.8	3.3
Germany	1			2.4	3.1	1.7
Denmark	0.751			1.2	0.8	1.6
Spain	0.724	0.77	1.6	2.2	2.4	2
Finland	1	0.819	1.3	1.7	1	2.4
France	1	0.752	1.7	2.5	2	3
Hungary	0.149	0.251	2	2.8	2.5	3.1
Ireland	0.698	1	1.1	2.2	1.3	3.2
Italy	0.853	0.835	1.9	3.1	3.6	2.6
Netherlands	0.726			1.6	1.6	1.6
Norway	0.808	1	1.5	2	1.7	2.3
Portugal	0.369	0.349	1.6	2.5	2.4	2.6
Sweden	0.949			1.3	0.9	1.7
Slovakia	0.192	0.143	1.4	2.6	2.8	2.5
United Kingdom	1	0.938	0.9	1.1	1.1	1

Source: Based on PMR Data Base, OECD and Eurostat data.

From a general perspective, the conclusion reached in previous analyses is now backed in the case of tertiary activities. These analyses include those carried out by Bassanini et al. (2001), who concluded that the evolution of the total productivity of factors during the 1980s has been negatively affected by the regulation observed in the goods markets. Empirical evidence also demonstrates that those countries with a lower level of development have a higher public intervention in goods markets and productive factors (IMF, 2004), and a lower level of efficiency, according to the aforementioned results.

One of the main results obtained is the evidence that those countries where the levels of regulation in services are higher show lower efficiency levels, not only in the field of tertiary activities, but also for the whole economy (Table 7.4).

In fact, correlation analyses (on the basis of Spearman's correlation coefficients, with negative and statistical significant values) and linear regression analyses (taking the efficiency levels as dependent variable and the regulation level of services markets and goods markets respectively) reveal the existence of a significant relationship (see Table 7.5).

Table 7.5 Influence of regulation and efficiency

Efficiency in economy = f (Services regulation)

	All markets		Services markets	
	Coefficient	P>t	Coefficient	P>t
Constant	1.293	0.001	1.445	0.005
Regulation	-0.277	0.046	-0.515	0.085
Spearman's rho	-0.5695	0.0422	-0.6685	0.0125

Source: Based on PMR Data Base, OECD and Eurostat data.

From a strictly descriptive perspective, Figures 7.3 and 7.4 show that when the initial regulation levels are high, their reduction coincides with more pronounced efficiency increases. More specifically, the available information for the transport sector enables the analysis of the evolution of efficiency in recent years through the Malquist Indices, considering the value added as an output, and the level of labour, investment and regulation of road and rail transport as inputs (sectoral data available).

Taking into consideration the period between 2000 and 2003, all countries under analysis (except for the United Kingdom and Belgium) have experienced an increase in the total productivity of factors, based on the low levels of regulation in this sector.

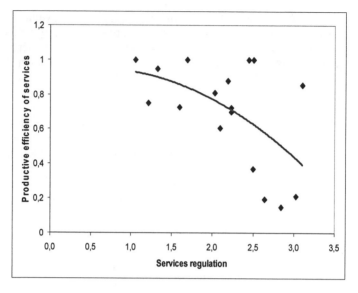

Source: Based on PMR Data Base, OECD and Eurostat data.

Figure 7.3 The influence of services regulation on the productive efficiency of services

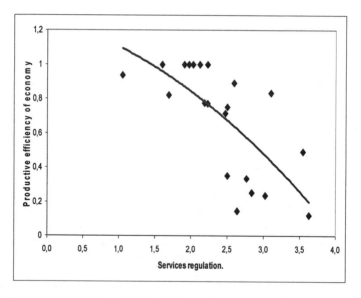

Source: Based on PMR Data Base, OECD and Eurostat data.

Figure 7.4 The influence of services regulation on the productive efficiency of economy

The trend of technical efficiency follows the same lines: Spain, Germany and Austria register an increased improvement in their levels. The levels of regulation registered by these three countries in the road and rail transport sector are among the highest in the sample. In the cases of Spain and Germany, a significant reduction has occurred in recent years. In Germany, in particular, this reduction has been concentrated in the entry of new companies in the field of road transport and public ownership in the rail sector. In Spain however, advances have been registered only in road transport, both in the entry of new companies to the sector and in the regulation of prices.

A highly positive evolution of technological change in the years under analysis can be observed. This highlights the positive influence not only from a static perspective, but also from a dynamic perspective, to the extent that the regulatory reform encourages the growth of the total productivity of factors and, consequently, the value added. Nicoletti and Scarpetta (2003) back this conclusion for all goods markets. However, the influence of the regulatory reform on the evolution of efficiency is more evident in the medium and long term than in the three-year period considered.

Table 7.6 Change in efficiency in the transport sector

	Change in productive efficiency 2000–2003	Total change in road and rail regulation	Rail	Road	Road and rail transport
Austria	1.103	-0.2	5.3	1.7	3.5
Belgium	0.831	-0.9	4.3	1.7	3.0
Germany	1.104	-1.0	3.8	1.3	2.5
Denmark	0.965	-1.1	2.6	0.5	1.6
Spain	1.097	-1.9	4.9	1.3	3.1
Finland	0.806	0.0	5.3	0.5	2.9
France	1	0.0	5.3	1.7	3.5
Ireland	1	-0.2	5.6	0.5	3.1
Italy	1	-1.2	2.6	5.5	4.1
Netherlands	1	-0.6	2.6	1.3	1.9
Norway	1	-0.6	4.3	1.0	2.6
Portugal	0.979	-1.4	3.8	0.5	2.1
Sweden	0.943	0.0	3.8	1.0	2.4
United Kingdom	0.97	-0.5	0.4	0.5	0.4

Source: Based on PMR Data Base, OECD and Eurostat data.

6. POLICIES TO REFORM AND IMPROVE REGULATION

Reform and Liberalization Guidelines

The objective of the reforms both from a theoretical perspective and in political and socio-economic practice is to improve the efficiency of regulations and markets, thus eliminating inefficient regulations and promoting those that imply advances in this respect. These objectives contribute to the improvement of national economies and their capacity to adapt to the changes occurring in increasingly globalized markets. At the same time, public interventions would gradually be reduced, and the role of the public sector would change from producer to regulator.

The attainment of these priority objectives requires the fulfilment of a series of conditions by the regulatory reforms carried out. Recent literature (Australian National University (2000) and the World Bank (2004)) has included important principles for better regulation in services, which can be summarized by the following parameters:

- Definition of clear objectives in the socio-economic field and a framework favourable to their implementation, on the basis of a complex economic and social context. In this sense, the convenience of identifying and boosting the links with other national or EU policies is set out.
- Neutral position of the regulator. There is a need to have independent/neutral regulators in charge of implementing the reform in a transparent and non-discriminatory manner, not only regarding the industry regulated but also political authorities. Within this framework, the reduction of discretional policy by the regulator is also included (Coghlan, 2000).
- In line with such an approach, respect for personal rights and liberties and, more specifically, for the autonomy of enterprises should be guaranteed.
- Together with the elimination of non-efficient regulation, two essential issues are presented: the definition of universal service and public service obligations, and the establishment of a new regulation. These are intended to protect and promote competition, with the general referent of minimizing public intervention in the markets. The priority objective is to restructure economic activities until the area with the characteristics of natural monopoly can be isolated, thus introducing higher competition levels in the other areas. This parameter is especially significant in the case of network services, where the characteristics of natural monopoly are observed in the network itself, and not in the production and distribution of services.
- Likewise, liberalization in price policies is intended to be promoted, thus increasing, where necessary, the association between controlled prices and cost levels. Nevertheless, the regulation possibilities based on the costs

tend not to encourage cost reduction, as these may not produce additional advantages in industry.

Within the European Union, certain national reforming processes have been initiated not only at a national level, but also from a supranational perspective. As a consequence, achievements include the rationalization and simplification of regulation in the markets, and particularly in services markets. These resulted in a reduction of the regulation levels in force in the late 1990s and the first years of 2000.

European Policies regarding the Simplification of Regulation

The Commission itself [5] has promoted the regulatory reform processes that are dealt with at a national level. This promotion was accompanied by the Commission's clear intent for a 'better legislation for growth and jobs in the EU',[6] in line with the Lisbon strategy, with the close and direct collaboration of Member States.

In particular, from the perspective that better regulation contributes to the achievement of higher growth and more and better jobs, the objective pursued by this line of action is to achieve simplification, which 'at Community and national levels can make regulation less burdensome, easier to apply and thereby more effective in achieving its objectives'. This objective develops into a process that tries to resolve the priorities highlighted in a consultation process carried out by the Commission, although the problems lie in the regulation of local, and mainly national, environment. This process can be identified under the name of 'better regulation'.

The measures applied thus far attempt, on the one hand, to guarantee that Member States' legislation develops according to a better regulation implying less costs for growth and creation of jobs and, on the other hand, to simplify the EU regulation itself. The observation of the progress made in the Member States reveals that 19 out of the 25 have implemented programs intended to improve regulation, and highlights the importance given to the impact assessment.

With regard to the simplification process in the context of the EU regulation, several intermediate objectives have been suggested on the basis of the experience of Member States:

- Simplification of legislation in force, and particularly that related to administrative processing. This process, which will be defined as an objective of the EU legislation from 2005, has already been initiated at national levels and has resulted in a reduction of related regulation in the majority of European countries (Table 7.7), as demonstrated by the information provided by the OECD concerning administrative regulation.
- Withdrawal or modification of pending legislations. In fact, the Commission has already suggested the withdrawal of an important part of

the proposals made (over 35 per cent) because: they do not meet the parameters established by this intent to improve legislation, under the terms set out in the Lisbon Strategy; they are obsolete; or they do not make an improvement compared to the previous situation. Some of these affect services regulation directly, including the prohibition of weekend truck traffic and sales promotion in the internal market.

- Improvement of new regulation. Public consultations intended to support the elaboration of new regulations and directives are worth mentioning.

Table 7.7 Evolution of administrative regulation

	Administrative burdens for corporation		Administrative burdens for sole proprietor firms		Sector specific administrative burdens	
	1998	2003	1998	2003	1998	2003
Austria	2.8	3.0	2.5	2.5	2.4	3.4
Belgium	1.5	1.8	1.0	1.5	1.3	1.7
Denmark	0.5	1.0	0.3	0.0	0.2	0.3
Finland	1.5	1.3	2.8	1.8	1.8	1.1
France	3.3	2.0	3.8	2.0	3.6	1.6
Germany	2.3	2.3	3.3	1.3	2.1	1.4
Greece	3.0	2.3	3.3	3.3	3.2	2.9
Ireland	1.5	0.8	0.8	0.3	0.5	0.3
Italy	5.5	2.8	4.3	2.8	4.7	2.1
Luxembourg	0.8	2.5	0.3	3.0	0.1	0.3
Netherlands	2.0	2.0	1.8	1.3	1.6	1.3
Portugal	2.8	1.5	1.8	1.8	1.8	1.8
Spain	3.5	2.8	4.0	4.0	3.5	2.4
Sweden	1.3	1.0	1.0	1.8	0.8	0.9
United Kingdom	0.8	0.8	1.3	0.5	0.8	0.6

Source: OECD.

Some of the sectors affected by this process of improvement and simplification of EU regulation are agriculture and food products, manufacturing industry and services, primarily financial and transport services; and, to a lesser extent, professional services. In this context, many directives have been reduced and summarized. For example, some concerning air transport (Council Regulations no. 2299/89, 3089/93 and 323/1999) were created to reduce the risk of abuse of a dominant position, although these were abolished due to the higher competition level in the sector, as it was predicted that this contributed to the improvement of market effectiveness and efficiency. Along the same lines, a future review of the directive regarding the supplementary supervision of credit institutions, insurance undertakings and investment firms in a financial conglomerate is projected (Directive 2002/87/EC).

7. CONCLUSIONS

According to the information analysed in this chapter, regulatory reform from an international and inter-sectorial perspective in recent decades (after the 1980s) has generated clearly positive effects in the field of services activities within the framework of the European Union. Especially in the late 1990s and first few years of the 21st century, an upwards trend has been maintained in the reduction of public intervention in the markets, not only strictly regarding regulation, but also in the existence of public ownership. This trend is included within the broader objective of rationalizing the effective regulation in the markets, by eliminating obsolete or inefficient regulations (to the extent that they create more costs than profits). The ultimate intention of this reform is to reduce the negative effects implied by the excess of regulation, essentially related to the decrease of efficiency in the markets, according to economic theory and the empirical evidence developed in recent years.

Traditionally, tertiary activities have been highly controlled by the public sector as a consequence of their own features – which imply the existence of market failures such as natural monopolies, externalities or imperfect information – and also due to the consideration of strategic products – which have led the public sector to guarantee its provision and to protect the sector from domestic and external competition. The incidence of regulatory reform in the services markets in this context has been clearly lower than in the production of goods. Therefore, the levels of regulation are still high in relative terms, thus limiting the positive effects generated by the process implemented, despite the significant advances achieved. Network services such as telecommunications and electricity services are clear examples. However, in some tertiary activities, such as water and rail transport, liberalization has been initiated with a relative delay, and its depth is lower in general terms (level of regulation), and particularly regarding the privatization of public ownership. A better balance is needed between liberalization and re-regulation. Professional services constitute another group of determining services. The rationalization of regulation among them has occurred at a slower pace, and they are still affected by important restrictions, mainly related to the free entry of companies in the sector and the educational requirements to carry out the relevant activity.

The empirical analysis performed demonstrates that there is a negative relationship between higher levels of regulation and efficiency achieved in the services markets under study. Moreover, the evolution of this efficiency is also characterized by the level of regulation. In this case, the research is limited to the transport and communications sector, given that this is one sector with available de-aggregated information in different periods of time. The results obtained lead one to conclude that some progress has been made regarding the total productivity of factors in virtually all countries, except for the United Kingdom, whose regulation levels in the year of origin are quite low. In contrast, Spain and Germany are among those countries dealing with greater reform and who are improving their technical efficiency to a larger extent (excluding technological change). However, much still remains to be done in both countries, as well as in many others. With regard to technical change, it is higher in those countries where regulatory reform has been more decisive, which reveals static and dynamic effects implied by market liberalization.

Under this approach, the process of improvement and simplification of regulation at an EU level takes on a special significance. The essential basis of this process includes the reduction and simplification of regulations in force, the improvement and reduction of pending provisions, and the introduction of improvement criteria in the new regulations. As regulation levels and positive effects generated in the services sector by regulatory reform – which also generates direct and indirect effects (as inputs of other activities) – are still high, there will be a need to continue making progress in the liberalization process of the service sector. However, this does not imply the withdrawal of regulation but rather, as evidence has shown throughout this chapter, its rationalization.

This rationalization will be carried out to the extent that only those measures implying an improvement regarding the lack of intervention and, consequently, an improvement of citizens' welfare will be maintained. As an example, the so-called services of general interest can be highlighted, including education and health, which have recently raised an important debate within the Framework Directive for the Internal Market of Services. The next two chapters – which address competition policy and internal market policy, respectively – will discuss in detail some key regulatory aspects of European market for services.

NOTES

1. Nuria Fernández participated in this chapter as main co-author.
2. Esfahani and Arkadani (2002).
3. Nicoletti and Scarpetta (2003).

4. Vickers and Yarrow (1991), Melle (1999), Kagami and Tsuji (2000), Gámir (1998, 2003), Fernández (1995), among others.
5. COM (2005)97, of 16 March 2005.
6. COM (2005)535, of 25 October 2005.

APPENDIX

Table 7A.1 Evolution of regulation in professional services, 1996–2003

	GMR (*) 03	Accounting 96	03	Architect 96	03	Engineer 96	03	Legal 96	03	Overall 96	03
Australia	0.9	3.2	1.8	0.0	0.0	0.0	0.0	4.4	2.2	1.9	1.0
Austria	1.4	3.5	1.6	4.4	2.1	4.4	2.1	4.3	2.1	4.2	2.0
Belgium	1.4	3.5	2.7	2.6	2.8	0.0	0.3	2.7	2.5	2.2	2.1
Canada	1.2	3.1	3.2	3.0	2.8	2.9	3.2	3.2	3.2	3.1	3.1
Czech Rep.	1.7	..	3.2	..	1.7	..	2.3	..	3.8	..	2.8
Denmark	1.1	2.1	1.2	0.0	0.0	0.0	0.0	2.1	2.0	1.1	0.8
Finland	1.3	2.4	2.2	1.0	1.0	0.0	0.5	0.0	0.3	0.8	1.0
France	1.7	3.0	3.0	1.8	2.1	0.2	0.0	2.3	2.8	1.8	2.0
Germany	1.4	5.1	2.8	3.3	3.1	3.8	3.1	4.5	3.6	4.2	3.1
Greece	1.8	2.9	2.0	..	2.5	..	2.8	4.9	4.5	..	2.9
Hungary	2.0	..	2.0	..	3.1	..	2.1	..	3.0	..	2.5
Ireland	1.1	2.0	1.6	0.0	0.7	0.0	0.0	2.8	2.8	1.2	1.3
Italy	1.9	1.4	4.0	4.3	3.1	4.0	3.8	3.6	3.6	3.3	3.6
Japan	1.3	3.0	2.2	2.5	0.9	2.0	2.8	3.7	3.3	2.8	2.3
Luxembourg	1.3	3.3	2.8	3.1	3.5	3.2	3.2	3.1	3.1	3.2	3.2
Netherlands	1.4	3.2	2.9	0.0	0.0	0.4	1.5	2.0	2.0	1.4	1.6
Norway	1.5	2.4	1.9	1.8	1.1	1.8	1.2	3.2	2.6	2.3	1.7
Poland	2.8	..	2.8	..	2.0	..	2.3	..	3.3	..	2.6
Portugal	1.6	1.9	2.8	2.0	1.6	3.7	1.6	3.4	3.6	2.8	2.4
Slovakia	1.4	..	2.2	..	2.6	..	2.4	..	3.7	..	2.8
Spain	1.6	3.1	2.1	3.5	2.5	3.0	1.5	4.0	3.6	3.4	2.4
Sweden	1.2	2.5	2.4	0.0	0.0	0.0	0.0	0.8	1.2	0.8	0.9
UK	0.9	3.2	2.1	0.0	0.0	0.0	0.0	2.3	2.1	1.4	1.1
US	1.0	2.6	1.7	..	1.7	2.4	1.9	2.9	1.8	..	1.8

Notes: * General Market Regulation.

Source: Based on Indicators of Product Market Regulation, OECD.

Table 7A.2 Evolution of regulation in network industries, 1996–2003

	Airlines		Telecom		Electricity		Gas		Post		Rail		Road	
	96	**03**	**96**	**03**	**96**	**03**	**96**	**03**	**96**	**03**	**96**	**03**	**96**	**03**
Australia	0.9	0.9	4.2	1.9	2.9	1.0	2.4	1.9	2.9	2.9	3.9	1.9	0.0	0.0
Austria	1.6	1.2	5.7	1.6	5.5	1.5	4.5	2.7	2.9	2.9	5.6	5.3	1.7	1.7
Belgium	1.4	0.0	4.6	2.1	4.2	1.3	3.7	2.6	3.7	2.9	5.6	4.3	3.5	1.7
Canada	1.5	1.0	1.2	0.8	5.0	3.7	0.6	0.5	3.7	3.7	3.0	3.0	0.5	0.5
Czech Rep.	..	4.4	..	..	..	..	5.2	3.6	..	3.2	..	2.3	..	3.0
Denmark	1.5	0.4	2.8	0.7	4.8	1.0	4.5	3.2	3.7	2.9	6.0	2.6	0.5	0.5
Finland	1.8	1.7	2.6	0.9	2.7	1.5	4.5	4.5	2.8	2.2	5.3	5.3	0.5	0.5
France	4.0	1.7	5.4	2.1	6.0	3.6	6.0	4.0	4.4	2.9	6.0	5.3	1.7	1.7
Germany	0.0	0.0	4.8	1.6	4.2	1.8	2.5	1.5	3.7	2.2	4.9	3.8	3.0	1.3
Greece	4.7	4.3	5.2	1.7	6.0	3.3	6.0	5.2	3.7	2.9	6.0	5.6	6.0	6.0
Hungary	..	5.6	..	..	..	..	4.2	3.4	..	3.5	..	3.8	..	2.5
Ireland	4.5	4.3	5.3	1.5	5.5	3.3	5.4	4.1	3.9	2.9	6.0	5.6	1.0	0.5
Italy	2.6	1.9	4.7	1.0	6.0	1.1	4.7	2.4	4.4	3.5	6.0	2.6	6.0	5.5
Japan	1.7	1.7	2.3	1.7	4.0	2.1	3.2	2.8	3.7	2.9	4.1	3.8	3.0	0.5
LX	..	..	6.0	..	..	..	4.5	3.4	..	2.7	..	..	..	..
NL	0.8	0.4	4.4	1.1	5.5	0.6	4.5	2.9	2.2	2.2	4.9	2.6	1.3	1.3
Norway	1.5	0.4	5.7	2.3	2.0	2.0	4.2	3.5	3.7	2.9	5.3	4.3	1.0	1.0
Poland	..	3.5	..	..	..	..	5.5	4.8	..	2.9	..	1.7	..	1.7
Portugal	4.7	3.0	4.6	1.5	4.5	2.3	5.5	4.1	6.0	2.9	5.3	3.8	1.6	0.5
Slovakia	..	4.2	..	..	..	..	..	3.7	..	3.4	..	1.9	..	1.5
Spain	4.0	1.0	3.3	1.2	3.7	0.5	4.0	2.5	2.9	2.9	5.6	4.9	4.8	1.3
Sweden	1.5	0.6	3.5	1.8	1.5	1.0	3.7	2.7	2.2	2.2	4.1	3.8	1.0	1.0
UK	1.4	1.4	1.2	0.5	0.1	0.0	3.0	1.7	3.7	2.9	1.5	0.4	0.5	0.5
US	0.4	0.0	0.5	0.2	3.3	2.3	0.5	0.4	3.7	3.7	3.0	3.0	0.5	0.5

Notes: For country abbreviations, see Table 3.3.

Source: Based on Indicators of Product Market Regulation, OECD.

8. European Union competition policy [1]

INTRODUCTION

The previous chapter has shown the extensive regulation of the service sector and the need to increase efficiency in its markets. A key to improving the efficiency and performance of a market is competition. This is the main aim of competition policy, an essential instrument of economic policy, particularly in services markets which are generally strongly regulated, and in the process of becoming more open and liberalized. There are different ways of promoting competition and this chapter deals with one of the main types: competition policy. Other methods of promoting competition are included in the subject matters in other chapters of this book.

Why is it necessary to have regulations defending and promoting competition in all countries and, in particular, in the EU? What guidelines prevail in EU competition policy? Does competition exist in services markets? Why is competition protection important within the service sector? More specifically, what regulations exist in the various tertiary categories? Which of the cases discussed by the European Commission illustrate the application of such rules? This chapter will address these questions, among others, in order to fully understand the current situation of European competition policy, especially within the tertiary sector, and also how it adapts to arising challenges.

This analysis is particularly significant considering that an efficient competition policy is the first step towards a real internal services market, which will be studied in the next chapter. If the structure of the common market and the behaviour of economic agents are not efficiently governed by the principle of free competition, it will be difficult to create an area where companies can establish and deliver their services with the same conditions throughout all the Member Nations.

1. RATIONALE FOR A COMPETITION POLICY

Competition policy is an instrument that enables the correction of market distortions, which threaten the efficient performance of the general economy. Therefore, virtually all countries have regulations in this respect. In the case of the European Union, these rules are also necessary to limit some consequences that could arise from the economic integration process. Although the opening up of markets increases social welfare and the efficiency of the economic system, it could encourage companies to restructure with the aim of taking advantage of possible scale economies derived from the larger market size. In this context, the EU competition policy establishes methods in order to restrict entrepreneurial dimensions and the development of anti-competitive practices. Additionally, the possible contradictions between national jurisdictions and the need to take into consideration the impacts of national approaches across borders also justify the adoption of a common competition policy (Pelkmans, 2006a). This *competition* policy co-exists with and complements competition *promotion* in some markets traditionally operated by state monopolies.

The principles supporting the EU competition policy include free market entry, independent decision making by companies and consumer sovereignty. These principles are intended to produce the beneficial effects that effective competition can provide for producers, final consumers and the general economic system. When companies face the pressure exerted by their direct competitors, they are forced to improve their cost structure, to increase their productivity and to constantly innovate in products and processes in order not to lag behind. Due to this, the final consumer therefore has the choice of a wide and varied range of higher-quality goods and services at lower prices. At macroeconomic level, this implies, to the extent permitted by the labour market, a greater control over inflation, as well as an increase in investment and medium- and long-term employment, which boosts economic growth and, ultimately, social welfare. In fact, recent researches have empirically proven that pro-competitive policies improve the economic performance of countries by means of increases in economic global productivity (Nicoletti and Scarpetta, 2003), innovation and technological diffusion (Aghion et al., 2001; Gust and Marquez, 2002). Hence, competition is a key element in increasing competitiveness through these channels. As a result, a proactive and effective competition policy is essential in order to achieve the Lisbon Agenda objectives.

Competition policy, regulation and liberalization are different instruments used to achieve the ultimate end of protecting and improving consumer welfare. However, according to the United Nations (2001) and the OECD (2002e), regulation and competition policy interact in different ways. Firstly, regulations can conflict with competition policy. Some regulatory measures designed to protect the public interest could create incentives for the emergence of behaviour that is contrary to the principles upon which the competition policy is based. Among these measures can be found legislation limiting the entry of new providers, promoting the coordination of prices or forbidding the publishing of rates, such as in the sector of professional services. Generally speaking, many regulatory rules 'limit competition more than is necessary for the purpose of achieving the regulation objectives' (United Nations, 2001). On the other hand, regulation can replace competition policy. In the case of natural monopolies, for example, the regulatory measures can be more appropriate for a direct control of exercising market dominance. Moreover, regulations can reproduce competition policy, that is to say, regulators can create instruments to prevent coordination and abuse in certain industries. Finally, the objectives of regulation can be achieved by methods that use market incentives, which are characteristic of competitive institutions. In particular, the coordination of both policies is vital within the framework of regulatory reforms intended to increase the competition level in certain sectors. A robust competition policy, correctly implemented by transparent and independent institutions with availability of resources should be the foundation for regulatory reforms implemented by countries (OECD, 1999, 2000c, 2005d).

There is a direct relationship between competition and liberalization. In fact, the opening of sectors that traditionally operated under monopolistic conditions is one of the areas of action of competition policy. The aim of liberalization is to increase the possibilities of choice of providers on the part of consumers, who can therefore benefit from a broader range of higher-quality goods and services provided at more affordable prices. As an example, consider the drop of average prices of telecommunications and air transport, liberalized at first. According to the European Commission (2005), the monthly average consumer expenditure on national calls fell 22.6 per cent between 1998 and 2003, while company expenditure on calls experienced a decrease of 13.5 per cent. With regard to international calls, the average cost decreased 41.6 per cent for private calls and 45 per cent for the business sector over the same period. In sectors where liberalization has not fully materialized (railway transport, postal services) prices do not show these trends. On the other hand, according to some estimates, the liberalization of network industries has enabled the creation of approximately one million jobs within the EU as a consequence of market growth.[2]

Competition policy is not neutral, not only regarding the behaviour of agents and markets, but also regarding other dimensions such as innovation, which often requires the entrepreneurial coordination in the different stages of the innovative process (Shapiro, 2002) and with which it sometimes could seem to be in conflict. However, the role of competition policy in basic research and invention is moderate. In the first case, pure research activities are considered to have characteristics of public goods, so the collaboration between companies is permitted (formation of consortia or joint ventures). Nevertheless, the competition policy can alter private companies' incentives to incur the necessary costs to innovate, since they affect the stages of commercialization of new technologies, diffusion of innovations in the economic system or elaboration based on the existing technologies. These processes are carried using licences, patents, intellectual property rights, alliances, concentrations, etc. If companies cannot appropriate the returns derived from innovating, competition policy can clearly hinder innovation. However, this has not been empirically proven, as the design of the competition policy oversees exemptions for certain cooperative behaviours within the framework of research and development. Moreover, as the antitrust policy fights abuses of a dominant position and agreements that restrict competition, it also encourages companies to use innovation as a 'clean' method to compete, against protectionist situations where there are no important incentives for innovation.

2. EU COMPETITION POLICY

In the ECSC Treaty (1951), the European Union adopted common competition rules with the purpose of avoiding the reappearance of cartels, which characterized the steel and coal industries in the period between wars. Articles 65 and 66 established the prohibition of certain agreements between businesses which might negatively affect competition, the power of the Commission to authorize specific alliances or impose fines, the control of state aids granted by the Member States and the need for notification of concentrations between companies. The Rome Treaty, signed in 1957, developed these elements, and currently governs the EU competition policy – together with some Regulations and Guidelines. The objective of 'ensuring that competition in the internal market is not distorted' is set out in Article 3 (g). To achieve this, various rules are established in Articles 81 to 89 (ex 85 to 94) regarding agreements between undertakings, abuse by one or more undertakings in a dominant position, state aid, and the liberalization of monopolised industries. Mergers between companies are not specifically regulated in this Treaty, but in special regulations. Each of these areas will be analysed in order to illustrate the general framework within which the services sector competition policy is included.

Restrictive Agreements between Companies – Cartel Control

Article 81 (ex 85) prohibits decisions, agreements and concerted practices between undertakings that may restrict or distort competition and affect trade among Member States. This prohibition affects particularly those agreements (whether vertical or horizontal) which: fix prices or any other trading conditions, limit production or market shares, restrict investment or technical development, share markets or sources of supply, or apply dissimilar conditions to equivalent transactions with other trading parties, thereby placing them at a competitive disadvantage.

There are block exemption regulations for certain categories of agreements, due to their importance in market performance or the advantages they can provide to the consumers.[3] As will be seen in section 4, there are also specific exemptions for certain sectors, for example transport. Also, agreements that comply with certain conditions (as specified in section 3 of Article 81) can be individually exempt from the EU competition law. These are alliances intended for the promotion of technical or economic progress in the interest of the consumers, but which in order to do so limit competition to a certain extent. Furthermore, agreements of minor importance (the *de minimis* principle), which do not noticeably restrict intra-EU competition or trade, can also be exempt. The European Commission can launch an investigation and impose fines of up to 10 per cent of the annual turnover of enterprises involved in alliances not included in these exceptions or those that are suspicious.

Abuse of a Dominant Position – Control of Monopolies

A company holds a dominant position in the market if its economic power enables it to operate without taking into account its competitors or consumers. In other words, it can influence competitive conditions without necessarily having to be subordinated to them. According to Article 82 of the Treaty (ex 86), the abuse of a dominant position affecting intra-EU trade is not compatible with the common market. The practices prohibited in this case are related to those established in Article 81, which has been previously analysed. This rule condemns the misuse of a dominant position in the market, not the position in itself, which could have been reached legitimately.

Modernization of EU Competition Policy

In 2004 the Modernization Package of competition policy[4] established new methods in order to improve the application of EU regulations, transferring responsibilities to the competition authorities and law courts of the Member States, on the one hand, and to businesses on the other. The key elements introduced by the reform are the following:

- *Removal of the centralized notification system and reduction of bureaucratic procedures.* Agreements between undertakings, that had to be previously notified to the European Commission in order to obtain authorization, are automatically considered to be valid; provided that no 'hardcore restrictions' are imposed to competition and that they are beneficial to the internal market according to the criteria set out in Article 81(3).[5] Therefore, the Commission loses the 'monopoly' for granting the exemptions.
- *Decentralization of the application of Articles 81 and 82 in national competition authorities.* The relationships between Community law and national law are regulated for the first time: when cross-border trade is affected, EU law will prevail.[6]

- *Direct application of EU competition law in Member States.* National courts of law, as well as competition authorities, have the power to fully apply EU regulations.
- *Creation of the European Competition Network,* whose aim is to coordinate the actions of the Commission and Member States and to improve their exchange of information.
- *Emphasis on economic analysis and the establishment of the position of liaison officer,* who will try to maintain a permanent dialogue with European consumers.
- *Broader powers for the European Commission,* not only regarding investigation (allowing officials to register private addresses, for instance), but also the possibility to issue fines.

A review of Article 82 has recently been started with the purpose of creating a methodology for evaluating the abuses of dominant positions, based on the analysis of their economic effects on competition and consumer welfare.[7] Similarly, the possibility of considering efficiencies derived from abusive practices as a compensation element is analysed. Such a review – if it concludes in the respective Guidelines – will enable competition authorities and companies in dominant positions to know with more certainty whether their conduct is lawful or not, as formerly the main reference has been the cases handled by the Commission.

Concentrations between Undertakings

Unlike agreements or alliances, concentrations between undertakings imply changes in their ownership in different ways: one or several companies taking exclusive control over another company; the fusion of companies to create a new company; or the acquisition of a company by one company which previously shared the control of this with another company. A risk of these types of operations is the reinforcement or creation of dominant positions, which can be detrimental to competition. However, these are not specifically regulated in the EC Treaty. In fact, a legal vacuum existed until 1989, which was only covered by the jurisprudence of the Court of Justice. Later, Regulation 4064/1989 enabled the *a priori* regulation of mergers establishing the requirement of previous authorization by the European Commission of all EU operations. The Community dimension is verified if simultaneously: all the companies involved have a joint worldwide turnover of over 5000 million euros, at least two of them have a Community-wide turnover of more than 250 million euros, and they do not achieve more than two thirds of their turnover in the same Member State. In these cases, the Commission assesses the operation in two investigative stages, on the basis of which it can directly approve the merger, submit it under certain conditions or prohibit it. In order to prohibit a merger, the criterion of creation or reinforcement of the *dominant position* (as described in Article 82) is used.

However, in highly centralized industries, the winding-up of a company as a result of a merger operation could lead to the tacit coordination of their actions by the few remaining participants, although a dominant position between them is not created or strengthened.[8] Regulation 139/2004[9], intended to regulate these cases, currently governs merger operations. The following are its key elements:

- *The notion of 'significant impediment to effective competition'* in the common market in order to prohibit a merger. A 'substantive test' based on economic guidelines will determine whether sufficient competition remains in the relevant market post merger and whether it guarantees the election capacity of consumers. Therefore, the Commission will also evaluate those issues which may not strengthen or create a dominant position, although they bring in their wake anti-competitive situations due to the performance of the companies involved in the operation (such as in the case of oligopolistic markets). Moreover, the Commission will take into consideration in its analysis the possible efficiencies arising from a merger transaction.
- *Consolidation of economic analysis.* In order to achieve this, the post of DG Competition's Chief Economist was created alongside a team of experts entrusted with advising mainly on those issues requiring advanced economic and econometric analyses.
- *Strengthening of the 'one-stop shop' principle.* The turnover thresholds used to define whether a merger must be assessed by the Commission have not been modified by this reform. Moreover, on the basis of such reform, mergers that affect three or more Member States shall also be directly notified to the Commission. The operations referral mechanism between the Commission and the Member States has been improved in order to guarantee that the most competent authority carries out the analysis of issues.
- *Procedural refinements.* Due to this reform, the terms of the Commission investigative stages are extended and more flexible, and its enquiring powers are more extensive.

State Aid

State aid favouring certain undertakings to the detriment of others can also alter open and fair competition between Member States. This is the reason why Article 87.1 of the Treaty (ex 92) considers incompatible with the common market, State aid affecting trade between Member States which distorts competition.[10] Such aid must involve the State or its resources and can be of diverse forms (subsidies, interest rebates, tax exemptions, guarantees, etc.).

The Member States must notify the European Commission of plans to grant an aid, which can be executed once its compatibility with the common market is approved (Article 88, ex 93). However, some simplifications have been introduced to this system according to Article 89 (ex 94). The aid granted for supporting small and medium enterprises (SMEs), research and development, environmental initiatives, employment and training schemes and those less than one hundred thousand euros (approved over a three-year period) will be exempt from that requirement.[11]

Other state aid granted but not included in the previous exemptions and not notified to the Commission, is considered illegal. If, upon the relevant investigation, the Commission concludes that the aid is not within the EU law, the Member State involved shall withdraw the measure and retrieve the aid.

In 2005, the Commission submitted a broad reform and modernization of the state aid policy, which will be concluded by 2009.[12] The main purpose of this action plan is to reduce the general amount of state aid, refocusing these on horizontal objectives. Within this program, the economic approach based on the analysis of market deficiencies will prevail as justification for the granting of state aid.

Liberalization

So far, the European policy seems to only protect competition from antitrust, mergers, abuses of a dominant position or state actions. However, EU regulations also try to introduce competitive elements in certain markets operating under monopolistic conditions, such as transport, energy, postal services and telecommunications.

Liberalization of these network industries is carried out on the basis of the existing differences between infrastructures, on the one hand, and delivery of services, on the other hand. Since the high investment costs linked to these industries makes the creation of additional competitive infrastructures inefficient, monopolistic structures continue to have a hold over these networks. Nevertheless, the services derived from these infrastructures could be offered within a competitive framework, provided that the monopolist allows suppliers to access and use the network. The infrastructure, therefore, results in an instrument for achieving competition.

In accordance with EU legislation, public undertakings and those which Member States grant special or exclusive rights shall be subject to the competition rules included in the Treaty – Article 86 (ex 90) –, always when the application of such rules guarantees the efficient performance of the particular tasks assigned to them. The European Commission is apt to supervise the verification of this, and to adopt and carry out the necessary directives or decisions.[13]

3. COMPETITION POLICY IN SERVICES

In the previous sections, competition has been analysed in general terms, without defining the situation of the different economic sectors. However, strong divergences can be observed between the liberalized manufacturing sector experiencing external and internal competitive pressures and services, which are frequently isolated from competition. Some inflexibility that restricts competitive behaviours can be found within the tertiary sector. It is worth highlighting the limited external competition affecting services. Services cross-border trade is more difficult compared to goods-producing sectors (Kox and Lejour, 2006). This hinders the development of competition at a national level and gives place, for example, to the existence of monopolistic licences, pricing outside of the market, limits to distribution or restrictions to the free delivery of professional services (Petitbó, 2000).

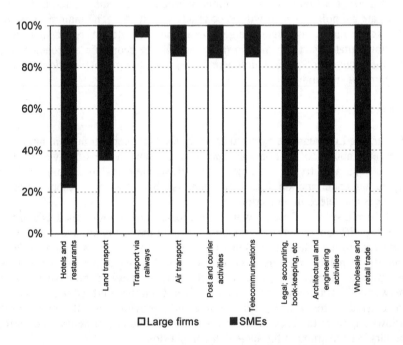

Notes: * For each category the available data for EU25 have been added. Data for 2002 have been considered for United Kingdom. Large includes enterprises with more than 250 employees, SMEs with 1 to 249. Wholesale and retail trade include repair of motor vehicles, motorcycles and personal and household goods. No information available for financial services.

Source: Based on Eurostat, 2006 (SBS).

Figure 8.1 Distribution of turnover by employment size classes, EU 25*, 2003

One of the factors explaining the limits to competition in services is market power. In some categories of the tertiary sector, companies with high market power may potentially restrict competitive behaviours. With regard to air and railway transport, telecommunications and postal services, large enterprises which represent, on average, 5 per cent of the total, accumulate almost 90 per cent of 2003 turnover and employees, as shown in Figure 8.1. By 2003, 63 per cent of the largest companies of the first category, 73 per cent of those of the second category and almost 65 per cent of postal services and telecommunications companies were located in France, Germany, the United Kingdom and Italy. These tertiary activities are normally characterized by oligopolistic market structures due to high infrastructure costs incurred by the provision of such services, which could result in the existence of natural monopolies. In this context, competition policy must accompany the regulatory reform in order to avoid companies taking unfair advantage of their dominant positions in the market. Traditionally, governments have created monopolies based on arguments such as avoiding the misuse of market power or guaranteeing a global access to networks. Nowadays however, their feasibility is questioned due to the impacts that technological changes and economic development have had on them (Rubalcaba et al., 2002). On the other hand, market power is much lower in hotels and restaurants, professional services and distributive trades, since these are fragmented services of monopolistic competition. In this case, large enterprises represent less than 0.10 per cent of the total, generating on average 24 per cent of the turnover and registering 20 per cent of employed persons. These fragmented market structures may reveal barriers to entry for certain organizational modes, such as large outlets in retail trade (European Central Bank, 2006). Regulatory reforms – particularly those regarding entry barriers – are the main tools to guarantee competitive conducts; competition policies can thus be used to inhibit anticompetitive behaviours (Hoj et al., 1995).

Market power has not been the only argument used to justify the intervention of the public sector in the services sector. As established in Chapter 7, externalities derived from certain tertiary activities, as well as information asymmetries, also justify state interventions. Limits to competition are explained not only on the basis of the inherent nature of services, which favours the market division at a local and international scale, but also according to government interventions undertaken within this sector. These actions have had different degrees of effect on the sector and thus adopted various forms: absolute public control of the delivery of certain services (i.e., railway transport and postal services); control of incorporation into professions by means of requirements such as membership to professional associations; control of certain activities through the granting of concessions to private companies (road passenger transport); establishing quotas (chemists), etc. According to the OECD (2000a), these national measures are the main restrictive factors to competition in tertiary activities.

Moreover, as demonstrated by the Public Choice School, imperfect state interventions intended to rectify market failures must also be noted. Measures adopted to safeguard competition can turn against it, creating barriers and inflexibilities that hinder the efficiency and productivity of the services involved.

There are services of an economic nature to which States impose specific responsibilities of public services in order to guarantee the fulfilment of citizens' basic needs. These services of general economic interest include transport, postal services, energy and communications, which have progressively become open to competition. Undertakings entrusted with the operation of these services are subject to the rules on competition, insofar as the application of such rules is not contrary to the interest of the Community, as stated in the previous section. In 2004, the European Commission decided to generalize its sectoral focus of EU policy regarding services of general interest rather than approving horizontal framework legislation.[14] This means that rules created shall be in accordance to the needs and specificities of each sector. In this context, the objectives presented are: the development of high-quality services of general interest with shared responsibility between the European Union, Member States and regional and local authorities on their definition, financing and control. With regard to the public financing of services of general economic interest, the European Commission decided in 2005 not to consider as state aid those guaranteeing the delivery of a specific public service with no overcompensations, which could result in cross-subsidies distorting competition in the sector.[15] Achieving a balance between the efficient market performance and the respect to competition rules, on the one hand, and the protection of general interest, on the other hand, appears to be an important challenge for the European Union and Member States.

Considering the cases handled by the European Commission regarding cartel and monopoly control during the period 2000–2005, it can be observed that the application of competition policy to services activities has surpassed that of goods. In this sense, competition policy follows the trend of structural changes experienced by modern economies. However, the weight of services in the application of competition policy does not entirely correspond to their participation in terms of value added generated by countries. Services have represented, on average, 59 per cent of the cases analysed by the Commission in accordance with Articles 81 and 82 of the Treaty; while its contribution to total value added is approximately 71 per cent, as analyzed in Chapter 3.[16] In contrast, goods register around one-third of value added and represent 41 per cent of the issues related to competition policy. Therefore, the proportions of competition-related cases do not correspond to those in force between economic sectors. Moreover, it is worth mentioning that the situation is not homogeneous within services. In the cases of energy, financial services, audiovisual services, transport and communications, competition effectively exceeds the relative economic participation of these sectors. Quite the opposite occurs in distributive trades, IT and professional services, since there is a deficit in the policy application when compared to the economic relevance of these services and the large amount of regulations and obstacles within them.

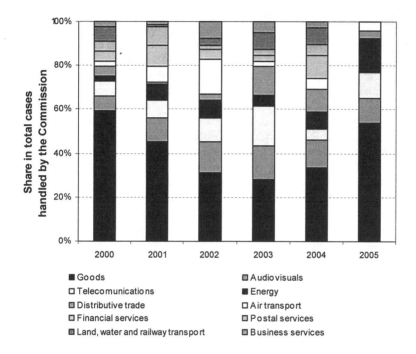

Notes: For each NACE code, the cases treated under Articles 81 and 82 of the Treaty and published in the European Commission website have been added. These were classified by years. Goods include manufacturing and the primary sector. Business services include professional and computer services.

Source: Based on the DG Competition website.

Figure 8.2 Application of competition policy to services, 2000–2005

Between 2000 and 2005, the Commission was constantly involved with the tertiary activities of telecommunications and audiovisual services. On average, these represented 12 per cent and 10 per cent, respectively, of the total cases analysed due to possible agreements between undertakings and abuses of dominant positions, as shown in Figure 8.2. In other services, intervention has fluctuated to a greater extent. For example, those cases regarding financial services represented 10 per cent of the total only in 2001 and 2004, while their participation in the rest of the period has been lower. The air transport sector has registered a gradual increase in the analyses implemented by the Commission since the year 2000, with the peak reached by 2002 with 15 per cent of total cases. Their importance, however, has decreased moderately over time. A similar situation occurred in distributive trades, where the interventions of the Commission reached their maximum in 2003. In the case of energy, competition cases have increased in latter years.

In the field of merger operations within the European Union, an upward trend until the year 2000 can be observed, followed by a fall which was overturned in 2004. Out of the 3022 cases notified to the Commission from 1990 (the year in which Regulation 4064/1989 took effect) until January 2006, the vast majority (85 per cent) was considered to be compatible with the common market in their first stage; conditions were imposed only for the approval of 5 per cent of the cases. Only 19 operations out of those analysed in the second stage were prohibited; that is to say, 0.6 per cent of total cases notified. According to Pelkmans (2006a), revisions of merger plans after informal interactions with the Merger Task Force and formal negotiations in the second stage of the process can explain this low rate of refusals. In sectoral terms, it can be observed that during the 1990s, mergers and acquisitions carried out in the services sector exceeded those in manufacturing. This is due to the impact of measures aimed at achieving an internal market. These measures were launched in the mid-1990s in the case of the tertiary sector, although they were completed earlier in the case of manufacturing.

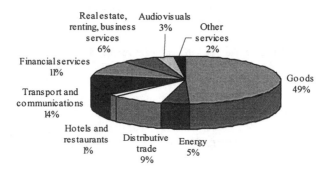

Notes: For each NACE code, the cases published in the European Commission website were added. Goods include the primary sector, manufacturing and construction. Other services include NACE codes L, M, N, O.90, P and Q.

Source: Based on the DG Competition website.

Figure 8.3 Mergers notified to the Commission by categories, 1990–2006

Regarding EU merger control, the trend is similar to that present in antitrust control. Between 1990 and 2006, the number of cases notified to the Commission regarding services has been slightly higher than that of goods. However, again in this case, the participation of services in competition is lower when compared to that registered in value added generated in economy. While such participation is, on average, 69 per cent between 1990 and 2006, only 50.6 per cent of the cases notified correspond to this activity, as shown in Figure 8.3.[17] On the other hand, 49 per cent of the mergers notified are related to goods, which represent one-third of the value added. In disaggregated terms, it can be noted that the participation in competition in a number of tertiary activities respect, to a certain extent, the dimension of this sector in economy. Such is the case of hotels and restaurants and distributive trades, where 1 per cent and 9 per cent of the mergers have been notified, while their participation in value added is of 2 per cent and 10 per cent, respectively. Moreover, regarding transport, communications and financial services, the proportions observed are not maintained, but the participation in the field of mergers exceeds that of the economy. Again, intra-sectoral heterogeneities arise regarding merger control.

With regard to state aid, the European Commission compiles a scoreboard in order to provide information about their situation and nature. Although a significant reduction in the level of global state aid was observed in the late 1990s, recent scoreboards show that this trend is stagnating. Total state aid granted by the EU15 during the period from 1994–2004 fell approximately 27 per cent. However, between 1994 and 1999, a remarkable drop of approximately 30 per cent was registered, while between 2000 and 2004, the aid was reduced only 0.03 per cent.[18] In 2004, the annual amount of state aid granted by the EU25 reached 62 000 million euros, which represents 0.60 per cent of the EU GDP. Germany, France and Italy have conferred the highest amount of aid. On the other hand, it can be noticed that the great majority of Member States devote their aid to horizontal objectives. Three-quarters of the total aid granted in 2004 by the EU25 was horizontal and mainly benefited environment (25 per cent), regional economic development (18 per cent), research and development (12 per cent) and small and medium sized enterprises (12 per cent).[19] One positive feature is that distortive state aid does not prevail in the service sector. Only 7 per cent of total state aid granted by the EU25 was aimed at tertiary activities; out of this percentage, 2 per cent corresponded to financial services and another 2 per cent to transport, excluding railways. Portugal grants the highest amount of aid to the financial sector, while the Netherlands is the leader regarding transport. The bulk of state aid (59 per cent) was granted to manufacturing, although the overestimation of data is expected due to specific measurement difficulties.[20] Approximately half of the aid granted to these sectors was in the form of subsidies, and, to a lesser extent, tax exemptions (32.4 per cent) and the granting of guarantees (10.3 per cent). It is worth highlighting that the sectoral distribution of aid is not homogeneous in all countries: Italy, Sweden,

Malta and Slovakia allocated 75 per cent of state aid to manufacturing and services, while 60 per cent were allocated to the agricultural and fishing sector in Austria, Estonia, Finland, Latvia and Lithuania. In Spain, Germany and Poland, aid granted to the coal industry is also worth mentioning.

4. CASE STUDIES ON SERVICES UNDER THE EUROPEAN COMPETITION POLICY

Given the importance attained by the services sector in the economy, in accordance with Chapter 3, the lack of competition in this sector is an important concern. It prevents the positive effects arising out of competition spreading throughout the economic system by means of the multiple interrelations that link them with other sectors. In this section, the competition rules in force in the main services sectors will be studied. The analysis will be complemented by some cases handled by the European Commission in order to illustrate, with examples, the application of such rules.

Telecommunications

In recent years, the telecommunications industry has experienced a significant change: from being a traditional public monopoly to being a much more complex industry where the number of operators and the amount of services to be delivered increased outstandingly. This has been heightened by technological change and the existence of potentially competitive activities within the telecommunications industry, such as the provision of local services in high-density and commercial areas, long-distance services and mobile. In turn, network provision, as well as residential telephony in rural or low-density areas, remains non-competitive (OECD, 2001e). The regulatory framework of this sector was created in 1990 with the Directive 90/388/EC, which has been amended five times.[21] This legislation promoted the opening of telecommunications and network markets and was completed in 1998. Taking into consideration the constant technical changes affecting electronic communications, the European Commission decided in 2002 to establish a new package of technologically neutral directives, which were flexible enough to adapt to them.[22] In this way, a new association was formed between EU competition rules and *ex ante* regulations of specific telecommunication sectors. Within the current framework, *ex ante* regulations of such sectors must be *proportional* to their existing competition restrictions. This means that in those markets where there are no suppliers with Significant Market Power (SMP), existing measures must be eliminated so that the agents' behaviour is only governed by the general competition rules. In contrast, in those markets where there are undertakings with a dominant position, additional regulations must be imposed to be applied together with such rules, with the purpose of avoiding their misuse. The concept of 'Significant Market Power' (SMP) used herein is in accordance with the definition of dominant position set out in Article 82 of the Treaty.[23] Additional regulations imposed on companies with SMP must be based on appropriate market analyses implemented by the National Regulatory Authorities (NRA) in association with the national competition authority. In its 2003 recommendation, the Commission suggested a list of eighteen markets (likely to be imperfect) where NRAs must focus their analysis in order to determine the need for *ex ante* regulations.[24] Regulatory projects arising from this analysis must be notified to the Commission so that it can verify their compatibility with effective EU laws and their contribution to the internal market. Thereafter, the Commission has one month to make observations: if specific aspects are doubted, a second investigation stage can be opened, and afterwards, if necessary, it can prohibit the adoption of the new regulations as it has 'veto authority'.[25] At present, a review of the current e-communications regulatory framework is under way. Nowadays, the biggest challenges the Community regulations must face are: on the one hand, achieving their complete and correct practical implementation by all Member States, and on the other hand, guaranteeing that the NRAs have the necessary faculties to carry out their regulatory role in a transparent, independent and impartial manner.

With regard to telecommunications, the Commission has carried out several enquiries, related primarily to the abuse of a dominant position by traditional operators. In 2003, Wanadoo Interactive, a subsidiary of France Telecom, and Deutsche Telecom were fined 10.35 million euros and 12.6 million euros, respectively, for this type of abuse in their relevant markets. Moreover, an increased regulatory certainty has boosted the pace of cross-border mergers and acquisitions in this sector, whose main objective is not only to take advantage of scale economies, but also to outline potential European and international strategies. Large national operators are already present in other markets, and investment has also been directed towards new Member States. For example, the Commission has authorized the Spanish company Telefónica to acquire Czech Český Telecom. Meanwhile, the acquisition of O2 has been subject to certain conditions.

Several telecommunications companies have received state aid in different ways. The European Commission has approved (with conditions) a guarantee granted by Germany that consists of a loan of 112 million euros to the mobile operator MobilCom for company restructuring. In 2004, the Commission demonstrated that French authorities had provided illegal aid to France Telecom, including special tax schemes and an advance awarded on condition of its status as a new shareholder, thus enabling the enterprise to gain access to better financial conditions in the market.

In spite of the fact that the liberalization process has not been completed in all Member States or in all important market areas, the opening of telecommunications to competition has so far benefited the consumers with lower prices, better services and a wider range of choices.[26] Nowadays, operators offer packages of low-cost telecommunication services including voice, broadband access and audiovisual content. However, further progress is needed regarding international roaming in order to increase competitive pressure. The telecommunication sector is extremely dynamic, which can translate as difficulties in seeing the difference between the effects generated by the technological changes and those arising from the gradual liberalization and introduction of competition. In practice, a reduced number of large enterprises still dominate the sector, as explained in the previous section. In fact, *ex ante* regulation and control elements present in this opening could eventually restrict the strengthening of competition.

Distributive Trades

The sector of distributive trades structurally constitutes a competitive market characterized by mainly small enterprises with relative facility to enter and exit it (Hoj, Kato and Pilat, 1995; Pilat, 1997). A distinction is usually made between direct trade with consumers (retail) and that carried out by the intermediaries of producers and distributors (wholesale).

Competition in this sector has traditionally been affected by a wide range of regulations that restrict the opening times of businesses, the set-up of large shops and the establishment of new stores in certain areas. Vertical agreements between different agents of the value chain with the purpose of controlling the purchase and sale of goods or services are subject to EU competition rules. According to these rules, almost all alliances are admitted, as long as the enterprise involved does not have market power.[27] Vertical agreements are exempt from the application of Article 81 provided that:

- Serious restraints on competition are not allowed, such as the imposition of resale prices on distributors or territorial or potential customer restrictions.
- The market share of the suppliers involved in the agreement does not exceed 30 per cent of the relevant market.
- Certain restrictions may be compatible with community competition regulations if a number of conditions are met.

Within this action framework, the European Commission has dealt with diverse cases. In 2002, for example, Nintendo and seven of its European distributors were fined 168 million euros due to their association, which hampered the commercialization of video games from low-cost countries to high-cost countries. On the other hand, concentration transactions within the distributive sector have been significant, representing on average 9 per cent of the total cases notified to the Commission since 1990, and 18 per cent within the services sector. In 2005, a joint venture was approved between Sephora (a retail store of cosmetic products) and the department store chain El Corte Inglés. In the same year, the Commission referred the proposal of acquisition by UK company Tesco of Carrefour retailing business in Slovakia to the national competition authorities, the Antimonopoly Office of the Slovak Republic. This is the first time a merger had been referred to a New Member State authority for its evaluation.

Sales and after-sales services of motor vehicles have their own competition rules, which are stricter than those applicable to the overall trade sector.[28] Among other measures, the rules grant retailers the possibility of selling more than one trademark in their stores and of keeping the 'availability clause', which allows dealers to supply cars that are identical to those of other Member States. In this way, cross-border purchases are promoted. Repair and maintenance services have also been affected by rules promoting distributors' and consumers' choice. Regulations in force were amended in 2002, following a series of serious infringements of the competition rules committed by manufacturers and car dealers. In 2005, for instance, Peugeot was fined 49.5 million euros for hindering the export of new cars from the Netherlands to consumers in other Member States.

Regulations detrimental to competition still exist in the distributive trades sector. The action of competition policy could be more in depth, as it still contains entry restrictions (for example, limited permissions granted to department stores), predatory pricing, collusion provision, abuses of a dominant position, and considerable influence of political interests. Furthermore, there are difficulties within local and regional competitions. A more ambitious competition policy would be more advantageous to consumers (the access of department stores to markets and fair competition practices would be easier) and for small stores and suppliers (in order to avoid the abuse of power by large department stores and to promote modernization of retailers).

Audiovisuals

At present, certain technological and commercial factors – such as the stagnating of the advertising market, the increase in costs to access high-quality contents and the complex transition towards digital stages – are causing the re-structuring of the audiovisual sector's competitive environment.[29] Taking these elements into consideration, the effective application of community competition policy is extremely important. In the field of sport broadcasting, the Commission has resolved several cases related to the joint sale of television rights in order to guarantee the public access to high-quality contents (UEFA, Bundesliga). In this way, the detrimental effects of exclusive joint sale on competition – production and technical developments restrictions, price conflicts and the strengthening of the position of companies with sufficient financial capacity to access the packages – are intended to be prevented. Included in these decisions is one of the major priorities of the European competition authorities: the development of new audiovisual modes, such as image transmission by mobile phones (3G).

Competitive difficulties associated with concentrations carried out within the audiovisual industry are principally related to the access to contents and the supply to final consumers. In this sector, Member States have the capacity to control business concentrations in order to guarantee the diversity of the media.[30] However, the European Commission also controls concentration transactions, bearing in mind that certain aspects of the audiovisual sector could result in higher degrees of concentration compared to other industries. As an example, specific conditions have recently been imposed on the acquisition of the Italian pay-television company Telepiú by the Australian media group Newscorp.

State aid that is granted to the audiovisual industry, and which does not threaten community exchanges and whose purpose is to promote cultural development, is compatible with the EU regulations in force, provided that certain criteria are met.[31] Within this framework, the Commission has approved certain aid schemes to support cinematographic activities, such as those granted by the German and Belgian governments. Moreover, public broadcasting services have also benefited from state aid.

It is fundamental for the competition policy to accompany the technological revolution in which audiovisual services are fully immersed. The actions taken by the Commission have not hindered the existence of dominant positions and practices contrary to competition in many countries. Barriers to competition are related to the granting of licences and the existence of exclusive agreements to access certain contents. In the case of printed media, it is important to advance towards the elimination of restrictions imposed by the Member States on retail booksellers. This will benefit final consumers and will favour modernization and the flexibility of the sector towards new technologies. Independent national regulatory authorities are crucial to support competition and diversity in the supply of audiovisual media.

Air Transport

Some areas within the air transport industry, such as aircraft operations, maintenance facilities and catering services, are potentially competitive. In contrast, infrastructures and certain airport services, including take-off and landing (slots), are usually not of this kind (OECD, 2001e). The opening of this sector to competition has gradually been carried out through three packages of liberalizing measures in 1987, 1990 and 1992. Until 2004, the Commission only had the faculties to apply the European competition policy to intra-EU air transport. It did not have the power to act in transatlantic alliances or other types of agreements between EU and non-EU operators. Regulation 411/2004,[32] created a framework for regulating these types of practices under which the Commission can grant block exemptions in air transport between the EU and third countries, as it already did concerning traffic between EU airports. In 2006, the exemption conferred on the IATA Conference (International Air Transport Association) concerning the establishment of tariffs in interline passenger transportation has been reviewed.[33] The use of a single ticket for flights operated by different airlines (interlining) brings benefits to consumers and enterprises. Nevertheless, the Commission considers the possibility of using other methods, whose effects on competition are less negative than pricing.[34]

Generally speaking, the Commission considers that alliances between airlines can be beneficial for passengers in that they expand networks, increase the frequency of flights, and improve the efficiency of the service. This is the case of the cooperation agreements signed between British Airways and SN Brussels Airlines, which were approved in 2003, or the alliance between Air France and Alitalia, which was authorized subject to conditions in 2004. Concerning concentrations between air companies, the European Commission has shown a favourable position toward consolidating the European air sector. In 2003, the merger between KLM and Air France was authorized, subject to conditions. Likewise, the increase in the participation of SAS in Spanair has been approved without objections, so the former has taken over the latter.

Compared to the mid-1990s, state aid granted to air transport companies have decreased considerably. However, this form of aid continues to be authorized, and recent years have even observed an increase within EU15. In 1994 and 1995, this aid exceeded 2500 million euros, while in the period from 2002 to 2004 the state aids granted were on average of 330 million euros, representing 20 per cent of the overall amount conferred on the transport sector. In contrast, state aid between 2001 and 2003 represented 18 per cent, and between 1999 and 2001, 12 per cent. Among the authorizations given in recent years, the Ryanair-Charleroi case is worth mentioning: the Commission considered the aid granted by the Belgian region of Valona and the public airport Charleroi to Ryanair to be compatible with the common market, since it enabled the use of a secondary terminal that was underused, reduced air congestion, and boosted the creation of new routes.

The liberalization of the air transport sector has had positive effects for consumers, who can now choose from a larger number of airlines, routes and timetables. Although promotional tariffs have increased, no downward trend can be seen in the prices of tickets that allow date and time changes. This implies that competition could intensify even more. In fact, as previously mentioned, business alliances still have the advantage of a certain immunity regarding competition policy, and state aid has not yet disappeared entirely. The emergence of low-cost airlines that use secondary airports not controlled by large enterprises is one of the most important incentives increasing competitive pressure. Actually, between 1998 and 2004, their participation in the sector has grown 16.8 per cent. The liberalization of airports, particularly concerning slots, could also increase effective competition.

Inland Transport (Rail, Road and Water Transport)

Taking into consideration the special characteristics of this sector, exceptions have also been stipulated regarding the application of EU competition legislation in relation to certain agreements and concerted practices that fix transport rates and conditions, apply improvements or establish technical co-operation, or the joint acquisition of transport equipment or supplies, among others.[35] This is the reason why the joint venture between Maersk and P&O Nedlloyd was approved in 2002, with the purpose of facilitating the movement of their containers between the seaports of Rotterdam, Bremerhaven and Hamburg, and the inland terminals located in Germany, Italy, Poland and Hungary.

As regards railway transport, several factors limit the development of effective competition: the lack of an appropriate separation between infrastructure managers and operators of the rail services, the non-existence of transparent mechanisms for the allocation of international train routes and the sparse competition regarding supply. In spite of this, some devices have been developed since 2001 aimed at achieving the integration of national railways into a single European passenger and freight rail network by 2010.[36] Discriminatory and exclusionary practices by operators already established in the market towards new operators can be observed in this sector. Subsidies granted to railways by EU15 amounted almost 25 000 million euros in 2004.[37] However, a large amount of the state aid is not notified to the Commission. Due to the absence of market opening, European countries do not consider financing in this sector strictly as state aid. On the other hand, state aid assigned by the Member States to road and inland water transport represented 13 per cent and 0.4 per cent respectively of the total amount allocated to transports (excluding railways) between 2002 and 2004 (65 per cent for maritime transport and 21 per cent for air transport). The Commission has recently accepted several aid schemes to compensate for additional costs of inter-modal transport. In 2002, for example, the Commission approved rescue aid to the Belgian company ABX, which provides logistical services for road transport, among others.

The railway transport sector is still closed to effective competition. It is necessary to limit the existing protectionism, accelerate the free access to rail infrastructures for passenger and freight transport, and control the state aid granted. Moreover, inland water transport does not fully benefit from competition, despite the fact that it is liberalized. To this end, it is essential to harmonize the different existing national regulations in this respect, which can distort the intra-EU competitive process.

Financial Services

One of the political priorities of the Commission is the integration of the European financial markets into a single market. In order to do so, the introduction of the single currency was complemented by the Financial Services Action Plan, which promoted freedom for the establishment and the provision of such services between Member States.[38] In 2005, the Commission released a White Paper with the intention of consolidating the integration process of the financial markets for the following five years following practical, economic and consumer criteria. This also established as key challenges the integration of retail markets and the effective application of existing legislation.

In order to complement these requirements, a sectoral investigation was launched, in 2006, regarding the situation of competition in basic retail banking – which started with payment cards – and insurance. This analysis is justified given the variability of prices between similar financial products among Member States, the increase of the banking concentration levels, intra-EU heterogeneity of banking benefits, and the barriers to entry into cross-border insurance markets.

The decisions taken by the Commission in this respect are varied and range from financial and monetary intermediation to market administration and insurances and pensions. In 2002, an Austrian bank cartel (comprised of eight banks) was fined 124.26 million euros. Moreover, in 2004, the Commission condemned Clearstream Banking AG and its parent company, Clearstream International SA (German institutions that provided securities liquidation, compensation and custody services), for double abuse of their dominant position in these markets. In the field of payment systems, the Commission's first report, issued in 2001, was related to Visa International. With regard to inter-bank commissions applied to cross-border transactions with payment cards, Visa adopted transparent criteria and objectives, and the Commission subsequently granted an exception in 2002.

The proportion of cross-border intra-EU acquisitions carried out in the financial sector is low compared to other sectors. Between 1999 and 2004, only 20 per cent of the total value of financial operations corresponded to this type of transaction; in other sectors, however, this value amounted to 45 per cent.[39] Those involved in this activity – in response to a Commission call – identified the legal and tax control schemes as well as the heterogeneous consumer-protection rules between Member States as the main restrictions limiting these types of operation. With regard to this situation, the Commission has maintained a favourable position towards cross-border banking acquisitions. In 2005, it authorized without objections the takeover of the Banca Nazionale del Lavoro by the Spanish group Banco Bilbao Vizcaya Argentaria, and the Banca Antoniana Popolare Veneta by the Amro Bank, a Dutch banking association. In other cases, companies have to comply with certain requirements in order to achieve the Commission's authorization.

Several cases of state actions leading to competitive market distortions have been detected in the financial sector. The German state was recently urged to recover 3000 million euros from the WestLB group and another six public banks. France, in turn, granted a guarantee to Caisse des Dépôts et

Consignations (CDC), which was transferred to one of its commercial subsidiaries, the investment bank CDC IXIS. This state aid will gradually be withdrawn in order to enable the company to adapt to the new situation during the transition period.

Undoubtedly, competition has become more intense in the field of European financial services in recent years, particularly regarding wholesale markets. However, some markets are still fragmented, and an improvement is recommended. Such is the case of retail financial services and insurance services, where elements restricting competition persist: entry restrictions, price differences between Member States, market power and vertical agreements. In these fields, final consumers and SMEs could benefit from lower prices and a wider variety of goods and services.

Professional Services

Liberal professions including legal, technical, accounting and pharmaceutical have been historically subject to regulations, state or self-imposed, with the purpose of protecting consumers from fraudulent and negligent practices. The establishment of qualification requirements and the membership of professional associations have controlled market entry. Furthermore, the behaviour within the market has been regulated by the fixing of prices and rates, as well as limits to advertising and multidisciplinary practices.

The policy of the European Commission consists of the full application of competition regulations to liberal professions, taking into consideration their specific features. In this sense, it does not question the existence of professional self-regulations, but their use at the expense of consumer welfare. In 2003, an analysis carried out by an independent entity revealed the large differences between levels of regulation between countries and professions (Paterson et al., 2003). Moreover, it concluded that those countries with the lowest level of regulation – Ireland, the United Kingdom, Denmark, the Netherlands and the Nordic countries – are not necessarily less efficient, but quite the opposite, as excessive regulation is a hindrance to the creation of employment and wealth. Also in 2003, the Commission conducted a collective exercise on the basis of the opinions gathered from customers, experts, professional associations and state bodies in order to make an inventory of the effective EU regulatory practices. Upon revealing this information, a Report on Competition in Professional Services was issued, which was subsequently completed with the analysis of this situation in the new Member States.[40] In such a Report, the countries are requested to scrutinize their professional regulations by applying a proportionality test. This test would seem appropriate in assessing to what extent the relevant regulation is objectively justified and serves the public interest. The Commission invites regulatory authorities and non-governmental organizations to jointly try and eliminate those rules which do not meet the criteria established. Moreover, they will explore the need to use accompanying pro-competitive methods to increase transparency and enhance consumer empowerment (active monitoring by consumer associations, publication of historical data, etc.). Recently, the Commission has advised that Denmark, the Netherlands and the United Kingdom are conducting significant reforms in this respect. Fewer reforms have been registered in Austria, Estonia, Hungary, Slovenia and Portugal, and analytical works have already started in another nine countries.[41] However, the fact that no advances in this field have been made in the Czech Republic, Cyprus, Finland, Greece, Malta, Spain and Sweden is cause for concern.

So far, several official decisions have been made regarding the provision of professional services. For example, the Commission has sanctioned the fixed prices set by Italian customs agents and the prices recommended by Dutch professional associations. In 2004, the scale of recommended minimum fees adopted by the Belgian Architects' Association was condemned.[42] However, certain professional regulations have also been admitted under specific circumstances. In the so-called Arduino case, for instance, the Commission permitted Italian lawyers to fix a fees scale, provided that this is justified by a public interest and that there is no delegation of responsibility or control by the state to private operators. Another judgement refers to the prohibition of multidisciplinary practices in the Netherlands in order to prevent conflicts of interests and guarantee the proper functioning of the office.[43] One consequence was the establishment of a legal precedent, by which the professional ethics and legal rules of those organizations that guarantee the proper exercise of the profession are excluded from the application of Article 81 (1) of the Treaty.

Despite the aforementioned actions, the area of liberal professions is still a sector closed to competition, although significant differences can be observed between Member States. This situation arises from the lack of national political determination to eliminate professional restrictions that affect the competitive process, on one hand, and, on the other, the reluctance to change that characterizes this sector. Rents derived from anticompetitive actions can be large, and sectoral interests are highly concentrated (Wise, 2001). Subsequently, liberal professions still constitute one of the economic sectors most distant from the competitive opening process and market integration.

Postal Services

Potentially competitive areas in the field of postal services include postal transport, delivery of express mail or packages and delivery of mail to high-volume business clients, especially in high-density areas. Door-to-door mail delivery in low-density residential areas is usually considered a non-competitive activity (OECD, 2001e). The Postal Directive adopted in 2002[44] currently governs this sector and its ultimate objective is to create an effective single market for postal services. The main resources needed to achieve this include the opening of the market with a staged reduction of the reserved area[45] and the liberalization of outgoing mail between Member States.[46] Moreover, this Directive prohibits – with some exceptions – cross-subsidization of services outside the reserved sector out of revenues from services in the reserved sector. It also proposes a study to be finalized by 2006, which will demonstrate the impact that an internal market for the postal services – presumably completed by 2009 – will have on each Member State. Based on the study's conclusions, the Commission will confirm with the European Parliament and the Council the full implementation of the internal postal market or determine any other necessary steps.

Although all Member States are progressively adopting the measures imposed by the Commission, different levels of liberalization currently exist in the postal sector. Sweden, Finland, Estonia, Germany, the United Kingdom, the Netherlands and Slovakia are those countries registering the greatest advances, according to a recent study (ECORYS, 2005). In fact, the former three have already liberalized the postal sector, and the others plan to do so before the date stipulated in the last Directive.

The intervention of the Commission in the postal sector is important in order to guarantee a quality service to users, mainly companies, at affordable prices throughout the EU, as well as to prevent anti-competitive practices by state and private operators involved in the delivery of the services. The decisions reached mainly condemn the abuse of a dominant position of some operators within the sector. The first verdict of this type was adopted in 2001 against the German postal operator Deutsche Post AG (DPAG) for using its revenue from the letters monopoly to finance services in the competitive commercial package market. However, no fine was imposed for this infringement because the economic cost concepts used to identify predation were not sufficiently developed at the time the abuse occurred. Furthermore, in 2001, the German operator was fined for intercepting, surcharging and delaying incoming cross-border letter mailings.[47] In that same year, the Commission fined the Belgian postal service operator De Post/La Poste 2.5 million euros for financing a new business-to-business mail service.

The European Commission has also adopted decisions regarding concentrations within the postal sector, such that these neither create nor strengthen dominant positions in the companies involved. For example, the Commission approved (under certain conditions) a joint venture between public postal operators from the United Kingdom (TPO), the Netherlands (TPG) and Singapore (SPPL). On the other hand, the takeover of DHL International Ltd in 2002 by Deutsche Post AG was authorized without conditions.

With regard to the postal sector, the Commission approved in 2002 the financial support that the Italian government provided to Poste Italiane during the 1990s. This approval was based on the fact that this aid did not exceed the costs of the task of supplying a public postal service. On the same basis, the

Commission also authorized the state aid granted by the British government to Post Office Limited (retail subsidiary of Royal Mail Group).

Competition is not yet deeply rooted in the postal sector. As in other services categories, significant differences between Member States and market areas can be observed regarding the advances of the liberalization process. The persistence of the reserved area, which acts as a legal barrier to the entry of new operators, limits competitive pressure. In practice, a group of large companies still dominates the sector, and traditional operators enjoy protection, for example, concerning payable taxes. This can also hinder the entry of new agents into the market and limit the competitive process.

5. CONCLUDING REMARKS

EU policy is intended to protect competition from certain unfair business and state practices, which could be detrimental to it, and to enhance the opening of some sectors closed to competitive pressure. Therefore, EU policy attempts to promote the positive effects that competition generates on the economic system in general and on consumers in particular. In the first case, pro-competitive policies improve productivity, innovation and technological diffusion that boost economic growth. In the second, competition allows consumers to choose within a wider range of higher-quality goods at lower prices. Given that the service sector accounts for nearly 70 per cent of employment and value added generated in advanced economies, the fact that many of them are still far removed from competitive pressure is an important concern. This is due to the specific features of services, to the presence of market power in certain categories of the sector, as well as to the maintenance of inefficient, and now unjustifiable, regulations.

The application of competition policy is not entirely in line with the importance of tertiary activities in terms of value added generated in the economy. Services have represented, on average, 59 per cent of the cases analysed by the European Commission in accordance with Articles 81 and 82 of the Treaty, and 50.6 per cent of the mergers notified. The situation, however, is not homogeneous within tertiary activities. On some occasions, competition policy is deemed to be unambitious (professional services, distributive trades); in other sectors (like postal services or communications) traditional operators are still protected, thus hindering the entry of new operators and, therefore, competition. Generally speaking, competition policy appears to be quite flexible, with many exceptions and exemptions, some of which are legitimate according to public interest, and others that can no longer be justified by this argument.

There is limited authority regarding the heterogeneity of criteria and policies of Member States. Regulatory differences between them and discrepancies in the adoption of the Commission rules result in asymmetries in the markets, thus hampering the attainment of an internal market. The level of competition achieved is uneven between Member States and sectors of a same market. Moreover, potential tensions are feasible between national traditions and the Commission's approach. No real updating has occurred regarding increasing market integration and globalization. Borders are gradually less important in Europe, and this is a main challenge for competition policy. In this sense, competition policy seems to need to prioritize higher economic content over legal content. In 2004, the Commission made a change in this direction with the appointment of the first DG Competition's Chief Economist and the modernizations of the application of Articles 81 and 82 and the Merger Regulation, which have introduced economic criteria to the Commission's analysis.

EU and national economic and political interests can have an influence on the direction of regulation on competition, as well as on the exemptions granted. The promotion of objectivity and transparency is necessary at both levels. The Commission has been criticized in recent years, as its decisions were not always based on strict and consistent analytical studies. However, its approach has currently become more economic, although some of its fields could provide companies with more legal clarity and security. Member States' governments are, in turn, likely to suffer internal pressures regarding the application of competition policy. This explains the slowness in achieving certain political objectives, such as the withdrawal of some state aids or, as in the field of professional services, the maintenance of detrimental regulations.

In summary, EU competition policy faces many challenges in the services arena. There are specific challenges for certain sectors; more general challenges concerning the way competition policy is designed and addresses the needs of services markets; challenges derived from increasing globalization trends and potential conflicts with the still highly heterogeneous regulation and uneven national competition policies; and finally, challenges regarding interactions with other policies. The accurate management of policies for facing these challenges should lead to better competition and market integration in European services.

It is worth highlighting the low participation of European consumers and the organizations representing them in the fight against anti-competitive behaviour. In contrast, private actions in the US legislature represent 90 per cent of the application of competition policy. Consumers need to raise their voices and hold more frequent discussions with the Commission. In this regard, the position of the liaison officer has been established within the DG Competition in order to approach competition and consumer protection policies. But this new policy-making still needs to deliver its performance.

Competition depends also on the procompetitive orientation of other EU policies. This is why competition policy cannot act in isolation. A good competition policy is vital to achieve a real internal market. Greater coordination between competition and the internal market is needed, such as in the case of the energy sector, with the recent takeovers concerning Eon-

Endesa and Suez-Gaz de France. On top of the coordination with the internal market policy, competition policy may also be complementary and coordinated with other service-related policies, as will be shown in Chapter 10.

Appendix – Cases Discussed in this Chapter

Wanadoo Interactive-COMP 38.233. Deutsche Telecom.- COMP 37.451. Telefónica/ Český Telecom. - M.3800. France Telecom/ Amena- M.3920. Germany/ Mobilcom-C/5/2003. France/ France Telecom.–C/13//A/2004 y C/13/B/2004. Nintendo - COMP/35.706. El Corte Inglés/ Sephora- Peugeot-COMP/36.623. UEFA- COMP/37.398. Newscorp/ Telepiú- M. 2876. Newscorp /Telecom Italia/ Stream- M.1978. Germany/ Audiovisual state aid - N 41/2004. Belgium/ audiovisual state aid - N 224/2004. British Airways / SN Brussels Airlines COMP/38.477. Air France / Alitalia- COMP/38.284. KLM/ Air France- M.3280. SAS/ Spanair- M.2672. Ryanair/ Charleroi-C/76/2002. Maersk /P&O Nedlloyd- COMP/38.086. Intermodal transport state aid: N/64/2003, N 623/2002, N 810/2002. Belgium /ABX- N/769/2002. Austrian bank cartel-COMP 36.571. Clearstream/ Euroclear Bank-COMP/38.096. Visa International- COMP 29.373. BBVA /BNL- M.3768. Amro Bank/ Banca Antoniana Popolare Veneta-M.3780. Germany/ WestLB-C/64/1997. France/CDC- C/2003/42/3. Custom agents /Decision 93/438/EEC. Dutch professional associations/ Decision 96/438/EEC. Belgian Architects Association/ COMP/38.549. Arduino- Case C-35/99. Wouters-Case C-309/99. Deutsche Post AG- COMP/36.915.. De Post/ La Poste-COMP/37.859. Deutsche Post AG/Germany- COMP 38.745. TPO/TPG/SPPL- M.1915. Deutsche Post AG/ DHL International Ltd-M.2908. Italy/Poste Italiane- C/47/1998. United Kingdom/ Post Office Limited - N/784/2002.

NOTES

1. Gisela Di Meglio has collaborated in the drafting of this chapter as a coauthor.
2. Commission Green Book of 21st of May, 2003 on services of general interest, COM (2003)270.
3. These include horizontal agreements promoting cooperation between undertakings for the improvement of goods or services by means of specialization, transfer of technology or R&D, as well as vertical supply and distribution agreements that improve coordination within a supply or production chain (facilitating, for example, cross-border sales in the case of the automotive sector).

4. Council Regulation (EC) no. 1/2003 of 16.12.2002 on the implementation of the rules on competition laid down in Articles 81 and 82 of the Treaty entered into force on 1.5.2004.
5. 'Hardcore restrictions' are those with negative effects on trade and which are expressly prohibited (for example, agreements among competitors fixing prices, sharing customers and dividing markets or limiting production).
6. According to the Guidelines, if agreements cover a market share of below 5 per cent and the turnover of companies involved in the corresponding products is lower than 40 million euros, they will not presumably affect intra-EU trade, so they remain under the authority of the Member State in question.
7. 'DG Competition discussion paper on the application of article 82 of the Treaty to exclusionary abuses', December 2005. Public consultation of this document will be open until March, 2006. Afterwards, the Commission will assess the preparation of Guidelines on the basis of such document.
8. Airtours/ First Choice case, M.1524, DO L 093 dated 13.04.2000
9. (EC) Council Regulation no. 139/2004 of 20.01.2004, on the control of concentrations between undertakings ('EC Merger Regulation').
10. However, this article includes a list of possible exceptions (87.2) and exemptions (87.3). The following are compatible with the common market: aid with a social character granted to individual consumers; aid to repair a damage caused by natural disasters or exceptional occurrences; aid to promote the regional economic development; aid to promote the execution of an important project of common European interest; aid to remedy disturbances in the economy of a Member State; aids to facilitate the development of certain economic activities or areas; aid to promote culture or heritage conservation; and any other aid specified by the Council on a proposal from the Commission.
11. They are only required to submit an information card upon granting of the aid.
12. COM (2005) 107 final: 'State aid action plan: less and better targeted state aid. A roadmap for state aid reform 2005–2009'.
13. On the basis of this, the Commission has prepared a Directive on the transparency of financial relations between the Member States and public undertakings: Directive 723/80, modified by Directive 2000/52.
14. White Paper on Services of General Interest. COM (2004) 374.
15. Those aids of less than 30 million euros per year granted to companies with a turnover of less than 100 millions euros are exempt from the requirement of notifying the Commission.
16. The cases considered are those published in the DG Competition website between 1990 and 2006. Regarding the value added, the average considered has been that corresponding to the EU15 during the period 2000 to 2003, according to the data available in the Groningen Growth and Development Centre Database.
17. The cases considered are those published in the DG Competition website between 1990 and 2005. Regarding the value added, the average considered has been that corresponding to the EU15 during the period 1990 to 2003, according to the data available in the Groningen Growth and Development Centre Database.
18. Total state aid in the sense described in Article 87.1 of the Treaty, including manufacturing, services, coal, agriculture, fishing and transport (except for railways).

19. COM (2005) 624 final 'State Aid Scoreboard, autumn 2005 update'. Employment received 4 per cent of state aid, 3 per cent was aimed at training, and the remaining 3 per cent corresponded to other horizontal objectives.
20. In the manufacturing sector, state aid includes those for general economic development and horizontal objectives such as research and development, SMEs, environment, energy, employment and training, for which the specific sector is not always known. Consequently, the data corresponding to this sector could be overestimated.
21. Directives 94/46/ EC, 95/51/EC, 96/2/EC, 96/19/EC and 99/64/EC.
22. Framework Directive 2002/21/EC, Directive 2002/19/EC on access to, and interconnection of, electronic communications networks, Directive 2002/20/CE concerning the authorization of electronic communications networks and services, Directive 2002/22/CE concerning universal services and users' rights, Directive 2002/58/EC concerning the processing of personal data and the protection of privacy in the electronic communications sector.
23. An undertaking will have a dominant position, whether individually or collectively, if it can operate regardless of the actions carried out by its competitors, clients or consumers.
24. Commission Recommendation 2003/311/EC on relevant product and service markets within the electronic communications sector susceptible to *ex ante* regulation. To regulate a market not mentioned in this recommendation, the NRA concerned shall request permission to the Commission and act in accordance with Article 7 of the Framework Directive.
25. In late 2005, the Commission passed 99 cases, using its veto authority on only four occasions (two against Finland, one against Austria, and one against Germany).
26. COM (2006) 68 dated 20.02.2006. European electronic communications regulation and markets 2005 (11th report).
27. (EC) Regulation no. 2790/1999 on the application of Article 81 (3) of the Treaty to categories of vertical agreements and concerted practices.
28. (EC) Regulation no. 1400/2002 on the application of Article 81 (3) of the Treaty to categories of vertical agreements and concerted practices in the motor vehicle sector.
29. European Commission, 2003, SEC 467, XXXIInd report on Competition Policy.
30. Article 21 (3) of the EC Merger Regulation.
31. Communication from the Commission on certain legal aspects relating to cinematographic and other audiovisual works. COM (2001) 534 final. For example, subsidies granted to audiovisual works (cinematographic or television) are limited to 50 per cent of their budgets. Moreover, audiovisual organizations should be free to spend part of their budgets in other Member States – not just in the aid-granting state.
32. EC Council Regulation 411/2004 of February 26th, 2004, which repeals the ECC Regulation no. 3975/87 and amends ECC Regulation no. 3976/87 and EC Regulation no. 1/2003 regarding air transport between the European Community and third countries. This Regulation came into force on May 1st, 2004. In scope: agreements or alliances between transatlantic air operators. Not in scope: mergers and acquisitions to which the EC Merger Regulation is applicable.
33. EC Regulation 1617/93 on the application of Article 81(3) to certain categories of agreements and concerted practices concerning consultations on passenger tariffs

on scheduled air services. Recently, this exemption has been renovated for a limited time (EC Regulation N° 1459/2006). Depending on the type of agreement, the date on which the block exemption expires differs. Once the exemptions conclude, the airline industry must evaluate if its practices are in accordance with EU competition rules.

34. Discussion and consultation documents available at http://europa.eu.int/comm/competition/antitrust/ others/

35. ECC Council Regulation no. 1017/68 of 19 July 1968, applying rules of competition to transport by rail, road and inland waterway. Official Journal L 175 dated 23.7.1968.

36. Directive 2001/12/EC of the European Parliament and of the Council of 26 February 2001, amending Council Directive 91/440/EEC on the development of the Community's railways. Directive 2001/13/EC of the European Parliament and of the Council of 26 February 2001, amending Council Directive 95/18/EC on the licensing of railways undertakings. Directive 2001/14/EC of the European Parliament and of the Council of 26 February 2001 on the allocation of railway infrastructure capacity and the levying of charges for the use of railway infrastructure and safety certification.

37. COM (2005) 624 final 'State Aid Scoreboard, autumn 2005 update'.

38. Financial Services. Implementing the framework for financial markets: Action Plan. Commission Communication of 11.05.1999 COM (1999)232. Its strategic objectives were: establishing a single market in wholesale financial services, making the retail markets open and secure, guaranteeing Community financial stability and eliminating tax obstacles which hinder the EU financial integration.

39. Cross-border consolidation in the EU financial sector. Commission Staff Working Document. SEC (2005) 1398.

40. Report on competition in professional services. Communication from the Commission. COM (2004) 83 final. Stocktaking exercise on regulation of professional services. Overview of Regulation in the new EU Member States. COMP/ D3/ MK / D(2004).

41. Professional services: scope for more reform. Communication from the Commission. SEC (2005) 405 final.

42. The Commission fined this association 100 000 euros. The amount reflects the facts that, upon warning, the Belgian Architects Association reconsidered and abolished this system in 2003, and also the gradual approach by the Commission in fining anti-competitive practices in the professions. It is worth mentioning that in its first decision concerning tariffs of professional bodies, the Commission did not impose a fine. In the second case, it imposed a symbolic fine of 1000 euros.

43. Known as the Wouters case.

44. Directive 2002/39/EC of the European Parliament and of the Council, amending Directive 97/67/EC with regard to further opening to competition of Community postal services.

45. The reserved area refers to the postal services reserve for the operators (whether public or private) providing universal services within national borders. According to the Directive, the weight limit shall be 100 grams from 1 January 2003, and 50 grams from 1 January 2006. These weight limits shall be applicable to ordinary domestic correspondence as well as to items of incoming cross correspondence.

They shall not apply if the price is equal to, or more than, three times the public tariff for an item of correspondence in the first weight step of the fastest category.

46. Except for those countries where the income from this mail is necessary to ensure the provision of universal service. Such is the case of Spain, Italy, Greece, Ireland, Portugal and Luxembourg, which have maintained their cross-border outgoing mail monopoly.

47. DPAG was only fined 1000 euros, due to the existing legal uncertainty at the moment the infringement occurred.

9. The internal market for services[1]

INTRODUCTION

The European integration process is one of the most significant political and economical projects that have taken place in the continent. The first agreement on the European Coal and Steel Community (ECSC, 1951), shortly followed by the European Economic Community (EEC, 1958) and the actual European Union (EU), which recently adopted the euro as common currency, represent, within modern history, steps of a magnitude without comparison in the rest of the world. The European founding fathers, Schuman, Monnet, De Gasperi, and Adenauer earnestly sought to create stable links between countries in order to guarantee peace and prosperity in Europe. The union of strategic coal and steel industries, essential to the military machine, appeared as the necessary first step for protecting the continent, basically from itself. During its modern history, the old Europe passed through trade integration in order to achieve economic, but also social, political and cultural goals.

In fact, since their foundation in the 1950s, one of the most important features of the European Communities had been trade integration among their members. An essential element of this process is the creation of an all embracing commercial market where people, capital, goods and services are allowed the freedom to move inside Europe as easily as within their own national boarders. The Single European Act (SEA, 1987) strengthened the principles of the Treaty with the intention of setting up by 1993 a single market including services even though, as will be seen, these activities remain at the back of the integration process. Due to the importance of the service economy and the actual behaviour of internal trade patterns, the development of an efficient service market is nowadays essential for the competitiveness of the continent and the welfare of its citizens, and therefore becomes one of the most relevant challenges the European political economy has to face.

This chapter presents the situation of the internal market for services commencing from two different perspectives: its necessity and justification on one side and existing barriers and the policy actions to remove them on the other. The following points will be presented: firstly, theories on economic integration and its positive outcomes will be introduced, with particular attention to all concerning services (Section 1), followed by the actual situation of the services market, which will be shown through a brief empirical analysis in order to present a clear view of the level of integration attained so far and to put forward evidence of its enhanced effects and its weaknesses (Section 2). It will also be shown how, although the goods market has been consolidating over the years and nowadays shows a high level of association, the same cannot be stated for the tertiary sector, which seems to be lagging behind in integration and displaying a difficult path impeding the emerging outcomes.

An overview of the legal framework governing the services sector (Section 3) will help to clarify the complex system of regulations behind the actual situation, trying to provide evidence of limitations and impediments. This insight is necessary in order to understand the wide array of barriers preventing the achievement of an internal market for services (Section 4). The recent policy actions are analysed (Section 5), in particular the 2004 *proposal for a directive on services in the internal market*, presenting goals, scope and impact assessments. As the proposal had a controversial reception by the different economic participants, the reaction provoked will be exposed and commented on. The chapter finishes with some concluding remarks.

1. ECONOMIC INTEGRATION AND SERVICES

The first reasons justifying the internal market for services come from the advantages of integration processes proved by international trade theories. Initially considered as a secondary branch of the study of international economics, the theory on economic integration experienced increasing interest during recent decades: researchers and stakeholders have made consistent progress in fields such as international macroeconomics, international monetary, international, intra-industry and regional trade theory since the first pioneering works of Viner (1950) on the impact of custom union formation on production. Such progress converted this into what is currently considered a complete research area. At the same time, the interest of the policy makers increased as they started wondering how these processes could be driven or influenced in order to reach higher levels of financial welfare and growth.

The last fifty years of European history are not the only example of economic integration process which deserves the attention of policy makers and researchers, cases of progressions in their early stages can be found all over the world.[2] All these cases show how economic integration is necessary based on the creation of integrated markets. From a trade point of view, integration processes are the consequence of the establishment of multilateral Preferential Trade Agreements (PTAs) among countries, generally from the same continent or world area and with a comparable level of development. It is interesting to note that, although the PTAs contradict the non discrimination principle, jointly with the reciprocity principle and the enforcement mechanism, one of the pillars of the GATT/GATS-WTO system, a special provision was included to approve the existence of free trade areas and custom unions in GATT's Article XXIV. Moreover, the positive experiences shown in the free trade areas constitute the good examples – or the best practices – for launching multilateral negotiations for further trade liberalizations. The benefits of existing trade agreements among members cause further requests at a global level. The role of geographical examples is particularly important in services, where market segmentation is so remarkable that step-by-step procedures are requested to prove the benefits of liberalization and this is also the way that advances in GATS are expected to be produced.

Literature distinguishes four different levels of integration characterized by the number and importance of the trade barriers removed among countries, and by other actions taken in order to harmonize the markets involved. The four phases are: *Free Trade Area,* where the countries involved eliminate custom duties and quantity restrictions; *Customs Union,* an integrated group of countries with the same customs and international commerce policy; *Common Market,* the freedom of movement is extended to factor as for products; *Economic and Monetary Union,* which means a common market implemented by financial integration.

The economic integration theory finds its roots in the first years of the 1950s when some models of international commerce were adapted to include the PTAs cases. As these models could only appreciate changes in custom fees and quantity restrictions, the so-called direct effects, microeconomics outcomes of the agreements were the only ones considered. No importance was given to indirect effects like trade and scale economy creation, intra-industry specialization, redistribution of welfare, pro-competitive results and, more generally, induced growth. These consequences of the integration process will be later named *dynamic effects,* in contrast with the *static effects,* the ones appreciated in the first models.[3] Some of the dynamic effects like a *production effect,* derived from the larger demands of products in which the country encloses competitive advantages, or a *consumption effect,* as a consequence of the trade creation, and a *trade diversion,* a mechanism affecting the allocation of resources, are the main conclusions of the theory conducted on the works of the period from the 1950s to the 1970s. The trade diversion effect was the object of particular attention.

Trade creation is beneficial for a country basically because it leads to the reduction of the inefficient allocation of resources, thus redirecting them to more efficient exploitations. Trade groups could also lead to distortions within the results of welfare inhibitions for participant countries. PTAs can create comparative intra-regional advantages, but comparative disadvantages if considered at a global level. The magnitude of these effects compensates, in some cases, the positive consequences drawn from the production and consumption effects.

The term 'dynamic effects' includes a wide range of outcomes: scale economies and the learning-by-doing outcomes, boosted by larger markets and by the consumption effect; FDI consequences on growth and the intensified competition enhanced by the higher number of enterprises acting in the same market. These are all effects that at that time needed a new theoretical framework to be studied. The first attempt of taking into consideration these aspects was through the models of imperfect competition and scale economies.[4] The theory's progressive opening which included dynamic effects and indirect barriers to trade inhibition was accompanied in following years by empirical studies that evaluated the consequences of the PTAs, especially under the commercial, welfare and competition points of view. The works of Smith and Venables (1988), among others, on the benefits of completing the European internal goods market deserve to be mentioned.

Attention can now be focused on the theoretical specific outcomes to be expected from the increasing market integration, those directly applicable to the services sector and in particular the predictable outcomes of the creation of a Single European Service Market. Should this sector integration benefit from the direct and dynamic effects? What would these effects represent in services markets?

The European Union has passed through all the previously described integration phases since the first steps in 1951. From an initial free trade area it developed into a customs union with common tariff and quotas during the 1960s, to later evolve towards a common market at the beginning of the 1990s when factors were formally set free for movement. Finally the economic and monetary union phase was achieved with the adoption of a single currency by twelve of its members in 1999. The actual debate centres on the effectiveness of this level of integration and on the positive upshots resulting from its strengthening.

At the time of its adoption, the Euro triggered an animated debate on the single currency with economists sustaining positions both for and against the single currency. Some maintained that the Euro zone was not an optimum currency area,[5] due to the rigidity of the markets, the lack of mobility of factors, the great heterogeneity among national economies and the lack of super-national mechanisms devoted to facing asymmetrical shocks. Benefits from economic integration will hardly emerge in a context where distortions affecting the single currency area performance persist. Among these market failures, high rigidity, heterogeneity and lack of mobility can be listed. There is a kind of incompatibility between a European optimum (or sub-optimum) currency area and an unfavourable political and economical reality, in the service sector among others.

What the literature defines as static and dynamic effects is perceived by the economy through phenomena enhanced by different aspects of the integration process. It can be stated that, in the case of services, they are particularly sensitive to improvements on the supply side, where the consumption and the production effects apply jointly. These advances of the supply side owing to the market integration can be appreciated by observing five different changes within the economy: a higher capacity of the economy to face asymmetrical shocks; increased elasticity; higher competition levels;

the development of more efficient companies (e.g., scale and scope economies); and the increase of structural changes leading to sector specialization.

Trade integration contributes to the consolidation of sectors at a continental level. These new large and continent-integrated sectors are more capable of facing asymmetrical shocks, such as a decrease in the demand side of a single nation or to a regional extent. In a large integrated market, the hit of a national crisis is received by the full economy and balanced by the stability of the partners reducing, in this way, its magnitude and avoiding a deepening of the problem at a local level. Given the fact that services represent 70 per cent of EU economies and that they are becoming more integrated into the global world, it is likely that more and more asymmetric shocks will be related to services.

Services are rather segmented activities in which monopolistic power is important (due to product differentiation, information asymmetries, regulations, or natural monopolistic or oligopolistic structures) and price elasticities are not as high as they would be in wider integrated markets. The single market brings by itself a higher elasticity of the supply side. This is the result of vertical and horizontal integrations occurring within and among sectors at a continental level and also the result of developing new scale and scope economies. Firms previously hampered by national borders can now act in an integrated way, thus increasing the overall efficiency of the economy. As changes in demand patterns are absorbed by a non-elastic supply side through changes in the production (and therefore employment) levels, an increased elasticity, due to integration, can shift these tunings towards price adjustments, thus leaving the employment less affected by demand shocks.

High importance is always attributed to the advantages consequent to an increase of competition in a sector. The most relevant effects of this situation are a reduction in general price levels and a rise in the quality of the products. The price reduction brings advantages directly to the consumers but also helps to increase the performance of the economy. This is particularly significant when referring the services sector, whose relevance in the supply chain has been underlined time and time again by literature (e.g., Rubalcaba, 1999; Kox, 2002). Above all the increase in quality consequent to the integration is experienced by the sector, through an increase in product diversity. Services competition is not, in fact, focused particularly on price competition, as firms are always pledged to attracting customers offering services adaptable, to a greater extent, to the client needs. Another positive outcome derived from a more competitive market which becomes visible during an integration process is the opening to the international competition of sectors traditionally developed within the national borders and affected by distortions of the free market owing to excess of regulations, corporative, monopolistic and oligopolistic situations. The removal, or at least the weakening of these barriers, creates, due to the harmonization that normally accompanies the integration, in some central sectors as financial or transport services, a potential boost for the growth of a large part of the economy.

Another way by which the advantages derived from market integration can be perceived within the service sector is from the structural changes that occur in involved economies. It is not merely the case of the change from an industrial economy to a services economy, but also a renovation in the specialization patterns within the two main sectors. The enlargement of the potential markets facilitates changes in specialization, which are particularly important if the actual global dimension of the markets and the consequent necessity of efficient economies acting in a competitive environment are taken into consideration, especially from the low-skilled intensive sectors point of view. Large markets, where services are left free to act, give the European economies the chance to gain new competitive advantages to replace sectors that are not at the head of the markets anymore.

2. THE MARKET INTEGRATION OF EU SERVICES

The previous section shows what has been the theoretical approach to the economic integration process by putting into evidence the expected positive outcomes. The incumbent questions are now whether there is European single market for services, and whether it achieves the expected positive outcomes. For these reasons, this section intends to provide a brief overview of the situation's empirical evidence and the trends of the Internal Market of Services. This section will take into consideration four different market trends: trade, FDI, prices and labour costs.

Empirical literature on market integration has generally focused on the relationship between intra and extra-trade flows as well as on price convergence among countries. Along these lines, analyses regarding the North American goods market have been carried out by McCallun (1995), Anderson and Smith (1999) and Wolf (2000), among others. Nitsch (2000) and de la Maisonnueve, De Serres and Hoeller (2001) propose investigations focusing specifically on the European Union goods market, concluding that market integration is higher within the EU than it is among OECD countries.

In services, the benefits of the internal market were empirically enumerated for the first time within the outcomes of the programme named *Cost of Non-Europe* in 1988. The same year witnessed the presentation of the *Cecchini report*, which has sought to quantify the potential benefits to be derived from the creation of the European Single Market. In 1996 the Commission published the results of a major study on the benefits of the unified market, highlighting its positive effects on specific key activities comprehended in the service aggregate. By that time, the financial sector had already increased sharply in cross-border branches and capital movements, and transport and distribution activities had reduced their costs and had improved in efficiency while telecommunications prices had fallen due to increased competition. Since the 1998 Cardiff European Council, the Commission has presented annual progress reports on the benefits and the necessary reforms of the internal market, including evaluations on the situation of the service sector. The main findings on the concerns of the service sector are the improved quality of citizens' lives, perceived and measured, and a general trend of price convergence among members due to the creation of the market. Considerable attention has also been paid to the evaluation of the potential benefits of the integration. In 2002 the Commission estimated the potential positive outcomes of the financial services integration at a 1 per cent increase of EU's GDP and 0.5 per cent of EU total employment.

Trends in Trade and FDI Statistics

As the first effect of an endorsed positive trend, one can expect to observe an increased volume of continental trade and foreign direct investments. As has been seen in Chapter 6, globalization sharply increased the international trade figures for services. In order to evaluate the effective intensification of the European transactions, a comparison between internal and external trade volumes, trends and FDI will be carried out. On the other hand, more dynamic effects of the process will also be taken into consideration, convergence trends in price levels of services and the remuneration of the labour factor in the different countries will be taken as indexes of the occurred establishment of the market. In these cases, a positive result would be attributed to the increased level of competition among enterprises performing in the sector at continental level.

In a single integrated market, the level of trade within common borders is supposed to be higher if compared with the levels outside. This is due, among other reasons, to the fact that companies share the same legal environment, business background and have to cover shorter distances in delivering their products. All these factors contribute to the fall in transaction costs and, consequently, to the rise of the trade level. Our first empirical attempt to answer the question of the effectiveness of the services market will be to concentrate on the side-by-side analysis between internal and external trade patterns, later seen as *intra* and *extra trade*. To evaluate the efficacy of the efforts engaged by the European and national institutions (and owing to the availability), we considered data on service trade, both intra and extra, regarding the aggregate EU15 covering the period from the establishment of the common market in 1992 until the most recent data obtainable. Figure 9.1 is a comparison, not only between intra and total trade, but also between goods and services commerce. It is not surprising that the goods exchange levels are higher than the services ones, since they represent around 70 per cent of the world trade. What is of more interest is the comparison of the differences between intra and extra trade in the two sectors, which suggests that goods market integration was already a reality in 1992 and followed a trend of increased integration, while the services sector lagged behind, presenting a less substantial index. The annual growth rate of the percentage difference between intra and extra trade shows that both internal markets are achieving a greater importance over time with services having a limited tendency to catch up. Since the institution of the market trade patterns had been more consistent within the Union's borders than with extra-European partners, this importance had not experienced any positive pressure despite the institutions' efforts over the considered period. After ten years the relevance of the internal market was the same measured at the moment of the official institution of the market for most of the considered sectors.

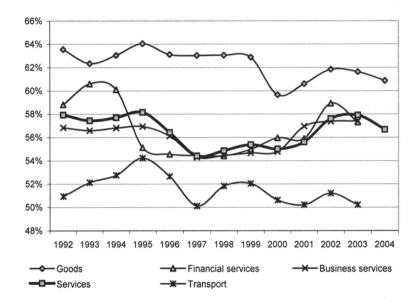

Source: Based on Eurostat data, New Cronos, 2006.

Figure 9.1 Intra trade on total trade, EU15

In a more specific analysis considering different services it can be noticed that, during the first twelve years of the official common market, most of the services tended to slowly increase the importance of the internal trade, but without a clear take off inclination in any of the considered cases with the exception of the telecommunications, which seems to be the only sector with strong continental integration propensities. In fact, if we consider the intra/extra trade ratio, the index for the communication services was only 1.19

in 1996 and grew until reaching the value of 2.01 in 2003 (exports). The second best performer when considering the same period is the Travel sector, which moved from the estimate of 1.69 to 2.21(exports).

Table 9.1 International trade integration, EU15: intra EU versus extra EU, 1996 and 2003

Ratio: Trade intra EU / Extra EU	1996		2003	
	Exports	*Imports*	*Exports*	*Imports*
Goods	1.72	1.71	1.61	1.62
Services	1.20	1.29	1.24	1.37
Transport	1.10	1.12	0.96	1.10
Travel	1.69	1.63	2.21	1.52
Communications services	1.19	1.18	2.01	1.90
Insurance services	0.64	2.00	0.90	2.24
Financial services	1.19	1.22	1.22	1.61
Personal and cultural services	1.21	1.03	1.22	1.11
Public services	0.72	1.41	0.83	1.26
Royalties and licence fees	0.75	0.60	0.56	0.64
Services between affiliated enterprises	1.32	1.23	1.36	1.49
Business services	1.14	1.36	1.09	1.54
- Information services	1.15	1.41	1.30	1.74
- Leasing	1.43	1.35	1.44	1.81
- Professional and technical services	1.13	1.47	1.08	1.46
- Advertising, market research	2.00	1.84	1.30	1.79
- Research and development services	1.38	1.80	0.81	1.06
- Technical consultancy	0.87	1.47	0.89	1.60
- Agricultural, mining, and on-site processing	1.27	2.63	0.78	1.91
- Other business services	1.14	1.36	1.05	1.52

Source: Based on International Trade Statistics, Eurostat New Cronos, 2005.

It should be noted that the exposed weakness of intra EU service market performance is partially due to the effect that globalization has on external trade patterns. In fact, the internal services market exchanges increased at an average rate of 6.1 per cent per year between 1992 and 2004, thus demonstrating a particular dynamism considering that the whole European economy in the same period grew at a rate of 2.3 per cent per year. This dynamism, which can be considered an effect of the market creation and of all the institutional efforts in this direction, does not appear as favourable when compared with the effects that globalization had on European *extra* trade in services, which increased at an average annual growth rate of 6.81 per cent in the same period. For example, the increasing integration of the global economy (e.g., trade with China and with the Eastern European countries) increased the range of differences between absolute and relative prices, and costs, which may explain part of the decreasing share on intra-trade in goods after 1995 and in goods and services between 2002 and 2004. However, some services are more committed to the internal market, like Communications or Travel services, although others are more keen to develop at a global level, as for example Marketing or R&D services, while the service aggregate is a good proxy for most of the other sectors.

Data describing trade patterns suggest that common market opportunities do not encourage European service companies to embark on the direct international selling of their products to the same extent as with manufactured and agricultural products in the past. The actual situation seems to describe a stationary market state without future perspective of a take-off in the integration levels in relative terms: exchanges are increasing in both intra and extra scenarios, and European operators are still no more inclined to conduct intra-EU business than extra-EU business.

All the services characteristics influencing their tradability described in Chapter 6 suggest that the internationalization of the service sector cannot be made only through the international trade channel and that it is necessary to pass through a combination of direct trade and foreign investments. Within the process of internationalization, the approach of service enterprises to new markets is normally planned through international strategies blending direct trade with the start-up of local affiliates, greenfield investments or mergers and acquisitions. The analysis presented now focuses on data regarding FDI and the foreign control of European services enterprises. Time series, regarding FDI stocks in the sector of the fifteen members of the European Union before enlargement, are available from 1995 to 2003, while comparable information on the foreign control aspect is obtainable for nine countries over the period of only one year. By looking at the foreign control of firms statistics, it can be observed that the presence in a different market is much more common among services than among manufacturing companies. In the EU in 1999, the reference year, the manufacturing companies controlled by foreign operators were (on average per country) less than 1000,[6] while in the services sector the amount was twice this value.

If the analysis moves to foreign investment patterns, it can be noted that the services sector represents the destination of the major part of the European investments. Figure 9.2 illustrates where manufacturing lags behind services in values and trends. The graph shows a take-off of FDI, which took place during the recent years of the past decade, as a two-way phenomenon with a single conclusion: intra-EU flows have been more dynamic than extra-EU flows. Since 1998, the gap between EU-directed investment and overseas-directed investment increased sharply, so that in 2003, 65 per cent of the total stock invested found its destination within the Union's borders. The services sector experienced a consistent increase: its annual growth rate between 1998 and 2002 showed an average of 32 per cent, while up until that year it was 'only' about 18 per cent. The performance of the service operators is even clearer when compared with the data from the manufacturing sector. In this case, the relatively low importance of this channel in the industry appears evident.

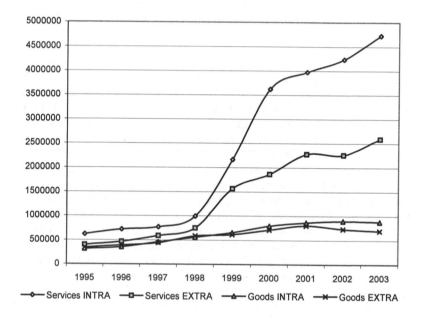

Source: Based on Eurostat, New Cronos, 2006.

Figure 9. 2 EU15 FDI stocks – origins and destinations (millions of euros)

From this brief description, it can be concluded that the consolidation of the services market at a European level seems to use foreign investments as a preferential channel. The direct presence of an enterprise in a Member State market appears to be considered the most appropriate means adopted in the companies' internationalization/Europeanization due to the special characteristics of the sector and the barriers to international trade. This way of providing services engages high fixed and sunk costs, thus blowing away many of the SMEs from the internationalization challenge.

Trends in Prices, Labour Costs and Productivity

From a company point of view, a large integrated market consists of advantages derived from expansion opportunities and the concerned positive externalities, but it also means the necessity of facing competition from foreign companies. The most efficient firms, present in national competitive markets, have the opportunity to operate all over the European Union, forcing the enterprises previously performing in a market with low levels of competition, to increase their organizational and productive effectiveness and reduce their mark-up, with the theoretical result of higher product quality and reduced price trends. This brings the features of formerly less competitive markets closer to those of the more efficient markets. From the point of view of European market integration, this can be interpreted as an empirical convergence of the price levels and cost factors in the tertiary sector. However, convergence will not be completed due to several factors regarding country specific differentiations. A form of price discrimination will persist due to the continuing distinctiveness of each national market. Examples of these factors could be national differences in local taxes, wage levels, preferences, scope of the national markets, transaction costs, asymmetric information or transport costs. All these reasons slow down the erosion of price and productivity differences.

Price level convergence can therefore be considered as an index of market integration. Several economic reports produced by the DG Internal Market evaluate progress through the analysis of this index.[7] Despite the statistical limitations[8], time series were used, covering the period 1995 to 2003, on price levels in the former 15 EU members. According to Barro and Sala-i-Martin (1991), among others in the current literature, a measure of the occurred convergence is the decrease in the variance of the data over time: this is referred as σ *convergence*. We interpret a reduction of the variance among prices as one of the consequences of market integration in the considered sector. As shown in Figure 9.3, again, the European goods market shows greater integration patterns. This result is not unexpected, as goods represented three times more trading than did services. Considering the trends of the variables, it can be seen that from 1995 until 1998 the impact of the installation and implementation of market policies can be appreciated in both sectors, while from this year onwards, both sectors seem to present a diminished trend. The implementation of these markets goes together in the considered period. The services market had, compared with the goods market, a catch-up outline due to its lagging position. The incomplete equalization of the dispersion levels confirms the presence of a range of factors in the sector, not affecting the goods market, thus impeding integration.

Unsurprisingly, more specific analysis shows heterogeneity in the results when different service sectors are compared. Firstly, it can be observed that the convergence of the service aggregate price levels is driven by the convergence of the *Consumer services* aggregate data since they show strongly correlated patterns: dispersion decreased by 52 per cent in the former case and 54 per cent in the latter. This is not the case for the *Government services*, as these activities are normally out of market and their price convergence within the EU presents the lowest relative value. Below the average variance are two sectors: *Transportation* and *Restaurants and Hotels*. These do not seem to show a high convergence in prices during the observed period, in the case of the latter an unexpected price divergence can be noted over the last four years. The only service sector that presents convergence outlines comparable with the goods market is the aggregate encompassing cultural and recreational services with a low level of dispersion and a 34 per cent decrease over the period.

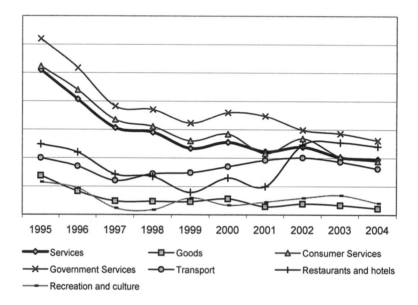

Source: Based on Eurostat, New Cronos, 2006.

Figure 9.3 Price variance in the EU 15 internal market

Since the inauguration of the common market in 1993, labour force and capital have been free to move and circulate within the Union's borders. Economic theories on international trade suggest that once production factors are set free to move worldwide, their costs and returns tend to equalize among countries. In accordance with this theory, the compensation and the productivity of the labour factor should converge within the same sector among different countries. Regarding these factors, employees' compensation levels and labour productivity in different sectors will be observed in order to obtain information on the integration process. The expected result is a decline in the dispersion of the considered values, which would indicate the internationalization and the real integration of the examined sector.

When observing this data, one must bear in mind that the integration process can encourage different economies to specialize in sectors where they present comparative advantages. This specialization is accompanied by a change in productivity that can raise the dispersion value of the specific sector. Furthermore, aggregate data such as the *total services* can include, at the same time, activities where specialization patterns took place and activities where productivity levels converged.

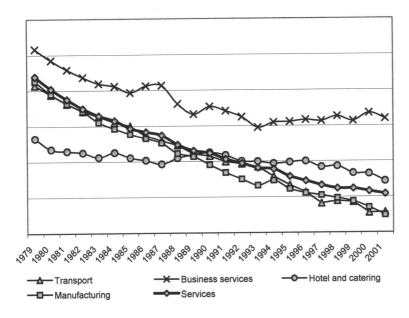

Source: Based on Eurostat, New Cronos, 2006.

Figure 9.4 Compensation convergence trends in the Euro Area

Data on employee compensation in the Euro-area[9] countries in different sectors show that compensation of the labour factor becomes closer in levels among the members. In particular, Figure 9.4 analyses the trend of the variation coefficient of employee compensation in total services, manufacturing and other service sectors in a time series, which runs from the late 1970s until the beginning of the new century. Following the DG Internal Market economic reports, the chosen variable to measure the dispersion is the coefficient of variation, rather than the standard deviation or the variance. In a series of compensation distributions over time, the latter measures may increase over time with inflation, and thus may influence the behaviour of the variance. The coefficient of variation avoids this effect, and thus the fundamental inequality observed does not rise because of price increases. A CV of 0.64, as it is the service figure for 1979, means that the maximum and minimum prices in the sector vary in a band of 64 per cent; the same figure for 2001 is 0.31 showing that prices across Europe are now 50 per cent closer than they were at the end of the 1970s. In the deeper analysis on the patterns of convergence in different periods presented in Figure 9.4, it can be noted that the manufacturing sector, once again, has driven the convergence in Europe. In any case, compensations are moving closer in the service sector of the Euro-area at an average speed of more than 3 per cent per year, but, in the example given, different progressions can be noticed.

The differences in compensation among countries are declining in all sectors observed, and the convergence seems linear over time. However, when studying economic activities that constitute the tertiary sector, it appears clear that the process of integration is greater in some economic areas than in others. Sectors like transport, for example, contribute actively to this convergence. International integration has been stronger in this sector due to less technical barriers, low levels of national irregularities or requirements, and less possibility of specialization. Areas like those included in the business services sector data show the lowest levels of convergence. This situation could hide a national or regional specialization, as mentioned previously. Other reasons behind this include the still-strong barriers regarding national borders: differences in national market regulation, companies' diverse, country-dependent needs, and language barriers which are especially resistant in these specialized and personalized services

The results are similar when studying the productivity levels: service and manufacturing levels seem to converge following a similar constant trend, but when the analysis is focused at an intra sector level, disparities are evident. For example the transport sector seems to follow the trend outlined by the goods and services markets, but the business services aggregate shows convergence patterns prior to the market creation and remains substantially unchanged until 2002.

Also common to both tests is that the process of integration from this point of view results in being slow and constant over time, with the reduction in the dispersion regarding services compensation of 25 per cent taking around twenty years, although this was without shocks. Another common characteristic is that integration occurs in a few specific economic areas, generally the most homogeneous areas which have low international intra industry penetration. The factor-market integration appears to be more gradual in contrast with the other economic fields observed and there is no particular evidence of take-off patterns during the past decade.

In summary, analyses on the convergence of price levels and factor remuneration reveal that the labour cost and return of the labour factor are converging gradually among European countries. This convergence seems to be slow and regular especially when considering the former data. Moreover services are less integrated than manufacturing and, even if this process continues, the remaining barriers are still hampering a greater integration. These facts reinforce, to some extent, the lack of integration in services markets previously identified in the section related to international trade. This is partially due to the fact that the majority of this sector's internationalization passes through the foreign direct investment and foreign control channel. In this field the increase in the intra continental volume with respect to the extra European volume shows evidently that an internal market for services has been taking shape and gaining importance since the end of the 1990s.

3. THE LEGAL FRAMEWORK OF THE INTERNAL MARKET FOR SERVICES

From the Treaty to the Strategy for an Internal Market for Services

Legal bases introducing and sustaining the idea of an internal market for services within the more comprehensive concept of services commerce in Europe can be found directly in the Treaty establishing the European Community.[10] Indeed Article 43 sets up the right of establishment in any of the Member States of the Union, applicable to every kind of European service provider. This freedom includes the right, for foreign operators, to take up and pursue activities under the same conditions laid down for its own nationals by the law of the country where such establishment is effected. At the same time Article 49 states that any kind of restriction on cross-border service provision between Member States is prohibited, should it be a legal act or a *de facto* situation as a consequence of different circumstances and local conditions. These two articles guarantee a complete legal framework for the existence of an internal market for services in Europe. In fact, in the international services trade, both operators selling services in a foreign country and providers establishing their economic activity in a different country in order to retail their services, are able to do so according to the principles here recognized. It must be noted that Article 49 of the Treaty identifies the existence of barriers beyond customs barriers and forces Member States to remove them. Taking into consideration all the articles included in Title I, Chapter II,[11] it can be affirmed that the Treaty forces Member States to modify any internal rule opposing the principles of the internal market. In practice, not only rules creating a direct discrimination between a national and a foreign operator, but also rules applicable to domestic and foreign providers which hinder or render less attractive any kind of cross-border provision of services, are banned by the agreement.

The aim of the entire legal framework sustaining the single market of services is to make the provision of services within the European borders as easy as within an individual country. The Treaty is not the only instrument working for this purpose, which is far too extensive to be achieved by simply putting into action the principles expressed. For example, if legal barriers, obstacles affecting the market development derived from legal constraints of Member States, are directly faced by the rules exposed above, the same cannot be stated for the large series of non legal barriers affecting the process of market unification. Non-legal barriers are those impediments arising from situations not regulated by legal frameworks, affecting each different stage of the economic provision of services, from the start-up of a company up until the distribution and the after-sales aspects. This will be disclosed in more detail later on in Section 4. Cultural and language barriers and the lack of knowledge concerning procedures or formalities are examples of these kinds of impediments. In order to resolve this situation several actions have been put into practice by the European institutions, originally to outline the way the internal market for services should be set up and later directed in order to remove almost all kinds of barriers.

Pressured by the consistent differences between the levels of intra European commerce of services and goods, the actions undertaken by the European Community during the decade of the 1980s were focused on the creation of formal rules to develop different strategies for the internal market, paying particular attention to the former sector. *The White Paper on the Internal Market* (1985) was the very first document promoting directly the services market, followed by the Single European Act,[12] signed under the Commission presidency of Jacques Delors. In this document, among other institutional reforms, the concept of a European market is set up. The Act, in fact, enabled the majority vote on hundreds of necessary directives for the removal of numerous barriers and other regulatory market impediments, becoming the blueprint for achieving free flows of goods, services, labour and capital.

However, due to the individual characteristics of the services sector, the legal framework created by the Treaty and the following acts was not enough to drive and control its complete continental integration. The sector presents a more complex situation than the manufacturing one. Indeed in some relevant sectors, like transport or financial and postal services, particular policies were created, excluding them from the competences of the general rules. The next section will concentrate on these specific cases. Other economic activities presented a strongly regulated situation at a national level and it is considered in some cases impossible and in others difficult and/or expensive for a foreign operator to enter into one of these markets: see the case of telecommunications, energy supply or postal services. The individual ways in which services are traded at an international level creates the necessity of specific, directed and individualized rules to stimulate their commerce and integration. Indeed even if the legal framework shaped during the 1980s and

1990s, like the White Paper or the Single European Act, put the services at the centre of the attention and set out the bases for a strong harmonization, especially driven by the affirmation of the mutual recognition principle, only the rules brought into being after the year 2000 managed to secure the policy makers full interest in this internal market for services.

As a result of the European Council of Lisbon 2000, the Commission presented a strategy aimed at eliminating the barriers hampering the internal market for services. The Internal Market Strategy for Services,[13] the first attempt by the European institutions to approach the problems directly and exclusively related to this issue, propelled integration through different legislative and non-legislative measures specifically aimed at problematic matters. It was also the first effort to recover, through a horizontal measure, the asymmetry that characterized the tertiary sector within the European legislative framework. Indeed, up to that year, some services had been treated under special regimes and others had been following the same framework designed for goods (Pelkmans, 2006a). The strategy is justified by the need of competitiveness arising in a society based on technology and information. In order to increase productivity in the European economy, attention was paid by the authorities to any kind of barrier, so as to free the movement of services and their spill-over effects across economic sectors. This strategy seeks the creation of an effective market through a horizontal approach. Its principles were: allowing services to move across national borders as easily as within a Member State; guaranteeing companies and consumers the right to benefit from the advantages of a single market; preserving the dynamic nature of the activities of the sector and maintaining a legislative coherence with other community actions.

Under the supervision of the Council of Lisbon, for the first time since 1962, the Commission also undertook an all-embracing analysis of the existing barriers to the free circulation of services and their aftermath on other economic sectors. The task culminated in the preparation of working papers that focused on some specific cases and on the whole situation of the sector: the report of the Commission on the state of the internal market for services (European Commission, 2002). The horizontal tactic is considered even more when the way to liberalization and integration crosses problems such as the delays in which the Member States transpose directives into national laws or the difficult legislative approach to services due to the high number of different sub-sectors that can be distinguished within the sector.

All the works revealed so far created the necessary background for the most recent legal assessment going in this direction, the Draft directive on services in the internal market, following the same action lines expressed in the former ones. The aim of removing barriers through legal harmonization, codes of conduct, development of measures directed to stimulate quality in services and a stronger collaboration among national authorities is the focus of the directive. Later in this chapter, a more in-depth analysis of the draft directive will be presented focusing especially on the principles and challenges of the proposal: how the objectives are planned to be achieved by the simplification of existing rules, the intensification of customer rights and a more effective application of the infringements proceedings, the evaluation of its economic impact and the different reactions provoked.

Sector Specific Directives and Complementary Measures: Some Examples

As well as the actions directed horizontally to the service sectors, a whole set of specific and complementary measures were created to facilitate the formation and development of an internal market for services. Since these acts harmonize the regulations and business habits at continental level, they contribute towards the creation of a complementary endowment upon which services can be developed, produced and traded within a European perspective. The vertical complementary community actions committed to specific aspects of the services economy contribute to the creation of a comprehensive framework.

Within the mentioned services strategy, it was also planned to review the existing directives related to the free movements of services paying particular attention to the telecommunications framework, the two directives on public service contracts, the directive on postal services, the directive on copyrights in the information society, the strategy on financial information, the takeover directive on public offers and the directive on VAT on online services. Along these same lines are the directives aiming to improve the international environment in which services act, such as the directive on the transparency of regulation or the new directive on the mutual recognition of professional qualifications.

Indeed, the cross-border provision of services is strongly hampered when a professional, whose competence is legally certified to run a function in an Member State, presents a qualification that differs from the one owned by the professionals performing the same work in another Member State. For this reason great attention was given by the European legislator to the regulations related to the recognition of professional qualifications. In order to create a complete framework extending the possibility of pursuing professional activities, two distinct methods are used. A series of sectoral directives cover a limited, but crucial, number of professions,[14] providing rules for the automatic recognition of diplomas. The principle sustaining these measures is that if a diploma gives access to a particular profession in a Member State, this access is recognized in the other Member States. The other regulated professions attested by diploma recognize qualifications according to the *General Recognition System* (GRS) criteria. The GRS was created in 1989[15] and has been continually enhanced. It shaped a system for the recognition of higher-education non-academic diplomas awarded on the completion of professional education and training of a duration of at least three years.

By 2007 a new directive on the recognition of professional qualifications[16] will be fully adopted and will replace the GRS and the sectoral directives. The measure, which affects in a prominent way the services sector labour market, means a simplification for the actual framework (there are 15 above-cited directives) and is supposed to lead to a streamlining and to facilitate recognition. Moreover, one of the goals of its application is to contribute to a further liberalization of services provision across countries.

Within the *horizontal group* can also be mentioned the harmonizing initiatives regarding contract law or the directive centring on the competence of Member States in the trans-national posting of workers. The safety of services or the cooperation in the area of consumer protection was also the centre of the policymakers' attention. The horizontal approach also includes initiatives directed to promote the provision of a high quality of services of general economic interest. A broad set of horizontal policy frameworks, complementary to the regulatory ones, will be presented in Chapter 10, many of which are based on the proposed actions for business-related services.

The group of *vertical programs* presents a high heterogeneity and touches a wide range of sectors. Beyond the specifically created regulations for some key sectors, such as financial, postal services and transport, there is another series of vertical actions directed to satisfy the specific needs of some economic areas. As an example, the *e-Europe Action Plan* can be mentioned. It consists in a proposal for a directive, in line with previous initiatives, with the intention of obtaining the highest benefits from the digitalization of the economy. Some proposals were elaborated in order to regulate some specific questions within the continental framework like the proposal for a directive on the reimbursement of health costs.

As a sector directly related to all the branches of the economy, the financial services always deserved the specific attention of the policymakers. An efficient financial sector characterized by high levels of competition and transparency is fundamental for the good functioning of a modern market economy. Furthermore there will not be a fully integrated market without integration in this sector. For this reason, the European institutions elaborated, during recent years, a full range of initiatives directed towards the several branches of the sector. Generally, all the European policies in the area are structured at two different levels: the wholesale level regarding all the instruments used by banks, insurances and investment companies; and the retail level treating all the financial instruments dedicated to consumers, such as accounts, mortgages or pension funds. The common aims of all the policies acting in this field are the same as those for the other services: the establishment of a far-reaching set of rules which would allow companies to establish new branches in different Member States, having compatible rules across borders, creating a European market for consumers.

The most important of all the finance-related actions endorsed is the Financial Services Action Plan set up in 1999. This was a five-year plan made up of 42 legislative measures acting at the wholesale and retail level. The measures committed to the former had the scope of promoting the integration of the financial services, as well as integrating the rules on securities and derivative products. The rules created for the latter concentrate on the transparency and the cross-border transactions. An evaluation undertaken in January 2006, shows that 98 per cent of the measures have been put in place (an expected result after five years), but that an effective and real integration of the market is lagging behind, fragmented by several national rules and regulations.

It is relevant to notice, when looking from a single market viewpoint, that a series of initiatives were committed to the harmonization of payment services. The creation of a market involves not only the creation of an integrated supply side, but also the harmonization of the demand side. To this extent, since July 2002, the intention of creating a European regulation in the sector had been put into action. In December 2005, the proposal for a directive on a new legal framework was presented by the Commission. The new five-year agenda is based on various principles and from now on interventions will not be horizontal and all-over embracing, but a set of specific legislations, such as the Mortgage Credit White Paper or the cross-border banking consolidation. The legislative attention will work jointly with other initiatives like tax harmonization or competition policies.

As previously mentioned, another sector whose fundamental economic importance made a specific policy endowment necessary is transport. In fact, the first perception of the Common Transport Policy (CTP) can be found directly in the Treaty of Rome in the Articles from 70 to 80. Even though these articles guarantee a framework to make the transport services part of a large integrated market, not much had been done by the institutions in this respect until the mid-1980s. The White Paper on the Internal Market was the first attempt of intervention, pursuing the liberalization and harmonization of the sector. During the 1990s, attention passed to infrastructural development and to the creation of projects of multi-modal transport networks through the continent. The sectoral approach had been left to one side in this period in order to approach a series of integrated policies such as pricing or environmental and social protection. The idea was that in order to enhance the sector, it had to pass through technology and the full exploitation of single market opportunities.[17]

The actual policy framework in this field finds its bases in the White Paper on the Future CTP: 60 measures created facing the most problematic topics of the sector at a continental level, such as congestion, pollution and accidents, especially considering the expected development of the sector which will experience, by 2010, a rise of 38 per cent in freight transport, of 24 per cent in passenger transport, and increased road congestion.

The creation of a real single transport market demands harmonization at a continental level. To achieve the aim of using the transport sector as a support in the complementation of other sectors, the treatment received by operators in the different countries should be more homogeneous than is currently the situation. To this extent, particular policies are needed in the fields concerning fuel taxation, road charging and sustainable mobility.

4. BARRIERS TO THE INTERNAL MARKET FOR SERVICES

So far we have discussed the situation of the internal market for services in Europe. The conclusions achieved appear clearer when the outcomes for the services are compared with the goods market. The different stages of integration accomplished by the two activities suggest that, from one side, the opportunity of a European market seems to be less suitable for service operators, and from the other, that intensive barriers obstruct the integration process affecting this field. Due to its multifaceted structure, the service sector is subject to complex dynamics, and the different activities which give shape to the sector present more particularities compared to those in manufacturing. This multiplies the number of barriers which the whole sector has to face during the market formation process, and renders the organization and application of an integration plan complex and difficult to accomplish, thus leaving a limited range of action for policy initiatives.

The Barriers

In this section, barriers affecting the formation of the internal market for services will be identified and described in line with the most recent institutional references on the subject. In fact, barriers are filed following a production process stage-level subdivision in accordance with the views expressed by the European Commission in the 2002 report on the situation of the market.[18] As mentioned, part of the 2000 Internal Market strategy consisted in the identification of the impediments within six phases which made up the business process, in order to obtain a comprehensive background on which to formulate the possible policy options to improve the benefits deriving from the integration. The six stages making up this scenario are: establishment of the service provider; use of inputs; promotion of the product; distribution; sales of the output; and after-sales support. All the barriers can also be classified into two groups, legal and non-legal. All the impediments derived from national legal constraints such as laws or regulations which cause discrimination between domestic and foreign operators belong to the former group, and all the difficulties not directly originated by public acts, for example, cultural and language barriers or lack of necessary information belong to the latter.

Table 9.2 Identification of the business process phases and relative barriers

Phase 1	Phase 2	Phase 3	Phase 4	Phase 5	Phase 6
SETTING UP	USE OF INPUTS	PROMOTION	DISTRIBUTION	SALES ACTIVITY	AFTER-SALES SUPPORT
Examples of rules impeding the integration process:					
Authorization regulations,	Administrative formalities	Bans on commercial communications	Specific legal form	Form and contents of the contracts	Difference in civil responsibility systems
Local regulations in the field	Disparity in tax and social protection	Content restrictions	Requirements of professional qualifications	Price regulation	Financial guarantees

Source: European Commission (2002) COM (2002) 441.

The relocation of a supplier implies a total rearrangement of the business model following the limitations present in the new market. These constraints normally consist of national regulations like licences, authorizations, technical or legal requirements, but also the bureaucratic nature of the necessary procedures is a barrier in itself. Barriers in this field are among the highest ones and are of all different kinds. This is possibly the hardest step to overcome by a firm with international ambitions. Furthermore, all the barriers affecting the process of establishment cause an increase in the associated fixed costs and since the high fixed costs are one of the main reasons why small and medium-size enterprises (SME) do not undertake the international path, the described barriers push to exclude these companies from the advantages of the internal market.

Difficulties concerning the use of inputs in providing services are principally related to the personnel recruitment. Obstacles are found in both cases: the mobilization of a company's actual staff or the engagement of local employees. The complexity of the administrative formalities and the characteristics of each individual law system for everything concerning social security and pension systems render this phase of the international expansion particularly complicated for firms. The lack of harmonization at an international level and lack of flexibility at a national level are currently perceived as the greatest impediments by service providers.

The promotion of the product is essential for every kind of business and it is even more important when an operator intends to enter into a new market. In this phase, providers face a high level of regulation. Indeed an increased number of different rules on advertising are present in every country and are often sector specific. In individual countries, for example, some service advertisements may require prior authorization by local authorities, like financial services, while others are subject to content restrictions, or are totally banned, as is the case of some professional services including law or engineering.

As aforementioned, services are subject to more complex dynamics at the time of distributing them internationally. Normally Member States regulations tend to submit foreign providers to the same requirements applied to domestic suppliers. In most cases, this discriminates against foreign operators that are in a position where they must double their efforts to match both authorities' requirements: those from their country of origin and those in the new market. For example some professional categories require in some Member States a registration with the national association, so that professionals occasionally providing services abroad must be registered and pay their contribution in every country in which they pursue the service. Specific legal forms are not agreed at European levels, and professional titles and qualifications are still hardly recognized, especially within high skilled professions. Again the red tape and its inconsistency among European countries can be pointed out as responsible for these deficiencies.

Concerning the barriers influencing the sales phase of the business production chain, the poor level of agreement continues to play a central role. Contracts, if compared between countries, often require different features so that firms need to constantly adapt their standards to the new forms as they confront new markets. Similar problems are found also when treating invoicing, accounting principles or VAT payments and reimbursements.

Services characteristics, such as the personalization of the product, are particularly relevant in the after-sales phase of production. Barriers in this field are, once more, related to the differences in regulations in the countries' systems. In the cross-border service provision, liability insurances, post sale obligations and responsibilities vary noticeably. Minimum insurance coverage, for example, can differ widely from country to country, for the same type of service provider. This means that firms must provide different kinds of services depending on the market they are operating in, with the obvious consequences for costs and quality of performance.

The supply chain is not the only aspect affected by the presence of barriers; the consumer side also faces impediments that slow down integration. Nowadays, the right of European consumers to utilize services from every country in the Union is signed on paper, but still partially unknown and seldom respected, so that purchasers still meet restrictions on the cross-border acquisition of services. These constraints make foreign providers more costly and, in general, less attractive reducing notably the level of competition and, consequently, the level of a firm's competitiveness with the well-known effects of high prices and low levels of quality and variety. Moreover, the major impediments from the service-user point of view are, firstly, the lack of information on the possible consumption of services produced in other countries, their availability, typologies and characteristics, and all this contributes to low competition; secondly, a lack of trust in buying cross-border, which is, at this time, due to the low information on consumer rights, rules and modalities of transaction.

Cost of the Barriers

Low levels of cross-border activities may entail negative effects with harmful consequences on European economies. The large gap between the vision of an integrated market, and therefore of an integrated economy, and the reality as experienced by European citizens and European service providers must be considered with particular attention. The loss of competitiveness enhanced by this situation disenables the growth of service companies with potential for expansion, independent of size or type of activity. The consequences of this gap do not exclusively affect the tertiary sector. Due to the central role played by the service industries in our modern economies, effects are spread throughout other sectors, thereby reducing productivity and growth, and influencing the potential for expansion of firms operating in other sectors affected by high prices and low quality levels of the services necessary to their production activity.

Protectionist barriers for services often damage the same companies they are supposed to protect. These barriers permit inefficiencies, avoid competitive environments and behaviours, close the market to new entrepreneurs, and hamper the development of internationalization strategies by the 'protected' companies. When a country, or a sector, raises barriers it starts a chain effect whereby other countries or sectors follow the same tactic to intensify their protectionism measures. In doing so, they impede international trade and encourage the black market. The lost growth pattern particularly affects SME firms, since their reduced dimensions do not permit an effortless availability of the resources needed to act at a European level. Barriers also affect final consumers with higher prices for services of a lower quality and variety.

Finally the effort of the administrations to maintain every single national structure of regulations and laws is a cost at the international level. A simplification in administrations in order to obtain a higher transparency and standardized procedures across countries will initially have a positive effect and would reduce executive formalities in the mid term. Obtaining such a positive outcome will stimulate the dynamics of the internal market.

Evidently the reduction of barriers does not consist in the removal of regulations in services. However, most of these rules are necessary frameworks in the consumer protection and are designed to guarantee the application of the same regime to everyone. The point is to identify a feasible level of heterogeneity and find a compromise for a sustainable governability.

These are actually two limits of the internal market integration, which is a process where services are called upon to compete internationally and to do this they need to operate in the best available environment.

5. THE DIRECTIVE ON SERVICES IN THE INTERNAL MARKET

According to the 2000 plan, a phase followed the contemplation of the difficulties hampering the internal market. In this phase, the Commission's role was to elaborate a package of initiatives intended to dismantle specific barriers and to stimulate the development of the services market. The analysis undertaken thus far suggests that the central needs on which to act are not sector-specific, but rather emerge with similar characteristics from different areas of the service sector. The lack of harmonization among national regulations, the high costs of establishment in other Member States and the low levels of cooperation among different administrations were faced by a unique horizontal instrument which, by using a combination of techniques, was capable of addressing all these barriers. To this end, in January 2004 the Commission presented its proposal for a directive on services in the internal market, which had been finally adopted by the European Parliament (EP) in November 2006 (European Council, 2006), after a long and complex debate.

This proposal, initially called by its promoting commissioner Frits Bolkestein '...potentially the greatest impulse to the internal market since its establishment in 1993', intends to apply pressure on the Member States to reduce administrative charges and the unreasonable bureaucracy impeding companies from providing cross-border services or from establishing themselves in other members' territory. In fact, since the internal market is still not exploiting the majority of its potential positive outcomes, all the analyses on the state of the market and the obstacles to its development were addressing the following essential aspects as the focus on which to concentrate their attention: commerce and FDI. Due to the similar characteristics presented by the barriers in the different sectors, a horizontal approach embracing the largest number of services possible was chosen.

At first, the activities covered by the directive were all the services provided as an economic activity, and not subject to specific communitarian reglamentation.[19] However, in February 2006 the European Parliament voted to reduce the scope of the directive, excluding services such as health care, gambling, temporary work agencies and several kinds of social services. Moreover, since the first version, all the services of a non-economic nature were excluded. In practice, all the services provided by the states to accomplish their public duties (such as public administration and justice or basic social, cultural and education services) were not included within the scope of the proposal. Finally, one should consider the case of the services of general economic interest. Since their definition is not clear, Member States have the right '...to define, in conformity with Community law, what they consider to be services of General Economic Interest, how those services should be organized and financed and what specific obligations they should be subject to'.[20]

The intention of the policymakers is to enhance the positive effects deriving from the launch of the single market for services which means an expansion of the production of the sector, increased employment, a raised level of productivity, lower price levels, higher quality and in general higher levels of welfare. There are three main challenges endorsed by the directive:

1. Freedom to establish a business in another Member State.

   With the intent of eliminating superfluous obstacles impeding and discouraging the operators, the proposal contemplates some administrative simplification such as the creation of *single contact points* for companies, the so called 'one-stop-shop', in order to make the complete relevant information on the requirements for becoming established in another Member State available. Furthermore, the directive includes a list of regulations not compatible with the principles of the single market, to be removed by the Member States and a list of regulations that the Member States shall examine to guarantee that its employment does not contradict the access of foreign providers to the internal market. The objective is the abolition of complex and costly procedures, which require a high number of authorizations and homologations, through the reduction of entailed documentation and the installation of computerized procedures.

2. Free trade between Member States.

   Originally, in order to strengthen the cross-border provision of services, the proposal planned to act by using different instruments among which we find the long debated country of origin principle (CoOP) implying that when a service supplier wants to provide his services in another Member State without a permanent presence there, he has to comply only with the administrative and legal requirements of his country of establishment. The principle was removed from the proposal after the vote of the European Parliament, although the directive reaffirms the consumers' right to receive/buy cross-border services. The directive also reaffirms the right of users to utilize services from every country of the Union, impeding Member States from imposing restrictions such as the authorizations to use services or discriminating rules raising the cost of foreign services.

3. Harmonization process aimed to increase mutual trust between members.

   In order to facilitate the establishment of providers and the free trade within the Union, the Commission considers essential the reinforcement of mutual trust among Members. However, there will be no unique market until a unique framework of rules is missing. Moreover such a heterogeneous system of prescripts can create a series of comparative advantages, some of them partially unintentional, without economic justification, but founded on legislative principles. Some of these advantages are actually keeping the European economy away from its optimal situation. The directive proposes here to harmonize legislations so as to guarantee protection for the consumers through common regulations on compulsory insurances, resolution of lawsuits or the information the provider is required to make available at the moment of supplying a service. Another important aim is the reinforcement of the mutual assistance between national authorities. It is an attempt to exercise an efficient control on the service activities under a clear distribution of competences. Complementary actions should include the development of inputs for companies aimed at increasing the quality of products, such as the introduction of voluntary certifications or cooperation with the chambers of commerce. It also aims to promote codes of conduct on particular questions such as the public advertising of regulated professions.

Potential Impact of the Policy Action

In practice, in order to understand the extent to which these efforts will become reality, different evaluation studies were undertaken. The first to be published was the Commission's official impact assessment,[21] which identified the main expected outcomes of the application of the directive, from its social implications to its overall effects on competition. Relevant works on the subject had also been presented by the OECD and the IFO Institute for Economic Research.[22] Four works were finally carried out by high standing economical analysis institutions; these applied empirical econometric models in order to give a clear view of the possible scenarios.

At the Commission's request, the impact assessment completed by the Copenhagen Economics (2005) is based on a general equilibrium model. By considering the different barriers in several sectors, and assigning corresponding costs and benefits, the model elaborates the impact of their removal by creating different outlines. The most conservative possibility estimates an increase of 0.8 per cent of Union's GDP, with a rise in employment of around 600 000 new jobs (0.3 per cent of total) and an expected increase in salaries of 0.4 per cent. Distorted price levels will be reduced by 7.2 per cent, improving the service consumption. The countries that perceive more advantages from the application of the proposal will be, on the one hand, those leading the service economy (i.e. the UK or the Netherlands) and, on the other, those presenting the highest levels of regulation (such as Italy or Austria). These prudent estimations, which are based on two-thirds of the services affected by the directive, represent 57 per cent of all the benefits the internal market has produced since its institution in 1993.

After the document was presented, the Dutch presidency of the EU Council requested another study, which this time was carried out by the CPB Netherlands Bureau for Economic Policy Analysis (2005). This analysis applies gravitational models based on the heterogeneity of the regulations within Europe. Table 9.3 shows that intra trade in services could rise by 30 per cent to 60 per cent, implying an increase of 2–5 per cent of total intra trade (goods and services). FDI could increase between 25 per cent and 30 per cent.

Table 9.3 Potential impacts of 2004 EU Services directive on trade and FDI in (commercial) services

	Minimum effects	Maximum effects
Total intra EU trade increase	**30**	**62**
of which:		
* Increase due to reduced heterogeneity in barriers to competition	25	51
* Increase due to reduced heterogeneity in explicit barriers to trade and investment	5	11
Total intra EU FDI increase (including rounding difference)	**18**	**36**
of which:		
* Increase due to reduced heterogeneity in barriers to competition	7	18
* Increase due to less FDI restrictions (level effect) [a]	11	16
* Increase due to reduced heterogeneity in state control	0	2

Notes: a. assuming that investors from other EU countries experience a 30 per cent reduction in the destination country's level of FDI restrictions.

Source: Kox et al., 2006, CPB.

In view of the parliament vote, the CPB (2006) elaborated a second impact assessment, which also considers separately the effects of the application of the CoOP. By applying a general equilibrium model, it shows that the full implementation of the original services directive could have increased European GDP by 0.5 to 0.7 per cent, which would mean a boost for the European economy of 32 to 74 billion euros. The estimated effect for European consumption is even larger, with a forecast of an increase by 0.5 to 1.2 per cent. With regard to the concerns of the CoOP, the report concludes that its application would have accounted for more than one-third of the trade increase and for about 40 per cent of the expected growth in GDP and consumption.

A third institute, Europainstitut (2005), elaborated a report that supplemented the previous studies using an econometric approach to estimate the effects the proposal could have on productivity, employment, value added and investments. In line with the previous forecasting, the results approximate the total derived growth of EU GDP by 0.69 per cent pushed by a value added increase of 1.65 per cent, considering the services originally covered. The effect on employment is calculated as 612 000 new occupations, while the FDI ratio is supposed to increase by 0.55 per cent.

The Political Debate

Undoubtedly the Service Directive has been one of the most disputed, controversial pieces of legislation in recent EU history. Almost three years passed since the presentation of the first version in January 2004 and the final vote of the EP in November 2006. In its first reading, the parliament approved more than 400 amendments; this is symptomatic of the difficulties encountered. Critics of the first proposal alleged that it was exposing public services, such as education and health care, to private competition with a consequent decrease of the quality of services, and asserted that workers' rights, as established by the national laws of the countries in the Union, were in danger after the application of the CoOP. Supporters emphasized that the proposal was the very first attempt to promote effective integration throughout the continent, making cheaper and improved services available to the EU citizens. Furthermore, the debate on the proposal was active in the French campaign on the European Constitution. It had been used as an argument by the 'no party'. Hardly ever had an economical directive been used as a political argument. In this case, it was converted into such a profitable electoral argument that part of the body of 'yes' voters assumed a critical stance that adapted the interventionist ideas so well considered in other sectors like agriculture. After the failure of the Constitution in France and the Netherlands, few optimists still believed in a successful outcome for the directive. Nevertheless, in February 2006 it passed through the plenary vote of the parliament, although with consistent dilution of its principles. Thereafter, the Commission presented a new proposal including the major part of the amendments voted, on which the council encountered a common position (July 2006). Negotiations brought the directive to a second and definitive reading by the EP at the end of the same year, and the plenary session of November finally adopted the text. Before enactment, it will have to be transposed by Member States into national law in the following three years.

With respect to the original version, the approved text presents a reduced scope, and the application of the CoOP had been buried. The directive's original scope was supposed to present a horizontal approach, and the results are unclear. The definition of an economic activity was open to interpretation and could create conflicts with other previous EU or Member State legislation. Moreover, a large majority of the European Parliament Members pushed for the exclusion of a series of services of general interest (education, electricity, postal services, water furnishing, etc.); gambling, health care, temporary work services and social services were also finally barred. The veto came even after the Commission clarified that the directive did not affect Member States freedom to define, organize and finance services of general interest at public level. The result reduces the horizontal harmonization impulse the proposal originally presented, leaving it less effective

However, the proposal's most controversial argument was the application of the CoOP. This is not surprising, as this step brings the highest number of changes to the actual state of the situation. From the CPB analysis exposed above, its results clearly show that the application of this principle would strengthen the integration of the market. Opponents argued that this principle would have involved a possible social dumping among Member States, and reduce wages and workers protection. These opinions seemed to be more of a reaction to the creation of the market, rather than a direct reaction to the CoOP. It can be noted, for example, that this principle had been working in the manufacturing sectors since the creation of the internal market, and that no downward spiral on social standards in those fields occurred in Europe. The proposal already contained several exceptions of the CoOP; the exception of the posting of the workers directive, for example, was assumed to prevail.

Nonetheless, a majority of critics founded their arguments on misunderstandings; others founded theirs on conflicts of interests and protectionism traditions; and the minority on the ambiguity of the initial proposal. National identities strongly affect public support to European integration (Carey, 2002). For example, it was stated that the directive pretends to liberalize public services and open them to competition, while its intention was to trigger competition in what are already market services – not to debate the public character of certain services and the Member States' competition in them. The same reasoning can be applied to the services of general economic interest (e.g., health care, postal services, energy) whose financial and territorial control lie in Member States' hands. The proposal intended to improve the cross-border supply of services and the establishment of operators abroad, without initiating liberalization processes or the suppression of monopolies.

A less-debated aspect is the transfer of bureaucracy now charged on companies and supposedly under administrations' responsibility. The directive enhances a simplification mechanism that forces national administrations into vast modernization, transparency and cooperation efforts that could meet several obstacles. Another less controversial aspect is mutual evaluation. This idea is to create an open and transparent system in order to eliminate disproportionate restrictions that undermine the principles of the Treaty. This actually reduces Member States' competence in certain fields and reduces potential future restrictions. The measure is in line with past directives, and it is the only way to obtain a truly harmonized sector. An internal market for services requires less heterogeneity in service regulation; otherwise asymmetric effects may appear.

In order to evaluate the directive, several additional observations have to be taken into consideration. The first is to cease the introduction of any new principles, out of respect for the Treaty of Rome. The directive basically intends to strengthen the Treaty's accomplishment, as it had in 1993 through the strategy on the internal market. The directive in its initial form was already 'watered down', with a number of services left out of the scope and several barriers left unconsidered. There is general agreement in the fact that only a full development of the assumptions of the directive, in cooperation with other specific actions, will lead to a total integration of the market. In any case, a major effort will have to be made to obtain a real internal market for services. It is likely that, beyond the Directive, future actions will have to combine the further development of horizontal specific principles with specific actions for specific sectors.

6. CONCLUSIONS

An integrated and structured European service market means an efficient economy in which potential macroeconomic shocks are smoothed out and competitive levels are high. This provides the EU with stable growth patterns in terms of welfare and employment and benefits to consumers who can take advantage of a variety of high quality and low priced services. Since its foundation, the EU has understood the magnitude of the profits derived from the internal market and, based on the Treaty, worked to construct horizontal measures such as the service action plan, and sector specific measures such as the directives on transport or financial services.

In order to present a clear view on the state of the market a brief explorative analysis on the figures regarding trade, FDI, prices and productivity was continued. It can be seen that the formation of the market is driven more by the FDI than by cross country service trade and that so far the process of market integration has been slow and is still incomplete.

Nevertheless, there are several barriers impeding the free movement of services within Europe and these affect every phase of the business process. One of the principal causes of the barriers is the high heterogeneity of national service regulations, which hampers the scope and potential effectiveness of policies toward a real internal market for services.

The strategy adopted by the Commission was to support the rules imposing respect of the principles of the Treaty, with a horizontal directive aimed at harmonizing and stimulating the internal market. Even if this measure has been highly criticized and its strength reduced, several complementary instruments can be utilized so as to continue the process of the creation of an internal European service market.

NOTES

1. Stefano Visintin has collaborated in the drafting of this chapter as co-author.
2. The Australia and New Zealand trade agreement (Anzcerta) was created in 1983, the North American free trade area (NAFTA) among Canada, US and Mexico has been a reality since 1992, the idea of a South American Common Market (Mercosur) appeared in 1995, and also Asian countries made their first steps towards more integrated east Asian markets within the Asean intergovernmental organization in recent years.
3. See Viner (1950), Meade (1955), Lipsey and Lancaster (1957).
4. See Krugman (1979), Helpman and Krugman (1985).
5. This argument was sustained by both the followers and critics of the single currency since the non-existence of an optimum currency area in itself does not deprive of authority the adoption of a single currency.
6. Personal estimation on Eurostat, New Cronos data, 2006.
7. See for example *Study on* 'Price dispersion in the Internal Market' 05/2001, or the more recent Evaluation of the Performance of Network Industries Providing Services of General Economic Interest, 12/2005.
8. The difficulty in collecting price indexes and value added deflectors in services, due to the lack of harmonization and statistical coverage, is widely recognized. In many cases, data are estimated as opposed to using real values. Data is adjusted using an EU15 price average.
9. The Euro area was chosen due to data availability.
10. Signed in Rome on 25 March 1957, last consolidated text published on *Official Journal C 325* of 24 December 2002.
11. From Article 28 until Article 31.
12. OJL 169, 29.06.1987
13. COM (2000) 888 final
14. Lawyers, architects, dentists, doctors, midwives, nurses, pharmacists and veterinarians.
15. Dir 89/48/EC.
16. Dir 2005/36/EC.
17. COM (92) 0494 Communication on the future development of the CTP; COM (95) 0302 CTP Action Plan 1995–2000.
18. See COM (2002) 441 final; and SEC (2004) 21.
19. The latter is the case of the financial, transport services, electronic communications, and network services for example.
20. Text of one of the amendments introduced by the parliamentarian vote.
21. IA COM (2004) 2 final.
22. See *The EU's Single Market: at your service?* by Line Vogt, OECD ECO/WKP (2005) 36 and the IFO 2005 project *Chances and Risks of a Modified General Framework for the Service Enterprises from the EU Service Directive.*

10. Complementary policies regarding services

INTRODUCTION

This chapter deals with complementary policies regarding services within a general framework, with descriptions of synergies, complementarities or, as the case may be, contradictions between the different types of services policies. The previous chapters described in detail the regulatory framework of services at a European level, as well as the steps that have gradually been taken in order to achieve improved market integration and to have more competition within the European Union. These kinds of policies are complemented by other non-regulatory policies – or, to be specific, primarily non-regulatory, although these policies may have implications on certain regulations.

The range of these other types of policies is extraordinarily broad; hence each of these would require a whole chapter. In the interest of space, this book provides a brief summary of only the main related policies. As stated in the book's introduction, specific sectorial policies such as those related to transport, tourism, education, health or general public services sectors have been excluded. As these would obviously require a separate study, just a few examples will be provided at the end of this chapter. Instead, this chapter will focus its attention on 'horizontal' policies, referring to services as a whole or, where applicable, those focused on business-related services.

This chapter will deal, in greater detail, with some questions previously considered, such as innovation or employment, where the implications regarding economic policy have not yet been mentioned. We shall also tackle, in greater depth, regional policy and quality policy, which are issues considered for the first time in this book and which could exercise remarkable influence in future years. Regional policy is very important when considering services, due to the fact that this policy has guided a large part of transport policy, and that it is now, for the first time in its history, expanding significantly to include a broad range of services linked to competitive and innovative regional needs. Quality policy is, in turn, an interesting example of the response to the challenges brought about by the necessity to catch up with what has already been developed in the goods market for decades. This chapter will also refer to policies that favour entrepreneurship, services information and knowledge, as well as some examples related to sectorial policies.

The assertions made in this chapter aim to cover two objectives: the justification and analytical framework for policy proceedings (next section), on the one hand, and the presentation and discussion of policies or proposals by the Commission at a European level, on the other (rest of the chapter). These objectives are not strictly linked to each other. The economic justification presented may or may not coincide with the motives leading the Commission to develop a specific policy, and hence different alternatives to those of the Commission. In fact, references to justify the different policies and establish interrelations are intended for all possible policies, at all levels, and not just for those of the European Commission.

It is worth mentioning that the majority of the policies presented in this chapter are in an incipient stage: these are recommendations and suggestions rather than specific policies with their own weight and budget. This is due to the recent advance of these kinds of policies, whose consolidation, where appropriate, will lead to a several-year-long process. Many of the specific recommendations contained in these pages are partially based on the works carried out by the European Forum on business-related services. This Forum was created by the Commission in 2003–2004 (DG Enterprise) in order to rely on the experience of experts, associations and services companies advising on the policies to be implemented. The author of this research has also participated in the works of the Forum, and contributed to many of the proposals formulated there, which will be summarized in the relevant sections. Nowadays, within the DG Internal Market and Services, the Forum has been re-established to support the single services market policy, where a different type of issue is presented as instrumental or complementary to the internal market, as the case may be. Stakeholders continue to play a role in shaping EU policies concerning services.

1. THE FRAMEWORK FOR SERVICES-RELATED POLICIES: OBJECTIVES AND SYNERGIES[1]

The previous analysis deduces the need to promote competition and regulation harmonization within the European Union in order to gain competitiveness and to confront the challenges set out in the chapters of this book. But this will only be achieved effectively if all services-related policies are coordinated so that a real complementary situation exists. In fact, the objectives of the complementary policies are the same as those of the regulatory policies, as described in the previous chapters: growth and employment, innovation, competitiveness, competition and market integration. Their achievement is the way to confront the stated challenges, such as comparative backwardness regarding productivity, competitive weaknesses within the globalization and offshoring process, R&D deficit or the heterogeneity of regulations and the lack of market integration and competition.

Complementary policies are imperative in order to achieve all the objectives of a services policy. Regulatory policies influence market conduct and aim to pursue particular objectives this way. However, although this is essential, it is not enough to achieve the specific objectives in areas such as services innovation or quality. Other policies must act directly on a series of intermediate objectives on which regulatory policies interact. Finally, the intermediate objectives help to achieve the predominant objective of growth and two other interrelated objectives: welfare and competitiveness. Figure 10.1 illustrates the different interactions between objectives.

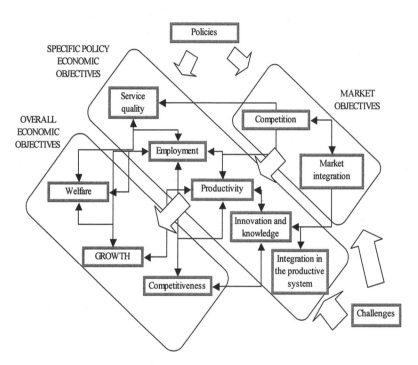

Figure 10.1 Interrelations of services policy objectives

Obviously, policies have a greater effect on some objectives than on others. For example, competition policy will particularly affect the competition in the internal market, although its application will benefit innovation and growth, as previously seen. Internal market is intended to improve market integration, but this also implies stronger growth and more employment. A policy of services innovation leads to a company' competitiveness, which takes advantage of these investments, and in doing so improves its competitive capacity and possibilities regarding growth and income.

Figure 10.2 shows the six major objectives analysed in the previous chapters, from which the main regulatory and non-regulatory policies are derived. In the cases of sectoral policies (transport, tourism, financial services, etc.) and policies on employment and qualifications, the attention must be paid to both categories. For example, labour market regulations, and also training and qualification policies (non-regulatory to a large extent) are a key factor concerning employment. The diagram includes those policies planned for the promotion of entrepreneurship, which is largely related to all the other policies, whether regulatory or non-regulatory, although particularly to policies on regulation, innovation and competition improvement. Innovation and R&D policy is also linked to regional policy and to that intended for the improvement of statistical and analytical knowledge on services, as will be seen further on.

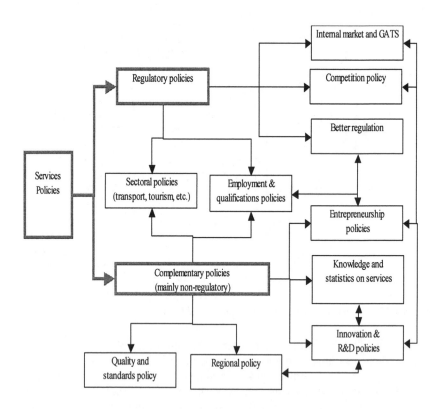

Figure 10.2 Policies for a competitive services economy

Complementary policies are necessary for various reasons. Firstly, to amplify the effects intended by legislative or regulatory policies. For example, competition or internal market policies are not sufficient to foster their pursued objectives. Competition policy is not enough to guarantee fair competition, but an economic framework is required which renders competition effective. Moreover, a policy on internal market is needed but is not sufficient for an internal market to function well. While a completely single market would be possible from a legal point of view, the companies could keep on operating in fragmented markets or on a small scale. In order to facilitate effective competition and market integration, other types of secondary tools would be required.

The second reason that justifies the complementary policies is the need to face specific problems derived from a framework traditionally orientated to goods industries or infrastructures. Quality, innovation or regional policies have usually been directed towards agriculture, manufacturing goods or infrastructures, and services have remained in a second or third position. Even those policies that are allegedly horizontal, with no sectoral priorities, have been designed in such a way that services have found limited space for their development. Some sectoral aspects have recently been taken into consideration in these and other policies, so that services have a greater scope of action.

The third reason arises as an effect of globalization. This has increased competition between countries, with companies requiring administrative support in order to reinforce some strategic areas, to define high-quality differentiated services, or to provide incentives to promote competitive production in less-developed regions. The challenges of globalization demand a combination of different policies in order to achieve a greater effectiveness of objectives regarding competitiveness.

Fourthly, some policies occasionally may pursue contradictory objectives, requiring an approach that reinforces synergies and minimizes conflicts. For instance, an interventionist regional policy for the promotion of public services could result in the distortion of competition, which prevents private companies from operating, and so the attainment of an objective (i.e., growth, employment or innovation in a region) may imply the reduction of competition and competitive capabilities in such a region. In the long term, however, this type of action generates a net damage, since the exclusion of the private sector could bring net losses in a local economy. A second example of possible contradiction in quality policies is the guarantee of high quality standards, which mean, without doubt, an initial benefit for the quality of services. However, this could also be a concealed protectionist measure to guarantee monopolistic incomes, for example, when quality standards are mandatory and hinder the entry of new agents. In the final analysis, the lack of competition has adverse effects not only on competition but also on consumers; theoretically, the ultimate effect on almost all objectives to be attained is clearly negative. A third example consists in liberalization without guaranteeing the appropriate regulatory conditions. The mere liberalization of certain sectors can generate problems associated with the abuse of market power or, if this process is not underpinned by regulatory measures, problems concerning investments and services guarantees for all or most potential consumers. For example, market competition and the sustainability of the sector must be ensured by means of investment guarantee systems. Generally, there is a need to coordinate regulatory policies and policies regarding internal market and competition, as seen in the 2006 debates concerning the directive on services in the internal market (some opposing opinions argue that the great heterogeneity of regulations within Europe could generate asymmetrical effects, which certainly reveals a deficiency in the process of European construction) or in the debate on the internal market of energy (where the need for DG Internal Market and DG Competition to work together in order to solve the contradictions arising from the current strategy of European economic construction has become evident).

Table 10.1 Necessary complementarity between services policies: some examples of competition policy

Specific initial objective	Policy developed	Potentially negative secondary effects	Specific secondary objective	Complementary policy
Complementary use of competition policy				
Removal of legal barriers	Internal market	Competition problems	Competition	Competition policy
Promotion of services in poor regions	Regional policy	Marginalization of private sector	Competition	Competition policy
Competitiveness vis-a-vis third countries	Quality policies	Concealed protectionism	Competition	Competition policy, internal market and GATS
Policies complementary to competition policy				
Competition	Liberalization of services sectors.	Lack of investments. Worse service	Sustainability of the sector, quality	Regulation
Competition. Defence against concealed state aid	State aid: limits to public services R&D	Services R&D deficit	Innovation and competitiveness	Services R&D&I policy

In fact, if the referred policies are taken into consideration jointly, some could be complementary to others: the regulatory ones to the non-regulatory ones, and also within each of the groups, as previously seen. This complementarity acts in all possible directions. A coherent approach to services policy requires the reinforcement of synergies among the different types of policies. Table 10.1 shows some examples regarding competition policy.

The contradictory or opposing effects of the application of policies can be reduced by a comprehensive view of services policies and a coordinated implementation. On many occasions, this vision is not produced, not only at a national, but also at a European level, due to the fact that each type of policy is designed and manipulated separately, with no apparent connection with the others. As far as the European Commission is concerned, there are two useful systems which reduce the incompatibility between policies: the system whereby each commissioner is obliged to follow and express his/her opinion on the pertinent issues of the rest of the Commissioners' College, and secondly, the existence of inter-services consultations where the affected services of each directorate general must deliberate on the issues of concern brought forward by other directorates general. However, except for transport and, to a certain extent, the financial sector, services continue to receive lower consideration in European policies.

When the European Commission changed in 2004, services were situated in a more prominent place (within the newly named Directorate General for 'Single Market and Services'), which raised expectations regarding the possibility of an encompassing approach to European services, similar to that intended by the Directorate General for Enterprise and Industry for the manufacturing industry. However, it seems that rather than a specific, complete and coordinated approach to the different services policies, the existing pretence (at least for the time being, as of February 2007) is the reinforcement of services in the internal market, which could serve to other initiatives. This is an important step, although insufficient. Complementary policies and their coordination should receive a higher ranking within the policy-making structure of the European Union.

It is worth mentioning that the emphasis on the services policies is not due to an 'a priori' principle that considers the development of specific services policies always necessary. On the one hand, in many cases horizontal policies developed for the whole economy are justified, and the only requirement is a greater attention to their implications and an adaptation to services. In this sense, services-specific policies (for example, for the internal services market) will co-exist with generic policies for all sectors (for example, employment policies) where appropriate. On the other hand (and due to the aforementioned reasons), beyond the debate between vertical and horizontal, the reinforcement of synergies and complementarities between policies are desirable, as shown.

2. INNOVATION AND R&D POLICIES

Chapter 5 highlighted the challenges of the EU regarding services innovation and R&D, which consist of a basic five: (1) The necessity to understand the special characteristics of services innovation; (2) The scarce orientation of R&D programmes and public funding to services; (3) Weaknesses in adequate measurements in the statistical system; (4) The need to direct innovation policies towards the specific elements of services innovation, including organizational aspects or 'unrecognized' diverse methods of developing R&D; (5) The limited suitability of the patent system, which implies the promotion of alternative systems for the protection of innovation, such as copyright.

Justification

There are numerous reasons to support the services innovation policy, which should be at least the same as those reasons which support innovation policy in the industrial sector (more detail in Rubalcaba, 2006, and den Hertog et al., 2007). Three types of arguments can be considered: context factors, market failures and systemic failures. With regard to context factors, the following points can be stated:

- The role of services innovation acts as a stimulant of innovation as a whole through intangible investments.
- With regard to the relatively low productivity of many services sectors and the limited use of ICTs in Europe, the consideration of interrelations between the different types of innovation, technology and non-technology is required.
- The recent deregulation and liberalization in many services sectors means that those companies leaving their protected market niches need new strategies and promotions in order to compete.
- The current process of services relocation to remote countries, or simply to countries with lower costs or higher specialization, forces companies in advanced countries to find new competitive innovation-based strategies.
- With only a few exceptions, the especially low participation rates of services and services companies in R&D programmes.
- The Lisbon strategy launched by the European Union in the year 2000 stated an objective to reach 3 per cent of GDP in R&D investment. It will be difficult to achieve this goal without the more active participation of services.

From the perspective of market failure, an innovation policy for services is completely justified. The problems regarding risk and uncertainty are typical of services activities, where investment risk is added to the intangible nature of new products and the asymmetrical information present in many markets, which includes significant limits to the perception of innovation due to its potential demand. The problems regarding the externalities and appropriateness of results are highlighted in the case of services, where patents have very limited efficiency. The inefficiency of the patent system is due to the fact that the reputation, personal nature and copyright of the service are the main appropriation tools, although the protection tools should be improved. The problem of indivisibility and scale economy is similar in both goods and services, although the predominance of services SMEs and the low structuring of R&D are distinctive features to take into consideration when launching a thorough analysis. Finally, the market power in services is particularly significant, with many structures that are far from those that are typical in high competition.

Together with these classical arguments applied to services, evolutionist theories suggest other arguments based on failures of the system, where services also play a key role. Infrastructural, financial and government systems are, in general, far from incorporating services as perpetrators of the innovation systems. Although there are some important exceptions, there is a lack of consideration regarding the advantages arising from services innovation for regional, national and European systems.

In spite of everything, there are three types of positions and arguments in favour of or against the implementation of an innovation policy specifically for services (Rubalcaba, 2006):

- Arguments in favour of maintaining the pro-industrial status quo: those countries leading in R&D are leaders in industrial R&D; the intangibility of results in services innovation hinders their assessment; the difficulties in patenting the results achieved in services; uncertain results; the competition policy is generally reluctant to authorize aids for the innovation in organizations; services are less productive, less innovative.
- Arguments in favour of a horizontality including services: there are organizational aspects of services which are necessary for the innovative production of companies within any sector; the role of productivity in knowledge-intensive services; the role of SMEs, mainly services SMEs; there are no theoretical reasons to justify the exclusion of services from the horizontal policies.
- Arguments in favour of a complementary and mixed (horizontal to all activities and vertical to the services sector) services approach: there are specific characteristics of services innovation (organizational aspects, patents, standards); advantages for all derive from services innovation (better competitiveness of companies offering and requiring services); the participation of services in R&D programmes and expenditure (currently 13 per cent over the total) should be increased.

Actions of the Commission

The European Commission has recently started to include services innovation in its initiative programmes, the majority of which is subject to discussion and with no foreseeable application for some years. The main works performed between 2002 and 2006 were:

- The Action Plan for Innovation (DG Enterprise and Industry), which includes actions towards organizational and services innovation to be launched during 2007.
- The existing proposal to assess actions regarding services in Member States (Reneser project; DG Internal Market and Services) and to identify the best practices, as in the case of the German programme on services R&D – a unique experience in Europe.
- The initiatives for considering investments in intangible services as an investment and not as an expense.
- The works aimed to include services innovation in the 7th Framework Programme. In this sense, it is worth mentioning the project entitled 'Foresight innovation in services,' launched by the DG Research in 2005.
- The inclusion of services in the recommendations of the Commission for Structural Funds (see next section).

Within the framework of the aforementioned European Forum, some additional priorities have been highlighted:

- Definition of an innovation policy for services, as technological aspects continue to dominate the EU services policy.
- Establishment, within the EU Framework Programme for Research and Technological Development, of a substantial research area aimed at improving productivity and competitiveness of the services sectors.
- Provision of support for the emerging discipline of 'services engineering',[2] directed to the promotion of methods and tools to be used systematically in the prototype and development of new services.

The works carried out by the Forum have also stressed the role of the assessment of intangibles for the improvement of the visibility, appropriateness and development of innovation in services activities: voluntary disclosure of intangible investment could provide greater confidence to investors and could also provide public authorities with a basis for introducing additional fiscal incentives (as is sometimes the case with R&D expenses being subject to tax relief). An adequate level of reporting on intangibles could probably be achieved using data that is currently available in companies. Within this framework, there are current initiatives to improve the information regarding intellectual capital and intangibles, offered as part of or supplementary to corporation or financial reports. However, there are some countries, e.g. Denmark, where this practice is more frequently followed than in others. The Commission also suggests contributing to the diffusion and promotion of good practices as a way to help companies. The promotion of specific training to managers, accountants and personnel related to innovation and services, constitutes one of the actions suggested.

In the statistical area, there is also a series of proposals in the statistical field to review definitions and to provide better coverage for services. This author advocates progress in various directions: improvement of CIS3 for a better coverage of services activities; assessment of alternatives or possible improvements following broader taxonomies in services innovation; new indicators within the framework of the necessary reviews of the Oslo Manual 2005; improvements in R&D statistics to improve the coverage of services activities and researches for the improvement of the Frascati manual; assessment of possible indicators from demand; new indicators for the needs of specific vertical services sectors; indicators of how services activities and companies are represented in R&D programmes; assessment of statistics oriented towards the existing services in national Member States.

The most important service innovation-related actions at EU level are taking place during 2007 and will last several years before consolidation. The most important initiative follows the stakeholders' consultation on a new Europe INNOVA activity: a European Innovation Platform for knowledge intensive services of October 2006. There seems to be an emerging consensus on the following elements: the European Innovation Platform should be implemented through public private partnerships, bridging between research institutes and KTOs, incubators, investors as well as innovation agencies; the European Innovation Platform should offer pooled service packages to be developed, tested and validated at sectoral level in order to better respond to the specific needs of potential high growth ventures active in service innovations; emphasis should be on service innovations instead of innovation in services in order to better reflect the linkages between manufacturing and services; addressing the needs and specificities of enterprises active in knowledge intense services is generally supported as it represents not only the most challenging segment, but also the most rewarding one in terms of economic growth and value added. A second initiative promoted by DG Enterprise on services innovations is developed under the Pro-Inno Europe actions, as instrument for new and better innovation policies for Europe in the area of services.

Innovation in Public Services

Finally, within innovation policies, a special section should be dedicated to innovation policies in public services, since, to a great extent, Chapter 5 and the previous implications of innovation policies and R&D are mainly intended for market services. The importance of innovation in public services has been studied by the Publin network, whose overall objective has been to contribute to the knowledge base for the European and national policy development in this area. This applies to the need for a broad based 'holistic' innovation policy that goes beyond the call for reform and increased efficiency, and which looks at learning and creativity in public institutions and at their interaction with private and non-governmental organizations and with various knowledge institutions (Windrum and Koch, 2007). The policy recommendations from this project (Koch et al., 2006) stress the key points such as investment in technological know-how, performance measures and evaluations, policy learning and pro-innovative spirit. This last point is particularly important for public administrations and can be formulated in this way:

- *Develop learning strategies.* Public managers and frontline employees interviewed by Publin report a lack of dialogue between different parts of the public system, horizontally and vertically, while at the same time underlining the importance of knowledge diffusion. Public institutions ought to develop in house learning strategies needed to find, understand and make use of competences developed elsewhere. Public institutions will normally benefit from developing inter- and intra-organizational networking, coordination and cooperation at all levels.
- *Encourage policy learning.* There is a tendency among some policy makers responsible for innovation, research and knowledge policies to neglect their own learning and innovation activities. Although participants of directorates, councils and ministries do learn actively through their day-to-day activities they often lack strategies for learning and innovation.
- *Encourage entrepreneurs.* Managers should encourage local entrepreneurs with sufficient vision and determination to push innovation processes through, for instance by giving them funding, responsibility and sufficient freedom. Incentive mechanisms can be viewed as a step towards this goal but not as an isolated substitute for it. Team spirit, which gives employees a sense of ownership of the innovations at hand, is important as it also widens the belief systems of the people involved and deals with risk aversion (development of participatory processes, demonstration of utility and acceptance of risk).

In fact, these recommendations are not yet accepted fully in the political direction of the Commission; examples exist in different countries or regions. At a community level, innovation policy in public services can presently be seen in five ways:

1. *E-government.* Admittedly, the efficient and effective delivery of public services – in particular e-government and e-health – has a significant potential for economic growth and for enabling new services. E-government is in itself an innovation source and allows a greater intra- and

inter-administrative connection, as well as improved or new delivery of services.

2. *Information exchange system between public administrations (IDABC).* According to the definition given by the Commission, IDABC stands for Interoperable Delivery of European e-Government Services to public Administrations, Businesses and Citizens. It uses the opportunities offered by information and communication technologies to encourage and support the delivery of cross-border, public sector services to citizens and enterprises in Europe, to improve efficiency and collaboration between European public administrations, and to contribute to making Europe an attractive place to live, work and invest.

3. *Better regulation.* The aim is to strengthen the confidence in quality regulation of other Member States (exchange of information and best practices). In line with this, the Commission has made 'impact assessments' compulsory for its own policies, while launching at the same time several initiatives to improve the efficiency of the regulation, as seen in Chapter 7.

4. *Public procurement.* The New Package for public procurement (with effective date in 2006) introduces several mechanisms to clarify, simplify and modernize the existing directives. Aside from introducing electronic procedures, there is an interesting aspect for services from a spatial point of view: the introduction of greater scope for a competitive dialogue between contracting authorities and suppliers can determine contract conditions. As commented throughout this book, the quality of services lies in the quality of co-production: there will hardly be a good co-production when the public sector contracts them in the same way as it purchases furniture or computers. The lack of homogeneous prices inevitably requires the negotiation of conditions between suppliers and customers. However, in public procurement this must be done in a transparent and competitive way. Although the ongoing reform implies a favourable shift in this direction, some questions remain unresolved, such as clarifying the functioning of competitive dialogue and analysing the experiences of those countries already using it, especially in ICT services and public works. Other outstanding questions emerge from the following points: public procurement is time-consuming and expensive, especially for small contracts; lack of transparency is a common perception in many countries; expertise often 'travels' with the contract, i.e. it does not remain with the procuring company after the contract ends.

5. *Public Private Partnerships (PPPs).* PPPs constitute one of the methods to promote the subsidiarity principle and to leave in the hands of the private initiative the joint provision of public services and services of general economic interest. Although there is an important development in Europe, as indicated in the Green Book of the Commission (2004),[3] a higher occurrence of these partnerships is still needed. Improved clarity is required in definitions, typologies and objectives, as well as in action

guides, practical studies, implications in cross-border co-operations, impact assessments, etc. The incorporation of competitive dialogue in the PPPs, as in the Public Procurement, seems to be particularly necessary. The Communication of November, 2005[4] makes a call for the clarification of game rules in Europe, particularly regarding concessions, for its subsequent development in 2006 and 2007.

3. REGIONAL POLICIES

The importance of services policies to regional development is justified primarily by the role of producer services, mainly advanced or knowledge intensive services (KIS) that act as facilitators of economic development. In addition, recent trends towards more delocalization or decentralization open the gate for obtaining new competitive advantages at regional level (trends identified in Chapter 6, underlying the role of new emerging economies or countries in the service provision, like Ireland, India or the Baltic states). The COM (2003)[5] states the importance of the regional dimension in its key policy message number 4:

> The provision and use of business-related services is limited in less developed regions and candidate countries, mainly affecting SME and convergence processes. In the context of globalization of the economy, business services operate as the brains of industry which may provide competitive advantage to those firms and regions which have easy access to advanced business services. By their own nature these services tend to cluster in core metropolitan areas which are well connected internationally. The development of regional markets for business-related services, in particular those related to advanced services facilitating innovation in SMEs, is a necessary element for the catching-up process of the less favoured European regions, including the accession countries. These services can also contribute to a more competitive regional environment and thus attract inward investment. Moreover, it is in the services sector where most of the new quality jobs that regional policy is trying to create will take place.

This paragraph summarizes the key justifying arguments for a services-oriented regional policy.

Concentration versus Decentralization

Most of the empirical evidence collected in the related literature reports high concentration rates of business services in certain areas, cities, regions or countries.[6] Many differences can be observed depending on the type of services whereby these producer services as a whole do not contribute in a significant way to economic and industrial decentralization. Business services locate together in certain places that offer relative advantages, creating a higher concentration than that observed in other economic sectors. Some manufacturing or traditional service sectors are usually highly adapted to the economic bases and structures, but business services location shows impressive concentration of activity in some places while in others the opposite applies. In any case, the phenomenon is rather complex and a great many factors interact together. A recent work (Merino and Rubalcaba, 2005), shows that KIS concentration is important when considering top EU international regions and cities. However, when these regions are excluded, concentration is relatively poor and less important than in other economic sectors. The remarkable role of capital cities, as shown for the EU in another previous work (Rubalcaba and Gago, 2003), reinforces the role of producer services to the establishment of new economic hierarchies and new central places in the global economy (Daniels, 1993).

Table 10.2 Factors explaining business service decentralization or concentration trends

Towards concentration	*Towards decentralization*
Geo-economic context	
Transaction and opportunity costs	Shrinking travelling costs
Proximity and client location	Shrinking communication costs
Income and economic development	ICT boost
Factor endowments	Decreasing marginal productivity
Productivity gains: skills and qualifications	Manufacturing economic bases
Service-oriented economy	
Environmental conditions	
Agglomeration economies	Environmental negative externalities
Innovative environment	Rise of prices and costs in demanded areas
Urban and regional conditions	Other limits to agglomeration economies
Market dynamics	
Presence of multinationals	Factor mobility
Reputation	Market transparency
Uncertainty	Integration
Trade barriers	
Entrepreneurial profiles	
Requirement for co-ordination	Specialization processes
Integration and concentration of knowledge	Steps towards global strategies
Service nature	
Intensive interactive co-productions	ICT dominance of co-production
Short-time co-productions	Commodification processes
	Long-time co-productions

Source: Rubalcaba and Gago, 2003.

Table 10.2 presents a summary of factors explaining the key elements behind business services concentration or decentralization. These factors can be divided into five categories, according to different aspects of service provision. Firstly, those factors related to the geo-economic context; secondly, those related to environmental conditions; thirdly, factors derived from market dynamics; and fourthly, those factors related to the entrepreneurial characteristics of firms. Finally, there is the very specific nature of services. For explanation of these factors see previous works (Rubalcaba and Gago, 2003; Rubalcaba and Garrido, 2005, Rubalcaba and Merino, 2005). The dialectics between concentration and decentralization establish a dynamic in services that reinforces regional convergence or divergence processes, as the case may be. In general, decentralization allows the convergence of emerging regions, while concentration in areas of higher international level makes the existing differences greater. For this reason, regional policy, since the 1980s, has tried to improve the delivery of regional services, with the intention of, where appropriate, convergence or non–convergence to the group of regions with the highest development and income. Therefore, business-support services have been developed using public and semi-public institutions and chambers of commerce, although on occasions some initiatives with a high presence in the private sector have been instigated.

Business-related Services versus Business-support Services

Leading cities and regions concentrate most of the highly qualified business-related services in Europe due to the interaction between different agents creating the service economy at regional level: private business-related service suppliers, clients of services (users), business support services and the institutional framework. Concerning these last two actors it is important to note that some of the most successful business service policies at the regional level are found in those regions already leading the international concentration of business services. Therefore, these kinds of service policies are not just 'social' policies for less developed regions.

Less developed regions normally have an important lack of private business-related services so the institutions and business support services act sometimes as substitutes of private business-related services. Therefore, the benefits of the complementarities between private- and public-oriented services are less relevant than in advanced regions. Moreover, developed regions export services to other regions, particularly less developed regions, and also import services from other competitive regions where prices are lower. In this sense, less developed regions have the possibility of developing competitive advantages and exporting services to top regions, following the current examples provided by Ireland or India. There are opportunities both for competitive regions based on low wages and for competitive regions producing high-qualified services.

To obtain these competitive advantages as well as the service endowments needed for local service users, policymakers promote the interaction already successful in top business-related services regions: interaction between suppliers and clients, between public and private services, between best practices and failure practices. In this context a business-related service policy should promote both the service supply and service demand, both private services and business support services, and the transformation of bad practices into best practices. The need to promote both top quality business support services and top business-related services was included in the COM (2003) 747: 'Both public and private services competing on an equal footing and exploiting synergies among them can contribute to this desirable development path'. The role of the private-public interaction is also recognized in the EU Guidelines for Cohesion and Structural Funds (2004):

> Business services should preferably be delivered by the private sector or by mixed public/private organisations. The services should be top-class, readily available, easy to access and responsive to the needs of SMEs. The quality of the services should be defined and monitored and there should be coherence between service providers, e.g. by establishing public-private partnerships and one-stop shops.

Figure 10.3 indicates the idea of the need for complementarities between the promotion of private-market business-related services and the promotion of business-support services. In the figure, three types of major impacts are identified for a regional policy on business-related services.

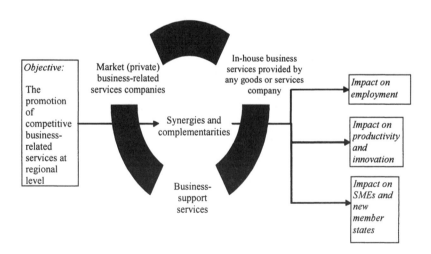

Figure 10.3 Complementarities between market services and business-support services in regional policy context

EU Regional Policies and Services

The Commission COM (2003) 747 also stated that:

> Programmes under the structural funds should seek to identify the constraints of a more balanced availability of business services. Policies to achieve this could include the identification of the demand for business services in the regions, the development of appropriate human resources and the promotion of the information society as business support tool.

After the message in that Communication, the Forum on business-related services has fixed a number of key characteristics that should be taken into account when developing a 'services-informed' regional policy: market transparency, and availability of information about services on offer, is low (there is a heavy reliance on referral from customers, rather than systematic attempts to seek out the highest quality service available, and comparison of competing offers on the basis of value for money); low barriers to entry, lack of standards and quality assurance schemes can also contribute to the difficulty of procuring high quality services in certain regions; there is also a tendency for services to localize in major urban centres (for example financial services, retail, design, and other knowledge intensive business related services), resulting in less easy access in more remote areas. Following these key elements, the Forum proposed a number of recommendations for raising awareness and good practice (European Forum on BRS, 2006):

- A multi-sectoral approach, combining public and private initiatives should be promoted, taking account of the transition to a services oriented economy.
- A good infrastructure of Business Support Services and private business-related services to start-ups and SMEs has to be developed. Specific measures should be introduced to ensure that businesses in all sectors have access to such services, particularly in the transition economies. For example, best practices could be spread such as vouchers for purchase of external services, access to finance via micro-loans, regional risk-capital funds.
- Links and networks between providers of business services, users, and business support services should be developed. These could take the form of 'meet-the-buyers' events, sector-specific symposia, and graduate fairs, etc.
- Exchange of best practices could be promoted to attract talent into the less developed regions, and particularly the transition economies, based on the real needs of enterprises, and to retain highly qualified workers and recent graduates.
- Raising awareness on the importance of services for regional development. Better information on the subject should be provided to policymakers in

the less developed regions. Education of the business environment (banks, accountants, and other service providers) on the availability and the need for high quality knowledge intensive business services and promotion of the possibilities and benefits of externalizing service functions would also contribute to the competitiveness of the regions.

- Knowledge on business-related services in the regions is not sufficient. Regional data bases of available business services would be useful and would stimulate increased demand and competition.
- In order to improve the evaluation of regional policies, further research is needed on the geographic distribution (mapping), availability and uptake of BRS in the regions.

Particular attention must be paid to the place of services in the Guidelines for Cohesion Policy, 2007–2013, to be approved during 2006 to orient the use of Structural and Cohesion Funds. These guidelines are made in the light of the renewed Lisbon strategy for growth and jobs, in such a way that programmes co-financed through the cohesion policy should seek to target resources on the following three priorities:

1. Improving the attractiveness of Member States, regions and cities by improving accessibility, ensuring adequate quality and level of services, and preserving their environmental potential.
2. Encouraging innovation, entrepreneurship and the growth of the knowledge economy by research and innovation capacities, including new ICT.
3. Creating more and better jobs by attracting more people into employment or entrepreneurial activity, improving adaptability of workers and enterprises and increasing investment in human capital.

For the first time services are included at the top of the EU policy agendas, after their inclusion in these 2007–2013 cohesion guidelines, in particular within the first two priorities. Services are recognized to play a major role in convergence processes: 'Along with efforts directed at basic infrastructure, action is required to modernise and restructure the productive capacity of regions by providing services to enterprises, particularly SMEs; by improving access to finance; by promoting RTD and innovation; by developing human resources; and by promoting the penetration, dissemination and take-up of ICTs'.

The place of services in the cohesion guidelines can be summarized as follows in Box 10.1. The Cohesion Fund plays the key role in support of Trans-European transport networks while, in turn, the Structural Funds should generally focus on the development of 'infrastructure' linked to measures to stimulate economic growth, including most of the proposals related to services.

BOX 10.1. SERVICES IN THE EU GUIDELINES FOR COHESION POLICY, 2007–2013

- **Business services and business support services.** Under the guidelines for 'Improving knowledge and innovation for growth', the role of business services to facilitate innovation and promote entrepreneurship is recognized. A call is made for providing business support services to enable enterprises, and in particular SMEs, to increase competitiveness and to internationalize, in particular by seizing the opportunities created by the Internal Market. Business services should prioritize the exploitation of synergies (e.g. technology transfer, science parks, ICT communication centres, incubators and related services, co-operation with clusters) and give more traditional support in the areas of management, marketing, technical support, recruitment, and other professional and commercial services. Business services should preferably be delivered by the private sector or by mixed public/private organizations.

- **Services of general interest.** Cohesion policy contributes to strengthening economic and political integration through, for example, developing infrastructure networks and access to services of general interest, raising the skills of the Community's citizens, enhancing the accessibility of remote regions and promoting cooperation.

- **Transport services.** To promote environmentally sustainable transport networks. Transport networks include public transport facilities, mobility plans, ring roads, increasing safety at road junctions, and soft traffic. They also include actions providing for accessibility to common public transport services for certain target groups (the elderly, disabled persons) and providing distribution networks for alternative vehicle fuels. Attention should be paid to improving the connectivity of landlocked territories to the Trans-European network (TEN-T).

- **Information society, e-service and public services.** The dissemination of ICT across the Union's economy represents a major lever for improving both productivity levels and the competitiveness of regions. The dissemination of ICT also encourages the re-organization of production methods and the emergence of new business and private services. The efficient and effective delivery of public services – in particular e-government and e-health – has a significant potential for economic growth and for enabling new services. Technology dissemination can contribute to regional development by favouring the creation and growth of poles of excellence in ICT activities and developing connectivity and networking among enterprises and SMEs in particular. Measures should encourage the development of products and services with a view to facilitating and stimulating private investment in ICT while guaranteeing competition in the ICT sector. Policy measures should also focus on improving innovation support services for SMEs with the particular objective of boosting technology transfer between research institutions and enterprises. Cohesion policy should also be used to develop skills needed in the knowledge economy and to develop content through the delivery of applications and services (such as e-government, e-business, e-learning, e-health), which provide interesting alternatives to other, often more costly, service delivery models. This is particularly relevant for remote and sparsely populated areas.

- **Services in rural areas.** The territorial dimension is of particular importance for urban and rural areas respectively. Cohesion policy can also play a central role in improving the situation of cross border and broader transnational areas as well as regions suffering from other handicaps due to their insularity, remoteness (such as the outermost or Arctic regions), sparse population or mountain character by promoting better accessibility, notably in the case of services of general economic interest, by sustaining economic activity and by promoting economic diversification on the basis of their endogenous capacities and natural endowments. For cohesion policy, action in favour of rural areas should contribute to ensuring a minimum level of access to services of general economic interest with a view to improving conditions in rural areas that is needed in order to attract firms and qualified personnel and to limit out-migration.

- **Rural areas and tourism.** Many rural regions depend heavily on tourism. These regions require an integrated approach dedicated to quality, focusing on consumer satisfaction and based on the economic, social and environmental dimensions of sustainable development. Actions should take advantage of, and seek to preserve natural and cultural assets which can have important positive spin-offs by protecting habitats and supporting biodiversity. The integrated approach should aim to have a positive impact on the tourism sector, the local economy, the people working in the tourism sector, visitors and the local population, as well as the natural and cultural heritage.

4. QUALITY AND STANDARDIZATION POLICIES

'Quality policy' is understood as all measures promoting the delivery of better services. On some occasions, these measures are related to the regulations included in other types of policies. Quality is one of the main consequences of those regulations tending to facilitate competition or the opening of markets. However, quality can be an express object of a policy affecting numerous aspects of the relationships between suppliers and customers, which is the case of standardization.

Justification

The problems of imperfect information (moral hazard and adverse selection) create an obstacle to quality, both for service providers and for clients. Problems arising from market segmentation and lack of transparency could be the objective of a business service policy on influencing prices and quality. First, it is necessary to observe the mechanisms supplied by the market to resolve these problems. State action is justified only if the market is not capable of adequately resolving the different situations. The following factors supplied by the market can be considered in relation to the problems of imperfect information and transparency.

- *Reputation.* Reputation is the first mechanism of the market which reduces the levels of adverse selection and moral hazard. The reputation of the provider guarantees a certain level of quality. Reputation is associated with a name and an image. For example, in business services, the company name is usually closely related to the name of the professionals who run the company, firm or consultancy. On occasions, reputation can stem not from a name or an image, but from the simple transmission by word of mouth of the good experiences of former customers.
- *Contractual clauses.* Contracts can be written in such a way as to specify guarantees in the case of services rendered not corresponding to an established minimum. The classic example is that of a lawyer who reaches an agreement with his client to receive payment only in the case of winning the lawsuit. In principle, this type of contract reduces moral hazard, as the effort made by the provider carries a greater guarantee. Adverse selection is not directly affected, though the fact that less-qualified businesses leave the market affects it indirectly. In any case, these solutions do not only have advantages. A link between salary and results is negative inasmuch as the success of services often depends on factors which are not controllable by either of the parties involved. Whether the best lawyer wins or loses a lawsuit does not only depend on his or her qualifications or effort, but on the interest, attitude and reason of the client and on the emotions and actions of the judge or jury. It is understandable that professionals endeavour to charge for their work and not for its end result.
- *Insurance.* Obtaining insurance linked to the service is one way of reducing the problems generated by imperfect information. There are insurance policies linked to the service which take effect in the case of failure or error. One example is security services, where provision of the service may be coupled with various insurance policies (for the guards, the objects or persons guarded and for the likelihood of errors in service).

- *Certification.* One of the most noteworthy phenomena in the world of services has been the extension and expansion of accreditation and certifications guaranteeing quality. As quality control is the key issue in problems of imperfect information, many business services providers seek to be accredited by institutions and organizations which guarantee the commitment of their members to comply with determined standards of quality. Thus, for example, the ISO 9000 in the world of consultancy is a basic certification of service which provides the customer with certain guarantees. But as these ISO-like rules do not focus on the real quality of services, more ambitious approaches are needed (the next section deals with this topic).
- *Professional requirements.* Public or professional organizations associated with qualifications also exist. Examinations, university degrees, diplomas, etc., are key instruments to guarantee quality in many business services. In addition, professional associations have the responsibility of serving as a quality upgrade of services.   Professional societies and associations themselves also emerge as a response to the issue of quality. They do so in an attempt to distinguish their members from other non-members as having higher quality requirements. Besides lending their name to their members, they ensure loyalty to their deontological principles and codes. Problems in this area arise in discussions on the voluntary or compulsory character of certain exams, certificates, membership of professional associations, price guides, technical requirements, etc. Trends are towards distinguishing between quality assurance (e.g., technical visa) and corporate protectionism (e.g., prices control). In any case, it is necessary to strike a balance between quality and entry barriers.
- *Training and qualification.* The problem of adverse selection is closely related to the educational system of a country – the quality of instruction and the different alternatives available in universities, technical studies, and professional education. Masters degrees and courses promoted by interested companies themselves reduce the level of adverse selection as they raise qualifications.   Professional societies and associations also promote courses and training methods for their members, with the same effect.
- *Concentration and competition in markets.* Low market transparency has a natural self-correcting mechanism according to the dynamic of the companies which constitute a sector. An expansion of companies in one determined area increases competition and, probably, the level of similarity improving quality as differential mechanism.
- *Information.* By producing tools for obtaining information (magazines, trade directories, membership lists, etc.), societies and associations also contribute to the reduction of low market transparency and non-comparability of markets. The consultation or publication of these works reduces the amount of imperfect information.

As has been shown, the set of market mechanisms for dealing adequately with imperfect information is broad. Within this context it is logical to ask what the role of the state is in a possible policy which might contribute to reducing further the information problems in markets. In this matter, past experience and consulted studies lead to clear conclusions:

1. Government is not necessarily more efficient than the market in providing incentives for the improvement of quality of service. Furthermore, individual incentives cannot be regulated by the state; therefore its work in this field must be secondary to the work of the market.
2. In the context of imperfect information, regulation by the state will have effects which will not be effective in the Pareto sense. That is to say, it is necessary to carry out interpersonal utility comparisons, evaluating who will benefit and who will be harmed by a particular measure.[7]
3. Government can and should support the actions of those private agents who create mechanisms for reducing information problems. To this end, among the possible positive measures which could be adopted are the following: promoting certifications and guarantees for quality of service, allowing legislation appropriate to these problems, improving the educational system, fostering the internationalization and deregulation of the sector. Government should also endeavour to maintain quick and efficient courts and legal operations. In this way, possible conflicts would have a more prompt resolution and the number of potential violations of service contracts would be reduced.
4. Government could carry out promotion actions in those segments of the market where service providers are not interested in having a presence and where, therefore, the structures of the existing markets are not developed adequately or do not have the same usefulness. Within this context, one might establish direct promotion in favour of SMEs and less-developed areas, which, as was already discussed, are the two segments which benefit the least from the producer services economy.
5. The state has a direct responsibility to foster mechanisms for the promotion of quality in public services and services of general economic interest. This also applies to services with implications on environmental or a user's security matters, as in the case of transport or leisure services such as amusement parks.

The Actions of the Commission and Services Standards

Community actions have focused on ensuring that the services provided have an environmental quality and guaranteeing the consumer's rights and security. Within these areas, several horizontal interventions have been developed – not specifically for services – although some are specific for certain sectors, such as in the case of fair transport or data protection in services of purchasing and sales over the Internet.

Other fields of quality policy remain unexplored at a European level, or they are in very early stages. In 1998, the Commission suggested some actions for the promotion of measures to improve quality and the access to business services certification, with a joint approach from the interested parties, and to also evaluate deficits in quality and support improvements.

Within the works carried out by the Forum on business-related services, the range of possible actions regarding the quality of services focuses on standards. The Forum considers that European standards are an essential feature of the internal market. For decades, they have enabled products to be manufactured and sold throughout the Union. In the field of information technology and communications, the role of standards is crucial. Now, they are increasingly used to support an internal market for services, to the benefit of both suppliers and users. The Forum states that the number of voluntary European standards available for services is extremely low compared to the sector's huge contribution to the Union's economy. Superficially that may not be surprising, since it is clearly harder to set norms for activities without obvious physical characteristics than it is for manufactured goods.

Standards have the advantage of providing a higher understanding between suppliers and customers, thus avoiding misunderstandings. In the case of services such as hotels, the star classification system, for example, has been used as a common reference to orientate customers, although these need other types of additional indications to ensure that their selection is correct. Standards can act as a guarantee of the quality being supplied, reduce the time spent explaining what is on offer, and strengthen negotiating positions. Suppliers should be able to expand their markets as customers become more aware of what is available and demand is stimulated for new services and products. This is particularly important in the context of services globalization and relocation, where many European services need a visible and standardized quality in order to compete with low-cost countries, and where quality is less pronounced.

According to the Forum, companies become more willing to pay a higher price for a service which they perceive as being innovative or of higher quality. This is particularly true where in-house services are outsourced to an external service provider. In such cases companies are also willing to pay a premium for the transfer of business risk to another company. Innovation in service delivery can be seen as making an increment with respect to what is accepted as the current standard practice, state of the art, or norm. In the absence of reliable means of assessing the current 'standard' level of services, too much attention is given to the price factor to the detriment of the quality factor. This is particularly the case in public procurement of services, which is almost exclusively driven by price.

Additionally, the advantage of standards is that they increase competition between suppliers, while allowing an augmented comparison of prices and services. This becomes a key instrument favouring competitive strategies for the benefit of the final users, company or individual consumer. Standards cannot be only referred to services as such, but also to certain production stages. Therefore, a standard on a specific stage can help in the improvement of efficiency, the reduction of costs and to innovation.

The Commission has already given the European standards organizations a formal mandate to identify priority areas where standardization of services would be most useful. In February 2005 CEN responded to the programming mandate by providing a comprehensive long-term strategy for services standardization, and outlining areas of future work, which will be discussed in the relevant committee with the Member State representatives. The CEN strategy takes account of discussions in the Forum working group which addressed the issue of standardization, in which CEN and a number of national standardization bodies were active participants.[8] According to these discussions, the overall strategy for services standardization should take account of the needs of industry, government and society (an analysis of the economic benefits of services standardization is urgently needed); indicate the areas in which standardization might be most appropriately pursued at national, European, or international level, or alternatively through industrial consortia;[9] and take account of the different types of standardization 'products' that are available. Where appropriate, standards for qualifications should also be developed. The Forum suggests a shift from regulation-imposed national service quality standards to a situation where quality standards become a desirable market asset (create EU quality hallmark for service providers), as well as a shift from a priori quality regulation to ex-post quality insurance (strengthen EU-wide liability rules regarding service quality and consumer protection, or promote EU-wide professional indemnity insurance for service providers, which at present are not always readily available, and differ between professions).

Within this framework of services standardization, a combination of horizontal and vertical approaches is produced. Horizontal standards are used as a basis for specific services applications, which often require an individual approach, depending on the companies' needs.

Other Actions favouring Quality

As stated at the beginning of this section, standards are a highly significant and necessary part of quality policy. However, other issues exist, some of which are susceptible to being conducted by the policymakers. More precisely, a review and critical valuation could be carried out of some of the existing regulations, such as those regulating liberal professions (often justified by the need for improved quality), legislation regarding the performance of contracts, guarantee clauses, regulations on the granting of licenses and certifications or the position of the quality of services within the public procurement criteria. There is still much to do regarding this issue and agreements with those affected are required through the use of evaluations and independent experts, together with other services policies that affect quality, either directly or indirectly. It is worth mentioning that, concerning quality (standards, public procurement), many initiatives are a response to the interest of companies offering services, by which the subsidiary promotion of an objective market need is pretended. This is also applicable to an essential dimension of services quality, which will be tackled in the following section: qualifications and capabilities of services suppliers.

5. EMPLOYMENT AND QUALIFICATION POLICIES

One of the features characterizing the services economy is the high weighting in its growth that is held by the human factor. The relative low use of physical capital and technology turns human capital into the indisputable protagonist of services economy. In this sense, those policies aimed at the labour market and employment exercise a direct impact on services.

Justification

Compared to what occurs in other areas of policy action, policies required regarding employment do not seem to differ in a significant way from those undertaken for the whole economy. Beyond the high relative importance of human capital in the production of services, there are no important specificities to justify special policies. When they do exist, employment policies usually coincide with other policies, such as those related to the internal market and competition, innovation or the regional area, with obvious effects on employment. However, general policies regarding employment are essential in the field of services. In spite of everything, there are specific elements in services economy reinforcing the need to deal with ambitious strategies for the growth of services employment.

In the report on employment in Europe 2004, the European Commission highlighted the importance of services in the employment strategy.[10] In order to deal with the requirements of services employment, the Commission started with the comparison between Europe and the United States. Despite the relative convergence between them in recent years, significant differences still remain. Although an improvement in the performance of services employment and the less favourable evolution of industry in the EU have reduced to a great extent the differences with the US regarding employment throughout the period between 1998 and 2003, the US still registers the highest employment rate in the services sector (55.4 per cent) and the lowest in industry (12.6 per cent), in contrast with the Member States of the EU. The differences in employment in the services sector between the EU and the US, which are very pronounced between women and older workers, show the possibility that this sector creates jobs that are not yet exploited in Europe. The imbalance, by sectors, between the US and the EU is higher in sectors that are comparatively low- or high-qualified, for example in low-waged sectors, such as wholesale and retail trade, hotels and restaurants, and high-qualified and high-waged sectors, such as real estate and business services, education and health and social services. The same can be stated regarding the disparities between the European Union and the United States by jobs: these are higher between services workers and sales assistants, on the one hand, and, on the other hand, between administrative assistants, jurists and managers. Within Europe, there are also positive cases. For example, in 2003, the employment rate in Denmark, the Netherlands, Sweden and the United Kingdom exceeded that of the United States. More specifically in Sweden, and also in the United Kingdom, the employment creation rates have been significant (as in the US) in low- and high-qualified services sectors, especially in high-waged jobs such as business services, education and health and social services. Chapter 3 highlighted the higher dynamics registered in the United States regarding the creation of employment in almost all services areas between 1979 and 2003, especially in distributive trades, transport and information-intensive services, not only with regard to employment, but also to added value. Europe has been more dynamic than the United States only in real estates services employment and the value added of telecommunications and professional services.

Different reasons explain the differences in favour of the United States. These can basically be grouped into four types of factors: those related to home consumption habits and structures of final demand; the differences in labour markets and salaries; the uneven establishment and impact of new technologies; and the heterogeneity in market sizes, regulation and competition levels.

In addition to the issue regarding the EU relative inferiority in dynamics when compared to the United States, the recent issue of services offshoring – tackled in Chapter 6 – adds to the arguments for improving those qualifications that are under relocation to countries with new competitive advantages. Current unemployment figures in Europe continue to be of concern, and services need to maintain a vigorous performance to absorb the unemployment generated in other sectors and within the services sector itself.

Policy Actions

There are three broad fields of action for a European employment policy in favour of services dynamics:

1. European framework for the reinforcement of services employment. The Lisbon Strategy and the growth and work programme for its development can be used as uniting elements of varied initiatives, reform programmes, employment strategies for individual countries, etc. The Directorate General for Employment (2004) suggested policies aimed at a real internal market for services, a higher participation of women and older workers in

the labour force, and the support of public expenditure in fields such as education and health and social services as a way to take better advantage of the employment possibilities in the services sector. The employment growth in the services sector should focus on the creation of services jobs, with comparatively high wages and productivity, such as business services, education, health and social services. For this purpose, the Commission states the need to exploit the indirect effects of the demand for industrial products on services employment, and the need to increase the final demand for services. The effects of the structural change and globalization on European economies could be an incentive to support measures of reintegration in the labour market through the Fund suggested in 2006.[11] In any event, in order to reach this action framework, it is necessary that the whole action on services exploits the synergies and complementarities between all areas mentioned in this book: all actions on services (regulations, trade, innovation, regional, etc.) affect employment in one way or another.

2. Improvement in operations and in the flexibility of labour markets. One of the reasons for the European backwardness compared to the United States with regard to employment is the rigid operation of its labour markets, overregulation in some countries, and, in general, lack of mobility. All this hinders the possibility of a real internal market where the advantages of economic integration can be used. The liberalization and integration of product markets could be reduced without the parallel liberalization and integration of labour markets. It is worth highlighting that a higher flexibility in labour markets does not mean *per se* a reduction in labour conditions or social welfare. Some services require flexible work, such as part-time jobs and teleworking, in order to reach their maximum expansion, which redounds on the welfare of those people accessing these types of jobs. This is the case of Dutch business services, where the high rates of part-time employees, mainly women, enable family life and working life to combine in sectors of low and high qualifications and wages. The mobility of the labour force within Europe should be another key focus of political attention in order to achieve the real integration of markets, for which many efforts, in economic and non-economic areas, are required.

3. Finally, there is a group of action proposals regarding skills and expertise, which lead to improvements in training systems and their adaptation to specific services needs. The justification of a training effort is based on the following five elements:

- Specific skills are required for effective, competitive operation services. In the current context of organizational changes and internationalization, a continuous upgrading of the specific skills of the employees and adaptability are important tools in overcoming skills shortages.

- Within the current globalization framework, higher specialization and differentiation of the project are required by means of quality. Neither issue is possible without the cooperation of workers providing new qualifications and expertise to the production process. This is particularly important in producer services. There are many qualifications (20 per cent) which potentially undergo offshoring trends towards emerging countries.
- Services innovation is extraordinarily linked to the acquisition of new skills or to the upgrading of existing ones, due to the importance of non-technology and with regard to the know-how of human capital.
- The improvements in qualifications and skills result in an increase in the motivation of workers, their loyalty to the company, and their disposition to undertake new challenges and adopt innovations.
- The services internal market requires major transparency in the EU education and training systems, permitting comparisons of merits and competencies of employees.

The Forum agrees with these recommendations, while suggesting at the same time some specific proposals regarding training and qualifications, such as (European Forum on BRS, 2005): the development of new concepts for vocational training (ensuring the greatest possible degree of flexibility and mobility in the context of the continuous social dialogue) or the creation of awareness of the necessary skills to support the increased specialization of the professional service firms, and the development of more value added services (e.g. personal management skills and teamwork skills). In addition to this, the application of certification of qualifications and competences, on a voluntary basis, would contribute to the mobility of the service providers and strengthen the transparency within service sectors (systems led by services companies themselves). This could be promoted by the Commission in line with what is foreseen in the field of voluntary standardization of services.[12] There is also an existing need to agree these objectives with those of the European Social Fund.

6. POLICIES THAT FAVOUR ENTREPRENEURSHIP

Entrepreneurship is one of the main engines of services economy, behind innovation, competitiveness and growth. Beyond the macroeconomic factors explaining the structural change, as outlined in Chapter 3, specialization changes in services are produced because some entrepreneurs are willing to take the risk of creating new companies or moving to new activity areas. In particular, the sector of business services is that with the highest rate of creation and also of destruction of new companies. Some leisure and personal services are also extremely dynamic.

All issues studied so far have been important in the encouragement of entrepreneurship, providing a favourable framework for its development and fulfilment. More specifically, the internal market offers an even broader field for entrepreneurship. Innovation, which is connected to the entrepreneurs and the administration support, could be decisive on many occasions. The reduction and improvement of regulations are necessary to simplify the game rules and eliminate the obstacles to the entrepreneur's work. Competition policy guarantees fair play between entrepreneurs and the administration, achieving a defence for the born entrepreneur. The improvement of qualifications and the education system have a direct effect on entrepreneurial capabilities. In summary, the group of policies treated in this book is essential for promoting entrepreneurship, especially in SMEs, but also in large enterprises.

The European Commission has a specific plan for the promotion of entrepreneurship. First, the Green Book[13] was drafted in 2003, followed by a wide consultation and then the drafting of an Action Plan in 2005.[14] A reference indicator is the independent work, representing 17 per cent over the European Union, although it is preferred by 47 per cent of the Europeans and the SMEs, considered to be essential in this policy.[15] The relationships between risks and remunerations are decisive to understanding the factors promoting entrepreneurship, among which the training and education of youth are highlighted. The Action Plan outlines a series of key actions related to five strategic areas. High on the agenda are fostering entrepreneurial mindsets among young people, reducing the stigma of failure, providing support for women and ethnic minorities, reducing the complexity of complying with tax laws, and facilitating business transfers. These five action areas are composed of 38 sub-actions, each of which analyses the estimated objectives and impacts. These actions, developed in 2005 and 2006, are complemented by other specific SME-related actions in five areas: promoting entrepreneurship and skills; improving SMEs' access to markets; cutting red tape; improving SMEs' growth potential; and strengthening dialogue and consultation with SME stakeholders.[16] None of these actions has been designed for the development of a specific services policy, although this can be the first beneficiary as it is the principal economic sector, and registers the highest percentages regarding SMEs and independent work, as well as the highest rates regarding the creation and dissolution of companies.

7. POLICIES FOR THE IMPROVEMENT OF STATISTICS AND KNOWLEDGE

Considering the backward situation of services regarding research works, particularly those of researchers and statisticians, it seems reasonable to start thinking about measures to improve this situation. This will be useful not only for researchers, but also for policymakers, services companies, professional associations, and society as a whole. Policymakers should take a particular interest in this deficit. With improved data and studies, they could form better judgements to make decisions, some of which need to be supported by objective information. Such is the case of competition policy which defines market share or dominant positions, or those policies requiring an impact assessment to justify its proportionality (e.g. internal market or quality). Obviously, not all services sectors are in the same position. Those such as transport, tourism and financial services are in a much more advanced stage than, for example, the majority of business-related services or personal and leisure services.

The lack of services statistics compared to industrial or agricultural statistics is evident for anyone who has looked for them in official sources. Until the beginning of 2000, the situation in National Accountancy, Structural Statistics or Statistics specific to the sector was very poor. The old NACE and product classifications provide a sparse representation of the most important and heterogeneous economic sector. For example, before adopting the Regulations regarding the Structural Business Statistics (SBS) of December 1996,[17] there existed only harmonized statistical data on extractive industries, the manufacturing industry, production and distribution of electricity and water, and also construction. Therefore, the application of the SBS Regulation, also covering business-related services and other services sectors, is considered a significant achievement. This was the result of the first services statistics elaborated at the end of the 1980s and from the adoption of various regulations designed for the reduction of the vast deficit. However, despite the advances undergone in the last twenty years, the current situation is far from ideal. Nowadays, services represent one whole part less in current classifications, without reduction of their heterogeneity. In the SBS Regulation, industry is covered by 241 different activities, against 32 for market services.[18] With regard to national accounts, the need to have more detailed information is even more pressing: users have to accept their residual classification as 'other market services.' The analysis is hindered by the addition of section K of the NACE, and should at least offer the distinction between knowledge-intensive services and operative services as an alternative aggregate.

The lack of statistics compared to those of other sectors is due to several reasons, such as the difficulties of measuring intangible and differentiated products (e.g., the difficulties of obtaining price indices in services sectors where prices are not homogeneous); the vast changes undergone in services economy; the budgetary limits of statistical offices during the 1990s, which hindered the increase of works on services projects without reducing budgets in other areas; and finally, the reluctance that is characteristic of the 'materialist' tradition, which has frequently affected those politically responsible.

The COM (2003) 747 describes a strategy for long-term services statistics. In this strategy, five key objectives regarding the structure of the services sector are outlined, including a description of the basic economic and employment variables, labour factor (labour qualifications, suitability, education, hours worked), technology and knowledge factor (use of ICTs, e-business, e-trade, R&D, innovation, immaterial assets); business interactions (externalization, services acquisition, networks, strategic alliances, franchises); the product of services (products, prices, productivity). The Strategy is being developed partly by Eurostat, and at times in collaboration with the OECD.

The services Forum considered the improvement of knowledge and services statistics to be of great importance, and therefore established the following three broad areas: knowledge society; competitiveness and productivity; and internationalization and globalization. Moreover, it suggested the creation of an information platform to be used as a meeting point and a place to diffuse works and studies regarding services, combining some typical observational tasks with others regarding the policy coordination and consultation affecting services. This proposal and many others have not been yet developed.

The European Association for Service Research (RESER) played an active role in the works to define these priorities carried out by the Forum.[19] The network, created in 1990, brings together numerous European services researchers, developing different initiatives such as the organization of an annual congress and the participation in similar international forums. Today, it comprises members from 25 countries and has developed its own strategy for relaunching services research in Europe, including works for the inclusion of services subjects in R&D programmes, and the improvement of information exchange methods and a higher collaboration among services researchers. Among the research priorities, eight are determined as priority areas: (1) Globalization, international trade, outsourcing; (2) Productivity and inter-sectoral relations; (3) Knowledge, innovation and ICT; (4) Employment, skills, training; (5) Markets, quality, prices, regulations; (6) Service management and marketing; (7) Regional and urban dimension; and (8) Non-market services, new public management.

8. EXAMPLES OF SECTORAL POLICIES

Besides the horizontal complementary policies and those referring to the whole of services, the Commission has some services-oriented policies. The most important is perhaps the one intended for transport and communications, although others also stand out, such as those regarding information society and tourism. Sometimes, these sectoral policies are highly regulatory (e.g., information society), while the content of others relates to best practices and information (e.g., tourism). This depends on the state, community or regional level of the competition in each sector or activity, and also on the priorities established by the policy-makers according to the importance given to each of the sectors in the process of European construction.

The information society policy is justified by the fact that the information society offers benefits to European business, society and culture only because it can deliver useful content and services. Digital content and services are therefore crucial to the information society, as well as being a potentially major source of new jobs themselves. Europe has assets in the sector,[20] but faces unique challenges in translating them into the information society. Although the software sector is currently dominated by American firms, the new landscape offers new opportunities to innovative companies. The Commission supports Europe's rich cultural and linguistic diversity, which must be developed as an asset and not allowed to disappear. Some European policies for the information society and related services are shown in Box 10.2.

Transport policies are probably the most important vertical services policies of the Commission, to the extent that they have their own Directorate General, although a major part of these policies focus on transport infrastructures rather than on services. The White Book on transport policy outlined the following goals in 2001: the rebalancing of the modes of transport; the removal of bottlenecks; the concerns of the users; and mastering the globalization of transport. In 2005–2006, an analysis of this book was carried out, and the actions of the Commission have been orientated to facilitate mobility as the most important asset for competitiveness, even taking congestion costs (1 per cent of GDP) and pollution (26 per cent of CO_2 emissions) into consideration. The current objectives are set within three axes: development (which implies the improvement of market competition and the promotion of new infrastructures), protection (the safety of travellers and workers), and innovation (to improve services quality). Within the latter objective, the programmes Galileo (satellite navigation), ERMTS (railways interoperability) and SESAR (harmonized air traffic) can be found.

BOX 10.2. POLICIES FOR THE PROMOTION OF THE INFORMATION SOCIETY

- **Copyright**: While digital technologies make content easier to transmit, creating a potentially huge market, they also make it easier to copy content. Hence the EU Directive on Harmonization of copyright and related rights in the information society, which moved Europe's copyright rules into the digital age in May 2001. Since then the European Commission has played a facilitating role to encourage the different stakeholders to tackle the issues together and find common ground.

- **Software patent**: In February 2002 the Commission presented a proposal for a Directive on the protection by patents of computer-implemented inventions. The goal is to harmonize the way in which national patent laws deal with inventions using software, as the differences between European countries form a significant barrier to trade in patented products.
- **Free and Open Source Software**: The eEurope 2005 Action Plan makes several references to the importance of free and open source software (F/OSS).
- **Public Sector Information:** The public sector is the single biggest producer of information in Europe, producing data on topics as diverse as economics, traffic flow and demographics. This is valuable raw material for new digital products and services, but there are a number of barriers preventing its exploitation. Hence the EU's Public Sector Information Directive of December 2003.
- **e-Inclusion:** ensuring that *all* Europeans can access this new generation of content and services is essential to both help bridge the gaps currently in our society and minimize the risk of a new 'digital divide' opening up.
- The Recommendation on Protecting Minors and Human Dignity in Audiovisual and Information Services was adopted in 1998 to provide guidelines for national legislation combating illegal and harmful content over any electronic media.
- **Television:** the 'Television Without Frontiers Directive', one of the EU's audiovisual policies, promotes the European broadcasting industry by ensuring the free movement of television broadcasting services throughout the EU; digital TV is also promoted.
- e-Content Programme. Launched in early 2005, this four-year programme aims to promote the take up of leading-edge technical solutions to improve accessibility and usability of digital material in a multilingual environment, addressing specific market areas where development has been slow: **geographic content, educational content, cultural, scientific and scholarly content**. The Programme also supports EU-wide co-ordination of collections in libraries, museums and archives and the preservation of digital collections so as to ensure availability of cultural, scholarly and scientific assets for future use.
- Information Society Technology (IST) research. While eContent focuses on using available technology, the EU's IST **research activities** are looking to the future. While almost all research activities involve software development of some sort, some **IST Strategic Objectives** focus on creating technologies crucial to the development of the digital content industry.
- The Media Programme (2001–2005) aims to strengthen the competitiveness of Europe's audiovisual industry. This includes preparing the sector for innovations such as the distribution and exhibition of digital films and finding ways to digitize – and hence preserve – Europe's rich archives of audiovisual material.

- The **Safer Internet Programme** funds activities dealing with illegal and harmful Internet content. It has a wide scope, covering **technologies** as diverse as 3G, online games and chatrooms; and dealing with **content** ranging from child pornography to racism. It was originally adopted for 1999–2002 and then extended for 2003–2004.

Tourism policy has no clear place within the Commission. However, the task of the small unit in the DG Enterprise is: to ensure that the interests of the tourism sector are taken into account; to improve knowledge on tourism and to contribute to the dissemination of information; and to stimulate co-operation across the board. A particularly interesting action is the Information Guide for the tourism sector. The objective of the Internet Guide for the tourism sector is to make available to actors in the tourism sector and to other interested people, a comprehensive and structured overview of various EU programmes, schemes, funds, initiatives and actions of potential interest. It provides Internet links to the homepages of the relevant programmes.

9. FINAL REMARKS

This chapter has briefly dealt with the overall policy framework of services-related policies in general, and, in particular, with main non-regulatory services policies, which are complementary to the regulatory ones seen in previous chapters, such as competition and internal market policies. The specificity towards services of these policies has been recently developed, thus the majority of thoughts outlined concern, on the one hand, theoretical justification advising action in these fields in order to favour the service economy and, on the other hand, recommendations of possible policy fields of action. Significant advances were only made in a few cases in recent years.

Theoretical justification for the development of one policy or the other does not only depend on the importance of services, but also on specific problems arising from innovation, regional localization, quality, employment and information. These five issues are related to three types of factors: deficit of comparative policy performance and delay regarding goods sectors, issues derived from the co-productive nature of services activities and market and systemic failures, or, as the case may be, from the need to apply new services-oriented policy performance criteria within existing community policies (as in the case of services in structural funds). On many occasions, these three factors act jointly to explain the need for a specific policy.

Nevertheless, the existing evidence and reports do not recommend just a focus on vertical approaches towards service companies (for instance, the horizontality promoted by OECD (2005c), but the needs of services companies are clearly undervalued in innovation policies (Miles, 2005; den Hertog et al., 2007). The only reasonable way out of this apparent contradiction is the promotion of service innovation, KIS-oriented in particular, as a dimension of innovation policies addressed to any economic sector. This direction has recently been suggested by the European Economic and Social Committee (2006) when claiming more support to service innovation in the context of a new EU industrial policy. The EESC opinion makes reference to the deepening division of labour within developed economies and the disaggregation of previously integrated vertical value chains. The type of economy which is developing is one in which services and manufacturing are integrated and complementary in nature. However, this services-industry inter-linkage has so far not been taken into account in the design of policy actions aimed at improving industrial competitiveness. The effect of such measures may be limited if they focus exclusively on industry and fail to address the impact on, and the challenges faced by the associated business-related service activities, such as globalization, skills, investment in research and innovation, and productivity improvement. A new challenge for industrial policy would be to examine the framework conditions which affect the supply, demand and quality of services on which industry depends for its continuing competitiveness.

At a European level, complementary policies and industrial policies related to services are in an initial stage, compared to the others under consideration in the previous chapters of this book. The integration of services within industrial policies is at a very early stage. Innovation and employment policies have been developed horizontally, providing many competencies to member states and regions, and yet are at a stage of reflection regarding the convenience or inconvenience of adapting to services needs.

The first important service innovation actions developed by DG Enterprise are being launched in 2007, and will take several years before consolidation. For the first time, regional policy includes ambitious objectives in terms of innovation and competitiveness, where services are clearly a priority, and again for the first time, within the recommendations of the Commission for 2007–2013 funds.

Quality policy – standards in particular – are still at an initial stage, the main role corresponding to private agents and associations requiring the support and guarantee of international institutions. The measures to promote entrepreneurship concern a wide range of actions and are awaiting the results of the action plan under development since 2005. Finally, advances in terms of statistics and research have been particularly important within the statistical framework, but are still insufficient for the knowledge needs of the sector. In brief, these are incipient actions, still not wholly developed, although with a great growth potential for future years.

NOTES

1. This section is based on a previous working paper Rubalcaba (2007).
2. An analogy with software engineering, also giving rise to an intangible product, seems more appropriate than its physical counterpart. In the absence of a base science (physics, chemistry, life sciences, etc.) the development of the service greatly depends on the processing of information and on the exchange of good practices. A specific example can be found in the field of design, where the demand for a platform for such an exchange seems to exist.
3. Green Book on public-private partnerships and community law on public procurement and concessions, COM/2004/0327 final
4. Communication on public-private partnerships and community law on public procurement and concessions, COM (2005) 569 final. Brussels, 15.11.2005
5. The competitiveness of business-related services and their contribution to the performance of the European enterprises, COM (2003) 747. December 2003.
6. The 1990s were very fruitful in works related to the regional location of producer services. See Marshall et al. (1987), Coffey and Polèse (1987), Hansen (1990), Bailly et al. (1992), Moulaert and Gallouj (1993), Senn (1993), Baró and Soy (1993), Marshall and Wood (1995), Cuadrado and Rubalcaba (1993), Daniels (1993), Cuadrado and Del Río (1993), Bonamy and May (1994), Esparza and Krmenec (1994), Illeris (1994, 1996), Illeris and Phillipe (1993), Rubalcaba (1999), Wood (2002), among others. Most of these works are region-oriented, although some of them also deal with urban implications in direction similar to the ones undertaken in the recognized works provided by Sassen's chapter (1990) on producer services or by Castells' discussion (1989) about the dialectics between centralization and decentralization of services.
7. This result, as well as a model of the problems of adverse selection and moral hazard as applied to services, can be seen in Holmstrom (1985).
8. As included in the works by the Forum, which also states that, although the programming mandate explicitly excluded standards in support of e-Europe policies, future work on services standardization should look closely at developments in the field of ICT standardization. As well as providing possible case studies of effective standardization, this area of work is important in developing the 'digital delivery' of services which currently involve a high level of personal interaction.
9. Particular attention should be paid to areas where industry standards have been developed by consortia, outside the framework of the standardization bodies.
10. Taken together, it seems that the EU is still far short of the Lisbon objectives and targets. Relative to the 2010 employment targets, the 2003 employment rates overall, of women and of older people, fall short by 7, 5 and 10 percentage points, respectively. Closing these gaps will rely heavily on the implementation of further labour market reforms to improve the employment prospects notably of women, older people and the low-skilled, and to foster employment creation in the services sector. It is also necessary to combat the recent increases in youth unemployment and in long-term unemployment (European Commission, COM (2004)239 final).
11. COM (2006) 91 final. Proposal for a regulation establishing the European globalization adjustment fund. 2006/0033 (COD) Brussels, 1.3.2006
12. The future European Qualification Framework is also recognized as an important and useful work in progress to promote and coordinate/harmonize sector-specific

education and training initiatives. Additionally, sector-specific actions to promote the acceptance and usage of the Europass should be launched (Forum on BRS, 2005).

13. European Commission (2003) Green Book. Entrepreneurship in Europe. Brussels, 21/1/2003. Document based on COM(2003) 27, final version.

14. European Commission (2004) Communication – Action plan: The European agenda for entrepreneurship COM(2004) 70 final

15. European SMEs are key to delivering stronger growth and more and better jobs – the two main objectives of the new Lisbon partnership for Growth and Jobs. They make up a large part of Europe's economy: there are some 23 million SMEs in the EU, providing around 75 million jobs and accounting for 99 per cent of all enterprises.

16. Commission Communication 'Implementing the Community Lisbon Programme - Modern SME Policy for Growth and Employment' (COM (2005)551 final of 10.11.2005).

17. Council Regulation (CE, EURATOM) no. 58/97.

18. See Eurostat: *Services Statistics: Strategy for Services Statistics – a Complement to the Strategy on Short-term Statistics* (doc. CPS 2002/46/4/EN), presented in the meeting of the Statistical Programme Committee, held in Palermo in September, 2002.

19. This author participated in the Forum as the President of RESER, appointed in 2004.

20. Europe's content sector alone – media, publishing, marketing and advertising – contributes around 5 per cent to Europe's GDP (some €433 billion), putting it ahead of Europe's telecommunications (€254 billion) industry. The information society thus presents new challenges and opportunities to a sector which already employs some 4 million Europeans.

11. Conclusions and final remarks

1. LEARNING FROM THE NEW SERVICE ECONOMY

Overall Conclusions from the Book

The first two parts of this book have endeavoured to present the analytical framework and main evidence regarding services activities in advanced economies, mainly in Europe. They have identified the content and behaviour of the new service economy, which is based on the growing interrelations between goods and services and on the crucial importance of services for modern economic growth. In order to do this, some analysis has been made of issues relating to employment, productivity, innovation and globalization. In contrast to the myths that regard services as less productive, less innovative and less tradable, we have encountered services – mainly knowledge-intensive services – whose behaviour is exactly the opposite, i.e. they act as generators of productivity gains, channels of innovation and active globalization players. In any event, services are very heterogeneous, and many of them in many countries lag behind and may slow down economic growth. All these topics serve to demonstrate how the new service economy poses new challenges that call for action in respect of research (better and more comprehensive service research), in respect of the business world (new opportunities emerging in the complex global service world) and in respect of policy-makers: services can no longer be excluded from policy initiatives and should feature not only as a sector deserving special attention but as a dimension of horizontal economic and industrial policies.

We have also analysed in this book the particular case of the European Union, which lags behind the United States in some key indicators. After exploring this in detail, the third part has highlighted other challenges faced in particular by the European Union, in areas such as regulation, competition policies and the internal market. The modest EU performance in some services areas is due not only to natural factors or the existence of different national realities, but also to the existence of artificial barriers, over-regulation and heterogeneous regulations, all of which hamper market integration, competitive gains and the free interaction of agents, which is at the basis of the new service economy.

With an eye to coping with all these challenges and problems at EU level, we have presented and discussed the European Commission's policies on services. Regulatory policies to guarantee the free provision of services and freedom of establishment should be accompanied by some standardization of the very varied regulations in Europe, in order to make the internal market in services more effective in economic terms and more accepted by citizens. Particular attention should be paid not only to the level of regulation and discriminatory barriers but to non-discriminatory barriers, competition restrictions and the heterogeneity of regulations too, where major obstacles to market integration have been identified. In addition, these regulatory policies should go hand in hand with non-regulatory complementary policies able to deal with market or system failures in areas such as innovation, regional development or SME entrepreneurship.

Main Research Contributions

After these overall conclusions from the book, the remarks in this final chapter are not intended to provide an exhaustive summary of all the issues dealt with, but rather to give an overview of the book's principal aspects and contributions, as well as some common elements that have arisen throughout the research.

The book begins by underlining the need to understand services as a dimension of any economic activity, rather than as a specific sector (Chapter 2). The service economy generates a whole economic anthropology, in which the aspect of free interaction is a key element in furthering the growth of the servindustrial society. In a world where any product is a goods–services compound, services highlight the intangible element that gives value added to products and a new driving force to the relationship between clients and suppliers. Services – and the related interaction between them – stop being just another sector and become a dimension of the social and economic system. Services are a dimension of any economic activity.

Given the presence of services in the new servindustrial society, it is not surprising that the service sector has increased its share in advanced economies and currently represents around 70 per cent of employment and value added (Chapter 3). The growth of services in recent years has been driven mainly by business services, and to a lesser extent by personal and leisure services and public services. Services have expanded for a number of reasons, ranging from the traditional theories of their slow productivity growth, the growth of income and the role of public sector – all valid reasons within their limits – to the integration between goods and services and the role of globalization. Some of these explanations apply more to producer services (e.g., sectoral interrelations) and others more to consumer services (e.g. income and socio-cultural changes). European services have grown less than those of the United States, prompting us to identify the sector's growth potential, particularly in some business and personal services. However, trends in Europe do not show clear convergence patterns in the way they undergo structural change, suggesting that their specific evolution is linked to national parameters. Convergence in common growth patterns is minimal, as can be seen from some business-related services.

Productivity has been the most widely discussed explanation for the growth of services (Chapter 4). The debate centres around two interrelated issues: the technical difficulties involved in statistically measuring service productivity, and the analytical difficulty in explaining services growth on the basis of related apparent productivities, which do not take account of any factor that is not statistically measurable in a traditional way. Data on apparent productivity show certain backwardness in the productivity of most service fields, albeit with significant exceptions. Moreover, not all productivity returns derived from services are easily recorded, as in the case of the industrial productivity growth arising from the use of producer services. In Europe, productivity underdevelopment is recorded mainly in technology user services and in some business services. Putting to one side cultural, social and statistical measurement reasons, this implies that part of the explanation could lie in the sectors' differing capacities to be efficient.

One of the key elements in obtaining higher profits in productivity and growth is innovation (Chapter 5). Despite the fact that services have traditionally been regarded as not especially technology-intensive (this being one of the main reasons for their low relative productivity), the data available show that services do not have to be less innovative than goods; on the contrary, European surveys on innovation demonstrate that some services are highly innovative. The difference lies in the non-technological and more organizational nature of service innovation, as well as in the higher impact on quality compared with goods, which are more highly characterized by technological innovations in the product and process fields and by cost impacts. From the viewpoint of innovation sources and obstacles, the differences between goods and services are not very significant. However, services have more difficulty in appropriating results (the patent system is not effective) and in obtaining finance from public funds (R&D programmes are channelled mainly towards goods, even when these are initially horizontal and no sectoral distinction is intended). Another challenge is Europe's backwardness in several innovation indicators compared with the United States, although there do appear to be some signs of convergence. Moreover, the statistical system needs to be improved if service innovation is to be measured more accurately.

Increased innovation and productivity are needed in order to meet the new competitive requirements arising out of globalization (Chapter 6). Services have been, and still are, active agents of globalization, although they themselves face the challenges of competitiveness. Services are starting to copy the relocation trends that have characterized manufacturing industry for the past thirty years. Services-offshoring is emerging strongly, although the statistics might lead us to think that it is not a very significant and generalized phenomenon. As an example, although important services are provided by India or, within Europe, by Ireland or the Baltic countries, this is far from a general fact and, besides, they are not detrimental to the growth of services in developed nations. Some potential employment is lost, but for the time being no net losses of employment have been registered in service sectors due to this phenomenon, in contrast to what happened in many European manufacturing industries from the 1980s and in some US ones from the beginning of the current decade. Business services stand out as among the most active services in globalization. The most significant trends towards international integration are not in international trade, where services seem to be stagnant at 20–22 per cent of the total, but in foreign direct investment and, more specifically, in mergers and acquisitions.

In order to see how policies could best respond to the challenges in employment, growth, productivity, innovation and globalization, the book has analysed public intervention via the reasons given to justify regulation of services (Chapter 7), which are usually regarded as superior to those justifying state intervention in the goods market. The traditional theory of regulation posits issues such as externalities (both positive and negative), monopolistic power or asymmetric information as factors dictating intervention in service markets, and more specifically in the markets of network services. The problem is that recent changes in services mean that some regulations in force since the 1950s and 1960s now either need to be revised or even (where appropriate) abolished. The liberalization of some services shows that it is necessary to think differently about state intervention and to sanction its use in favour of competition and the private sector: interventionist positions are not currently justified, as they normally hide protectionist interests. The negative correlation between over-regulation and economic efficiency seems to be clear. Europe has especially suffered from an excess of interventionism, and a policy aimed at promoting competitive services should re-regulate and open the way to a greater prominence of private or social agents, in line with the principle of subsidiarity. EU policies on better regulation are moving in the right direction.

In Europe, there are two key regulatory policies that affect services: competition policy and internal market policy. Both share the aim of increasing competition between the Member States of the European Union, so they are directed at commercial and investment operations between countries. For this purpose there are directives, control mechanisms, infringements and case law from the European Court of Justice. Competition policy (Chapter 8) guarantees the performance of those articles of the Treaty drafted to safeguard the correct application of market criteria within the Union; it also controls agreements, mergers and acquisitions and monopolistic power, which can be related to the abuse of dominant positions that restrict competition. The number of cases in services under the EU competition policy is more or less proportional to those of their economic weighting, if compared to the goods market, and are directly related to market power. Virtually all services are affected by this policy, although professional services and distributive trades have until recently remained largely outside this picture. In the case of professional services, the Commission prefers initial action to be taken by the Member States and the sectors alone, and this has frequently created a self-regulation or protection detrimental to competition. Competition policy faces several challenges, such as the necessary cooperation between EU and national policies, changes in the scale of markets due to the emergence of globalization in traditionally separate service markets, and the protectionist resurgence in some countries in 2006, influenced by, among other things, the disillusion created by the French and Dutch 'no' votes on the European Constitution Treaty the year before. This has also affected the internal market policy for services (Chapter 9).

The internal market policy requires more decisive action on services, according to the most important documents drafted as part of the Lisbon Strategy. The low level of services integration in Europe is explained, beyond the natural barriers, by the presence of artificial obstacles limiting the growth of sectoral competitiveness and hindering the opening-up of sectors to markets and improvements in innovation and productivity that affect the overall economy. However, the Commission's reports – drawn up by its many directorates-general – almost unanimously highlight the importance of creating an internal market for services at least similar to that for goods. This contrasts strongly with the bitter controversy surrounding the Directive proposed by the Commission in December 2004, which was politically exploited in the French referendum on the Constitution by those in favour of the 'yes' and the 'no' votes, and was severely cut back and amended by Parliament in February 2006. The country-of-origin principle gave rise to many misunderstandings and conflicting interests, and was widely criticized, despite the exceptions already included in the Commission proposal and the potential advantages identified by the independent studies carried out. Now that a rather limited Directive has been approved in November 2006, any move towards an internal market for services will have to take alternative paths and may follow a more vertical, sector-by-sector approach. Nowadays, it seems necessary for the internal market to go hand in hand with action to reduce the heterogeneity of regulations (thereby avoiding asymmetrical effects) and boost complementary policies (thereby smoothing and preparing adjustment mechanisms).

Apart from the mainly regulatory Commission policies, there is a series of mainly non-regulatory policies, and also complementary policies, aimed at responding to market failures and systemic failures in services (Chapter 10). Promoting competition and market integration through internal market and competition policies is not enough to achieve the objectives of growth, competitiveness and social welfare. Preference must be given to a comprehensive services policy which includes direct impacts on some of the intermediate objectives influencing business efficiency: innovation and R&D policies, so that services can be included in those policies and programmes that have so far largely excluded them; regional policy, so that the use of services – particularly knowledge-intensive services – can be supported in those regions with convergence problems and a lack of market services;

quality policy, so that the standardization processes carried out by services companies and organizations can be expanded, thus making up the time lost with respect to goods standardization and providing services better able to acquire a competitive edge through quality – in a context where offshoring is led by costs; employment and qualification policies, so that the training needs arising out of the new service economy and continued specialization can be identified; information and knowledge policy, so that statistics, analysis and research on all these issues can be improved; policies to promote entrepreneurship, which is decisive in the sectors with the highest business start-up and cessation rates. Vertical policies can be included too, in order to boost the development of specific sectors, along the lines of what the Commission does with transport and communications. A problem that arises from the group of policies developed for services is the lack of coordination and exploitation of possible synergies between them, and between the Commission policies and those of the Member States. On some occasions, certain contradictory effects or asymmetric effects arise in various directions. In this case, it would be advisable for the European Commission, maybe through the DG Internal Market and Services, to take on a higher profile among the full range of service policies and not only among those relating strictly to the internal market. The integration of services within a new industrial policy, as a horizontal dimension useful for business economic performance, may also lead to a new role of DG Enterprise and Industry for developing service-related policies.

2. FINAL REMARKS ON POLICY IMPLICATIONS

Policy Options

To conclude, a brief reflection on the work carried out is proposed, ranging from the most ontological aspects of the service economy to the most specific implications of economic policy. There is not just one policy; different options are possible, and they should take account of the natural order of the actions to be taken. For instance, one aspect to be considered is that all policies under analysis are key elements in promoting entrepreneurship and free initiative in the world of services. Service entrepreneurs will be more motivated to innovate, take risks and grow internationally if they encounter more competition, more transparency, fewer regulations and less protectionist markets, clearer game rules within Europe, as well as support in those markets where public intervention is required because of market and systemic failures (R&D, more developed regions, education and training, statistics and research). Public services too will be more likely to modernize if they are included in programmes for innovation and for interaction and cooperation with private or social-initiative services. Moreover, public services need 'entrepreneurs' to produce higher-quality services at lower costs. Finally, services depend more than goods on the motivation of suppliers for co-production. Political action should be geared towards creating conditions where the motivation of suppliers and clients is as high as possible, in order to obtain maximum growth and social welfare.

The issue of motivation leads us to conclude the trajectory of this book at its starting point. Development of the services ontology resulted in considering the principle of free interaction – two or more parties working jointly and freely for the achievement of a mutual interest – as the key to development of the service economy. Because of the need to observe the principle of free interaction, political action should give priority to competition, free initiative and entrepreneurship, cooperation with the private sector, education and training, and research and knowledge. Interventionism, protectionism, corporatism and conservatism restrict free initiative, the spirit of change and adaptation to new realities. However, States should not give way to inaction, as might appear defensible from a short-sighted liberalist perspective, but should promote everything that favours economic operation and intervene only when the private sector does not act or where market and system failures have to be corrected. In this sense, the subsidiarity principle is defended here, since the State is promoting rather than substituting social initiative where possible. It is not by chance that all the aforementioned complementary policies require the active intervention of social representatives: companies and researchers, in order to comply with administrations' needs on R&D and innovation, training and skills; professional associations and accreditation bodies, in order to create standards that will subsequently be guaranteed at an international level; business-support services and private representatives, so that they work jointly under the best possible model of regional development and an efficient use of services. As has already been said, interaction between the parties is one of the guarantees for the success of all these policies.

Principles for Services-related Policies

Bearing in mind the above considerations and indeed the whole of the foregoing analysis, extracted below – as a personal reflection – are a series of basic principles for political action, which the author considers to be consistent with the new service economy and its challenges:

- *Freedom.* Freedom as a principle of action means support for social and private initiative, for plurality and for unrestricted competition. It is a way of avoiding negative State interferences in services, which in many sectors have been the engines of economic growth through their own vitality rather than by State initiative. All this is set within the framework of a necessarily regulated system and a competition policy in which the State should play an active part in promoting the service economy, with a view to encouraging the freedom of those representatives who will be able to build a thriving service economy. This also implies emphasizing the co-productive and interactive aspects of regulations on services: a start has been made on this, for example, by allowing for competitive dialogue in public procurement and by devising programmes in some countries to match support for innovation and R&D to service needs.

- *Subsidiarity*. This principle is related to the previous one. The first thing to note is that subsidiarity means more than the higher levels – Commission, Federal state, states – not intervening when lower levels (states, regions) can do so. This interpretation is very useful for policy purposes but can sometimes bring with it a protectionist use of the principle, which thus becomes a defender of the status quo. It also and more fundamentally means that state intervention – EU/federal, national or regional – should ensure that social initiative plays a leading role in competition, internal market, R&D or regional policies. With that in mind, the bottom-up criterion must be applied whenever possible to the formulation of policies (as in voluntary service standards) by companies or civil society. The State should promote rather than substitute social initiative.

- *Horizontality*. Services have been presented from Chapter 2 onwards as a dimension of overall economic activity and not merely as an economic sector. With that in mind, political action should deal with services not just because they are numerous and their relative weighting in industry is higher, but because a primary objective is to integrate the service dimension into horizontal policies. This does not mean that vertical policies cannot sometimes be applied to specific sectors (e.g. transport, tourism, cultural services). The idea is mainly to promote a horizontal services policy – across all sectors – as a way to reinforce the new service economy (e.g. those cross-sectoral policies aimed at strengthening knowledge-intensive services as a source of growth, employment and competitiveness). The horizontality criterion should lead to a convergence of service-related policies and industrial policies, as suggested by Pelkmans (2006b) when explaining Europe's industrial policy and the role of the internal market for services, and also by the opinion from the European Economic and Social Committee (2006) on services and industry. Moreover, the full range of horizontal industrial policies may meet the needs of services and the incipient service-related policies.

Operating the New Services Economy in an Old Europe

In the case of Europe, one further principle – realism – should be added to the three that were enumerated above. Becoming aware of the challenges arising out of globalization or the backwardness of productivity, innovation and competition implies that decisive action is needed, although it must be characterized by a realistic appreciation of the difficulties of the European construction process and the difficult path towards the integration of markets and societies. It is perhaps clearer in the field of services than in goods that the construction of Europe cannot only be focused on the free movement of goods and capital, but that less heterogeneous regulations are required, as well as a certain social integration to bind services: a pro-European aim is essential, and this is not always a given among the European population or the various governments.

On the basis of the realism principle, firm but moderate steps should be taken towards the strengthening of a service economy in Europe. This would be the result of a social process that extends beyond the economic field. As has been stated throughout this book, services have the capacity of combining the local and the global, the diverse and the standard, the distant and the near. In the past, fairs and exhibitions were a central axis of the European economic unit: a service which localized the global and globalized the local. Nowadays, services aim to play a similar role: without them, a powerful and prosperous Europe, from which other world nations and developing countries could also benefit, would not be possible. A decisive development of the service economy can bring to light new ways of combining the global and the local, the European and the national, beyond interventionist or nationalist reductionisms. European services need 'more Europe' to solve their problems and face their challenges.

The time has come for the service economy and the European construction project to agree on new powers and renewed energies. This task is the responsibility of everybody (entrepreneurs and consumers' associations, research community, education system, media, etc.), not only of statesmen, although they are in charge of guiding the process, as were Europe's founding fathers in the post-war period and other politicians have been since. Nowadays, there is no danger of severe war within Europe, and this lends encouragement to the process of common construction. However, at this difficult beginning of the 21st century, Europeans are responsible for believing in themselves and contributing, as far as is possible, to the welfare of the whole world. Let us hope that services can be used as a channel to achieve these objectives!

References

Aghion, P., Harris, C., Howitt, P. and Vickers, J. (2001), 'Competition, Imitation and Growth with Step-by-Step Innovation', *Review of Economic Studies*, **68** (3), 467–92.

Aharoni, Y. (ed.) (1993), *Coalitions and competition: the globalization of professional business services*, London and New York: Routledge.

Aharoni, Y. (1999) 'The role of reputation in global professional business services', in Aharoni, Y. and Nachum, L. (eds), *Globalization of services: some implications for theory and practice*, London and New York: Routledge.

Aharoni, Y. and Nachum, L. (eds) (2000), *Globalization of services: some implications for theory and practice*, London and New York: Routledge.

Aiginger, K. and Landesmann, M. (2002), 'Competitive economic performance. The European view', *Harvard University WIFO Working Paper*, 179.

Anderson, M.A. and Smith, S.L.S. (1999), 'Do National Borders Matter? Canada-US Regional Trade reconsidered', *Review of International Economics*, **7** (2), 219–227.

Antonelli, C. (1999), *The microeconomics of technical change*, London and New York: Routledge.

Australian National University and Productivity Commission (2000), *Achieving better regulation for services*, Conference proceedings aus info, Canberra, November.

Bacon, R. and Eltis, V.A. (1976), *Britain's economic problem: too few producers*, London: MacMillan.

Bailly, A., Coffey, W., Paelinck, J.H.P. and Polèse, M. (1992), *Spatial Econometrics of Services,* Aldershot: Avebury.

Baily, M. and Gordon, R. (1988), 'The productivity slowdown, measurement issues and the explosion of computer power', *Brookings Papers on Economic Activity*, 2, 347–420.

Baker, G.P. (2007), 'The impact of business-services use on client industries. Evidence from input-output data', in Rubalcaba, L. and Kox, H. (eds), *Business Services in European Economic Growth*, London: MacMillan/ Palgrave.

Baldwin, R. and Cave, M. (1999), *Understanding regulation. Theory, strategy and practice*, Oxford: Oxford University Press.

Barcet, A. (1987), *La montée des services, vers une économie de la servuction*, Doctoral thesis, Lyon: Lumière Lyon II University.

Barcet, A. (1991), 'Production and service supply structure: temporality and complementarity relations', in Daniels, P. and Moulaert, F. (eds), *The changing geography of advanced producer services*, London and New York: Belhaven Press.

Baró, E. and Soy, A. (1993), 'Business service location strategies in the Barcelona metropolitan region', in Daniels, P.W. et al. (eds), *The Geography of Services*, London: Frank Cass.

Barro, R.J. and Sala-i-Martin, X. (1991), 'Convergence across States and Regions', *Brookings Papers on Economic Activity*, 1, 107–82.

Bassanini, A., Scarpetta, S. and Hemmings, P. (2001), 'Economic growth: the role of policies and institutions. Panel Data evidence from OECD countries', *Economics Department Working Papers*, 283.

Baumol, W. (1967), 'Macroeconomics of unbalanced growth: the anatomy of urban crisis', *American Economic Review*, 57 (3), 415–26.

Baumol, W. (1985), 'Productivity policy in service sector', in Inman, R.P. (ed.), *Managing the service economy. Prospects and problems*, Cambridge: Cambridge University Press.

Baumol, W. (1989), *Productivity and American leadership. The long view*, London: MIT Press.

Baumol, W. (2000), 'Services as leaders and the leader of the services', Inaugural lecture, International Conference on the Economics and Socio-Economics of Services, June 22 and 23, 2000, Lille, France.

Baumol, W., Blackman, S. and Wolff, E. (1985), 'Unbalanced growth revisited: asymptotic stagnancy and new evidence', *American Economic Review*, 75 (4), 806–17.

Bell, D. (1973), *The coming of post-industrial society*, New York: Basic Books, Inc.

Berndt, E.R., Cutler, D., Frank, R., Griliches, Z., Newhouse, J. and Triplett, J. (1998), 'Price indexes for medical care goods and services: an overview of measurement issues', *NBER Working Paper*, 6817, Cambridge, Massachusetts.

Beyers, W.B. (2005), 'Services and the changing economic base of regions in the United States', *The Service Industries Journal*, 25 (4), 1–16.

Beyers, W.B. (2007), 'Outsourcing tendencies in the producer services in the United States', *Outsourcing and offshoring in services. Facing the global challenge*, in Camacho, J.A. and Rubalcaba, L. (eds), Cheltenham, UK: Edward Elgar (forthcoming).

Bhagwati, J. (1987), 'International trade in services and its relevance for economic development', in Giarini, O. (ed.), *The emerging service economy*, Oxford: Pergamon Press.

Bhagwati, J. (2004), *In Defence of Globalization*, Oxford: Oxford University Press.

Boden, M. and Miles, I. (eds) (2000), *Services and knowledge-based economy*, London: Continuum.

Bonamy, J. and May, N. (1994), *Services et mutatons urbaines: questionnements et perspectives*, Paris: Anthopos, Economica.

Browning, H.L. and Singelmann, J. (1978), *The emergence of a service society*, Springfield: National Technical Information Service.

Bryson, J.R. and Daniels, P.W. (eds) (2007), *The handbook of service industries in the global economy*, Cheltenham, UK: Edward Elgar.

Bryson, J.R., Daniels, P.W. and Warf, B. (2004), *Service worlds: people, organisations and technologies*, London: Routledge.

Camacho, J. and Rodriguez, M. (2007), 'Integration and diffusion of KIS for industry performance', in Rubalcaba, L. and Kox, H. (eds), *Business Services in European Economic Growth*, London: MacMillan/Palgrave.

Camacho, J.A., Rubalcaba, L. and Bryson, J.R. (eds) (2007), *Outsourcing and offshoring in services. Facing the global challenge*, Cheltenham, UK: Edward Elgar (forthcoming).

Carey, S. (2002), 'Undivided loyalties: is national identity an obstacle to European integration?', *European Union Politics, 3*, 387–413.

Castells, M. (1989), *The informational city*, Oxford, UK and Cambridge, US: Blackwell.

Clark, C. (1940), *The conditions of economic progress*, First edition, London: MacMillan.

Clarke, T. and Pitelis, C. (1994), *The political economy of privatization*, London: Routledge.

Coase, R.H. (1960), 'The problem of social cost', *Journal of Laws and Economics, 3*, 1–44.

Coffey, W.J. and Bailly, A.S. (1990), 'Services activities and evolution of production system: an international comparison', *Environment and Planning A, 22* (12), 1607–20.

Coffey, W.J. and Polése, M. (1987), 'Trade and location of producer services', *Environment and Planning A, 19* (5), 597–611.

Coghlan, P. (2000), *The principles of good regulation*, paper presented at the Productivity Commission and Australian National University Conference Achieving Better Regulation of Services, Canberra, Australia, 26–27 June.

Collechia, S. and Schreyer, P. (2001), 'ICT investment and economic growth in the 1990s: is the United States a unique case? A comparative study of 9 OECD countries', *OECD STI Working Paper*, 2001/7, Paris: OECD.

Conway, P. and Nicoletti, G. (2006), 'Product market regulation in the non-manufacturing sectors of OECD countries: measurement and highlights, *Economic department working papers*, 530, OECD.

Conway, P., Janod, V. and Nicoletti, G. (2005), 'Product market regulation in OECD countries: 1998–2003', *Economics Department Working Papers*, 419.

Cooke, P.N. (1988), 'Flexible integration, scope economies and strategic alliances: social and spatial mediations', *Environment and Planning D: Society and Space, 6* (3), 281–300.

Copenhagen Economics (2005), 'Economic Assessment of the Barriers to the Internal Market for Services', study commissioned by the Enterprise Directorate General of the Commission,

CPB Netherlands Bureau for Economic Policy Analysis (2005), 'The free movements of services within the EU', Kox, H., Lejour, A. and Montizaan, R., CPB Document 69.

CPB Netherlands Bureau for Economic Policy Analysis (2006), 'The trade-induced effects of the Service Directive and the Country of Origins Principle', de Bruijn, R., Leijour, A. and Kox, H., CPB Document 108.

Cuadrado, J.R. and del Río, C. (1993), *Los servicios en España*, Madrid: Pirámide.

Cuadrado, J.R. and Rubalcaba, L. (1993), 'Regional Trends in Business Services Supply in Spain', in Daniels, P.W. et al. (eds), *The Geography of Services*, London: Frank Cass.

Cuadrado, J.R., Rubalcaba, L. and Bryson, J. (eds) (2002), *Trading services in the global economy*, Cheltenham, UK: Edward Elgar.

Cullis, J.G. and Jones, P.R. (1987), *Microeconomics & Public Economics. Defense of Leviathan*, Oxford: Basil Blackwell.

D'Alcantara, G. (1987), 'Reflections on some basic concepts for services economy', in Akerhurst, G. and Gadrey, J. (eds), *The economics of services*, London: Frank Cass.

Daniels, P.W. (1993), *Service industries in the world economy*, Oxford: Blackwell.

Daniels, P.W. and Moulaert, F. (eds) (1991), *The changing geography of advanced producer services*, London: Belhaven Press.

De Bandt, J. (1989), 'Can we measure Productivity in Service Activities?', in Bressand, A. and Nicolaïdis, K. (eds), *Strategic Trends in Services : an Inquiry into the Global Service Economy*, New York: Harper and Row.

De Bandt, J. and Gadrey, J. (eds) (1994), *Relations de service et marchés de services*, Paris: CNRS Editions.

De Groot, H. (1998), *Macroeconomic consequences of outsourcing*, Center Discussion Paper, 9843.

De Jong, M.W. (1992), 'Networks of services provision: a customer-oriented approach', 2nd RESER Forum: networks in services, spatial development and the Single European Market, 2–4 September, Portsmouth.

De la Maisonnueve C., De Serres, A. and Hoeller, P.(2001), 'The Width of the Intra-European Economic Borders', *OECD Economic Department Working Papers*, 304, Paris: OECD.

Deardorff, A.V. (1985), 'Comparative advantage and international trade and investment in services', in Stern, R.M. (ed.), *Trade and investment in Services: Canada/US Perspectives*, Toronto: Ontario Economic Council.

Delaunay, J.C. and Gadrey, J. (1987), *Les enjeux de la societé de services*, Paris: Presses de la Fondation Nationale de S. Politiques.

Den Hertog, P. and Bilderbeek, R. (1999), *Conceptualising service innovation and service innovation patterns*, Utrecht, NE: Dialogic.

Den Hertog, P., Rubalcaba, L. and Segers, J. (2007) 'Is there a rationale for services R&D and innovation policies?', *International Journal of Services Technology and Management*, **8**, forthcoming.

Dunning, J.H. (1993), 'The internationalisation of the production of services: some general and specific explanations', in Aharoni, Y. (ed.), *Coalitions and competition: the globalization of professional business services*, London and New York: Routledge.

ECORYS (2005), 'Development of competition in the European postal sector: Research & Consulting for the European Commission', Rotterdam: DG Internal Market.

EIS Expert Report (2005), 'Evaluating and comparing the innovation performance of the United States and the European Union', Prepared for the Trendchart Policy Workshop 2005 by Dosi, G., Llerena, P. and Labini, M.S., June.

Eldridge, L. (1999), 'How price indexes affect BLS productivity measures', *Monthly Labor Review*, February.

Enderwick, P. (1989), *Multinational Service Firms*, London and New York: Routledge.

Esfahani, H.S. and Arkadani, A.T. (2002), 'What determines the extent of public ownership?', Working Paper, University of Illinois.

Esparza, A. and Krmenec, A. (1994), 'Producer services trade in city systems: evidence from Chicago', *Urban Studies*, **31** (1), 29–46.

Europainstitut (2005), 'The European single market for services in the context of the Lisbon agenda: macroeconomic effects', Vienna University of Economics and Business Administration, Breuss F. and Badinger H., December 2005.

European Central Bank (2006), 'Competition, productivity and prices in the Euro area services sector', Occasional Paper Serie 44.

European Commission (2001), *European Competitiveness Report 2001*, Brussels: European Commission.

European Commission (2002), 'The state of the internal market for services', COM (2002) 441final, Brussels: European Commission.

European Commission (2003a), *The competitiveness of business-related services and their contribution to the performance of European enterprises*, Communication from the Commission to the Council and the European Parliament, COM (2003): 747, Brussels: European Commission.

European Commission (2003b), *European Competitiveness Report 2003*, Brussels: European Commission.

European Commission (2004), *BRS: a key driver of European competitiveness. An enhanced economic analysis*, DG Enterprise Working Paper, December.

European Commission (2005), *EU competition policy and the consumer*, Luxembourg: Office for Official Publications of the European Communities.

European Council (2006) *Common position adopted by the Council with a view to the adoption of a directive of the European Parliament and of the Council on services in the internal market*, DIR 10003/06, Brussels.

European Economic and Social Committee (2006), *Interactions between services and European manufacturing industries CCMI/035. Own-initiative opinion of the European Economic and Social Committee*, 13 September 2006, EESC 1146/2006.

European Forum on Business-Related Services (2005), *Final report*, European Commission, Brussels: DG Internal Market.

European Forum on Business-Related Services (2006), *Final report*, European Commission, Brussels: DG Internal Market.

European Innovation Scoreboard (2005), *Comparative analysis of innovation performance*, European Trend Chart on Innovation.

Evangelista, R., Sirilli, G. and Smith, K. (1998), 'Measuring innovation in services', *IDEA Papers series*, STEP group.

Farrell, D. (2004) *Can Germany win from outsourcing?* San Francisco: Mckinsey&Company.

Farrell, D. (2005), 'Offshoring: value creation through economic change', *Journal of Management Studies*, **42** (3), 675–83.

Fayol, H. (1916), *La administración industrial y general en 1916*, reprinted in 1961, Buenos Aires: El Ateneo.

FEDEA (1987), *Public enterprises in Spanish industry*, Madrid: FEDEA.

Fernández, Z. (1995), 'Formas de privatización de empresas', *Economistas*, **63**, 14–20.

Fisher, A.G.B. (1935), *The clash of progress and security*, London: Kelley.

Fisher, A.G.B. (1939), 'Production, primary, secondary and tertiary', *Economic Record*, **15**, June.

Fitzsimmons, J.A., Anderson, E., Morrice, D. and Powell, G.E. (2004) 'Managing service supply relationships', *International Journal of Services Technology and Management*, **5** (3), 221–32.

Fixler, D. and Siegel, D. (1999), 'Outsourcing and productivity growth in services', *Structural Change and Economic Dynamics*, **10**, 174–94.

Fourastié, J. (1949), *Le grand espoir du XXème siècle*, Paris: PUF.

François, J.F. (1990), 'Producer services, scale and the division of labour', *Oxford Economic Papers*, **42** (4), 715–29.

François, J.F. (1993), 'Explaining the pattern of trade in producer services', *International Economic Journal*, **7** (3), 23–31.

François, J.F. and Reinert, K. (1995), 'The role of services in the structure of production and trade: stylised facts from a cross-country analysis', *CEPR Discussion Paper*, 1228, London: CEPR.

Freeman, C. and Soete, L. (eds) (1987), *Technical change and full employment*, Oxford: Basil Blackwell.

Fuchs, V.R. (1968), *The service economy*, New York: National Bureau of Economic Research.

Gadrey, J. (1994), 'Les relations de service dans le secteur marchand', in de Bandt, J. and Gadrey, J. (eds), *Relations de service, marchés de servicies*, Paris: CNRS Editions.

Gadrey, J. (1996), *Services: la productivité en question*, Paris: Desclée de Brouwer.

Gadrey, J. and Gallouj, F. (1998), 'The provider-customer interface in business and professional services', *The Services Industries Journal*, **18** (2), 2–15.

Gadrey, J., Gallouj, F. and Weinstein, O. (1995), 'New modes of innovation. How services benefit industry', *International Journal of Service Industry Management*, **6** (3), 4–16.

Gadrey, J., Noyelle, T. and Stanback, T. (1992), *La productivité dans les services aux Etats-Unis et en France*, Paris: Ministere de la Recherche.

Gago, D. and Rubalcaba L. (2007), 'Innovation and ITC in service firms: towards multidimensional approach for impact assessment', *Journal of evolutionary economics*, **17**, 25–44.

Gallouj, F. (1994), *Economie de l'innovation dans les services*, Paris: L'Harmattan / Logiques Economiques.

Gallouj, F. (2002), *Innovation in the service economy: the new wealth of nations*, Cheltenham: Edward Elgar.

Gallouj, C. and Gallouj, F. (1996), *L'innovation dans les Services*, Paris: Economica.

Gámir, L. (1998), 'Privatización, eficiencia y transparencia', **ICE**, 772, 27–44.

Gámir, L. (2003), 'Las privatizaciones en España y sus efectos sobre la competitividad', *Revista del Instituto de Estudios Económicos*.

Ganz, W. and Meiren, T. (2002), 'Service research today and tomorrow. Spotlight on international activities', Stuttgart: Fraunhofer-IRB.

Gelauff, G. and Lejour, A. (2006), 'The New Lisbon Strategy. An estimation of the economic impact of reaching five Lisbon targets', Report prepared for DG Enterprise of the European Commission, Central Planbureau, The Hague.

Gershuny, J. (1978), *After industrial society?*, London: Macmillan.

Gertler, M.S. (1988), 'The limits of flexibility: comments on the post-fordist vision of production and its geography', *Transactions Institute of British Geographers*, **13**, 419–32.

Giarini, O. (ed.) (1987), *The emerging service economy*, Oxford: Pergamon Press.

Giarini, O. (1988), 'Les nouvelles conditions du progrés économique: de la rigidité de l'offre à l'économie de service', *Revue d'Eonomie Industrielle*, I trimester.

Giarini, O. (2002), 'The globalisation of services in economic theory and economic practice: some conceptual issues', in Cuadrado, J.R., Rubalcaba, L. and Bryson, J.R. (eds), *Trading Services in the Global Economy*, Cheltenham, UK: Edward Elgar, 58–77.

Giarini, O. and Stahel, W.R. (1993), *The limits to certainty facing risks in the new service economy*, 2nd revised edition, Dordrecht, Boston and London: Kluwer Academic Publishers.

Gönenc, R., Maher, M. and Nicoletti, G. (2001), 'The implementation and the effects of regulatory reform: Past Experience and Current Issues', *OECD Economic Studies*, 32, Paris.

Green, L., Howells, J. and Miles, I. (2001), *Services and innovation: dynamics of service innovation in the European Union*, Final report, PREST & CRIC, Manchester: University of Manchester.

Greenfield, H.T. (1966), *Manpower and the growth of producer services*, New York: Columbia University Press.

Griliches, Z. (1992), *Output measurement in the service sector*, Chicago: University of Chicago Press for NBER.

Griliches, Z. (1999), 'R&D and Productivity Growth: Recent Evidence and the Uncertain Future', in Barrel, R., Mason, G. and O'Mahoney, M. (eds), *Productivity and Competitiveness*, NIESR/Cambridge University Press.

Grubel, H. (1995), 'Producer services: their important role in growing economies', in Felli, E., Rosati, F.C. and Tria, G. (eds), *The service sector: productivity and growth*, Heidelberg: Physica-Verlag.

Gullickson, W. and Harper, M. (1999), 'Possible measurement bias in aggregate productivity growth', *Monthly Labor Review*, February.

Gusinger, S. (1992), 'Rhetoric and reality in international business: a note on the effectiveness of the incentives', *Transnational Corporations*, 1–2.

Gust, C. and Marquez, J. (2002), 'International Comparisons of Productivity Growth: the Role of Information Technology and Regulatory Practices', International Finance Discussion Papers, 727.

Hansen, N. (1990), 'Do producer services induce regional economic development?' *Journal of Regional Science*, 30 (4), 465–76.

Haukens, J. (1996), *Innovation in the service economy*, STEP Report, December, Oslo.

Helpman, E. and Krugman, P. (1985), *Market Structure and Foreign Trade: Increasing Returns, Imperfect Competition and the International Economy*, Cambridge, Mass.: MIT Press.

Heston, A. and Summers, R. (1992), 'Measuring final product services for international comparisons', in Griliches, Z. (ed.), *Output measurement in the service sectors*, NBER, Chicago: The University of Chicago Press.

Hill, T.D. (1977), 'On goods and services', *The Review of Income and Wealth*, 4.

Hipp, C. and Grupp, H. (2005), 'Innovation in the service sector: the demand for service-specific innovation measurement concepts and typologies', *Research Policy*, 34 (4), 517–35.

HLIG – High Level Independent Group (2003), *An agenda for growing Europe: making the EU economic system deliver (Sapir Report)*, Brussels: European Commission.

Hoj, I., Kato, T. and Pilat, D. (1995), 'Deregulation and Privatisation in the Service Sector', *OECD Economic Studies*, 25, 37–73.

Holland, S. (1972), *The State as entrepreneur; new dimensions for public enterprise*, London: Weidenfeld & Nicolson.

Holmstrom, B. (1985), 'The Provision of Services in a Market Economy', in: Inman, R. (ed.), *Managing the Service Economy: Problems and Prospects*, London: Cambridge University Press.

Howells, J. (1988), *Economic technological and locational trend in European services*, Aldershot: Avebury.

Howells, J. (2001), *The nature of innovation in services. Innovation and productivity in services*, Paris: OECD.

Howells, J. (2004), 'Innovation, consumption and services: encapsulation and the combinatorial role of services', *The service industries journal*, **24** (1), 19–36.

Howells, J. and Tether, B. (2004), *Innovation in services: issues at stake and trends*, INNO-Studies 2001: Lot 3 (ENTR-C/2001), The Community Innovation and SMEs Programme.

Illeris, S. (1989), *Services and regions in Europe*, Aldershot: Avebury.

Illeris, S. (1994), 'La localisation des producteurs et utilisateurs de services', in Bonamy, J. and May, N. (eds), *Services et mutatons urbaines: questionnements et perspectives*, Paris: Anthopos, Economica.

Illeris, S. (1996), *The service economy: a geographical approach*, Chichester: John Wiley & Sons.

Illeris, S. and Phillipe, J. (1993), 'Introduction: the role of services in regional economic growth', in Daniels, P.W. et al. (eds) *The Geography of Services*, London: Frank Cass.

IMF (2004), *World economic outlook. Advancing structural reforms*, April, IMF.

Jansson, J.O. (2006), *The economics of services: development and policy*, Cheltenham, UK and Northampton, MA, USA: Edward Elgar.

Kagami, M. and Tsuji, M. (2000), *Privatization, deregulation and economic efficiency, a comparative analysis of Asia, Europe and the Americas*, Cheltenham, UK: Edward Elgar.

Kendrick, J.W. (1985), 'Measurement of output and productivity in the service sector', in Inman, R.P. (ed.), *Managing the service economy, prospects and problems*, Cambridge: Cambridge University Press.

Koch, P., Cunningam, P., Schwabsky, N. and Hauknes, J. (2006), *Innovation in Public Services: summary and policy recommendations*, Published by NIFU STEP Studies in Innovation, Research and Education.

Kok, W. et al. (2004), 'Facing the challenge – The Lisbon strategy for growth and employment', Report from the High Level Group chaired by Kok, W., Brussels.

Kox, H. (2002), *Growth challenges for the Dutch business services industry: international comparison and policy issues*, The Hague: CPB Netherlands Bureau for Economic Policy Analysis.

Kox, H. (2004), 'The contribution of business services to aggregate productivity growth', in Gelauff, G. et al. (eds), *Fostering productivity growth – patterns, determinants and policy implications*, Contributions to economic analysis series, 263, Amsterdam / Boston: Elsevier Science.

Kox, H. and Lejour, A. (2006), 'Dynamic effects of European services liberalization: more to be gained', in *Globalization Challenges for the EU and Finland*, Helsinki: Prime Minister's Office – Economic Council of Finland.

Kox, H. and Rubalcaba, L. (2007a), 'Analysing the contribution of business services to European economic growth', *Bruges European Economic Research Papers*, 9, January.

Kox, H. and Rubalcaba L. (2007b), 'The contribution of business services to European economy', in Rubalcaba, L. and Kox, H. (eds), *Business Services in European Economic Growth*, London: MacMillan/Palgrave.

Krugman, P. (1979), Increasing Returns, Monopolistic Competition and International Trade, *Journal of International Economics*, 9, 469–79.

Krugman, P. (1996), *Pop internationalism*, Cambridge, Massachusetts: The MIT Press.

Landesmann, M.A. and Petit, P. (1995), 'International trade in producer services', *The Service Industries Journal*, 15 (2), 123–61.

Lebow, D. and Rudd, J. (2001), 'Measurement error in the consumer price index: where do we stand?', *Board of Governors of the Federal Reserve System*, December.

Leo, P.Y. and Philippe, J. (2005), 'Business Services, the New Engine of French Regional Growth', *The Service Industries Journal*, 25 (2), 141–61.

Li, H. (1999), 'State factories in transition – openness, competition and productivity', *Journal of Development Economics*, 58, 429–62.

Licht, G. and Moch, D. (1999), 'Innovation and information technology in services, *The Canadian Journal of Economics*, 32, 363–83.

Lipsey, R. and Lancaster, K. (1957), 'The General Theory of Second Best', *The Review of Economic Studies*, 24 (1), 11–32.

Lucas, R. (1988), 'On the mechanisms of economic development', *Journal of monetary economics*, 22, 3–42.

Maddison, A. (1980), 'Economic growth and structural change in the advanced countries', in Leveson, I. (ed.), *Western economies in transition: structural change and adjustment policies in industrial countries*, Boulder: Westview Press, 41–60.

Mann, C.L (2003), 'Globalisation of IT services and white collar jobs: the next wave of productivity growth', *International Economics: Policy Briefs*, December 2003.

Markusen, J.R. (1989), 'Trade in producer services and in other specialized intermediate inputs', *American Economic Review*, 79, 85–95.

Markusen, J.R. (2005), 'Modelling the offshoring of white-collar services: from comparative advantage to the new theories of trade and FDI', National Bureau of Economic Research, Working Paper 11827, December 2005.

Maroto, A. and Cuadrado, J.R. (2006a), 'La productividad y los servicios. La necesaria revisión de la imagen tradicional', *Información Comercial Española*, 830.

Maroto, A. and Cuadrado, J.R. (2006b), *La productividad en la economía española*, Colección Estudios, Madrid: Instituto de Estudios Económicos.

Maroto, A. and Rubalcaba, L. (2008), 'Services productivity revisited', *Service industries journal*, 28 (3), forthcoming.

Marshall, J.N. (ed.) (1988), *Services and the uneven development*, Oxford: Oxford University Press.

Marshall, N. and Wood, P. (1995), *Services & Space. Key aspects of Urban and Regional Development*, Singapore: Longman Singapore Publishers.

Marshall, N., Damesick, P. and Wood, P. (1987), 'Understanding the location and role of producer services in the United Kingdom', *Environment and Planning A*, 19, 575–96.

Martini, M. (1990), 'Implicazioni statistiche dell'analisi dei servizi resi alle imprese. Criteri di identificazione e classificazioni', Luxembourg: Internal Document of Eurostat.

Martini, M. (1992), 'L'offerta di servizi innovati per le imprese nell'area metropolitana milanese', Collana Europa, SIPI.

McCallun, J. (1995), 'National Borders Matter: Canada–US Regional Trade Patterns,' *American Economic Review*, 31 (3).

McGuckin, R.H., Spiegelman, M. and van Ark, B. (2005), 'The retail revolution. Can Europe match U.S. productivity performance?', Perspectives on a Global Economy, Research Report R-1358-05-RR, New York, The Conference Board.

McKinsey Global Institute (1993), *Manufacturing Productivity*, San Francisco: McKinsey&Company.

McKinsey Global Institute (2003), *Offshoring: Is it a win-win game?*, San Francisco: McKinsey&Company.

McKinsey Global Institute (2005), *The emerging global labour market*, San Francisco: McKinsey&Company.

McLean, D. (1997), 'Lagging productivity growth in the service sector: mismeasurement, mismanagement or misinformation?', *Bank of Canada Working Paper*, 97–6, Ontario.

Meade, J. (1955), *The theory of Custom Unions*, Amsterdam: North Holland Publishing Company.

Megginson, W.L. (2004), *The financial economics of privatization*, New York: Oxford University Press.

Melle, M. (1999), 'Algunos resultados efectivos de las privatizaciones en España: una primera aproximación', *Economía Industrial*, 330, 141–58.

Melvin, J.R. (1989), 'Trade in producer services: a Hecksher-Ohlin approach', *Journal of Political Economy*, 97, 1180–96.

Messina, J. (2004), 'Institutions and service employment: a panel study for OECD countries', *European Central Bank Working Paper*, 320.

Messina, J. (2006), 'The role of product market regulations in the process of structural change, *European Economic Review*, 50, 1863–90.

Metcalfe, J.S. and Miles, I. (eds) (2000), *Innovation systems in the service economy. Measurement and case study analysis*, Boston: Kluwer Academic Publishers.

Miles, I. (1995), 'Service, innovation, statistical and conceptual issues', Working group on innovation and technology policy, DSTI/ESA/STP/NESTI, 95/12, Paris: OECD.

Miles, I. (1999), 'Foresight and services: closing the gap?', *The service industries journal*, **19** (2), 1–27.

Miles, I. (2000), 'Services innovation: coming of age in the knowledge-based economy', *International Journal of Innovation Management*, **4** (4), 371–89.

Miles, I. (2005), 'The future of R&D in services: implications for EU research and innovation policy', Foresight on services and R&D, Section 1, Main report, Platform foresight, Report prepared for DG Research, European Commission.

Miles, I., Andersen, B., Boden, M. and Howells, J. (2000), 'Service production and intellectual property', *International Journal of Services Technology and Management*, **1** (1), 37–57.

Moulaert, F. and Gallouj, C. (1993), 'The locational geography of advanced producer firms: the limits of economies of agglomeration', in Daniels, P.W. et al. (eds.), *The Geography of Services*, London: Frank Cass.

Muller, E. (2001), 'Knowledge, innovation processes and regions', in Koschatzky, K. , Kulicke, M. and Zenker, A. (eds), *Innovation networks: concepts and challenges in the European perspective*, Heidelberg: Physica-Verlag, 37–51.

Nicoletti, G. and Scarpetta, S. (2003), 'Regulation, productivity and growth', World Bank Policy Research Working Paper, 2944.

Nicoletti, G. and Scarpetta, S. (2005a), 'Regulation and economic performance: product market and productivity in the OECD', *Economics Department Working Papers*, 460.

Nicoletti, G. and Scarpetta, S. (2005b), 'Product market reforms and employment in OECD countries', *Economics Department Working Papers*, 472.

Nitsch, V. (2000), 'National Borders and International Trade: Evidence from the European Union', *Canadian Journal of Economics*, **33** (4).

Noyelle, T.J. (1983), 'The rise of advanced services', *Journal of the American Planning Association*, Summer.

Nusbaumer, J. (1984), *Les services: nouvelle donne de l'economie*, Paris: Economica.

Nusbaumer, J. (1987a), *The service economy: lever to growth*, Boston: Kluwer.

Nusbaumer, J. (1987b), *Services in the global market*, Boston: Kluwer.

O'Farrell, P.N. and Hitchens, D.M.W.N. (1989), 'Producer services and regional development: key conceptual issues of taxonomy and quality treasurement', *Regional Studies*, **24** (2).

O'Farrell, P.N. and Hitchens, D.M.W.N. (1990), 'Producer services and regional development: a review of some major conceptual policy and research issues', *Environment and Planning A*, **22**, 1141–54.

O'Mahony, M. (2002), 'Productivity and convergence in the EU', *National Institute Economic Review*, **180**, 77–82.

O'Mahony, M. and van Ark, B. (2003), *EU productivity and competitiveness: an industry perspective. Can Europe resume the catching-up process?*, Brussels: Enterprise publications, European Commission.

Ochel, W. and Wegner, M. (1987), *Service economies in Europe: opportunities for growth*, London: Pinter, and Boulder, CO: Westriew Press.

OECD (1993), *Proposed standard practice for surveys of research and experimental development – Frascati Manual*, Paris: OECD.

OECD (1996), *Measuring value added in services*, Paris: OECD.

OECD (1999), *Regulatory Reform in the United States*, OECD Reviews of Regulatory Reforms, Paris: OECD.

OECD (2000a), *The service economy*, STI Business and industry policy forum series, Paris: OECD.

OECD (2000b), *Employment in the service economy: a reassessment*, OECD employment outlook, Paris: OECD.

OECD (2000c), *Regulatory Reform in Spain*, OECD Reviews of Regulatory Reforms, Paris: OECD.

OECD (2001a), *Measuring productivity – OECD manual, measurement of aggregate and industry-level productivity growth*, Paris: OECD.

OECD (2001b), *The characteristics and quality of service sector jobs*, OECD Employment Outlook 2001, chapter 3, 89– 128.

OECD (2001c), *What services for what society? How should the services provided by financial intermediaries in a modern society be measured?*, STD/NA(2001) 13, Paris: OECD.

OECD (2001d), *OECD Science, Technology and Industry Scoreboard 2001 – Towards a knowledge-based economy*, OECD: Paris.

OECD (2001e), *Restructuring Public Utilities for Competition: Competition and Regulatory Reform,* Paris: OECD.

OECD (2002a), *Workshop on services*, Working party on statistics, 10–11 December, Paris.

OECD (2002b), 'Report of the OECD Task Force on the Treatment of non-life insurance in the National Accounts and Balance of Payments', STD/NA(2002) 6, Paris: OECD.

OECD (2002c), 'Report of the OECD Task Force on Software measurement in the National Accounts', STD/NA(2002)2, Paris: OECD.

OECD (2002d), *Regulatory Policies in OECD Countries. From Interventionism to Regulatory Governance*, Paris: OECD.

OECD (2002e), *Regulatory Policies in OECD countries*, OECD Reviews of Regulatory Reforms.

OECD (2004a), *Understanding economic growth*, Paris: OECD.

OECD (2004b), 'Globalisation of the ICT sector' Draft chapter 2 in Information Technology Outlook 2004. Presented for the Eurostat-OECD Expert Meeting on Trade-in-Services Statistics.

OECD (2005a), *Growth in services. Fostering employment, productivity and innovation*, Paris: OECD.

OECD (2005a), *Enhancing the Performance of the Services Sector*, Paris: OECD.

OECD (2005b), *Growth in services. Fostering employment, productivity and innovation*, Paris: OECD.

OECD (2005c), *Promoting innovation in services*, Working party on Innovation and Technology Policy, 14th October 2005, OECD, Prepared by Tamura, S., Sheehan, S., Martinez, C., and Kergroach, S., Paris: OECD.

OECD (2005d), *Competition Law and Policy in the European Union*, Paris: OECD.

Oulton, N. (2001), 'Must the growth rate decline? Baumol's unbalanced growth revisited', *Oxford Economic Papers*, **53**, 605–27.

Paige, D. and Bombach, G. (1959), *A comparison of national output and productivity*, Paris: OECD.

Pain, N. and van Welsum, D. (2004), 'International production relocation and exports of services', *OECD Economic Studies*, 2004/1, 38, Paris: OECD.

Parker, A. (2004), *Two-speed Europe: why 1 million jobs will move offshore*, Forrester Research Inc.

Pascual, U. (2002), 'Private property vs. the ejido sector in Yucatán: technical efficiency effects with slash-and-burn agriculture', 7th Biennal Conference of the International Society for Ecological Economics. Sousse (Tunisia), 6–9 March 2002.

Paterson, I., Fink, M., and Ogus, A. (2003), 'Economic impact of regulation in the field of liberal professions in different Member States', Vienna: Institute for Advanced Studies (IHS).

Pavit, K. (1980), *Technical innovation and British economic performance*, London: MacMillan.

Pelkmans, J. (2006a), *European Integration, Methods and Economic Analysis*, Harlow, England: Pearson Education Limited/3rd revised edition.

Pelkmans, J. (2006b), 'European Industrial Policies', *Bruges European Economic Policy Briefings*, **15**, July.

Petit, P. (1986), *Slow growth and the service economy*, London: Francis Printer.

Petitbó, J.A. (1997), 'La defensa de la competencia', *Economía Industrial*, 318.

Petitbó, J.A. (1999), 'Desregulación, liberalización y competencia. Tres instrumentos con los mismos objetivos', *Economistas*, **82**, 42–58.

Petitbó, J.A. (2000), 'La Defensa de la Competencia en el ámbito del Sector Servicios', *Información Comercial Española*, 787.

Petty, W. (1690), *Political Arithmetick*, London. Vol. 1 of *The Economic Writings of Sir William Petty*, Cambridge: Cambridge University Press, 1899.

Pilat, D. (1997), 'Regulation and Performance in the Distribution Sector', *OECD Economics Department Working Paper*, 180.

Pilat, D. (2005), 'Spain's productivity performance in international perspective', presented in OECD Workshop on Measurement of Productivity, October 17–19, Madrid.

Pilat, D. and Wölfl, A. (2005), 'Measuring the interaction between manufacturing and services', OECD Science, Technology and Industry Working Papers, 2005/5, Paris: OECD.

Pilat, D., Lee, F. and van Ark, B. (2002), 'Production and use of ICT: a sectoral perspective on productivity growth in the OECD area', *OECD Economic Studies*, **35**, 2002/2, Paris: OECD.

Piore, M.J. and Sabel, C. (1984), *La segunda ruptura industrial*, Madrid: Alianza Universidad.

Porat, M.U. (1976), *The information economy*, Doctoral thesis, Stanford: Stanford University.

Porter, M. (1990), *The competitive advantage of nations*, London: Macmillan.

Raa, T. and Wolff, E. (1996), 'Outsourcing of services and the productivity recovery in U.S. manufacturing in the 1980s', *Journal of Productivity Analysis*, **16**, 149–65.

Riddle, D.I. (1986), *Service-led Growth, the role of the service sector in World Development*, New York: Praeger.

Robert, D. (2004), 'Services on the production line', *Financial Times*, April 14, 21.

Roberts, G. and Shines, E. (2003), 'Service industries go global: how high-wage professional jobs are migrating to low-cost countries', *Financial Times*, 20th August 2003.

Roberts, J. (1999), *Multinational Business Service Firms*, Aldershot: Ashgate.

Romer, P. (1986), 'Increasing returns and long-run growth', *Journal of political economy*, **94**, 1002–37.

Romer, P. (1990), 'Endogenous technical change', *Journal of political economy*, **98**, 71–102.

Ros, A.J. (1999), 'Does ownership or competition matter? The effects of telecommunications reform on network expansion and efficiency', *Journal Regional Economy*, **15**, 65–92.

Rubalcaba, L. (1994), *Fairs and Exhibitions in the European Economy*, Brussels / Luxembourg: Eurostat / Commission of the European Communities.

Rubalcaba, L. (1999), *Business services in European industry: growth, employment and competitiveness*, Brussels / Luxembourg: European Commission DGIII-Industry.

Rubalcaba, L. (2002), *Competitividad y bienestar en la economía española*, Madrid: Ediciones Encuentro.

Rubalcaba, L. (2004) 'Innovation in services: current statistical needs and proposals for a better coverage', *Services sector statistics – Future needs and possible answers*, Workshop 29/30 June 2004, Luxembourg: European Commission DG Enterprise and Eurostat.

Rubalcaba, L. (2006), 'Which policy for innovation in services?', *Science and Public Policy*, **33**, 10, 745–756.

Rubalcaba, L. (2007), 'Services in European policies', *Bruges European Economic Paper Briefings*, n°. 16.

Rubalcaba, L. and Cuadrado, J.R. (2002a), 'Services in the age of globalization: explanatory interrelations and dimensions', in Cuadrado, J.R., Rubalcaba, L. and Bryson, J. (eds) *Trading services in the Global Economy*, Cheltenham, UK: Edward Elgar.

Rubalcaba, L. and Cuadrado, J.R. (2002b), 'A comparative approach to the internationalization of service industries', in Cuadrado, J.R., Rubalcaba, L. and Bryson, J. (eds) *Trading services in the Global Economy*, Cheltenham, UK: Edward Elgar.

Rubalcaba, L. and Gago, D. (2001), 'Relationships between services and competitiveness: the case of Spanish trade', *The Service Industries Journal,* **21** (1).

Rubalcaba, L. and Gago, D. (2003), 'Location and role of innovative business services in European regions: testing some explanatory factors', *The Service Industries Journal*, **23**.

Rubalcaba, L. and Gallego, J. (2006), 'The participation of business-related services in public R&D programmes: their particular role in EU Framework Programmes', Paper prepared for the European Commission project: evaluation of the R&D needs on business-related services enterprises, Utrecht, The Netherlands.

Rubalcaba, L. and Garrido R. (2005), 'Urban concentration of European business services and the role of regional policies', in Carrillo F.J. (ed.), *Knowledge Cities: approaches, experiences and perspectives*, Oxford: Butterworth-Heinemann / Elsevier.

Rubalcaba, L. and Kox, H. (eds) (2007), *Business Services in European Economic Growth*, London: MacMillan/Palgrave.

Rubalcaba, L., Fernández, N. and Cuadrado, J.R. (2002), 'The quality of regulation in services: an international outlook', *SERVILAB Working Paper*, 4.

Rubalcaba, L. and Merino, F. (2005), 'Urban demand-supply interactions in business services', *The Service Industries Journal*, **24**, 163–80.

Sapir, A. (1993a), 'The structure of services in Europe: a conceptual framework', *European Economy*, **3**, 83–98.

Sapir, A. (1993b), 'Sectorial dimension', *European Economy*, **3**, 23–40.

Sapir, A. and Lutz, E. (1981), 'Trade in services: economic determinants and development related issues', World Bank Staff Working Paper 410, Washington.

Sassen, S. (1990), *The Global City*, New York, London, Tokyo: Princeton.

Scarpetta, S. and Tressel, T. (2002), 'Regulation, productivity and growth: OECD evidence', *Economic Policy*, **18** (36).

Schreyer, P. (1998), 'Information and communication technology and the measurement of real output, final demand and productivity', *STI Working Papers*, 1998/2, Paris: OECD.

Schreyer, P. (2001), 'Computer price indices and international growth and productivity comparisons', *Statistics Working Papers*, STD/DOC(2001)1, Paris: OECD.

Schreyer, P. and Pilat, D. (2001), 'Measuring productivity', *OECD Economic Studies*, **33**, 2001/II, Paris: OECD.

Schumpeter, J.A. (1934) *The theory of economic development. An inquiry into profits, capital, credit, interest, and the business cycle*, Cambridge and Massachusetts: Harvard University Press.

Schumpeter, J.A. (1939), *Business cycles: a theoretical, historical, and statistical analysis of the capitalist process*, New York and London: McGraw-Hill.

Schumpeter, J.A. (1942), *Capitalism, socialism and democracy*, London: Unwin.

Senn, L. (1993), 'Service activities, urban hierarchy and cumulative growth', in Daniels, P.W. et al. (eds), *The Geography of Services*, London: Frank Cass.

Shapiro, C. (2002), 'Competition policy and innovation', OECD STI Working Papers 2002/11.

Sharpe, A., Rao, S. and Tang, J. (2002), 'Perspectives on negative productivity growth in service sector industries in Canada and the United States', presented in the Workshop on Service Sector Productivity, Brookings Institution, May 2002, Washington D.C.

Sharpe, C. and Wernerheim, M. (1996), 'The emperor's new clothes: a critical evaluation of the producer services concept', 43rd North American Meeting of the Regional Science Association, 14–16 November, Washington D.C.

Sichel, D. (1997), 'The productivity slowdown. Is a growing unmeasurable sector the culprit?', *The Review of Economics and Statistics*, **79** (3), 367–70.

Simon, H.A. (1945), *Administrative behaviour*, New York: Macmillan.

Singelmann, J. (1978), *From agriculture to services: the transformation of industrial employment*, Beverly Hills: Sage Publications.

Slifman, L. and Corrado, C. (1996), 'Decomposition of productivity and unit costs', *Occasional Staff Studies*, OSS-1, Federal Reserve Board, Washington D.C.

Smith, A. (1776), *An inquiry into the nature and causes of the wealth of nations*, reprinted in 1976, Oxford: The Clarendon Press.

Smith, A. and Venables, A. (1988), 'Completing the Internal Market in the EC: Some Industry Simulations', *European Economic Review*, **32**, 1501–25.

Soete, L. and Miozzo, M. (1989) *Trade and Development in Services: A Technological Perspective*. Maastricht Economic Research Institute on Innovation and Technology (MERIT), Report No. 89–031.

Stanback, M. (1979), *Understanding the service economy*, Baltimore: Johns Hopkins University Press.

Stanback, M., Bearse, P., Noyelle, T. and Karasek, R. (1981), *Services: the new economy*, Totawa, NJ: Allenheld & Osmar.

Stare, M. (2005), 'Regional Landscape of Services in Candidate Countries', *Service Industries Journal*, **25** (4), 477–491.

Stare, M. (2007), 'Service development in transition economies: achievements and missing links', in Bryson, J.R. and Daniels, P.W., *The handbook of service industries in the global economy*, Cheltenham, UK: Edward Elgar.

Stare, M. and Rubalcaba, L. (2005), 'Outsourcing of services from the CEEC – current potentials and new challenges', XVth International RESER Conference, Granada, Spain, September 2005.

Stigler, G.J. (1956), *Trends in employment in the service industries*, Princeton, NJ: Princeton University Press.

Stiglitz, J. (2002), *Globalization and its discontents*, New York: Norton.

Stiroh, K. (2001), *Information technology and the US productivity revival. What do the industry data say*, New York: Federal Reserve Bank of New York.

Sundbo, J. (1998) *The Organization of Innovation in Services*, Roskilde: Roskilde University Press.

Taylor, F.M. (1911), *The principles of scientific management*, New York: Harper.

Tether, B. (2005), 'Do Services Innovate (Differently)? Insights from the European Innobarometer Survey', *Industry and Innovation*, **12** (2).

Triplett, J. and Bosworth, B. (2002), '"Baumol's disease" has been cured: IT and multifactor productivity in US services industries', presented in the Brookings Workshop on Services Industry Productivity, Brookings Institution, September, Washington D.C.

UNCTAD (1989), 'Services in the world economy', Trade and Development Report 1988, New York: United Nations.

UNCTAD-Roland Berger (2003), 'Service offshoring takes off in Europe – In search of improved competitiveness', UNCTAD, June 14.

United Nations (2001), *Consumer protection, competition, competitiveness and development*, TD/B/COM.1/EM.17/3.

Valery, N. (1987), 'Factory of the future', *The Economist*, May, **30**, 3–18.

Van Ark, B. and McGuckin, R. (2002), 'Changing Gear–Productivity, ICT and Services: Europe and the United States', *Research Memorandum* GD-60, Groningen: Groningen Growth Development Centre.

Van Ark, B. and Piatkowski, M. (2004), 'Productivity innovation and ICT in old and new Europe', *Research Memorandum*, GD-69, Groningen: GGDC.

Van Ark, B., Inklaar, R. and McGuckin, R. (2003a), 'ICT and productivity in Europe and the United States. Where do the differences come from?', Research Memorandum, May, Groningen: GGDC.

Van Ark, B., Melka, J., Mulder, N., Timmer, M. and Ypma, G. (2003b), 'ICT investment and growth accounts for the European Union 1980–2000', Research Memorandum, GD-56, Groningen: GGDC.

Van Ark, B., Broersma, L. and den Hertog, P. (2003c), *Services innovation, performance and policy: a review. Synthesis report in the framework of the SID project (structural information provision on innovation in services)*, The Hague: Directorate General for Innovation, Ministry of Economic Affairs.

Van Welsum, D. (2003a), 'International trade in services: Issues and concepts', *Birkbeck Working Papers in Economics and Finance*, 04/03, London: Birkbeck College.

Van Welsum, D. (2003b), 'Foreign direct investment and exports of services', *Birkbeck Working Papers in Economics and Finance*, 03/03, London: Birkbeck College.

Van Welsum D. (2004), 'In Search of Offshoring: Evidence from U.S. Imports of Services', *Birkbeck Working Papers in Economics and Finance* 02/04, London: Birkbeck College.

Van Welsum, D. and Reif, X. (2006), 'The share of employment potentially affected by offshoring – an empirical investigation', Working Party on the Information Economy. DSTI/ICCP/IE 2005 8/Final 23 February 2006, Paris: OECD.

Van Welsum, D. and Vickery, G. (2004), 'Potential Offshoring of ICT Intensive Using Occupations', paper presented to the STILE conference, Measuring the Information Society, European Trade Union House, Brussels, September 30–October 1, 2004.

Van Welsum, D. and Vickery, G. (2005) 'Potential offshoring of ICT-intensive using occupations', DSTI Information Economy Working Paper, DSTI/ICCP/IE(2004)19/FINAL, Paris: OECD.

Veljanovski, C. (1987), *Selling the state. Privatisation in Britain*, London: Weidenfeld and Nicholson.

Vickers, J. and Yarrow, G. (1991), 'Economic perspectives on privatisation', *Journal of Economic Perspectives*, **5**, 111–32.

Vijselaar, F. (2003), 'ICT and productivity growth in the Euro area: sectoral and aggregate perspectives', presented in the IVIE Workshop on Growth, Capital stock and New Technologies, Madrid: Fundación BBVA.

Viner J. (1950), *The custom union issue*, New York: Carnegie Endowments for International Peace.

Vittadini, G. and Barea, M. (1999), *La economía del non profit. Libre expresión de la sociedad civil*, Madrid: Encuentro.

Vogt, L. (2005) *The EU's Single Market: at your service?*, OECD ECO/WKP(2005)36, OECD Economics Department, Paris: OECD.

Windrum, P. and Koch, P. (2007) *Innovation in public services: Management, creativity and entrepreneurship*, Cheltenham, UK: Edward Elgar.

Windrum, P. and Tomlinson, P. (1999), 'Knowledge-intensive services and international competitiveness: a four country comparison', *Technology Analysis and Strategic Management*, **11** (3), 391–408.

Wise, M. (2001), 'Competition in Professional Services', *OECD Journal of Competition Law and Policy*, **3** (4), 53–109.

Wolf, H. (2000), (Why) Do borders matter for trade?, in Hess, G. and van Wincoop, E. (eds), *Intranational Macroeconomics*, Cambridge University Press.

Wolff, E. (1999), 'The productivity paradox: evidence from indirect indicators of service sector productivity growth', *Canadian Journal of Economics*, **32** (2), 281–308.

Wölfl, A. (2003), 'Productivity growth in service industries. An assessment of recent patterns and the role of measurement', *STI Working Paper*, 2003–7, Paris: OECD.

Wölfl, A. (2005) 'The service economy in OECD countries', *STI Working Paper*, 2005/3, Paris: OECD.

Wölfl, A. (2007) 'Business services and Baumol's cost disease', in Rubalcaba, L. and Kox, H. (eds) *Business services in European economic growth*, London: MacMillan/Palgrave.

Wood, P.A. (1991), 'Flexible accumulation and the rise of business services', *Transactions of the Institute of British Geographers*, **16**, 160–72.

Wood, P.A. (2001), *Consultancy and innovation: the business service revolution in Europe*, London and New York: Routledge.

Wood, P.A. (ed.) (2002), *The business service revolution in Europe*, London: Routledge.

World Bank (2004), *Doing business in 2004: Understanding regulation*, Washington: The World Bank, The International Bank for Reconstruction and Development, and Oxford University Press.

Young, A. (1996), 'Measuring R&D in Services', *STI Working Papers*, OECD/GD, 96-132, Paris: OECD.

Zenker, A. (2001), 'Innovation, interaction and regional development: structural characteristics of regional innovation strategies', in Koschatzky, K., Kulicke, M. and Zenker, A. (eds) *Innovation networks: concepts and challenges in the European perspective*, Heidelberg: Physica-Verlag, 207–22.

Index